With thanks and
very best wishes!
Adrian

One World Archaeology

Series Editors:
Heather Burke, *Flinders University of South Australia, Australia*
Gabriel Cooney, *University College, Dublin, Ireland*
Gustavo Politis, *Universidad Nacional del Centro, Buenos Aires, Argentina*

For further volumes:
http://www.springer.com/series/8606

Adrian Myers · Gabriel Moshenska
Editors

Archaeologies of Internment

 Springer

Editors
Adrian Myers
Stanford Archaeology Center
Stanford University
Stanford, CA, USA
adrianmyers@stanford.edu

Gabriel Moshenska
Institute of Archaeology
University College London
London, United Kingdom
g.moshenska@ucl.ac.uk

ISBN 978-1-4419-9665-7   e-ISBN 978-1-4419-9666-4
DOI 10.1007/978-1-4419-9666-4
Springer New York Dordrecht Heidelberg London

Library of Congress Control Number: 2011927917

Printed on acid-free paper

Springer is part of Springer Science+Business Media (www.springer.com)

It was quite dark in the centre of the compound ... In each hut, cold and dead from the outside, a hundred prisoners, each with his own private problem, crowded into family intimacy. Each darkened hut seething inside with living cells, loving, hating, chaffing, wrangling.

The Wooden Horse, Eric Williams, 1949:35

Acknowledgements

The editors offer their deepest thanks to Gabriel Cooney, Katherine Chabalko, Isaac Gilead, Teresa Krauss, Lynn Meskell, Tim Schadla-Hall and Barbara Voss for their advice and support during the creation of this book. In addition, we are particularly grateful to John Schofield for his guidance and encouragement to both of us over several years, and for his input during the planning stages of this volume and the conference session it emerged from. For financial support we thank the Stanford Archaeology Center, the Stanford Department of Anthropology, University College London Institute of Archaeology and the Leverhulme Trust. Our heartfelt thanks to the contributors to the book and to the affective WAC 6 session in Dublin, as well as to the WAC 6 organizing committee and the One World Archaeology series editors. Finally, our thanks to our significant others for their patience and support.

Contents

Contributors

Iain Banks Centre for Battlefield Archaeology, University of Glasgow, Glasgow, Scotland, UK

Jeff Burton Manzanar National Historic Site, Independence, CA, USA

Gillian Carr Institute of Continuing Education, University of Cambridge, Cambridge, UK

Eleanor Conlin Casella School of Arts, Histories & Cultures, University of Manchester, Manchester, UK

Wayne Cocroft English Heritage, Cambridge, UK

Gonzalo Compañy Political-Cultural Memory Research Group (E.I.Me.Po.C.), Universidad Nacional de Rosario, Rosario, Argentina

Mary Farrell Coronado National Forest, Tucson, AZ, USA

Gabriela González Political-Cultural Memory Research Group (E.I.Me.Po.C.), Universidad Nacional de Rosario/CONICET, Rosario, Argentina

Alfredo González-Ruibal Heritage Laboratory, Spanish National Research Council, Santiago de Compostela, Spain

Vesa-Pekka Herva Department of Archaeology, University of Oulu, Oulu, Finland

Gabriel Moshenska Institute of Archaeology, University College London, London, UK

Adrian Myers Stanford Archaeology Center, Stanford University, Stanford, CA, USA

Harold Mytum School of Archaeology, Classics and Egyptology, Centre for Manx Studies, University of Liverpool, Liverpool, UK

Leonardo Ovando Political-Cultural Memory Research Group (E.I.Me.Po.C.), Universidad Nacional de Rosario, Rosario, Argentina

Nota Pantzou Museum of Political Exiles of Ai Stratis, Athens, Greece

Louise Purbrick School of Humanities, University of Brighton, Brighton, UK

David Rossetto Political-Cultural Memory Research Group (E.I.Me.Po.C.), Universidad Nacional de Rosario, Rosario, Argentina

Melisa Salerno National Council for Scientific and Technical Research, Buenos Aires, Argentina

John Schofield Department of Archaeology, University of York, York, UK

Oula Seitsonen Department of Geosciences and Geography, University of Helsinki, Helsinki, Finland

Judith Thomas Mercyhurst College, Mercyhurst Archaeological Institute, Erie, PA, USA

Lindsay Weiss Stanford Archaeology Center, Stanford University, Stanford, CA, USA

Andrés Zarankin Federal University of Minas Gerais, Belo Horizonte, Brazil

About the Editors

Adrian Myers is a PhD candidate in the Stanford Archaeology Center at Stanford University. For his dissertation research he is running excavations at a Prisoner of War camp that held German *Afrika Korps* soldiers in a national park in Canada during the Second World War.

Gabriel Moshenska is a Leverhulme Trust Early Career Research Fellow at UCL Institute of Archaeology. He works on the history of archaeology, public archaeology, and the archaeology and anthropology of Second World War Britain.

Chapter 1
An Introduction to Archaeologies of Internment

Gabriel Moshenska and Adrian Myers

Abstract In this opening chapter, we introduce the developing field of archaeologies of internment. We first illustrate the prevalence of modern forms of institutional internment around the world since the final decades of the nineteenth century. Second, we offer a tentative definition of "internment" and describe what is meant by an "archaeology of internment," including a review of previous research in the field. Third, we situate the archaeology of internment within an interdisciplinary context, and discuss some of its potential strengths and unique contributions. Fourth, and finally, we introduce and contextualize the chapters in this volume, and suggest some possible directions for future research.

The Experience of Internment

Internment, past and present, is in the news. During the writing of this intro-duction, US President Barack Obama is under fire for not closing the infamous Guantánamo Bay prison camp as promised, and the British government is defend-ing the internment of children of asylum seekers in immigration detention centers. At The Hague, Radovan Karadžić is on trial for alleged war crimes, includ-ing running concentration camps in the former Yugoslavia in the early 1990s. In Buenos Aires, former Argentinean president General Reynaldo Bignone has just been imprisoned for crimes including running a secret detention and torture cen-ter in the 1970s. The leader of the neo-fascist British National Party, Nick Griffin, was questioned on television about his belief or disbelief in the existence of the

G. Moshenska (✉)
Institute of Archaeology, University College London, London, UK
e-mail: g.moshenska@ucl.ac.uk

A. Myers
Stanford Archaeology Center, Stanford University, Stanford, CA, USA
e-mail: adrianmyers@stanford.edu

A. Myers, G. Moshenska (eds.), *Archaeologies of Internment*, One World Archaeology, DOI 10.1007/978-1-4419-9666-4_1, © Springer Science+Business Media, LLC 2011

Nazi extermination camps. The phenomenon of internment clearly has widespread resonance in society today.

The experience of internment is a common thread that links Winston Churchill, John McCain, Günter Grass, Nelson Mandela, Kurt Vonnegut, and Pope Benedict XVI. Internment has inspired powerful and influential books, including *The Gulag Archipelago* and *If This is a Man*, as well as popular films, such as *The Great Escape*, *Empire of the Sun*, and *Bridge on the River Kwai*. Despite their inherent restrictions, sites of internment have become spaces of intellectual and philosophical expansiveness: prisoners on Robben Island, South Africa, drafted the constitution for a new nation; Antonio Gramsci revolutionized Marxist philosophy in his *Prison Notebooks*; a group of rabbis in Auschwitz put God on trial; and Gerhard Bersu pioneered the archaeology of the Isle of Man (Chapter 3 by Mytum, this volume).

The long, varied, and often dark history of internment has played a significant role in shaping societies and cultures worldwide. It touches all the inhabited continents, the sea (e.g. Casella 2005) and, in the age of extraordinary rendition, the sky (e.g. Fastabend et al. 2004; Grey 2007). Internment stretches through time from the distant past to the present day and into the foreseeable future. The practice and experience of internment has been a powerful force in the forging of nation-states, in waging war and, some would argue, in maintaining peace (e.g. Cucullu 2009).

This book draws together studies from around the world with a shared interest in the material and historical traces of internment. It is based in part on a conference session held at the Sixth World Archaeological Congress, and we hope to invoke the ethos of that organization through the recognition that the past, with all its oppressions and injustices, is physically and socially materialized in the present. In this introduction, we examine some of the issues and concepts that make the archaeology of internment a coherent, if novel, field. Following this opening, we begin with a consideration of the word "internment" and argue for an inclusive and flexible conception of the term. The following section examines whether there is a need for an archaeology of internment, the precedents for work in this area, and the range of disciplinary contexts and influences on what is a highly interdisciplinary field of study. The next section of the introduction briefly discusses the contributions to this volume, highlighting connections and contrasts as well as some emergent themes for the discipline as a whole. The final section considers potential future directions for archaeologies of internment, which we anticipate will remain a vibrant field for years to come.

What is Internment?

In the most general archaeological sense, incarceration or internment might be described as the practice of organizing material culture and space to control and restrict the movement of a person or a group of people. Sites of internment can range in scale from a single room or building to entire landmasses. In the chapters of this book we see internment sites defined as physically bounded spaces, with either human-made boundaries such as fences and walls, or natural boundaries such as rivers or deserts. Landscapes of slavery and other coercive spaces bounded by fear or threats of violence are a separate but closely connected area of study.

There is currently some debate as to whether internment should be distinguished from imprisonment, and the contributors to this volume have taken a range of perspectives on this question. One useful if highly subjective definition of internment drawn from the chapters of this book might be all forms of unjust imprisonment: those that are not the result of a fair and equitable legal process. These forced movements serve social, political, economic and military ends and are often organized around conceptions of racial, ethnic, political and social otherness. The distinction between just and unjust laws and imprisonment is of course usually ambiguous. It is commonplace in criminology to state that prisons have little to do with justice and everything to do with brutal social control by elites. On similar grounds, some anarchists and prison abolitionists argue that all prisoners are political prisoners (e.g. Kropotkin 1927; Davis 2005; Davis and Rodriguez 2000).

A key theme in the history of internment is the notion of the camp, which is typically a newly built collection of more-or-less ephemeral structures designed for communal living, often bounded by a fence or other barrier, with that perimeter patrolled by armed guards. The internment camp is often modeled closely after the army camp, with the barrack as the archetypal structure in both contexts (Fig. 5.3). The architectural relationship between the army barrack and the internment barrack was perhaps formalized through the Hague Convention of 1899 (and later the Hague Convention of 1907 and the Geneva Conventions of 1906, 1929, and 1949) which stated that Prisoners of War (PoWs) must be held under conditions similar to the soldiers of the jailing nation (Geneva Convention 1988; Roland 1991; Vance 1992, 2000).

Everdell (1997) traces the first internment camp for civilians to the late nineteenth century. These "reconcentration camps" were established by the Spanish in Cuba, tested in 1869 and fully implemented in 1896. This system was set up to separate the Cuban rebels from the civilians: after rounding up the civilians and confining them in barbed-wire enclaves, anybody not locked up could be assumed to be a rebel (see also Netz 2004). The Spanish invention was first criticized, then rapidly copied, by the Americans in the Philippines in 1899 and by the British in South Africa in 1900 (Agamben 1997; Everdell 1997; Kessler 1999). Following the establishment of these earliest camps at the end of the nineteenth century, the First and Second World Wars were critical moments in the expansion of these technologies. Though an archaeology of internment should not be temporally bounded, the evidence does seem to suggest a particular association between the internment camp and the twentieth century, and perhaps even more specifically with what Hobsbawm called the "short twentieth century": that period of "accelerated modernity" which began with the start of the First World War (González-Ruibal 2007, 2008; Hobsbawm 1994).

Prominent and widely known historical examples of internment abound. Internment of PoWs has been a common practice for centuries and formed the basis for some of the earliest international laws. Today the most notorious examples of internment, such as Camp Delta at Guantánamo Bay, Cuba, are in violation of both national and international law (Rose 2004; Margulies 2006; Myers 2010). Where conflicts polarize ethnic communities, members of particular groups are often interned both to prevent their acting as spies or saboteurs, such as Germans in Britain in both World Wars (Bloch and Schuster 2005), or to prevent their joining insurgencies in colonial contexts, such as the Kikuyu in Kenya during the Mau Mau Uprising (Firoze and O'Coill 2002). Other examples of ethnic selection of internees, such as the Serb-run camps in the Bosnian War, were part of a wider scheme of genocide and ethnic cleansing (Campbell 2002). Labor camps, where prisoners are forced to work, existed most infamously in Nazi Europe (Chapter 5 by Myers, this volume) and the Soviet Union (Applebaum 2003), and these harsh penal methods remain in use in China and elsewhere today (Shaw 2010). In these cases the perceived need to isolate a population can conflict with the need to locate them close to their workplaces, whether rural and agricultural as in the case of Chinese forced laborers, or largely urban and industrial as in the Nazi case.

Internment and labor camps aim to control bodies, but some are expressly aimed at controlling minds, as shown in several chapters of this book (e.g. Chapter 4 by González-Ruibal, this volume). In post-war Europe "de-Nazification camps" tried to instill ideas of democracy in the German population (Herz 1948). Since 1957, Chinese dissidents and political prisoners have been sentenced to periods in "re-education through labor" camps. Internment camps are often used to control groups and populations on the move. Refugees, asylum seekers and "illegals" are interned in large numbers for defying national borders, those most arbitrary and often dehumanizing divisions of space (Dow 2004).

In the aftermaths of wars, violent conflicts and natural disasters, large populations of displaced persons are often housed in refugee camps—which have been shown to be a direct descendant of the internment camps of the Second World War (Malkki 1995). In 1945, as the war in Europe was ending, millions of displaced persons (DPs), including demobilized soldiers, Holocaust survivors and bombed-out civilians, were put into camps so that their movements could be regulated (e.g. Malkki 1995; Burström 2009). Internments of this kind are often defended as a means of providing food and shelter, as well as helping to prevent epidemics. In post-war Europe, many of the camps used to house displaced persons had previously held PoWs, political prisoners, forced laborers and soldiers. The institutional and material similarities that enabled these divergent yet connected uses are of significance to archaeologists attempting to understand the past uses of space through traces surviving in the present.

What is the Current State of the Archaeology of Internment?

In photographs, films, art and literature, the internment of civilians and soldiers in temporary or hastily constructed camps is often represented by a recurring set of material symbols, including barbed wire, watch towers and cell blocks. Barbed wire, a nineteenth-century American invention, is perhaps especially notable as both material reality and metaphor: it has inspired a surprisingly wide body of academic and popular writing (e.g. Liu 2009; Netz 2004; Razac 2000; Krell 2002; Vischer 1919). On a smaller scale we think of the uniforms, restraints and the prisoners' bodies themselves: shaved, shackled, starved or simply confined. But despite their iconic material manifestations, many of these camps have disappeared entirely or are only visible as traces. The brief but awesome power and significance of these structures belie their physical fragility and transience: today even some of the largest and most notorious camps have virtually disappeared from view (e.g. Gilead et al. 2009). As the people who experienced these spaces grow older and die, most of what we can learn about these spaces will come from archaeology.

If internment is a controversial practice, then the history and archaeology of internment is no less problematic. The conflict and controversy begins with the creation of a prison or camp and extends into the future, even to a time when nothing remains but a "site." Former internment camps are now museums, education centers and World Heritage Sites—as well as fields, forests, and urban residential neighborhoods.

Where interpretations and presentations of buildings or artifacts are present, these are continually and sometimes violently contested (Dwork and Van Pelt 1996:354–378). Thus the study of internment inevitably includes the study of its contested history and contested commemorations (Ashplant et al. 2000; Purbrick et al. 2007; Logan and Reeves 2009). With these conflicts come ethical and methodological quandaries: archaeologies of violence and violently contested pasts present complex problems that must be addressed from the outset (Meskell and Pels 2005; Moshenska 2008, 2010). The comparative novelty of archaeological approaches to internment is reflected in the scope of the published literature, which largely consists of site reports, with relatively few comparative studies or syntheses. Nevertheless there is growing interest in this field and it is reasonable to predict that in the coming years a greater number and range of articles and monographs will begin to appear.

There is an apparent dearth of archaeological research into the first generations of concentration camps: some investigation into the early South African Boer War concentration Camps is apparently ongoing but there are no publications to date (Willem Boshoff personal communication 2008). There is no known archaeological research, and apparently very little historical research of any kind, on the early civilian concentration camps in Cuba and the Philippines, and there is a single known report on the archaeology of internment from the First World War (Francis 2008).

A handful of archaeologists have begun to direct their research at the vast complex of camps that were built in Europe during the Second World War, such as Ronald Hirte's work at Buchenwald concentration camp near Weimar, Germany. Hirte excavated a number of war-era dumps "resulting in a collection of several thousand found objects, primarily simple articles of everyday life in the camps" (Hirte n.d.). Many of these artifacts were made by hand or personalized by camp inmates, serving as a reminder of the rich potential for a biographical approach to internment camp artifacts. An international team is currently working at the Sobibor extermination camp in Poland, conducting survey, geophysics and excavations toward an "archaeology of extermination" (Gilead et al. 2009). This project is an example of how archaeologists can become entangled with the subject of their own study: two of the project director's family members were murdered at Sobibor during the Holocaust.

One of the best-known projects focusing on this era occurred at Stalag Luft III, the Second World War PoW camp, made famous by the 1963 film *The Great Escape*. This interdisciplinary project involved remote sensing and excavations, one of the goals being to locate the escape tunnels *Tom*, *Dick* and *Harry* made famous in the film (Pringle et al. 2007; Doyle et al. 2010). This work is perhaps most useful in its demonstration of the utility of geophysical techniques at such sites: remote sensing work successfully located the *Dick* escape tunnel, which was confirmed by subsequent excavations. The excavations also uncovered remains of the tin can tunnel ventilation system and an escape kit that had been left in the tunnel shaft.

Just as the Second World War brought internment camps to Europe, it also initiated (or expanded) the systems of camps in America, Australia, Canada, South Africa and other nations. In the United States the archaeology of this period has focused on researching the internment of Japanese American civilians. An anthropological research-driven approach to Japanese American internment has been instigated by Bonnie Clark at the University of Denver (Clark 2008; Skiles and Clark 2010). In 2008 Clark's first full field season at the Granada Relocation Center in south-eastern Colorado examined the lives of women and children in the camp, as well as the gardening activities of the internees. A successful program of community collaboration and public interpretation was also developed, with former internees and descendants, among others, visiting the site and working with the archaeologists.

Burton has authored and co-authored an impressive collection of archaeological reports on the sites of the former Japanese American Second World War camps in America (e.g. Burton 1996; Burton et al. 1999). His work includes an overview of the archaeological resources as well as more detailed reports on a selection of specific sites. The archaeology of PoW camps in Britain is also a developing field of research but the published literature is largely limited to descriptive reports and assessments of "what survives and where" (Thomas 2003a, b).

During the Second World War, captured Axis soldiers were sometimes transported from continental Europe, Africa and elsewhere for internment in North America, Australia, South Africa, and elsewhere. The theory behind this policy was that in the event of a successful invasion of Britain the PoWs might become newly available to the Axis armies. Thus thousands of men were transported across oceans to be interned in camps on other continents. The United States Department of Defense has completed a comprehensive historical assessment of all of the Second World War PoW camps built on its lands (Listman et al. 2006), providing a significant resource for future archaeology. Other reports exist for Second World War era PoW camps in Australia (Austral Archaeology 1992) and Canada (Myers 2009).

An exception to the usual cursory reporting of Second World War PoW camps is found in the work of Michael Waters of Texas A&M University. Waters and his research team investigated Camp Hearne, a Texas PoW camp that held 5,000 German prisoners; the result of their work was published as the full length monograph *Lone Star Stalag* (Waters 2004). Waters reconstructs daily life in the camp based on his comprehensive archival, oral-historical and archaeological research. Waters' treatment might serve as a model for other research projects at North American PoW camps.

The archaeology of internment camps, as a specific area of interest for archaeologists, has reached a critical developmental moment. Increasing attention is being paid to the relevant sites, there is a growing awareness of the research within the wider discipline and, most importantly, the archaeologists working on internment in the recent past are starting to talk to each other. A number of detailed methodological statements on internment site studies have begun to appear, highlighting some of the practical issues in archaeologies of internment (Gilead et al. 2009; Pringle et al. 2007). The critical archaeological study of internment sites has been revitalized by Eleanor Casella's research, and particularly her book *The Archaeology of Institutional Confinement* (2007), which examines imprisonment and internment in America from a historical-archaeological perspective. Casella's work sets out a program for an archaeology of internment that examines the material manifestations of both the social policies of internment and the responses of the individuals who experienced it.

Despite these important advances, much of the work in the field remains unpublished and reports are sometimes difficult to obtain. Limited funding appears to be a serious challenge for archaeologists, and the majority of research on internment sites has been conducted by contract archaeology firms, as attested by the generally descriptive nature of many reports. However, Burton's work on the internment of Japanese Americans stands out as a model for Cultural Resource Management (CRM) reports that go beyond the basic descriptions and listings. The results of CRM work in general should be better recognized as a valuable research resource; Clark's anthropological project, for example, benefits from an earlier report prepared by a contract firm (Ellis 2004). In light of Casella's recent work and the developments described above, it would seem that now is an appropriate time both for critical assessments of the research to date, and a discussion of new approaches and areas of study.

Disciplinary Contexts

Where should we locate the archaeology of internment as a discipline? Like the young but well established interest areas of the archaeology of the recent past (Buchli and Lucas 2001; Harrison and Schofield 2010; Fortenberry and Myers 2010) and twentieth-century conflict archaeology (Saunders 2004; Schofield 2009), the archaeology of internment crosses a number of traditional disciplinary boundaries. The archaeological element in the studies in this book includes methodologies, theoretical frameworks and institutional and professional allegiances. Perhaps most fundamentally, archaeology refers to the focus on historical material culture, which can be approached from a number of directions other than those traditionally archaeological. Thus archaeologists studying internment will find themselves working as or with historians, archivists, oral historians, criminologists, architects and others. Fields such as human geography, heritage studies, museum studies and architectural history will have much to offer and much to gain from close working relationships.

Though boundaries are malleable, there does seem to be a particular association between the archaeology of internment and the wider field of archaeologies of modern conflict (Schofield et al. 2002). These studies have emerged from battlefield archaeology and historical archaeology, and focus on the theme of conflict in its broadest sense, including both physically violent and nonviolent forms. The archaeology of modern conflict examines contested spaces, sites, bodies and objects, and through these processes engages with contested pasts, making it a strong contender for a disciplinary home for studies of internment.

The nascent archaeology of recent internment also needs to consider its neighbors. These include archaeologies and ethnographies of prisons, schools, workhouses, leprosaria, monasteries and reform establishments such as boys colonies, as they contribute much to the closely related discussions on institutional life (Beisaw and Gibb 2009; Casella 2007; Spencer-Wood and Baugher 2001). There is a particularly rich literature on archaeological approaches to nineteenth-century prisons (Best 1987, 1992; Casella 1999, 2000a, b, 2001a–d, 2005). Studies of the archaeology of internment camps in earlier eras, such as the PoW camps of the American Civil War, are also relevant (Avery et al. 2008; Bush 2000, 2009; Thoms 2000, 2004). An argument could also be made for the relevance of bounded landscapes, such as reservations and sites of exile (Doughton 1997), plantation and urban slavery in the American South (e.g. Epperson 2000), military installations such as army camps (Schofield et al. 2006a) and contemporary maximum security prisons (e.g. Mears 2008; Pizarro and Stenius 2004).

What Can We Hope to Learn?

What can the material remains of internment spaces tell us about the organizations and societies that shaped and were shaped by them? As an introduction to this issue, here is another question: why do some prisons and internment camps closely resemble planned utopian communities: or, why have some utopian communities been designed like prisons (Van Bueren 2006)? The key to this juxtaposition is the notion that arrangements of material culture and space can manipulate or control human behavior. Hospitals display a similar spatial patterning, with an emphasis on widespread, accessible public spaces and small, confined private spaces. Hillier and Hanson (1984) highlight the contrast between modern prisons, hospitals and other public buildings on the one hand, and traditional homes on the other. They conclude that prisons are "reversed buildings" in which structures or arrangements of space embody and reinforce social ideas: "they are expressions and realizations of these organizing principles in a domain that is more structured than the world outside the boundary" (Hillier and Hanson 1984:184). It is through this lens that we should approach the archaeology of internment.

The arrangement of space in internment camps and buildings is an important area for archaeological study. For example, some forms of internment separate male and female internees while others, like most PoW camps, are exclusively male. These forms of segregation can often be witnessed in the archaeological record, either through the division of space and duplication of facilities, or through possible gender-specific artifacts and other material traces. The control and expression of prisoners' sexuality is a key element of internment, and one that is often neglected in historical studies, although one source uncharacteristically reveals that a few British PoWs in the Second World War declared "home or homo by Christmas!" (Morison 1995). Rape and sexual violence are common features of internment, both as forms of torture and coercion, and as a result of the increased vulnerability and dependence of the internees. Internment camps have been used to facilitate systematic rape (Diken and Laustsen 2005).

If the material culture of internment ranges from portable objects to buildings, settlements, landscapes and landmasses, then there are substantial opportunities for archaeological perspectives on these diverse elements. We might ask what food was available to the internees and their guards, where it was sourced, how and where it was prepared and consumed. From this information we can begin to examine the economic structures of internment, including perhaps the internal economy of trade and exchange between internees (e.g. Myers 2008, 2009; Valentine and Longstaff 1998). In many internment camps and prisons, varying degrees of malnutrition have been used as a means of control, keeping prisoners physically and psychologically weakened and distracted. Discussions of food feature prominently in historical accounts and memoirs of internment (e.g. Arct 1995; Spiegelman 2003; Williams 1949). Archaeological investigations of internment sites can provide insights into both the official food economy of the site and the unofficial economy of contraband, trade, bribery and hoarding (Chapter 5 by Myers, this volume). This use of archaeology as a source for ethno-historical studies of internment has a range of possible applications.

Archaeologists might contribute to the study of the economics of constructing and running internment sites. Internment is almost always expensive for governments or military groups, but is often extremely profitable for the private sector. The Nazi SS, in cooperation with German manufacturing titans such as Krupp and Bayer, made sure that their concentration and extermination camps extracted income in every possible way from the labor, possessions and corpses of the internees. Today, alliances between the US Department of Defense and contractors such as Kellogg, Brown & Root, and the privatization of the internment of asylum seekers in Europe have enriched a select few while draining the pockets of the taxpayers. To study the infrastructure of internment, we can examine what was constructed, when and by whom, and how much they profited from it.

What can an archaeological approach that reads between the lines of official and technical accounts of internment tell us about the internees themselves, their lives, strategies, personalities and forms of physical or mental escape? We know that these factors are most strongly affected by the aims of the internment: to control, contain, punish, protect, exploit and murder. Thus the formation and re-formation of individual and group identities is an important factor in the study of internment; for example, in the control, regulation and personalization of spaces through graffiti, violence, threats or consensus.

One of the recurring themes or mythologies of internment is, unsurprisingly, freedom and escape. This includes spiritual freedom, physical freedom or a more personal sense of liberation. These can be gained through petty control of time and space, through escape attempts, and not uncommonly through drug use or suicide (e.g. Human Rights Watch 2008). All of these activities leave their traces in the archaeological record: the archaeology of escape tunnels and escape equipment is a recent development in this field (Pringle et al. 2007). The scope for archaeological contributions to our understanding of internment is wide, both in the unique perspectives these offer and as part of a multidisciplinary approach to sites of contemporary resonance and significance.

In This Book

How, then, have researchers begun to apply these potential forms and foci for the archaeology of internment in practice? The chapters in this book are case studies from the broadly defined disciplines of contemporary and historical archaeology, as applied to practices of internment ranging across more than a century of world history. Weiss (Chapter 2) examines the sinister continuities between the use of camps to control workers in the diamond fields of late nineteenth-century South Africa and the later use of civilian internment camps in the same areas during the Boer War. This revealing comparison of colonial oppression and wartime exigency exposes the brutal inhumanity they share: the conflation of killing and working to death echo back to slavery, and forward to the Holocaust. Weiss convincingly argues that the paranoia around the illicit trade in diamonds based on theft from mines led to a form of control over workers' bodies that matched or exceeded that of an actual internment camp. Combined with routinely fatal working conditions, the economic logic of the diamond industry and the colonial project as a whole have controversially been compared to economic aspects of the Holocaust (Lindqvist 1996). Weiss considers the peculiar socio-legal circumstance of the bodies of the diamond miners, stripped of the presumption of innocence and accordingly their physical freedom. The study of the confined body is a fascinating one that will continue to grow in archaeologies of internment.

Banks' comparison of work and prison camps in Second World War Scotland (Chapter 7) is analogous to Weiss' study, but it highlights a very different equivalence. While the work camp was built to accommodate "friends" (the Canadian guest workers), the PoW camp was built for "enemies." However, these "enemies" were protected by international conventions. To the extent that the two camps are comparable in form, the common practicalities of accommodating groups of young single men seemingly outweigh the ideological differences. Banks' analysis draws on detailed archaeological studies of both sites, and his comparison of the different roles of the fences, one to imprison and one to demarcate, highlight the challenges of interpreting the archaeological record of even the very recent past.

González-Ruibal's account of the internment and concentration camps of the Spanish Civil War and its aftermath (Chapter 4) paints a grim picture of brutality and deprivation analogous to that of the Nazi concentration camps. Most of these internment sites were reused structures—such as schools, bullrings and religious buildings including monasteries and seminaries. González-Ruibal argues that the use of religious buildings was a conscious element of a larger plan to mould "rebels" or "reds" into "good Catholic Spaniards." The policies of widespread forced labor or "redemption through work" also reinforced this idea, employing a range of dehumanizing and de-individualizing techniques of social engineering on a large contingent of the population deemed a sub-human mass of "red scum." The theme of forced labor is a recurrent one throughout this volume, linking this paper to Weiss' study of diamond mining, the studies of Finnish and Arizonan road-building camps and Myers' consideration of material culture in Auschwitz, with its famous slogan *Arbeit Macht Frei*. In Chapter 4, by González-Ruibal, the concept of forced labor cuts across another key theme in internment, that of social engineering—including, for example, the removal of a category of people from society to change the nature of that society. This can be simply for physical separation, as in Chapter 11 by Pantzou, Chapter 3 by Mytum, and Chapter 8 by Carr; for a period of reform or re-education, as in Chapter 4 by González-Ruibal; or as a step toward mass murder, as in Chapter 5 by Myers and Chapter 12 by Zarankin and Salerno.

Myers' study of the Auschwitz concentration/extermination camp complex (Chapter 5) examines this symbol of the Holocaust from a material culture perspective. This unusual viewpoint highlights the brutally materialistic world of the death camp in which people's possessions and later their bodies were harvested on an industrial scale to feed the war economy and ideological bloodlust of the Nazi regime. Stripped of their belongings, the few objects the inmates possessed took on immense practical and symbolic significance, as Myers shows: losing your spoon, hat or clogs often amounted to a death sentence. At the same time, the small minority of prisoners employed in processing the possessions of new arrivals at the camp were able to access a super-abundance of material, including food, some of which they stole or smuggled into the camp, sustaining the black market among the prisoners.

The archetypal internment camps in popular consciousness are probably those from the Second World War, due in part to the considerable body of writing produced by former PoWs from this period. Thomas' study of a PoW camp for German prisoners in Texas (Chapter 9) is an exemplary exposition of the form and function of these sorts of camps, and of the survival, significance and vulnerability of their archaeological traces. The historical background research includes a series of vignettes that illuminate the nature of everyday life in the camp, including endless complaints about food, half-hearted escape attempts, petty corruption and badly paid labor. The documented accounts attest to haphazard adherence to standard camp building patterns and the continuous adaptation and rebuilding of aspects of the infrastructure: a cautionary tale for any archaeologists seeking literal embodiments of internment ideologies.

Whatever the rationale for the location of PoW camps, whether convenience or security, climate was not usually a consideration. From the Texan heat we move to the extreme cold of Northern Finland, where Seitsonen and Herva (Chapter 10) excavated a camp built for Soviet prisoners in the Second World War. From an archaeological perspective, the German guards, though numerically fewer, were inevitably richer in portable and disposable material culture than their more numerous Soviet captives. But Seitsonen and Herva describe the difficulties the Germans experienced in adapting their military tactics and technology to the frozen landscape, and the archaeology backs this up, with a significant amount of Finnish material culture mixed in with the German goods.

The civilian internment camps of the Second World War are less numerous and less known than the military PoW camps. These tended to be less regulated and regimented due in part to the legal and constitutional ambiguities surrounding their use, as well as the more diverse populations they enclosed. Carr's study (Chapter 8) looks at the small but significant number of civilians from the Channel Islands, already living under German occupation, who were held in camps in Germany for the latter part of the war. In contrast, Mytum considers German civilian internment on the Isle of Man (Chapter 3) in both the First and Second World Wars, providing a parallel to the accounts collected by Carr. Stories from civilian internment such as these often mention the crushing boredom of life behind the wire, and the psychological impact of the restrictions and lack of privacy. Presumably PoWs, in contrast to civilians, can be expected to have become at least somewhat accustomed to boredom, petty controls, and communal living during their pre-internment military lives.

Like Carr's and Mytum's chapters, Farrell and Burton's study of the Catalina Prison Camp (Chapter 6) examines civilian internment during the Second World War. Like Thomas' chapter, it is based on CRM work in the USA, and like the camp in Seitsonen and Herva' chapter it involves road construction. Unlike these studies, Farrell and Burton's site of internment heritage has a hero: Gordon Hirabayashi, a Japanese American student who argued that the internment of American citizens of Japanese descent was unconstitutional and unethical. Hirabayashi was given a short prison sentence, which he served at the Catalina camp in Arizona. In the 1980s, Hirabayashi's case was re-examined and his resistance became part of the civil rights narrative. Hirabayashi's internment at the camp, albeit brief, was used to challenge a decision to not add the camp site to the National Register of Historic Places. Farrell and Burton's study highlights the complexities of formal commemoration and commemorative practices at sites of internment, a recurring theme throughout this book. Narratives of oppression and resistance often come into conflict with real or perceived guilt and shame, including conflicting conceptions of victim, perpetrator and bystander. Meanwhile in some cases such as those described by González-Ruibal (Chapter 4) and Compañy et al. (Chapter 13) the sites can become foci for revisiting or refighting the original conflicts.

Several of the chapters describe the use of landscape features as technologies of internment. One of the most common types of geography used for imprisonment is islands, as in the famous cases of Alcatraz and Robben Island, and the Isle of Man (Chapter 3 by Mytum, this volume). Pantzou's study of the Greek island of Ai Stratis (Chapter 11) shows how the isolation and natural boundaries of islands have been used over time for the exile or banishment of individuals, as well as for the internment of larger groups. Ai Stratis has a long history of housing political prisoners during a number of periods from 1929 through to the end of the Greek Junta in 1974. Despite the official policy of erasing the traces of closed internment camps, and the earthquake that devastated the area in 1968, Pantzou shows that the material evidence of imprisonment can still be found on the island. Pantzou raises the issue of dark or uncomfortable heritage, a central theme in studies of internment, and a key element in the socio-politics of remembering and forgetting events that divided a nation.

Many of the post-1945 authoritarian regimes that have practiced mass internment of civilians are located in Latin America (see Funari et al. 2009). Notorious sites of internment include the Chilean National Stadium and the Naval Mechanics School in Buenos Aires. Zarankin and Salerno examine the history of clandestine detention centers in Argentina (Chapter 12), focusing on the 2002 excavation of the *Club Atlético* site, where around 1,500 political prisoners were held, tortured and murdered in 1977 before the site was razed to conceal the evidence of the crime. As with the excavation of the Gestapo headquarters in Berlin in 1985 (discussed below), survivors of the Argentinean detention centre and relatives of victims took part in the archaeological work on the site. This suggests a valuable social impact of conducting the archaeology of contested sites as a public or community archaeology, accessible to those affected by the site so that the excavation or survey project itself can become an arena for articulating and contesting different memory narratives (Moshenska 2007, 2010). In a related study, Compañy et al. (Chapter 13) describe the survey and recording of another detention centre *El Pozo* in Argentina, where again the survivors and relatives of victims chose to visit the site repeatedly to interact with the archaeologists and the space in an intensely emotional environment that challenged the desirability of emotionally disconnected research on sites of painful heritage such as these.

Schofield and Cocroft's study of the Stasi Hohenschönhausen prison (Chapter 14) took the form of *dérive*-like organized wanderings around the landscape context of the jail, mapping and photographing the abandoned factories and other buildings as well as the Stasi complex itself. Since the study was carried out, the prison featured prominently in the successful film *The Lives of Others*, which portrayed not only the offices of the Stasi, but also the residential complexes where employees lived and indeed where many of them still live. Schofield and Cocroft's photographs depict a once-feared centre of power reduced to a decrepit shell, and their discussion of the site reflects on the paradox that the popular culture depiction of internment camps are sometimes better known than the tangible historic sites themselves. It was in Berlin that the excavation of internment sites began, with the Active Museum's 1985 excavation of the Gestapo headquarters, including the cell-block in the basement, which is now a museum (Rürup 1996; Baker 1990; Moshenska 2010).

Purbrick describes recording the site of the Long Kesh/Maze prison in Northern Ireland (Chapter 15) from its closure and abandonment in 2000 to its near-total demolition beginning in 2006. For a time there were plans to reuse rather than redevelop the site, and several of the infamous H Blocks were cleaned out and redecorated, including painting over the numerous iconic murals and graffiti in both the Loyalist and the Republican blocks. Some of these artworks survived, and Purbrick discusses these in relation to the rich symbolic tradition of political murals in Northern Ireland, many of which are increasingly being regarded as heritage sites or civic artworks worthy of preservation. The murals in the Long Kesh/Maze site, on the other hand, are "orphan heritage" with no proximate community to advocate for their significance (Price 2005). Purbrick reflects on the extreme difficulty facing anyone who might have wanted to preserve or memorialize the H Blocks and their artworks, and raises the question of whether their loss is in fact a positive step in moving toward reconciliation in the affected communities. Material remains and the archaeological processes we devote to them drag painful and difficult pasts into the here-and-now: their power and significance cannot be underestimated, but we should not be afraid to ask whether in some cases material loss and the erasure of memory might not be a necessary stage in conflict resolution.

Future Directions for the Archaeology of Internment

Where do we go from here? The papers in this volume demonstrate the diversity of the field as well as its strength. The archaeology of internment has emerged as a distinct field with links to areas of study including material culture, heritage and tourism, history, museums, anthropology, human geography, planning, psychology, penology, public health and public policy. It is closely associated with conflict archaeology, historical archaeology and indigenous or postcolonial archaeologies. The overview of recent and contemporary work contained in this book, together with assessments of previous work in the field, not only shows a dynamic and exciting new discipline beginning to find its feet, but also highlights opportunities for growth, development and expansion.

The corpus of work on modern internment camps suffers from major gaps: archaeological reports on the earliest era of modern internment camps (in Cuba, the Philippines, South Africa, and elsewhere) are virtually nonexistent. Similarly, there is only one known report on a camp from the First World War. The particular knowledge and skills developed in the context of archaeology conducted at Second World War era camps, where a significant amount of research has already occurred, might be deployed at these earlier sites of internment. Such a program would clearly provide critical information and understanding about the genesis of the modern internment camp.

Archaeologists' engagements with the material remains of the recent past are growing in number, confidence and quality. A significant number of these studies have focused on contested pasts: episodes of historic violence, oppression or injustice that resonate in the contemporary world. It is within this context that we hope to see archaeologies of internment grow and develop. Perhaps the most valuable outcome of the long view on internment and internees that this work offers could be a critique of the practice of internment in the present day. One of the largest groups of people interned today are refugees, migrants and asylum seekers, displaced by conflict, natural disasters or economic privations. The hardships suffered by these people are exacerbated by their unjust criminalization when they seek to cross borders in search of a better life. The internment of young children in these camps and detention centers is particularly repellent.

The world is as full of civilian internment camps as it has ever been since their inception in the late nineteenth century, and they remain both symbols and technologies of inhumanity. Hopefully some of the outrage engendered by studying archaeologies of internment can help to change this shameful situation.

References

Agamben, G. 1997 The Camp as the Nomos of the Modern. In *Violence, Identity, and Self Determination*, edited by H. De Vries and S. Weber, pp. 106–118. Stanford University Press, Stanford.

Applebaum, A. 2003 *Gulag: A History*. Doubleday, New York.

Arct, B. 1995 *Prisoner of War: My Secret Journal*. Michael Joseph, London.

Ashplant, T., G. Dawson, and M. Roper 2000 *The Politics of War Memory and Commemoration*. Routledge, London.

Austral Archaeology 1992 Loveday Internment Camp Archaeological Survey. Unpublished Report Prepared for the South Australian Department of Environment and Planning by Austral Archaeology.

Avery, P.G., P.H. Garrow, J.A. Sichler, K.D. Hollenbach, and N.P. Herrmann 2008 Phase III Archaeological Investigations at 38FL2, The Florence Stockade, Florence, South Carolina. Unpublished Report Prepared by Mactec Engineering and Consulting for the Department of Veterans Affairs, National Cemetery Administration, Washington, DC.

Baker, F. 1990 Archaeology, Habermas, and the Pathologies of Modernity. In *Writing the Past in the Present*, edited by F. Baker and J. Thomas, pp. 54–66. St. David's University Press, Lampeter.

Beisaw, A. and J. Gibb (eds.) 2009 *The Archaeology of Institutional Life*. University of Alabama Press, Tuscaloosa.

Best, S. 1987 Auckland's First Courthouse, Common Gaol and House of Correction: A Preliminary Report on The Initial Salvage Excavation. Unpublished Report Prepared for the New Zealand Historic Places Trust, Auckland Regional Committee.

Best, S. 1992 The Queen Street Gaol: Auckland's First Courthouse, Common Gaol and House of Correction (site R11/1559). Unpublished Report Prepared for the Department of Conservation, Auckland Conservancy.

Bloch, A. and L. Schuster 2005 At the Extremes of Exclusion: Deportation, Detention and Dispersal. *Ethnic and Racial Studies* 28(3): 491–512.

Buchli, V. and G. Lucas (eds.) 2001 *Archaeologies of the Contemporary Past*. Routledge, London.

Burström, M. 2009 Selective Remembrance: Memories of a Second World War Refugee Camp in Sweden. *Norwegian Archaeological Review* 42(2): 159–172.

Burton, J. 1996 Three Farewells to Manzanar. National Park Service Publications in Anthropology 67. Western Archaeological and Conservation Center, Tucson, Arizona.

Burton, J., M. Farrell, F. Lord, and R. Lord 1999 Confinement and Ethnicity: An Overview of World War II Japanese American Relocation Sites. National Park Service Publications in Anthropology 74. Western Archaeological and Conservation Center, Tucson, Arizona.

Bush, D. 2000 Interpreting the Latrines of the Johnson's Island Civil War Military Prison. *Historical Archaeology* 34(1): 62–78.

Bush, D. 2009 Maintaining or Mixing Southern Culture in a Northern Prison: Johnson's Island Military Prison. In *The Archaeology of Institutional Life*, edited by A. Beisaw and J. Gibb, pp. 153–171. University of Alabama Press, Tuscaloosa.

Campbell, D. 2002 Atrocity, Memory, Photography: Imaging the Concentration Camps of Bosnia– The Case of ITN Versus *Living Marxism*, Part 2. *Journal of Human Rights* 1(2): 143–172.

Casella, E. 1999 These Women Subject'd to Strict Separate Treatment: An Archaeology of Penal Confinement. *Historic Environment* 14(2): 11–16.

Casella, E. 2000a "Doing Trade": A Sexual Economy of 19th Century Australian Female Convict Prisons. *World Archaeology* 32(2): 209–221.

Casella, E. 2000b Bulldaggers and Gentle Ladies: Archaeological Approaches to Female Homosexuality in Convict Era Australia. In *Archaeologies of Sexuality*, edited by R. Schmidt and B. Voss, pp. 143–159. Routledge, London.

Casella, E. 2001a Every Procurable Object: A Functional Analysis of the Ross Female Factory Archaeological Collection. *Australasian Historical Archaeology* 19: 25–38.

Casella, E. 2001b Landscapes of Punishment and Resistance: A Female Convict Settlement in Tasmania. In *Contested Landscapes: Landscapes of Movement and Exile*, edited by B. Bender and M. Winer, pp. 103–120. Berg, Oxford.

Casella, E. 2001c To Watch or Restrain: Female Convict Prisons in 19th Century Tasmania. *International Journal of Historical Archaeology* 5(1): 45–72.

Casella, E. 2001d *Your Unfortunate and Undutiful Wife, Chained Letters: Convict Narratives.* Melbourne University Press, Melbourne.

Casella, E. 2005 Prisoner of His Majesty: Postcoloniality and the Archaeology of British Penal Transportation. *World Archaeology* 37(3): 453–467

Casella, E. 2007 *The Archaeology of Institutional Confinement.* University Press of Florida, Gainesville.

Clark, B. 2008 Artifact Versus Relic: Ethics and the Archaeology of the Recent Past. *Anthropology News* 49(7): 23.

Cucullu, G. 2009 *Inside Gitmo: The True Story Behind the Myths of Guantánamo Bay.* Collins, New York.

Davis, A. 2005 *Abolition Democracy: Beyond Prisons, Torture, and Empire.* Seven Stories Press, New York.

Davis, A. and D. Rodriguez 2000 The Challenge of Prison Abolition: A Conversation. *Social Justice* 27(3): 212–218.

Diken, B. and C. Laustsen 2005 Becoming Abject: Rape as a Weapon of War. *Body & Society* 11(1): 111–128.

Doughton, T. 1997 Unseen Neighbors: Native Americans of Central Massachusetts, A People Who Had "Vanished". In *After King Philip's War, Presence and Persistence in Indian New England*, edited by C. Calloway, pp. 207–230. University Press of New England, Hanover.

Dow, M. 2004 *American Gulag: Inside U.S. Immigration Prisons.* University of California Press, Berkeley.

Doyle, P., L. Babits, and J. Pringle 2010 Yellow Sands and Penguins: The Soil of "The Great Escape". In *Soil and Culture*, edited by E. Landa and C. Feller, pp. 417–429. Springer, New York.

Dwork, D. and J. Van Pelt 1996 *Auschwitz, 1270 to the Present.* W.W. Norton & Company, New York.

Ellis, S. 2004 Camp Amache, Prowers County, Colorado: Site Management, Preservation, and Interpretive Plan. Unpublished Report Prepared by SWCA Cultural Resources (SWCA Project No. 6818-058 and Report No. 2004-48).

Epperson, T. 2000 Panoptic Plantations: The Garden Sights of Thomas Jefferson and George Mason. In *Lines that Divide: Historical Archaeologies of Race, Class, and Gender*, edited by S. Mrozowski, J. Delle, and R. Paynter, pp. 58–77. University of Tennessee Press, Knoxville.

Everdell, W. 1997 *The First Moderns: Profiles in the Origins of Twentieth-Century Thought*. University of Chicago Press, Chicago.

Fastabend, D., E. Hanlon, R.A. Route, and D. MacGhee 2004 *Detainee Operations in a Joint Environment: Multi Service Tactics, Techniques, and Procedures*. United States Department of Defense, Washington.

Firoze, M. and C. O'Coill 2002 The Missionary Position: NGOs and Development in Africa. *International Affairs* 78(3): 567–583.

Fortenberry, B. and A. Myers (eds.) 2010 Special Journal Issue on "Perspectives on the Recent Past". *Archaeologies* 6(1): 1–192.

Francis, P. 2008 *The World War I Internment Camp on Mount Revelstoke: First Archaeological Assessment*. Report available from Cultural Resource Services, Western and Northern Service Centre Parks Canada Agency, Calgary.

Funari, P., A. Zarankin, and M. Salerno 2009 *Memories from Darkness: Archaeology of Repression and Resistance in Latin America*. Springer, New York.

Geneva Convention 1988 Geneva Convention for Revision of the Geneva Convention of 1906: Convention Relative to the Treatment of Prisoners of War Signed at Geneva, July 27, 1929. In *The Laws of Armed Conflicts: A Collection of Conventions, Resolutions, and Other Documents*, edited by D. Schindler and J. Toman, pp. 341–364. Nijhoff, Dordrecht.

Gilead, I., Y. Haimi, and W. Mazurek 2009 Excavating Nazi Extermination Centres. *Present Pasts* 1: 10–39.

González-Ruibal, A. 2007 Making Things Public: Archaeologies of the Spanish Civil War. *Public Archaeology* 6(4): 203–226.

González-Ruibal, A. 2008 Time to Destroy: An Archaeology of Supermodernity. *Current Anthropology* 49(2): 247–279.

Gramsci, A. 1971 *Selections from the Prison Notebooks*. Lawrence & Wishart, London.

Grey, S. 2007 *Ghost Plane: The Inside Story of the CIA's Secret Rendition Programme*. Janaca, Auckland Park.

Harrison, R. and J. Schofield 2010 *After Modernity: Archaeological Approaches to the Contemporary Past*. Oxford University Press, Oxford.

Herz, J. 1948 The Fiasco of Denazification in Germany. *Political Science Quarterly* 63(4): 569–594.

Hillier, B. and J. Hanson 1984 *The Social Logic of Space*. Cambridge University Press, Cambridge.

Hirte, R. n.d. Found Objects, The Buchenwald and Mittelbau-Dora Memorials Foundation. http://www.buchenwald.de (Accessed 24 April 2010).

Hobsbawm, E.J. 1994 *The Age of Extremes: The Short Twentieth Century, 1914–1991*. Michael Joseph, London.

Human Rights Watch 2008 *Locked Up Alone: Detention Conditions and Mental Health at Guantanamo*. Human Rights Watch, New York.

Kessler, S. 1999 The Black Concentration Camps of the Anglo-Boer War, 1899–1902: Shifting the Paradigm from Sole Martyrdom to Mutual Suffering. *Historia* 1(44): 110–147.

Krell, A. 2002 *The Devil's Rope: A Cultural History of Barbed Wire*. Reaktion Books, London.

Kropotkin, P. 1927 *Kropotkin's Revolutionary Pamphlets*. Vanguard Press, New York.

Lindqvist, S. 1996 *Exterminate All the Brutes. One Man's Odyssey into the Heart of Darkness and the Origins of European Genocide*. Free Press, New York.

Listman, J., C. Baker, and S. Goodfellow 2006 Historic Context: World War II Prisoner-of-War Camps on Department of Defense Installations. Department of Defense Legacy Resource Management Program, Project Number 05-256. Department of Defense, Washington, DC.

Liu, J. 2009 *Barbed Wire: The Fence that Changed the West*. Mountain Press, Missoula.

Logan, W. and K. Reeves 2009 *Places of Pain and Shame: Dealing with "Difficult Heritage"*. Routledge, London.

Malkki, L. 1995 Refugees and Exile: From "Refugee Studies" to the National Order of Things. *Annual Review of Anthropology* 24: 495–523.

Margulies, J. 2006 *Guantánamo and the Abuse of Presidential Power*. Simon and Schuster, New York.

Mears, D. 2008 An Assessment of Supermax Prisons Using an Evaluation Framework. *The Prison Journal* 88(1): 43–68.

Meskell, L. and P. Pels 2005 *Embedding Ethics*. Berg, Oxford.

Morison, W. 1995 *Flak and Ferrets: One Way to Colditz*. Sentinel, London.

Moshenska, G. 2007 Oral History in Historical Archaeology: Excavating Sites of Memory. *Oral History* 35(1): 91–97.

Moshenska, G. 2008 Ethics and Ethical Critique in the Archaeology of Modern Conflict. *Norwegian Archaeological Review* 41(2): 159–175.

Moshenska, G. 2010 Working with Memory in the Archaeology of Modern Conflict. *Cambridge Archaeological Journal* 20(1): 33–48.

Myers, A. 2008 Between Memory and Materiality: An Archaeological Approach to Studying the Nazi Concentration Camps. *Journal of Conflict Archaeology* 4: 231–245.

Myers, A. 2009 Canadian National Parks Internment Camp Archaeology Project: 2009 Field Season Final Research Report. Permit #JNP-2009-2217. Available from Parks Canada.

Myers, A. 2010 Camp Delta, Google Earth and the Ethics of Remote Sensing in Archaeology. *World Archaeology* 4(3): 455–467.

Netz, R. 2004 *Barbed Wire: An Ecology of Modernity*. Wesleyan University Press, Middletown.

Pizarro, J. and V. Stenius 2004 Supermax Prisons: Their Rise, Current Practices, and Effect on Inmates. *The Prison Journal* 84(2): 248–264.

Price, J. 2005 Orphan Heritage: Issues in Managing the Heritage of the Great War in Northern France and Belgium. *Journal of Conflict Archaeology* 1(1): 181–196.

Pringle, J., P. Doyle, and L. Babits 2007 Multidisciplinary Investigations at Stalag Luft III Allied Prisoner-of-War Camp: The Site of the 1944 "Great Escape," Zagan, Western Poland. *Geoarcheology: An International Journal* 22(7): 729–746.

Purbrick, L., J. Aulich, and G. Dawson (eds.) 2007 *Contested Spaces: Sites, Representations and Histories of Conflict*. Palgrave Macmillan, New York.

Razac, O. 2000 *Barbed Wire: A Political History*. The New Press, New York.

Roland, C. 1991 Allied POWs, Japanese Captors and the Geneva Conventions. *War and Society* 9(2): 83–102.

Rose, D. 2004 *Guantanamo: The War on Human Rights*. The New Press, New York.

Rürup, R. 1996 *Topography of Terror: Gestapo, SS and Reichssicherheitshauptamt on the "Prinz-Albrecht-Terrain": A Documentation*. Verlag Willmuth Arenhövel, Berlin.

Saunders, N. (ed.) 2004 *Matters of Conflict: Material Culture, Memory and the First World War*. Routledge, London.

Schofield, J. 2009 *Aftermath: Readings in the Archaeology of Recent Conflict*. Springer, New York.

Schofield, J., D. Evans, W. Foot, and C. Going 2006a Thematic Characterization: Recording England's Army Camps, 1858–2000. In *Re-Mapping the Field: New Approaches in Conflict Archaeology*, edited by J. Schofield, A. Klausmeier, and L. Purbrick, pp. 58–63. Westkreuz-Verlag, Berlin.

Schofield, J., W. Johnson, and C. Beck (eds.) 2002 *Matériel Culture: The Archaeology of Twentieth Century Conflict*. Routledge, London.

Schofield, J., A. Klausmeier, and L. Purbrick 2006b *Re-Mapping the Field: New Approaches in Conflict Archaeology*. Westkreuz-Verlag, Berlin.

Shaw, V. 2010 Corrections and Punishment in China: Information and Analysis. *Journal of Contemporary Criminal Justice* 26(1): 53–71

Skiles, S. and B. Clark 2010 When the Foreign Is Not Exotic: Ceramics at Colorado's WWII Japanese Internment Camp. In *Trade and Exchange: Archaeological Studies from History and Prehistory*, edited by C. Dillian and C. White, pp. 179–192. Springer, New York.

Spencer-Wood, S. and S. Baugher 2001 Introduction and Historical Context for the Archaeology of Institutions of Reform. Part I: Asylums. *International Journal of Historical Archaeology* 5(1): 3–17

Spiegelman, A. 2003 *The Complete Maus*. Penguin, London.

Thomas, R. 2003a PoW Camps: What Survives and Where. *Conservation Bulletin* 44: 18–21.

Thomas, R. 2003b *Prisoner of War Camps (1939–1948)*. *Project Report, Twentieth Century Military Recording Project*. English Heritage, London.

Thoms, A. (ed.) 2000 Uncovering Camp Ford: Archaeological Interpretations of a Confederate Prisoner-of-War Camp in East Texas. Unpublished Report of Investigations No.1, Center for Ecological Archaeology. Texas A&M University, College Station.

Thoms, A. 2004 Sand Blows Desperately: Land-Use History and Site Integrity at Camp Ford, a Confederate POW Camp in East Texas. *Historical Archaeology* 38(4): 72–92.

Valentine, G. and B. Longstaff 1998 Doing Porridge: Food and Social Relations in a Male Prison. *Journal of Material Culture* 3: 131–152.

Van Bueren, T. (ed.) 2006 Daring Experiments: Issues and Insights about Utopian Communities. *Historical Archaeology* 40(1): 1–186.

Vance, J. 1992 The Politics of Camp Life: The Bargaining Process in Two German Prison Camps. *War and Society* 10(1): 109–126.

Vance, J. (ed.) 2000 *Encyclopedia of Prisoners of War and Internment*. ABC-CLIO, Santa Barbara.

Vischer, A. 1919 *Barbed Wire Disease: A Psychological Study of the Prisoner of War*. John Bale, London.

Waters, M. 2004 *Lone Star Stalag: German Prisoners of War at Camp Hearne*. Texas A&M University Press, College Station.

Williams, E. 1949 *The Wooden Horse*. Harper & Brothers, New York.

Chapter 2
Exceptional Space: Concentration Camps and Labor Compounds in Late Nineteenth-Century South Africa

Lindsay Weiss

Abstract This chapter explores and compares the causes and effects of colonial labor camps and concentration camps in nineteenth-century southern Africa. This comparison is an attempt to understand the relationship between the lethality of wartime camps and labor camps in the modern era. While concentration camps and worker labor camps were established according to ostensibly different power regimes and causal factors, British wartime concentration camps established different camps for Boers and Africans—the latter being structurally identical to preceding labor camps established on the South African Diamond Fields.

Introduction

This chapter is an attempt to understand the phenomenon of the camp through events that occurred in late nineteenth-century colonial southern Africa. I will explore the camp both through the lens of war and the lens of labor, exploring both the creation of closed worker compounds for miners working on the Diamond Fields and the subsequent establishment of British wartime concentration camps during the Anglo-Boer War of 1899–1902. The colonial context reveals important contiguities between camps associated with wartime (and thus state-sanctioned modes of killing) and those labor camps which perpetrated more mundane forms of killing. The point of comparing these two forms of the camp (wartime camps and "work"-time camps) is to understand the seamlessness with which the more visible sovereign violence of the camp has long intersected with a more dispersed, biopolitical mode of state- and market-sanctioned violence.

This historical case study problematizes the contemporary distinction between "state killing" and the more amorphous condition of "letting die"—a distinction

L. Weiss (✉)
Stanford Archaeology Center, Stanford University, Stanford, CA, USA
e-mail: lmweiss@stanford.edu

A. Myers, G. Moshenska (eds.), *Archaeologies of Internment*, One World Archaeology, DOI 10.1007/978-1-4419-9666-4_2, © Springer Science+Business Media, LLC 2011

that frequently occludes the lethal workings of neoliberal markets and states today (Povinelli 2008:512). Concentration camps, labor camps and sites of institutionalized violence are central to our engagement with the dispersed workings of violence and power in late modernity, particularly as we attempt to examine these institutional forms in a global context (Buchli and Lucas 2001; Casella 2007; Gonzalez-Ruibal 2008).

The First Camps: The 1886 Closed Labor Compounds

It is important to examine the camps that existed at the peripheries of overt warfare. In the case of colonial South Africa, problems of labor, mineral wealth, speculative fever and security concerns emerged with the discovery of diamonds in the 1870s and subsequently with the discovery of gold on the Witwatersrand reef in the 1880s (Turrell 1982; Worger 1987). These concerns revolved around securing the profits of diamonds from illicit trade, precipitated closed worker compounds and labor barracks, and set the administrative and architectural groundwork for aspects of apartheid. As Van Onselen explains,

> [b]y their very nature the concentration camps, prisons and compounds exercised a high degree of control over their black inmates. *This was not solely a wartime exigency*, for these institutions represented the vanguard of those oppressive instruments that continued to function under the post-war administration (Van Onselen 1978:79, emphasis added).

The suspension of ordinary law and the juridical state of the exception were both events which, in South Africa, *preceded* the emergency of a wartime state and largely centered on the exceptional conditions of black markets thought to be siphoning the profits of the diamond trade away from monopolist coffers (Worger 1987). The worker compounds of the early mining companies of the Diamond Fields not only segregated and incarcerated laborers for the duration of their contract, but they also relied upon strategic suspensions of the law—invoking a state of exception, even if only for the purpose of commodity security. The relationship between the 1880s labor compounds of diamond mining companies such as De Beers and the subsequent network of industrial labor systems under apartheid later raised concerns among company directors about comparisons to the infamous relationship between the I.G. Farben corporation and the Nazi regime (Ibhawoh 2008:281).

Even as the space of the camp came to center around wartime detainment, the camp's suspension of political and physical life, as well as the biopolitical production of race in South Africa, was always intricately interwoven with the material and speculative economies occupying sites of mineral wealth and production (Hayes 2001). The discovery of mineral wealth in South Africa accelerated a twinned production, one of the actual substances of diamonds and gold, the other of war for secure access to these goods. Both processes produced a class of laborers who were presumptive criminals and whose "bare life" materialized within the space of the camp (Agamben 1998).

The Precedent of Concentration Camps and Labor Camps in Southern Africa

In 1939, the British government reluctantly issued their White Paper on Nazi concentration camps in response to anti-British Nazi propaganda in which concentration camps were portrayed as having been "invented" by the British army during their war campaigns in South Africa (Struk 2004:28). Hitler's Minister of Propaganda, Josef Goebbels, had notoriously traced the term "concentration camps" to this British implementation of internment camps during the Anglo-Boer war of 1899–1902 in South Africa, attempting to situate the architectural and political precedent for Nazi concentration camps within British imperial rule (Stanley 2006:7).

These British camps had resulted in thousands of deaths due to disease, overcrowding and unsanitary conditions. Historians have recently suggested that the pivotal colonial precedent for the Nazi camps in fact emerged within the context of 1904 colonial South-West Africa, where German colonists actively inflicted a policy of *Vernichtung* (annihilation) upon the Herero and Nama under the military directives of General Lothar von Trotha (Lindqvist 1996; Madley 2005). These German colonial camps were produced as a result of Ratzel's notion of *Lebensraum*, or "living space." According to this idea, the colonial mandate for more space became paramount in order to accommodate the expanding populations and markets of the ruling race, precipitating the mass dispossession and relocation of Herero and Nama people into what were termed *Konzentrationslager*. Hitler was known to have read Ratzel's *Anthropogeographie* when writing *Mein Kampf* in prison, and the Nazi death camps may have been similarly inspired by *Lebensraum* (Ratzel 1899; Lindqvist 1996:145).

In British southern Africa the ravages of colonial encroachment following the discovery of diamonds and gold have been depicted as unfolding according to a far more pragmatic capitalist tack. Historian Benjamin Madley suggests that had British imperialist Cecil Rhodes "not decided that funding such a [genocidal] war would be prohibitively expensive, Southern Rhodesia might have become, like German South West Africa, a site of genocide" (Madley 2005:431). The analogy of British wartime camps to Nazi concentration camps has been viewed, largely, as a product of the distortions of the memorializing and mythologizing of the Afrikaner martyrdom under the apartheid regime (Stanley and Dampier 2005). The estimated 28,000 deaths which the condition of these camps brought about have not been understood as the result of an explicitly genocidal project but instead as the result of what has been termed an unfortunate case of "collateral damage" (Stanley and Dampier 2005).

The connection between the nineteenth-century German and British colonial concentration camp system in southern Africa fades, however, when the full story of the British administration of camps is examined in detail (Madley 2005). Tens of thousands of Africans died in camps, as a direct result of forced labor, inadequate shelter, negligible food supply and nonexistent medical attention: some war camps established for African detainees were reported to be subsisting on nothing more than rotting animal carcasses (Kessler 1999; Warwick 1983:149). Under the supervision of the Native Affairs Department, these camps created conditions of radical poverty and despair. Importantly, the notion of the superfluity of African life first emerged within the camps for profit and mineral wealth, camps which seem to have escaped eventful equivalence with sovereign-issued camps established for warfare and explicit territorial expansion, though their market-based motivations were no less lethal (Povinelli 2008).

The Diamond Fields of South Africa

In southern Africa, the discovery of mineral wealth began with the rush for diamonds in the northern frontiers of British colonial territories. The Diamond Fields emerged in the 1870s after a series of prominent diamond finds, with thousands of prospectors congregating around the confluence of the Harts-Vaal Rivers in what is today known as the Northern Cape Province of South Africa. While this region was swiftly incorporated as a British Protectorate (Worger 1987:17), the rule of law and police enforcement were frequently seen as inadequate to the community's preoccupation with the specter of rampant illicit diamond trading. The impetus for isolating African laborers from the general population of the fields was the result of widespread anxiety over the rumors of rampant illicit diamond buying. Anxiety over illicit diamond buying had already led to a series of exceptional legal moves, many of which were implemented under the Diamond Trade Act of 1882: for instance, suspending presumption of innocence and placing *onus probandi* upon the African discovered with diamonds on his person—a process handled by special illicit diamond buying courts (Smalberger 1974).

In the wake of several sharp declines in diamond prices, and the flooding and depletion of diamondiferous soil lenses on the fields, mass paranoia emerged about the ubiquity of illicit diamond buying. Failing prospectors may have questioned whether their claims were truly running out of diamondiferous soil, or whether concealment and illicit trade were the cause of their misfortunes. This widespread suspicion catalyzed the containment scheme which would see diamond diggers fenced in. Key proclamations and movements had led up to this event, including the Searching Ordinance 11 of 1880, establishing a comprehensive searching system for miners exiting the mines, and the Diamond Trade Act of 1882, which codified a set of trapping laws and punishments for illicit diamond buying (Smalberger 1974:410–412). Despite these laws, it was the growing sense of the *inadequacy* of these various searching ordinances and legislative security measures which gave rise to the consensus that some sort of camp or enclosed compound would be the only viable solution.

The synthesis of penal and labor architecture at Kimberley in the 1880s provides an important precedent for the subsequent urban formations of Johannesburg and other labor centers in southern Africa (Bozzoli 1981:71–72; Home 2000). The twin processes of proletarianizing and criminalizing southern African migrant laborers have been lost to some degree in the process of chronicling colonial projects of labor control. Yet, it is this criminalization in its built form and spatial logics which continues to resonate with urban landscapes in post-apartheid South Africa and marks a genealogical foundation for contemporary discourse of criminal violence and disorder in the postcolony (Comaroff and Comaroff 2006). During the outbreak of violence between British colonial forces and Boer commandoes at the end of the nineteenth century, while the Boer concentration camps were explicitly modeled after "protective custody" for purposes of wartime security, African concentration camps, in contrast, were conceived of with the goal of establishing "the supply of native labor to the Army" (Warwick 1983:149). Thus, in 1901, the Native Refugee Department was created, inmates characterized as receiving "aid" from the British army, yet in reality Africans were compelled by military force to enter what were self-supporting camps. Inmates were promised that for their loyalty to the British they would receive Boer farms at the end of the war (Kessler 1999:123). Instead, refugees were released from the concentration camps either to private employers, to return to labor on their original farms, or to join compound systems in the gold mines on the Witwatersrand (Kessler 1999).

The Birth of the Closed Compound on the Diamond Fields Circa 1886

In January 1885, the process of compounding officially began when one of the three major amalgamated companies, the "French Company," marched 110 African workers into a set of closed barracks, where they were detained for 6 months (Worger 1987:144). The architecture of segregated worker housing was widely replicated in industrial areas throughout southern Africa, with suburban cantonments for European supervisors and closed barracks for African laborers. This style of labor incarceration was thought to really be about securing cheap labor (workers notoriously leaving the fields during poor wage conditions), but it is also important to understand that this architectural precedent was formulated according to the question of the laborers as presumptive diamond thieves. Thus, this architecture infused the labor environment with all the issues of the camp: security, custody and the biopolitical administration of human life (Smalberger 1974; Worger 1987). Worker housing at the diamond mines became a disciplinarian-bachelor space for African laborers, and a private residential area for European laborers.

When the compound became "closed," it became a penal landscape. The architect of the compound, Thomas Kitto, a mining inspector from Cornwall, had been commissioned in 1879 to write a report on the Kimberley mines; Kitto explicitly based his architectural proposal on Brazilian Diamond Field slave lodges (Turrell 1982:57). Kitto was effectively advocating the architecture and regimented lifestyle of slave labor as a form of disciplinarian reform—the only alternative being a scenario in which the African laborer would remain "a lean, trembling debauch" (Worger 2004:70). Referring to the Brazilian slave barrack system, he describes the proposed security enclosure for African laborers:

> The blacks are lodged in barracks, which are built in the form of a square, the outer wall being much higher than the inner wall; the roof slopes inside. The entrance to the place is by a large gate, over which at night hangs a powerful lamp ... Men and women answer to the call of their names while passing out at the gate in the morning and in the evening when entering. They retire to rest early, and an overseer locks up the premises each night ... in another 22 years, or thereabouts, all will be free; by which time ... they will be ripe for the occasion. I believe the natives of South Africa, under European supervision, are capable of being made almost–if not quite–as good as the blacks of Brazil, provided they are dealt with in the same manner. (Kitto 1882 cited in Turrell 1987:97)

Robert Turrell states that the Kimberley compounds "were indeed, intended to pre-vent theft, and they later grew to be *structurally identical to convict stations* with entrance and exit tunnels to the mine, wire mesh over the barracks and detention cells for workers to flush out stolen diamonds when their contracts expired" (Turrell 1982:65).

The searching system that African laborers underwent at the end of their labor contract was almost exactly the same as that practiced at the Diamond Field's enor-mous central prison (Simons and Simons 1983:25). The convergent architectural signatures which stretched from Brazilian slave barracks to South African labor compounds and ultimately to concentration camps, demonstrate how easily sys-tems of confinement and criminalization incorporate and transfigure landscapes. The penal pedigree of the compound space, in its extra-legislative capacity to order and punish by race, was an architectural product of a "state of exception" in which the security of commodity flow came to usurp extant political and legal infrastructures, and ultimately came to inform the broader move toward containment of Africans who appeared to be "living large" without "visible means of support" (Turrell 1982:57). It was through the compounds, the prisons, labor depots and camps that Rhodes and other mining capitalists "came to define the black worker not as a legitimate part of an economic structure or of a growing city but as a presumptive criminal" (Worger 1987:111).

From Barrack to Compound to Concentration Camp

A little over a decade after the implementation of the closed compounds on the Diamond Fields, the first wartime implementation of the concentration camp occurred in South Africa, during the Anglo-Boer War of 1899–1902 (Agamben 1998:166). Considered by some to be the first modern war of the twentieth century, it began in 1899 between British colonial soldiers and Boer commandoes primar-ily over the territorial right to recently discovered gold-bearing regions—part of the wider "scramble for Africa" (Pakenham 1979). The motivations and political alliances were complex (Ally 1994: De Kiewiet 1966), but "whatever the ideology, the motive for the Boer war was gold" (Hobsbawm 1987:66).

British forces eventually put the Boer commandos on the defensive and combat moved toward guerilla-style tactics, precipitating the infamous scorched earth policy of the British. This involved the building of block-style forts, strung together with barbed wire and the burning of Boer homes and farms (Pretorius and Slater 2001). Central to this strategy, led by Lord Kitchener, was the building of concentration camps. Beginning in 1900, thousands of civilians, mainly women and children, were brought to approximately forty concentration camps in attempts to limit the mobility and subversive capabilities of these individuals. These concentration camps resulted in high mortality rates. One estimate is as high as 50,000 deaths in the course of only a few years, approximately a third to a half of the confined.

Much as with European worker housing, the war camps for Boer women and children were less explicitly disciplinarian as they were emphatically residential—and this distinguished them as the first modern form of concentration camp, "with the appearance of something like government custody rather than of government punishment" (Netz 2004:140). Echoing the landscape of the Diamond Fields from decades earlier, the South African landscape came to be crisscrossed with barbed wire and blockhouses, and controlling roving Boer commandos (Netz 2004:142). Camp administrators found it increasingly difficult to perpetuate the rhetoric of British humanitarianism in the face of forcible enclosure (Netz 2004:144).

Within the Boer camps power was asserted through the controlled meting out of food and privacy, with priority afforded to those families thought to not be linked to Boer commando fighters. Camps established for southern African refugees were operated according to an entirely different vision; inhabitants were expected to build their own shelters and dwellings; privacy, domesticity as well as food and basic medical care were methodologically neglected (Kessler 1999). The public veneer of "protective custody" in the instance of the exclusively African camps gave way to "disciplined existence" and extractive labor, extracted according to the presumptive criminality of the African—who, either voluntarily or involuntarily, would otherwise have become complicit with the dispersed guerilla campaigns of the Boers. The logic of security in colonial South Africa, both in the context of mineral extraction as well as in guerilla warfare, came to center around apartheid-style concentration camps.

Discussion

The social topography of the illicit diamond trade, questions of security and the "commodity-exception" were the formative discourses for the first detainment camps in southern Africa. This point conceptually realigns the early compounds of the Diamond Fields with security concerns that re-emerge in the twentieth-century militarized reforms of the National Party of South Africa under P. W. Botha (Louw 2004:88), and, more broadly, discursive anxieties that continue to circulate about crime and race in the contemporary South African neoliberal landscape (Comaroff and Comaroff 2006). The broad-reaching social effects of the compound's disciplinarian effects were not limited to the material architectural form of the actual compounds but circulated throughout the southern African landscape. By 1889, there were 10,000 Africans living in closed compounds at any given moment (Meredith 2007:157), yet on any given month, thousands of these laborers were being rotated with newly contracted laborers. The net effect of these sorts of spaces, and their work of removing previous habits and dispositions, effectively radiated across the entire southern African landscape with each new rotation of miner contracts. The hallmark of apartheid-style policies was about a negativity of space—as much about removal and relocation as it was about the imposition of disciplinarian spaces (Bremmer 1999; Judin and Vladislavic 1998; Robinson 1999).

The closed compound, like the concentration camp, seemed to address the inadequacy of either legal or renegade justice upon African migrant laborers as they became icons of the widespread perception of illicit trade and theft. They came to personify cracks in the surefire get-rich-quick life of the rush camp that seemed to threaten the general well-being of colonial project. This contains an obvious analogy to the Nazi obsession of the Jew "everywhere and nowhere," the figure that anti-Semitism classed as simultaneously economically all-powerful and subhuman, a figure at the root of Germany's historical failures (Arendt 1966:87). The excess of violence that created these camp landscapes was rooted in fantasies of unbridled wealth, both colonial and totalitarian alike (Arendt 1966:87). It is this syncretism between the traditional legislative form of sovereign exception and the biopolitical administration of labor that marks the contemporary space of the camp.

What was most obviously at stake in the construction of the compound spaces was the immediate suspension of the rights of citizenship, which came to set a profound precedent for the urban existence of twentieth-century South Africans. As Mahmood Mamdani put it, "[b]etween the rights-bearing colons and the subject peasantry was a third group: urban-based natives, mainly middle- and working-class persons...[n]either subject to custom nor exalted as rights-bearing citizens, they languished in a juridical limbo" (Mamdani 1996:19). Within this disenfranchised limbo came the historical process by which compound-dwellers and their dependents experienced a broad and debilitating set of suspended rights, dealing a crippling blow to any emergent sense of political or personal possibilities. It was this sort of suspension of full citizenship within the urban context that was to persist and become the hallmark of apartheid-style civil society.

In *A Bed Called Home* (1993), Mamphela Ramphele examines the effects of the hostel and compound culture in the urban South African context. Her conclusion is a powerful one, and it draws directly from the material conditions of camp life in making the comparison between life in the Nazi camps and life in the twentieth-century South African worker hostels. Above all, it signals how profoundly these artificially demarcated spaces came to signal an entirely different political universe of rights and needs—and how powerfully these sensibilities came to blur with the razor wire and fences and brittle planking within which this environment was constructed. It evidences the potent way that even the most artificially constructed physical habitudes come, from this initially brittle and foreign implementation, to occupy what can be called a profound phenomenological space of dwelling for the resident. Citing an account of life in a concentration camp, Ramphele attempts to convey life in the compounds:

> Shut up behind barbed wire, robbed of all rights including the right to live, we had stopped regarding freedom as something natural and self-evident. Gradually the idea of freedom as a birthright became blurred. . .[it] has to be earned and fought for, a privilege that is awarded like a medal. It is hardly possible for people to live for so many years as slaves in everyday contact with fascists and fascism without becoming somehow twisted, without contracting a trace of that dry rot unwittingly and unwillingly. (Kovály 1988 in Ramphele 1993:134)

The similarity of the experiences is rendered most explicit when the dehumanizing process of preparing the laborer to leave the compound is understood in detail. The final process of leaving the labor camps—which extended into the mid-twentieth century—was profoundly dehumanizing. Political disenfranchisement, by comparison to the merciless and traumatizing prioritization of the diamond over the workers privacy, health and bodily autonomy, would have imperceptibly become a natural state of affairs.

> For one week they have to live naked, and in complete imprisonment, not being allowed any communication with their comrades of the 'compound'. They have to wear hard leather fingerless gloves of enormous dimensions, which prevent them from using their hands, and oblige them to take their nourishment like four footed animals. Their belongings are taken away and searched, and during the week they have but a blanket belonging to the company to cover them. Their bodies are examined in every part, and never was this expression used with stricter exactness. Their teeth even are examined; and if they have swallowed some precious stone; the gloves prevent the possibility of their handling it to swallow it again. (O'Rell 1894:269)

This somatic process was enacted on every single one of the tens of thousands of workers who left the compounds, and marked a foundational set of biopolitical impositions that primed the labor system for the twentieth-century apartheid project.

The effects of compounding and camp sequestering were more than just spatial separation; however, these spaces were enacted through an absolute segregation of modes of consumption, exchange, socialization, access to privacy, sexual practices, childrearing, leisure activities, eating and sleeping. The workings of incarceration operated through a mesh of associated material culture, architectural landscapes and objects of disenfranchisement (Casella 2007:84). Within the compound, as soon as one set of potentialities was restricted, almost immediately emerged a new sort of life, and with it, the "internalization of hostel [compound] life" that culminated in the twentieth-century phenomenon of refusing, on the part of hostel dwellers, to revert to domestic unit-style accommodations—a refusal that Ramphele understands within the broader debates surrounding prisoner reentry (Ramphele 1993:8 in Mamdani 1996:262). While it is true that firm solidarities, distinctive practices, moral economies and subcultures also emerged in these spaces such as the hidden network of informal rules, known as *mteto* (Crush 1994:314; Moodie and Ndatshe 1994), it is also true that during the critical late twentieth-century years of resistance to apartheid, the practices of these hostel dwellers had come to be derided by African urban township residents, that they were dismissed as *ama-overalls* (those who wear overalls) and marginalized from full inclusion within the struggle against apartheid (Mamdani 1996:263).

Local debates surrounding the establishment of African concentration camps hinged around a very similar set of topics, essentially the camps were subject to a great deal of complaints by local shopkeepers who had lost business. In response, Major G. F. de Lotbinière, acting head of the Transvaal Native Refugee Department, wrote to the Deputy Administrator of the Orange River Colony, validated the conditions of his internment system by citing the precedent of the worker compound system, explaining "that he had, 'developed a *compound system* providing everything the Natives may require in the camps themselves. . .keeping the Natives together in the camps as far as possible'" (Kessler 1999:122 emphasis in original). This was because the newly established Native Refugee Department was, in reality, charged with the twin task of supervising African refugees, and "also for recruiting workers from among them to release those mineworkers in military employment" (Warwick 1983:149).

These camps preceded and surpassed the wartime impetus for "protective custody," their framework for profitable containment reproduced the established tradition of closed compounds for labor, a project which, in turn, had been explicitly based on the architecture and disciplinarian concerns of the slave barracks in Brazil. This material and architectural genealogy, it is imperative to underscore, was not only established in response to the exceptional circumstances of the present, but called upon successive colonial states of exception, each moment facilitating massive appropriation of laboring bodies—and the relegation of those unable to labor to the state of what the Nazis termed *Lebensunwerte Leben*, or "lives unworthy of life" (Madley 2005:438). This would be a spatial enactment and imperial tradition employed in the mid-twentieth-century Eastern Europe where Nazi governors, such as Hans Frank of Poland, would proclaim that "that the region shall be treated like a colony [in which] the Poles will become the slaves of the Greater German Empire" (Madley 2005:438).

Conclusion

The implementation of worker compounds and concentration camps in British southern Africa in the late nineteenth century problematizes the discrete consideration of wartime labor camps, detention camps and labor compounds that were ostensibly solely about labor. The genealogy that links the establishment of these historical camps traces some contiguities of the biopolitical project, which reinscribed the laboring body as a sort of *Homo sacer* (as a figure both sacred and subhuman). The workers' presumptive criminal condition intrinsically demanded their excision from the fabric of society and which ultimately entered them into the bare life of the camp, a state which arguably exceeded their physical containment within the confines of the camp (Agamben 1997, 1998). It is important to emphasize, however, that for all their wire meshes, panoptical towers, rigorous scheduling and denuding of privacy, these spaces never obtained any hermetic sort of state of exception outside of their abstract conceptualization. These spaces continually set into motion flows of people, commodities, and contraband, and fantasies of limitless profit which collectively constituted a transfiguring force which always exceeded the bounds of the modern political sovereign power as construed within Agambenian terms.

The materiality of the Diamond Fields, the story of the flows of diamonds, and the spatial refiguration of this trading population as well as the subsequent wartime concentration camps which emerged in the scramble for gold, all contribute to an important historical contextualization of the story of the camp. This materially inflected narrative demonstrates that narratives about colonial and financial speculation were always complexly intertwined with political projects of racial rule and even genocide. The contiguities between the colony and metropolis illustrate the readily transposable wartime state of exception and broader political and economic concerns about risk, security and profitability. The archaeology of the contemporary past has enormous potential for illustrating the genealogies of contemporary notions of dispersed and domestic enemies, both real and conjured, as well as how such discourses ultimately precipitate exceptional forms of detainment and continue to produce global sites of apartheid.

References

Agamben, G. 1997 The Camp as the Nomos of the Modern. In *Violence, Identity, and Self-Determination*, edited by H. de Vries and S. Weber, pp. 106–118. Stanford University Press, Stanford.

Agamben, G. 1998 *Homo Sacer: Sovereign Power and Bare Life*. Stanford University Press, Stanford.

Ally, R. 1994 *Gold and Empire: The Bank of England and South Africa's Gold Producers, 1886–1926*. Witwatersrand University Press, Johannesburg.

Arendt, H. 1966 *The Origins of Totalitarianism*. Harvest, New York.

Bozzoli, B. 1981 *The Political Nature of a Ruling Class: Capital and Ideology in South Africa, 1890–1933*. Routledge, London.

Bremmer, L. 1999 Crime and the Emerging Landscape of Post-Apartheid Johannesburg. In *Blank: Architecture, Apartheid and After*, edited by H. Judin and I. Vladislavic, pp. 48–63. Nai Publishers, Rotterdam.

Buchli, V. and G. Lucas 2001 *Archaeologies of the Contemporary Past*. Routledge, London.

Casella, E. 2007 *The Archaeology of Institutional Confinement*. University Press of Florida, Gainesville.

Comaroff, J. and J.L. Comaroff 2006 *Law and Disorder in the Postcolony: An Introduction*. University of Chicago Press, Chicago.

Crush, J. 1994 Scripting the Compound: Power and Space in the South African Mining Industry. *Environment and Planning D: Society and Space* 12: 301–324.

De Kiewiet, C. 1966 *The Imperial Factor in South Africa*. Russell & Russell, New York.

González-Ruibal, A. 2008 Time to Destroy: An Archaeology of Supermodernity. *Current Anthropology* 49(2): 247–280.

Hayes, P. 2001 *Industry and Ideology: IG Farben in the Nazi Era*. Cambridge University Press, Cambridge.

Hobsbawm, E. 1987 *The Age of Empire, 1875–1914*. Pantheon, New York.

Home, R. 2000 From Barrack Compounds to the Single-Family House: Planning Worker Housing in Colonial Natal and Northern Rhodesia. *Planning Perspectives* 15: 327–347.

Ibhawoh, B. 2008 Rethinking Corporate Apologies: Business and Apartheid Victimization in South Africa. In *The Age of Apology: Facing up to the Past*, edited by M. Gibney, pp. 271–286. University of Pennsylvania Press, Philadelphia.

Judin, H. and I. Vladislavic 1998 *Blank: Architecture, Apartheid and After*. Distributed Art Publishers, New York.

Kessler, S. 1999 The Black Concentration Camps of the Anglo-Boer War, 1899–1902: Shifting the Paradigm From Sole Martyrdom to Mutual Suffering. *Historia* 1: 110–147.

Kitto, T. 1882 *Report on the Diamond Mines of Griqualand Wes by the order of H. E. Col. C. Warren, Administrator*. University of Cape Town Smallberger Papers.

Ková́ly, H. 1988 *Prague Farewell*. Gollancz, London.

Lindqvist, S. 1996 *Exterminate All the Brutes*. New Press, New York.

Louw, P. 2004 *The Rise, Fall, and Legacy of Apartheid*. Praeger, Westport.

Madley, B. 2005 From Africa to Auschwitz: How German South West Africa Incubated Ideas and Methods Adopted and Developed by the Nazis in Eastern Europe. *European History Quarterly* 35: 429–464.

Mamdani, M. 1996 *Citizen and Subject: Contemporary Africa and the Legacy of Late Colonialism*. Princeton University Press, Princeton.

Meredith, M. 2007 *Diamonds, Gold, and War: The British, the Boers, and the Making of South Africa*. Public Affairs, New York.

Moodie, T. and V. Ndatshe 1994 *Going for Gold: Men, Mines, and Migration*. University of California Press, Berkeley.

Netz, R. 2004 *Barbed Wire: An Ecology of Modernity*. Wesleyan University Press, Hanover.

O'Rell, M. 1894 *John Bull & Co.: The Great Colonial Branches of the Firm: Canada, Australia, New Zealand, and South Africa*. Charles L. Webster & Company, New York.

Pakenham, T. 1979 *The Boer War*. MacDonald, London.

Povinelli, E. 2008 The Child in the Broom Closet: States of Killing and Letting Die. *South Atlantic Quarterly* 107(3): 509–530.

Pretorius, F. and C. Slater 2001 *Scorched Earth*. Human & Rousseau, Cape Town.

Ramphele, M. 1993 *A Bed Called Home: Life in the Migrant Labour Hostels of Cape Town*. David Philip, Cape Town.

Ratzel, F. 1899 *Anthropogeographie*. J. Engelhorn, Stuttgart.

Robinson, J. 1999 (Im)mobilizing Space–Dreaming of Change. In *Blank: Architecture, Apartheid and After*, edited by H. Judin and I. Vladislavic, pp. 163–171. David Philip, Rotterdam.

Simons, J. and R. Simons 1983 *Class and Colour in South Africa 1850–1950*. International Defense and Aid Fund for Southern Africa, London.

Smalberger, J. 1974 I.D.B. and the Mining Compound System in the 1880s. *South African Journal of Economics* 42: 399–410.

Stanley, L. 2006 *Mourning Becomes. . .: Post/Memory and Commemoration and the Concentration Camps of the South African War*. Manchester University Press, Manchester.

Stanley, L. and H. Dampier 2005 Aftermaths: Post/Memory, Commemoration and the Concentration Camps of the South African War 1899–1902. *European Review of History* 12: 91–119.

Struk, J. 2004 *Photographing the Holocaust: Interpretations of the Evidence*. I.B. Tauris, London.

Turrell, R. 1982 Kimberley: Labour and Compounds, 1871–1888. In *Industrialisation and Social Change in South Africa*, edited by S. Marks and R. Rathbone, pp. 45–76. Longman, London.

Van Onselen, C. 1978 "The Regiment of the Hills": South Africa's Lumpenproletariat Army 1890–1920. *Past & Present* 80: 91–121.

Warwick, P. 1983 *Black People and the South African War, 1899–1902*. Cambridge University Press, Cambridge.

Worger, W. 1987 *South Africa's City of Diamonds*. Yale University Press, New Haven.

Worger, W. 2004 Convict Labour: Industrialists and the State in the US South and South Africa, 1870–1930. *Journal of Southern African Studies* 30: 63–86.

Chapter 3
A Tale of Two Treatments: The Materiality of Internment on the Isle of Man in World Wars I and II

Harold Mytum

Abstract The Isle of Man was used by the British government for civilian internment during both World Wars, and in both cases this greatly altered the population levels on the island. The authorities organised, housed, and controlled the internees very differently in each conflict, however. This chapter explores the different material experiences of male internees in the First World War camps at specially built Knockaloe and at a requisitioned holiday camp at Douglas. These will be contrasted with the Second World War when internees lived in camps created from adapted boarding houses at several resorts around the coast. These two internment strategies affected both locals and internees in very different ways.

Introduction

The British government used the Isle of Man for internment during both World Wars. In each case this greatly altered the population levels on the island and introduced a substantial number of civilian aliens to an island previously accustomed only to newcomers from Britain and Ireland. The methods of organising, housing, and controlling the internees greatly differed materially in each conflict, however, as did internees' responses to their fate.

In the earlier conflict, the initial internment location was a requisitioned holiday camp at Douglas. This quickly became inadequate to cope with the numbers, and the authorities thus augmented this with a purpose-built camp at Knockaloe. The British government selected German national civilian males and captured merchant seamen for internment. In the later conflict, many requisitioned hotels and boarding houses housed civilian internees at several resorts around the coast. Barbed wire demarcated several adjacent properties designated as camps: Douglas, Onchan, Peel, Ramsey,

H. Mytum (✉)
School of Archaeology, Classics and Egyptology, Centre for Manx Studies,
University of Liverpool, Liverpool, UK
e-mail: h.mytum@liverpool.ac.uk

A. Myers, G. Moshenska (eds.), *Archaeologies of Internment*, One World Archaeology,
DOI 10.1007/978-1-4419-9666-4_3, © Springer Science+Business Media, LLC 2011

33

and Rushen for women. These contrasting strategies affected both locals and the internees in very different ways, as did the varying length of time that internees were held, and the types of people billeted together in the various forms of camps on the island.

Internment was clearly a physical, material condition. Much has been made of the psychological impact of this in the form of "barbed wire disease", recognised by some at the time (Vischer 1919), and discussed at length with reference to art (Behr and Malet 2004; Hinrichsen 1993). However, scholars have not analysed the material conditions that gave rise to this phenomenon and which constrained and controlled so much of life in the camps. That these material conditions were so different in the Manx camps in the two World Wars creates opportunities for comparison between contexts where some, at least, of the variables remained fixed. This study outlines a project in its early stages which aims to understand the various material conditions of internment of the Isle of Man. This comparative approach focuses on the First World War but sets that experience against those of the later conflict, and with other material conditions elsewhere where archaeological interests in internment are more developed (Burton et al. 1999; Thompson 2006).

Disciplinary Context

Research into the twentieth-century internment by the British government has only developed recently, first with an emphasis on the central decision-making and organisational structures (Bird 1986), followed by concerns regarding anti-German sentiment, of which the confinement of aliens formed a part (Panayi 1991; Cesarani 1993). Academic interest crystallised on the fiftieth anniversary of the start of internment during the Second World War, with an interdisciplinary volume that also briefly considered earlier internment (Cesarani and Kushner 1993), and with other edited collections produced by the Research Centre for German and Austrian Exile Studies a decade later (Behr and Malet 2004; Dove 2005).

Another strand of publication was that of the internees themselves, with some earlier autobiographies from the First World War (Cohen-Portheim 1931; Dunbar-Kalcreuth 1940) together with accounts by those who dealt with them (Hughes 1926). A few internees composed accounts of internment from the later conflict at the time (Lafitte 1988), but most wrote them some time after events (Bailey 1959; Stent 1980); Kushner and Cesarani (1993:5–10) discuss this reticence and consider that it was due to a combination of the limited duration of most internments combined with the wish to become integrated within postwar British society. Overt criticism of the internment process and experience after the war would have undermined this, especially given that the rest of the population had also suffered in various ways.

While many scholars suggest that internment has remained marginalised in historical analyses of both the First and Second World Wars, Panayi (2005) notes that research to date has had some impact on the wider narratives of the period. Many scholars note the contemporary relevance of such studies given the continued tendency for governments to limit the freedom of civilians; the World Archaeological Congress session from which this volume arises can perhaps be seen as a reflection of our contemporary concerns with recent policies such as those pursued at Guantánamo Bay, where the boundaries between military and civilian have become blurred.

Historians have investigated the policies, attitudes, and experiences using documented sources, and recent scholars have increasingly valued the accounts of those who experienced internment in some way. But other sources, including material evidence, have received limited attention. While the Stobbs camp newspaper, *Stobsiade*, has been noted as a source (Horne 2002), and the potential of the Isle of Man (Manx) newspapers produced at Knockaloe are being revealed (Kewley Draskau 2009), only the visual arts produced by internees at the time of their incarceration have received more widespread analysis (Behr and Malet 2004; Hinrichsen 1993). The most important published research on other material culture has been that of Cresswell (1994, 2005), not only reviewing the range of products from the various camps, mainly those items now curated by Manx National Heritage, but also noting others in private possession.

An archaeological perspective on internment within the British Isles is even more recent than that of historians, being produced by a combination of interest in conflict studies (Carman and Carman 2006), the fiftieth anniversary of the Second World War that first focused on the military but has gradually widened its scope (Schofield et al. 2002), and the more general trend that has recognised the value of the material remains of the recent past, military (Schofield 2005) and otherwise (Tarlow and West 1999; Mytum 2002). Relatively few archaeologists have investigated this phenomenon of internment, though this volume reflects much of the current work. Cresswell's pioneering research on the Manx material culture indicates the potential, but individual items or categories of artefacts have not been explored in great depth (but see Callow 2009).

At many levels, the dominant cultural, social, and physical structures controlled and constrained inmates (and indeed those managing them), yet agency is also extremely visible. This varies from actions of those in command of the camps, right down to minor acts of resistance by internees. The dynamic of structure and agency was played out continuously in all forms of negotiation within the camps and between these and wider authorities and communities. The everyday studied in the domestic context by Bourdieu (1977) formed the fabric of life in a rather more communal form within the camps. That very routine not only created a structure, but also the environment within which psychological damage could occur, so the agency of authorities, external groups, and the internees themselves expanded human experience and action beyond that framework. This activity might be for some other purpose such as economic gain or resistance to authority, or just for its own sake to maintain morale and motivation. Actions, and any of the products thereof, were highly conditioned by the material world of enclosure and limited physical resources. The internment camp allows aspects of structure and agency to be examined in a clear and defined way, with many of the variables controlled and defined; this can be considered in terms of group and individual agency and structures at a variety of levels.

Internment on the Isle of Man can be studied archaeologically across two comparative perspectives. One is of time: the First, versus the Second World War. The other is of varied perception: official management, the internees, and the local population. This combination allows analysis following constraints of structure: official nature of internment, rules, regulations, layout of camps and habitations, against personal and group agency such as newspaper editorial groups and individual artists and craftsmen amongst the internees and reactions to internment by the locals. These greatly varied from xenophobia to sympathy, and were differently constructed, articulated and physically expressed in each conflict.

The First World War

The Isle of Man is an independent Crown Dependency, with the Queen as head of state. As the First World War got under way, prevalent feelings regarding German aliens within the United Kingdom were manifested in direct action. The British government established a Civilian Internment Camps Committee, and its delegates visited the Isle of Man in September 1914 to find out whether a suitable location could be provided for these people. They considered Cunningham's Holiday Camp appropriate with limited alteration, and before the end of the month the first internees arrived. By this time the barbed wire had been erected, security lighting installed, and guard huts placed at appropriate locations (Sargeaunt 1920:58–60). Despite limited consultation, the island generally accepted its role as a secure holding area for aliens.

Douglas Camp

The Douglas Camp initially continued largely in the form of the existing and well-established holiday camp, with tents and chalets for sleeping and communal buildings for eating and social activities, as they were used by young working-class men from the mill towns of Lancashire for their summer break. The camp also provided a range of recreational resources such as tennis courts. The Douglas Camp structure was therefore not a de novo design and was partly dictated by the form of the existing holiday camp and the available adjacent land, notably on the opposite side of Victoria Road where communal huts were built. Unfortunately, no accurate plan survives, but it is clear that the Camp was split into three sections: Privilege, Ordinary, and Jewish. Here the materiality of the existing camp not only created opportunities, but also limitations for both the managers and internees.

Aspects of the camp design were probably partly influenced by the layout of temporary military tented camps, such as those used by the part-time British Territorial Army volunteers on summer exercise camps (Evans 2006). Control existed for the holidaymakers: young men only, and with alcoholic drink prohibited, but this was obviously enhanced for the internees. Nevertheless the structure of concepts and physical layout of controlled access, organised activity, and a mix between small group sleeping and larger communal eating and entertainment spaces, created a material world that was relatively easily adapted for internment purposes.

Internees enjoyed additional exercise at Douglas during the first part of the war by marches into the countryside, escorted by guards. While the facilities were initially relatively comfortable, tensions increased rapidly as autumn began to turn to winter and as overcrowding became more acute. Limited space and many having to sleep in tents in the stormy autumnal weather created dissatisfaction that spilled over into protests, described by the authorities as "a riot", on 19 November 1914. The guards shot dead five of the internees as they contained the riot and restored order (Sargeaunt 1920:58–60). The material conditions of the camp had led to a destabilisation that had to be addressed. Although the guards' actions were vindicated in the subsequent official enquiry, it was clear that changes had to be made, and as the existing camp could not be expanded given its location, an additional site was required. Here we see a clear case of internee agency, unsuccessful at one level in that the riot was quashed, but successful in the longer term, with subsequent changes and improvements in the material and social conditions of the internees. Agency led to changes in the structure, and part of that structural change was to be more sensitive to internee wishes, which in turn led to further changes within the camps.

Knockaloe Camp

Sargeaunt (1920) notes that only one place could be found for a camp on the whole of the island, and even that had its topographical difficulties. Knockaloe Moar had been used as a temporary camp site for the Territorial Army volunteers, and the authorities chose this site near the western town of Peel despite its clear problems with drainage (Fig. 3.1). Initially, a camp for 5,000 was planned and contracts were rapidly drawn up and allocated. As Panayi (1993:58–60) has emphasised, it was the sinking of the *Lusitania* in May 1915 that altered the speed and scale of internment, and the planned camp was to be augmented as around 1,000 men a week were being held, creating an interned population in the British Isles of over 32,000.

Buildings constructed using locally available timber by a Douglas builder formed the first incarnation of Camp 1, which was in some respects architecturally distinct from the later additions. Thereafter, Sargeaunt (1920) records that developments were taken back under the management of the government office. Local tradesmen were employed, but many within the increasing numbers of those interned had skills which could be applied to the tasks. Eventually there were four contiguous but discrete camps, which contained a total of 23 compounds, each for 1,000 men.

The structure of corporate military life inspired the structuring of the camps, and despite some slight differences caused by topography and the shapes of the camps

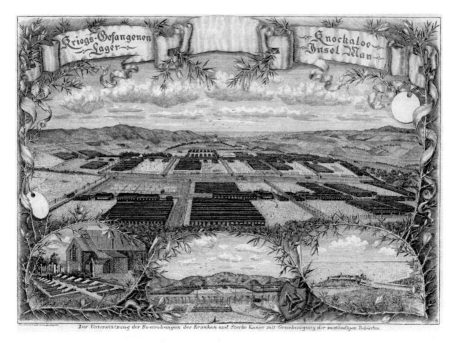

Fig. 3.1 Steel engraving produced at Knockaloe Camp, Isle of Man, showing aerial view of the whole camp. *Bottom left* are the internees' graves at the nearby Patrick Church and *bottom right* Peel Castle (Courtesy of Manx National Heritage)

(dictated largely by existing field patterns), all were similar at a planned level. The physical infrastructure of the camps is recorded in photographs, and illustrations made by the internees in various formats such as cartoons, sketches, paintings, and woodcuts. Some plans survive which show the layout of the camps and compounds, with the various types of buildings within. Unlike the Douglas arrangement, which had a large central communal building, each compound contained a number of discrete structures that included long huts for sleeping and general living, a latrine block, and a dining room. The huts of Camp 1 were distinct from those in the other camps, the latter being standard military issue prefabricated structures that could be combined end to end to create the long dormitory huts of the preferred design for the internment camp as a whole. Camp 1 also had a slightly smaller exercise area, a fault which supposedly led to greater illness in this camp than in others (Hughes 1920). Nevertheless, the overall design was one of uniformity, and to a pattern acceptable to military planners and bureaucrats, allowing forms of management such as security, controlled movement, feeding, and exercise that sat easily within existing knowledge and practice.

Knockaloe Camp was constructed with a modular structure based around 1,000 internees. Evans (2006:5) has noted in his study of English army camps that by the First World War the infantry battalion consisted of 1,000 men managed by 35 officers. The Knockaloe camp also was a recognisable unit as the division, which contained 12 infantry battalions organised into three brigades, an artillery brigade and other units, creating a force of some 20,000 men. Therefore the final size of Knockaloe, reaching 23,000 internees and to which should be added its own support staff of guards and administrators, was not significantly larger than the units being housed together within the context of the war. Other large camps at the time, such as that of the Northern Command Depot at Ripon, North Yorkshire, may also have influenced the designs. These precedents may explain why this one large camp was allowed to develop, and how the administrative structures could expand to manage such a large concentration of people with all their material needs.

When used for army purposes, the standard Armstrong Hut was 60 feet long and 20 feet wide, able to accommodate 30 soldiers (Evans 2006:5). The support buildings, such as dining rooms, were of a significantly larger span at 28 feet. A battalion's camp space was 1,100 by 500 feet, with the officers' mess and living quarters on one side of the parade ground, and on the other were barracks either side of a spine of sergeant's mess and communal facilities such as showers, dining room, and cook house. Ancillary buildings, including all those needed for horses and general stores, also flanked the parade ground. Elements of this design can be seen at Knockaloe, but many of the service facilities such as the bakery were centralised, and the arrangements for commissioned and non-commissioned officers were unnecessary.

The concept of packing the accommodation huts together and leaving a large open space for exercise mirrored that of the battalion camp unit. Here again the established structure of institutional organisation well established for the military could be adapted relatively easily to the purpose of internment. The different nature of the actors, however, led to some of these spaces being used for atypical purposes. Until excavation takes place which might reveal illicit activity that remained undetected, the range of known actions are largely those explicitly agreed with the camp management and recorded in various official sources, or which were acquiesced to and so survived the censor's pen in correspondence or the camp newspapers. However, the local police did uncover various examples of black market activity, as presently being researched by Jennifer Kewley Draskau (personal communication 2009), and some can also be identified in Manx prison records.

The internees often gave over their compound dining room to other uses (see below), instead choosing to eat in their linear accommodation huts. The authorities allowed this flexibility, as their greatest concern was to prevent any further rioting as experienced at Douglas, and to create positive activity that would promote physical and mental health. Resident medical staff and also visiting Red Cross delegations regularly assessed the internees. Reporting of good conditions was important as the German authorities also had interned British residents in Germany, and the matching treatment of these civilians was of considerable concern to the British government. The dining rooms were converted to a range of purposes, with some containing one activity at one end, and a different one at the other. Alternatively, dining rooms could change their role throughout the day. These larger communal spaces were places where group agency could create different locales, the most important being teaching rooms, workshops, theatres, and concert halls. Physical health remained good in the camps, partly because of the intense level of medical observation and the limited opportunities for industrial accidents or those associated with over-indulgence of alcohol. The authorities encouraged many sporting and cultural activities as well as gardening (Cresswell 1994).

A Comparison of Douglas and Knockaloe

At Douglas Camp, the infrastructure was already in place for the summer holidaymakers, and at Knockaloe an elaborate system of water provision and sewage disposal developed, the latter being pumped uphill across the site and over the cliff into the Irish Sea (Sargeaunt 1920). Given the still rudimentary sewage arrangements in many urban slum areas from where many of the internees would have been brought, these conditions were better than some would have experienced at home. It should also be noted that many would have previously lived in relatively cramped conditions with many people to a room in such tenements, and so the communality of the accommodation huts would not have been such an atypical experience for all. However, middle-class men, not fortunate enough to be placed in the privileged camp at Douglas, may have found the conditions traumatic.

The access routes to Knockaloe, however, were distinctly worse than in civilian life. The poor drainage meant that the timber buildings were all raised off the ground, but the walkways rapidly became muddy tracks and were lampooned in cartoons with men pictured on stilts. These were improved to some extent by the laying of railways sleeper tracks that not only provided drier lines of movement, but also emphasised how unsatisfactory were the surface conditions in the exercise areas within the compounds. The Douglas privilege camp, much smaller and still retaining elements of its holiday camp landscaping, had laid paths, lawns, and garden beds that created a contrasting aesthetic, though this did not probably apply to the Douglas ordinary camp with its communal huts. The physical conditions in the various elements of the two camps created alternative patterns of movement within the compounds, different aesthetic experiences, and would have affected the ways in which internees interacted with each other.

The logistics of constructing, maintaining, and supplying such a large number of people had significant material consequences. A contemporary map of Knockaloe indicates the layout of the whole camp, with its four separate camps, each in turn split down further into compounds. Documentary sources also give a certain amount of information regarding provision of water and sewage, roadways, and specialist structures such as hospitals. Few structures survive from the time of the camp, however, and most of these resilient structures were the stone buildings already on the farm that reverted to earlier uses after the end of the war; even traces of the specially built railway are not immediately visible. It is at present unclear, therefore, how far these official sources represent an ideal or reality, nor how these images changed in their composition over time. They are products of, and indeed part of, the structure of camp management, though through agency of internees, alternative images of the camp exist against which the official sources can be compared. Photographs are also informative, though the purposes of the pictures varied and all need to be deconstructed even when apparently simple action shots (Mytum forthcoming). Most photographs are clearly carefully composed set pieces, and need to be studied at a number of levels to reveal what messages they were meant to convey, and what else may be discerned from them. The same applies to the relatively large number of photographs from the Douglas Camp. Unlike in some Australian camps, photographs were not taken and processed by the internees themselves.

The Douglas and Knockaloe camps each contained an eclectic mix of recent arrivals to Britain from Germany, reflecting strong trade links across the North Sea. Many of the internees had lived in Britain almost all their lives, were often married to local girls, and had children, some of whom were fighting and dying in the British army. The camps contained not only Germans, but also Austrians, Hungarians, and Turks, the latter creating a small but culturally distinct group, though little research has been carried out on them (see Saunders 2003:116). As time went on, the shared experiences within the camps created more commonality, although political, religious, and class differences remained. Nevertheless, the long-term internment experience was itself acting on the psyches and identities of all those held in the camps.

Historical and literary research has begun on the newspapers produced by various groups within both Douglas and Knockaloe camps. Although controlled by the censor, and sometimes printed outside the camp by a Peel printer, they still reveal a great deal of cultural information. Some publications were also produced in Camp IV at Knockaloe (Cresswell 1994:28). Kewley Draskau (2009) has identified within these sources changes in perception and identity from 1914 onwards, and here we can discern the ways in which agency of a small number of writers, editors, and illustrators, influenced many within the camp as evidenced by the art and writing produced by internees over time, and by their letters to the newspapers. The disparate internees had varying degrees of association with Germany, some being recent economic arrivals in Britain, others well integrated and with their native language almost forgotten. The newspapers demonstrate a gradual move towards a revived and more widely felt German nationalism, and a romantic and idealised notion of the German homeland from which they were all excluded.

The widespread anti-German sentiments of the British population, combined with those powerfully in support of the German nation within the camps, created a dynamic that moved the dominant popular camp ideology towards the latter position. Despite censorship of the newspaper texts and the content and style of the illustrations, these modified attitudes and behaviours in what became a largely German-speaking environment. To examine this phenomenon in the form of layout and style of the publications—in their materiality—is an exciting avenue yet to be pursued, and Kewley Draskau's textual analysis demonstrates one aspect of this process. To what extent publications emulated British or German pre-war publications, or whether they deliberately created new, camp-specific styles, has yet to be discovered. The publications were illustrated, often by skilled artists including cartoonists, and although censorship was undoubtedly a constant influence on style and content, the overall appearance of the papers clearly reflects underlying cultural norms combined with context-specific tensions and concerns.

Interestingly, the internees felt a growing identity with the island, though an ambivalent one. The site of their incarceration, the island, was also seen as a temporary home; the impact of the place is seen not only in the newspaper writings, but even in the use of the Three Legs of Man symbol by the internee Hozinger for his knitting factory in Hamburg following his release (Kewley Draskau 2009:102–103). Locals could be relatively sympathetic to the internees, despite official propaganda and draconian punishments for providing unofficial rations and supplies. Some of the craft products still held by families on the island were received as gifts in return for kindnesses or unofficial economic activities when internees were out of the camps on work parties.

Internees made few attempts at escape, and these were never successful. They often resembled farce, with disconsolate sodden escapees handing themselves into police stations, or being stranded in Peel harbour on stolen boats without oars. Instead we mainly see internees concentrating on the construction of lives within the camp, within a surreal single-sex world where ethnicity, class, occupation, and other identities were variously maintained, irrelevant, challenged, or dangerous. One manifestation of internment was the provision of theatre in which all roles had to be played by men (Fig. 3.2). This was reported in the camp newspapers, and photographic evidence also survives (Cresswell 1994:33–35). Those with established

Fig. 3.2 Sketch of internee costumed theatrical performance with orchestra, actors, and scenery in Douglas Camp, Isle of Man (Courtesy of Manx National Heritage)

theatre and music skills could create a role for themselves within the camp. For others, including those who in civilian life would never have been able to take part in such activities, there was an opportunity to discover abilities previously untapped and widen their cultural and educational experiences (Rachamimov 2006). The agency of the internees involved many aspects of creativity—and potentially resistance—not only through performance but also creation of sets, costumes, newly composed reviews and plays, and the editing and adaptation of published plays. These, too, could create or reflect many of the feelings being represented in the newspapers, as do many of the watercolours and sketches by internees.

Other items of printed material culture that indicate resistance, and the eating away of time through years in camp, are evidenced through Christmas and New Year cards and calendars. Christmas was itself turned to political effect, being celebrated as an explicitly German (as well as religious) festival (Kewley Draskau 2009:100–101). In contrast, other items, such as the carved bone work, often convey escapist or uncontentious designs, such as the many vases made from cattle shin bones and carved with tulip or rose designs (Fig. 3.3). More obviously a protest, but cloaked in a classical and so perhaps acceptable guise, were representations of Prometheus chained to a rock used in a range of media. Many items—including pin cushions, ashtrays, and napkin rings—can be seen as souvenir items, and a number incorporate Manx symbolism and iconic views, or have *Isle of Man* carved onto

Fig. 3.3 Examples of carved bone produced in Knockaloe Camp, Isle of Man (Courtesy of Manx National Heritage)

them (Cresswell 1994:52–55). These may have been linked not only to potential markets, but also advertised from whence the products had come and reinforced the internees, carving these items where they were incarcerated. Competitive displays of products within the camps (Cresswell 1994:25–27) provided mutual support and respect, producing a sense of achievement and solidarity in creating material worlds that took the focus off the communal huts and compounds. Similar displays took place in other camps, for example at the Liverpool Holsworthy camp in New South Wales, Australia (Thompson 2006).

The other main focus of production was linked to earning money as well as creating activity which consumed time. This introduces the agency of another important organisation, the Society of Friends (Quakers) Emergency Committee. The Quakers could not condone violence, but wished to help those suffering through war (that in itself being part of their ideological structure). In the Manx context, the most important figure was James T. Baily, who managed, after some resistance, to obtain official recognition as Industrial Advisor at Knockaloe (Hughes 1926:66–70), though his relationship to the Douglas Camp was less effective. He organised efforts for the internees to earn money producing a wide range of craft products, despite being under close observation from the police and government given his non-combatant status. Two aspects of structure impeded such craft activity: bureaucratic impediments at the camp, and limitations for distribution and sale of the products. Baily managed to overcome both of these to a certain extent, allowing a modest scale of production at both Knockaloe and Douglas camps (Thomas 1920:66–81). A wide range of products included boxes, toys, furniture, textiles, brushes, and baskets (Cresswell 1994, 2005). Many were similar to those produced in other camps (Saunders 2003; Thompson 2006), but attribution to Manx camps is often possible through family connections of the owners or through motifs or text carved onto the objects.

Some natives on the Isle of Man profited from the contracts to supply the camps, and the Cunningham family, owners of the Douglas Holiday Camp, benefited considerably from improvements there and also enhancement of the facilities by internee labour at their farm at Ellerslie. Elsewhere on the island, improvements to infrastructure through the labour of the internees included management of the Ballaugh curragh to increase willow production for baskets, and the straightening of the Sulby River. The economic impact of the loss of tourism, however, was profound and although a few made money out of the war, most did not. This can be contrasted with the Second World War pattern of internment which did at least attempt to address some of these issues.

The Second World War

In the Second World War the Isle of Man was used for a range of military functions, including a fighter base at Andreas and various training establishments such as Jurby and Ronaldsway (the latter would later become the island's international airport).

Cunningham's Holiday Camp was once again taken over, but this time for naval training. Radar sites were established at Dalby and Cregneash, and various coastal defences were put in place. Internment was once more a significant feature of the wartime island, but instead of constructing large camps on this occasion, many of the numerous hotels and boarding houses were requisitioned for internees. The authorities put most hotel furniture into storage and partially refitted the buildings for their adapted use (Cresswell 1994). Barbed wire encircled groups of adjacent boarding houses and hotels to define each camp (Chappell 1984). Those along the Douglas sea front had wire set up part-way across the promenade to prevent internees getting to the beach, though bathing parties were organised under supervision; a similar arrangement was applied at Ramsey (Fig. 3.4).

The two reactions to internment—adapted or specially constructed camps as opposed to slightly adapted boarding houses and hotels—created very different

Fig. 3.4 Part of Mooragh Camp at Ramsay, Isle of Man, with the barbed wire divisions across the promenade (Courtesy of Manx National Heritage)

physical experiences of internment for each World War. Compared to Knockaloe, the later camps were designed for much smaller groups, though some were larger than the basic compound unit in the Knockaloe Camp. The more robust buildings, with smaller units of space and a more domestic atmosphere, created different dynamics and tensions, and their location within an urban environment emphasised a different form of isolation than those in the rural backwater of Knockaloe, or even Douglas Camp near what was then the edge of the town. From an economic perspective, the later strategy was much less disruptive than in the First World War when the requisition of most of the ferries and the abandonment of annual holidays by factory workers destroyed the main income stream from holidaymakers on which many of the towns depended. In the Second World War the displaced and sometimes then-homeless hoteliers and landladies of Douglas and Ramsey received compensation for the use of their properties (though largely only after the end of the war), while in contrast those in the Rushen Women's Camp at Port St. Mary and Port Erin continued to obtain per capita payment for all those billeted in their boarding houses throughout hostilities and actually received year-round income rather than their peacetime seasonal trade.

Throughout the island, the authorities converted rows of terraced small hotels into internment sites, with their inevitable barbed wire but often otherwise scenic sea views. These have been captured in some of the art produced by internees, many of whom were cultural, ethnic, political and religious refugees from Europe. In the Second World War many did not remain interned for the duration but, once assessed as low risk, could live elsewhere. Many returned to Britain to contribute to the war effort, others moved to the Married Camp established in the south of the island, within what had been part of the Women's Camp. This relatively limited period of incarceration and the greater turnover of internees created different structures within and between camps, and also altered the forms of agency chosen by the inmates.

Agency by internees can be placed in two broad categories: cultural and political activities to make the best of circumstances, and attempts to leave and help the British war effort. Refugees, including Jews, intellectuals, political activists, and artists of many kinds, continuously lobbied for release to take part in the war, while the Nazis or Nazi sympathisers attempted to increase support for their views within the camps and to undermine the British establishment. The dynamics of these two opposing groups within the same camps in itself created many tensions and actions but these are not very visible in the surviving material culture. Besides camps for those considered German, whether Gentile or Jew, there were also camps for Italians (Sponza 2005), and small numbers of other nationalities.

Attitudes to internment varied perhaps even more than in the First World War, in part because many had already experienced persecution and were worried about Nazi invasion. Some attempted to obtain freedom to support the war very quickly, others settled into making the best of life within the camps. The interpretation of the late prehistoric and Viking periods of the island's history was greatly strengthened by the internment of archaeologist Gerhard Bersu, which allowed him to excavate several key sites on the island. Chappell (1984:97) suggests that Bersu and his wife, who undertook much of the surveying, were immersed in their work, oblivious to the war. The excavations were supported by the archaeological establishment in Britain, already familiar with Bersu's groundbreaking work at Little Woodbury on Salisbury Plain in the late 1930s after the Bersus' emigration from Germany following persecution. The projects were allowed within the structure of appropriate external work by Inspector Cuthbert and supported by work parties of internees who were happy to labour on the excavations as a break from the drudgery of incarceration. The quality of work was extremely high for the time, and benefited from the lack of time constraints on completing the fieldwork. The published results appeared after Bersu's death (Bersu 1977; Bersu and Wilson 1966), and the excavation archive is substantial (Evans 1998).

The most frequently quoted cultural product of Second World War internment on the Isle of Man was perhaps the Amadeus Quartet, though even this was not actually formed in the camp and only some members met there. Many forms of artistic activity could flourish within the confines of the internment setting, where a lot of time and also strong emotions could be combined in sometimes stunning examples of art in a variety of media (Cresswell 1994). A number of well-established artists had fled Nazi persecution as their art was not acceptable within Germany, and so the quality of work could be very high, despite problems with regard to materials (Behr and Malet 2004; Hinrichsen 1993; Stent 1980). Newspapers were also produced in many of the camps, and a great deal of education and training was provided by many of the interned intellectuals (Chappell 1984).

Unlike in the First World War, some women and children were interned and a substantial camp was established for women alone; this held up to around 4,000 internees in early summer of 1940 (Kochan 1993:147), before many were allowed to live with their husbands in the Married camp once their status had been clarified. The women's camp consisted of a large portion of the southern tip of the Isle of Man, fenced off with barbed wire to include the two coastal settlements of Port St. Mary and Port Erin, both of which contained a number of small hotels and boarding houses that could be devoted to billeting the female internees and their children.

The management of the women's camp differed in a number of other important ways from those of the men (Stent 1980:186–198). From a material perspective, the very definition and control of movement of internees was completely different. Unlike the numerous discrete, individually controlled camps for the men, no other barbed wire was erected to control the women. This single fence, which could be largely forgotten or ignored, did not embed itself on the consciousness of the female internees, unlike the men who, as noted above, used the wire as a constant motif of their incarceration.

The limited control within this relatively large area meant that many choices of interaction could be experienced, not only with other internees but also with the local population. This was even more the case as the boarding house owners remained in residence in the women's camp, obtaining payment per internee per day and running the boarding houses, though using internee labour (Stent 1980:192). The physical and social constraints were thus far less stressful than for the men, but other aspects of treatment created alternative tensions. Some of these problems may have been due to the particular inclinations of the first Commandant, Dame Joanna

Cruickshank, whose own agency created difficulties by her insensitive arrangement of internees within the boarding houses and in the rules she enforced.

The British government assessed all alien females and classified them according to their perceived risk to the state. Those deemed *A* or *B*, required internment, but as this process was more selective for women than men, a high proportion of those held, especially for a long period, were Nazi sympathisers and in a few cases dedicated fascists (Lafitte 1988:117). This created stronger sets of tensions than in the male camps, though it has been noted there too. Brinson (2005) has studied the impact of the Nazi faction, and its self-styled leader Wanda Wehrhan, where material conditions in the early days of internment often led to the same house containing both Jews and Nazis. Dame Cruickshank reluctantly adopted segregation as a way of solving these problems, first setting aside the Windsor House and the Ard Chreg boarding houses for Nazis, though gradually more establishments became of this kind as many of the Jewish women were released to go home or to be with their husbands at the Married camp if they were still interned, leaving the category *A* Nazi sympathisers behind. Cruickshank only allowed one issue of a camp newspaper, as she would not accept that the Jewish and Nazi women could not cooperate in its production (Brinson 2005:105). Her replacement, Inspector C.R. Cuthbert, was deputed from Scotland Yard in 1941 to run both the women's camp and that of the newly established married camp (Brinson 2005), and he managed to resolve some of the difficulties, though this was made much easier by the reuniting of families shown to be of low risk.

The more open environment of the women's camp was attractive to the children, who could treat the experience as an enforced holiday, as is indicated by reminiscences from those involved (Cresswell 1994:52). Education was provided, though this was inconsistent over time and not satisfactory for all ages (Kochan 1993:156–157). It must be remembered that many had moved from the cities that suffered massive bombing raids, practical constraints on travel, and privations of supply that made many features of the women's camp life no worse physically than for those living through the war on the British mainland. The psychological elements of internment could still be significant (Stent 1980:197), and the women found the controlled and cramped environment involving shared rooms and indeed beds more problematic, it would seem, than many of the men (Kochan 1993). Internees' reminiscences emphasise this, often able to compare their own experiences with those of their spouses in other camps on the island (Spiro 1993:239). It is noteworthy that the women produced far less art or literature than the men, but did engage in craftwork (Fig. 3.5). Knitting and dressmaking was encouraged for a while by the introduction of tokens that could be used in a limited internal economy, but other forms of work were not available. A pattern of Service Exchange allowed a non-monetary economy to develop with reference to personal services and products. Whether this was due mainly to official constraints on activities and supplies, or cultural expectations of many of the women themselves, is uncertain.

The Second World War internment on the Isle of Man was, for most, shorter-term and in institutional structures more physically close to local civilian life than the internment in the First World War. The running of the camps with a mixture of

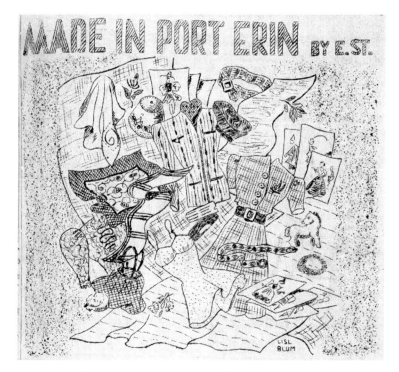

Fig. 3.5 Illustration from the male camp newspaper *The Onchan Pioneer,* illustrating the products made in the Women's Camp at Port Erin, Isle of Man (Courtesy of Manx National Heritage)

British and Manx management and control linked to a delegated internee hierarchy was similar for the two wars. The later war produced more vocal opposition within the camps and outside, including in the media and parliament, as many of those interned were demonstrably no threat to Britain.

Conclusions

Documentary sources available from official archives, diaries, and autobiographies of both contemporary locals and internees demonstrate the different perspectives and experiences of the various actors. The material evidence consciously produced by the internees can be set besides their writing, while the site-based evidence will be the only way of expanding beyond the limited (and staged) photographic record of the material realities of camp life. The First World War is now beyond oral history, and the Second is rapidly passing beyond memory. Yet the role of internment in the history of the Isle of Man is gradually being recognised as a valid subject of interest, in no small part due to the enthusiasm of Manx National Heritage in curating all that can be obtained. This material, and more data that can be acquired through archaeological investigation, can allow issues of structure and agency to be explored in a variety of contexts from both World Wars.

This distancing in time—removing potential conflicts of interest—may be why this volume, and the World Archaeological Congress session on which it is based, can now be offered. It may be that historical archaeology has joined the "past" up with the "present". Certainly the archaeological interest in recent conflict is now established (Schofield et al. 2002; Schofield 2005). But it could be argued that, from a Manx perspective, it is also because this past is now both relevant to current debates on identity, incomers, and the island's place in the world, but distant enough for it to be culturally safe on the island.

Acknowledgements I would like to thank Yvonne Cresswell and Jennifer Kewley Draskau for all their help and encouragement as I have begun to explore internment on the Isle of Man, and the ways in which an archaeological perspective can contribute to this subject. Both have made valuable suggestions that have improved this paper.

References

Bailey, L. 1959 *Craftsman and Quaker: The story of James T. Baily*. George Allen & Unwin, London.

Behr, S. and M. Malet (eds.) 2004 Arts in Exile in Britain, 1933–1945: Politics and cultural identity. *Yearbook of the Research Centre for German and Austrian Exile Studies,* Vol. 6. Amsterdam, New York.

Bersu, G. 1977 *Three Iron Age Round Houses in the Isle of Man.* Manx Museum, Douglas.

Bersu, G. and D. Wilson 1966 *Three Viking Graves in the Isle of Man.* Society for Medieval Archaeology Monograph Series 1. Society for Medieval Archaeology, London.

Bird, J.C. 1986 *Control of Enemy Alien Civilians in Great Britain, 1914–1918.* Garland, New York.

Brinson, C. 2005 "Loyal to the Reich": National Socialists and Others in the Rushen Women's Internment Camp. In *Totally Un-English? Britain's Internment of 'Enemy Aliens' in Two World Wars.* Yearbook of the Research Centre for German and Austrian Exile Studies 7, edited by R. Dove, pp. 101–119. Rodopi, Amsterdam.

Bourdieu, P. 1977 *Outline of a Theory of Practice,* translated by R. Nice, Cambridge University Press, Cambridge.

Burton, J., M. Farrell, F. Lord, and W. Richard 1999 *Confinement and Ethnicity: An Overview of World War II Japanese American Relocation Sites.* National Park Service Publications in Anthropology 74. Western Archaeological and Conservation Center, Tucson.

Callow, S. 2009 Bone as Material Culture of Conflict: from Napoleonic Prisoners of War into Twentieth Century. Paper delivered at the 2009 Conflict Archaeology Conference at the Royal Logistics Corps Museum, Deepcut, Camberley, UK, July, 2009.

Carman, J. and P. Carman 2006 *Bloody Meadows: Investigating Landscapes of Battle.* History Press, Stroud.

Carr, G. and H. Mytum (eds.) forthcoming *Cultural Heritage and Prisoners of War: Creativity Behind Barbed Wire.* Routledge, New York.

Cesarani, D. 1993 An Alien Concept? The Continuity of Anti-Alienism in British Society Before 1940. In *The Internment of Aliens in Twentieth Century Britain,* edited by D. Cesarani and T. Kushner, pp. 25–52. Cass, London.

Cesarani, D. and T. Kushner (eds.) 1993 *The Internment of Aliens in Twentieth Century Britain.* Cass, London.

Chappell, C. 1984 *Island of Barbed Wire: The Remarkable Story of World War Two Internment on the Isle of Man.* Hale, London.

Cohen-Portheim, P. 1931 *Time Stood Still: My Internment in England, 1914–1918*. Duckworth, London.

Cresswell, Y. 1994 *Living with the Wire*. Manx National Heritage, Douglas.

Cresswell, Y. 2005 Behind the Wire: The Material Culture of Civilian Internment on the Isle of Man in the First World War. In *Totally Un-English? Britain's Internment of "Enemy Aliens" in Two World Wars*. Yearbook of the Research Centre for German and Austrian Exile Studies 7, edited by R. Dove, pp. 45–61. Rodopi, Amsterdam.

Dove, R. (ed.) 2005 *Totally Un-English? Britain's Internment of "Enemy Aliens" in Two World Wars*. Yearbook of the Research Centre for German and Austrian Exile Studies 7. Rodopi, Amsterdam.

Dunbar-Kalcreuth, F. 1940 *Die Mannerinsel*. Paul List Verlag, Leipzig.

Evans, C. 1998 Constructing Houses and Building Context: Bersu's Manx Round-House Campaign. *Proceedings of the Prehistoric Society* 64: 183–201.

Evans, D. 2006 *Army Camps: History and Development, 1858–2000*. English Heritage, London.

Hinrichsen, K. 1993 Visual Art Behind the Wire. In *The Internment of Aliens in Twentieth Century Britain*, edited by D. Cesarani and T. Kushner, pp. 188–209. Cass, London.

Horne, J. 2002 The German Connection: The Stobs Camp Newspaper 1916–1919. *Hawick Archaeological Society Transactions* 26–32.

Hughes, W.R. 1920 Chapter IV. The Internment Camps. In *St. Stephen's House. Friends' Emergency Work in England 1914 to 1920*, edited by A.B. Thomas, pp. 43–56. Friends' Bookshop, London.

Hughes, W. 1926 The Internment Camps. In *St. Stephen's House: Friends' Emergency Work in England 1914 to 1920*, edited by A. Thomas, pp. 43–81. Emergency Committee for the Assistance of Germans, Austrians and Hungarians in Distress, London.

Kewley Draskau, J. 2009 Relocating the Heimat: Great War Internment Literature from the Isle of Man. *German Studies Review* 32(1): 82–106.

Kochan, M. 1993 Women's Experience of Internment. In *The Internment of Aliens in Twentieth Century Britain*, edited by D. Cesarani and T. Kushner, pp. 147–166. Cass, London.

Kushner, T. and D. Cesarani 1993 Alien Internment in Britain During the Twentieth Century: An Introduction. In *The Internment of Aliens in Twentieth Century Britain*, edited by D. Cesarani and T. Kushner, pp. 1–22. Cass, London.

Lafitte, F. 1988 *The Internment of Aliens*. Libris, London.

Mytum, H. 2002 A Comparison of Nineteenth and Twentieth Century Anglican and Nonconformist Memorials in North Pembrokeshire. *Archaeological Journal* 159: 194–241.

Mytum, H. forthcoming Photographs at Douglas Camp: deciphering dynamic networks of relationships from static images. In *Cultural Heritage and Prisoners of War: Creativity behind Barbed Wire*, edited by G. Carr and H. Mytum, Routledge, New York.

Panayi, P. 1991 *The Enemy in Our Midst: Germans in Britain During the First World War*. Berg, Oxford.

Panayi, P. 1993 An Intolerant Act by an Intolerant Society: The Internment of Germans in Britain During the First World War. In *The Internment of Aliens in Twentieth Century Britain*, edited by D. Cesarani and T. Kushner, pp. 53–75. Cass, London.

Panayi, P. 2005 Marginalized Subject? The Historiography of Enemy Alien Internment in Britain. In *Totally Un-English? Britain's Internment of "Enemy Aliens" in Two World Wars*. Yearbook of the Research Centre for German and Austrian Exile Studies, edited by R. Dove, pp. 17–26. Rodopi, Amsterdam.

Rachamimov, A. 2006 The Disruptive Comforts of Drag: (Trans)Gender Performances Among Prisoners of War in Russia, 1914–1920. *The American Historical Review* 111(2): 362–382.

Sargeaunt, B. 1920 *The Isle of Man and the Great War*. Brown and Sons, Douglas.

Saunders, N. 2003 *Trench Art: Materialities and Memories of War*. Berg, Oxford.

Schofield, J. 2005 *Combat Archaeology: Material Culture and Modern Conflict*. Duckworth, London.

Schofield, J., W. Johnson, and C. Beck (eds.) 2002 *Materiél Culture: The Archaeology of Twentieth Century Conflict*. Routledge, London.

Spiro, A. 1993 Internment Testimonies: Anna Spiro. In *The Internment of Aliens in Twentieth Century Britain*, edited by D. Cesarani and T. Kushner, pp. 236–241. Cass, London.

Sponza, L. 2005 The Internment of Italians 1940–1945. In *Totally Un-English? Britain's Internment of "Enemy Aliens" in Two World Wars*. Yearbook of the Research Centre for German and Austrian Exile Studies, edited by R. Dove, pp. 153–163. Rodopi, Amsterdam.

Stent, R. 1980 *A Bespattered Page? The Internment of His Majesty's "Most Loyal Enemy Aliens"*. Deutsch, London.

Tarlow, S. and S. West 1999 *The Familiar Past? Archaeologies of Later Historical Britain*. Routledge, London.

Thomas, A.B. (ed.) 1920 *St. Stephen's House. Friends' Emergency Work in England 1914 to 1920*. Friends' Bookshop, London.

Thompson, S. 2006 New South Wales Migration Centre, Objects Through Time, Liverpool Holsworthy Internment Collection c.1914–1918 http://www.migrationheritage.nsw.gov.au/exhibition/objectsthroughtime/holsworthy/

Vischer, A. 1919 *Barbed Wire Disease: A Psychological Study of the Prisoner of War*. John Bale, London.

Chapter 4
The Archaeology of Internment in Francoist Spain (1936–1952)

Alfredo González-Ruibal

Abstract Between 1936 and 1952 Spain was transformed into an immense prison. Hundreds of internment camps were established by General Franco all over the country: some of them were purpose built; others reused older buildings and spaces. No less than half a million people passed through the camps and many thousands died in them due to ill-treatment, hunger, disease, and executions. The Franco regime produced a complex typology of camps, articulated with other spaces of punishment, which was fundamental in disciplining its subjects and reconstructing the nation along totalitarian lines. In recent years, historical research on the camps has grown exponentially, but the materiality of the sites themselves has rarely been taken into consideration. Here, the Spanish camps will be studied archaeologically as a technology of repression. Toward understanding the Spanish camps in their wider context, the similarities and dissimilarities with Nazi Germany and Fascist Italy will be pointed out. Finally, I will scrutinize the contentious place of the camps in the collective memory of Spaniards today.

Introduction: The Rationale of Spanish Internment Camps

The aim of this chapter is twofold: On the one hand, I would like to present the case of the Spanish internment camps and outline the possibilities that their archaeological study offers—the case of Francoist Spain is interesting for the particular combination of archaic and modernist elements which is obvious both in ideology and in material culture; on the other hand, I would like to use this topic to problematize notions of domination and resistance that are prevalent in the discipline today—especially in, but not limited to, archaeologies of identity and postcolonial archaeologies. I argue that the analysis of modern strategies of control

A. González-Ruibal (✉)
Heritage Laboratory, Spanish National Research Council, Santiago de Compostela, Spain
e-mail: alfredo.gonzalez-ruibal@iegps.csic.es

A. Myers, G. Moshenska (eds.), *Archaeologies of Internment*, One World Archaeology, DOI 10.1007/978-1-4419-9666-4_4, © Springer Science+Business Media, LLC 2011

and punishment provides a more realistic perspective on the ambiguities, and limits, of resistance and on the powerful effect of domination. An overly optimistic vision of agency among the subalterns downplays the iniquities of power, and the sufferings these cause.

In Spain, between 1936 and the early 1950s, hundreds of internment camps and prisons were established by General Francisco Franco. Approximately half a million people passed through the camps and many thousands died in them due to ill-treatment, hunger, disease, and executions. The Franco regime (1936–1975) produced a complex range of camps, interwoven with other spaces of punishment, which was fundamental in disciplining its subjects and reconstructing the nation along totalitarian lines. In recent years, historical research on the camps has grown considerably (Lafuente 2003; Molinero et al. 2003; Rodrigo 2005), but the materiality of the sites themselves has rarely been taken into consideration. In fact, very little is known about daily life in concentration and labor camps, or about the mechanisms of punishment and discipline employed in them. Whereas personal memories and oral testimonies have proliferated recently (Ríos et al. 2008:144), there are very few photographs that may illustrate everyday life in the camps (Rodrigo 2008:228), and the majority of those that do exist are propagandistic. These circumstances make archaeology invaluable in exploring the iniquities of the Spanish *univers concentrationnaire*.

Concentration camps have often been considered as quintessentially modern (Bauman 1989; Everdell 1997:116–117). However, in this chapter I will ask: *Just how modern were Francoist concentration camps*? And, *what were the differences and similarities with other internment centers of the time*?

General Franco's regime was the only fascist dictatorship in the 1930s and 1940s that needed a civil war to impose itself (Casanova 2004:5). Germany's path to totalitarianism was relatively peaceful and (ostensibly) democratic, and Italy's fall into fascism was remarkably bloodless. The difficulties encountered by the Spanish generals in establishing a right-wing dictatorship may in part explain the extreme violence that plagued the process, and the varied brutal technologies of repression that marked the wartime and postwar period. There are other reasons, too: Franco's commanders, like Franco himself, were well-seasoned *Africanistas*, that is, soldiers of the colonial army formerly stationed in Morocco. What they did was import colonial tactics to Spain: raids, plunder, rapes, mass killing of civilians, and aerial bombings were all common in Morocco. Concentration camps themselves were first tested in the colonies—in Cuba during the war of 1895–1898 (Izquierdo Canosa 1998; Chapter 1 by Moshenska and Myers, this volume)—before being employed elsewhere. Colonial wars were based on the dehumanization of the enemy, which allowed metropolitan armies to give the indigenous population the most ruthless treatment (Lindqvist 1996; Zimmerer 2004).

Social and biological evolutionism offered intellectual support to this dehumanization of the other, and justified genocides, forced labor, and the systematic occupation of overseas territories. However, dehumanization practices and beliefs that mingled racism and classism were increasingly imported into Europe (Zimmerer

2005), a situation that strongly helped the emergence of total war (Ferguson 2007). During the Spanish Civil War (1936–1939), *Reds*, a blanket term applied to all those who backed the Republic, came to replace the *savage*: enemies were considered to be no more Spaniards than the Moroccans or Guineans. The Republican side was portrayed as Anti-Spain by the Francoist faction and its supporters were caricatured as absolute evil (Sevillano 2007). As colonial wars intended in the last instance to civilize the natives, the Spanish Civil War had for the Francoists the avowed aim of *españolizar* (Spaniardizing) the nationals that went astray and eliminating those who could not be reconverted. Internment camps played an important role in this scheme.

Franco purposefully protracted the conflict to get a better hold of the country. The future dictator knew that the majority of the population was against him and he systematically refused any armistice to put an end to the war that would imply a referendum. Knowing that the Spaniards were not with him does not mean that he did not have the right to rule Spain. He was, as the motto read, *Caudillo de España por la gracia de Dios*: Chief of Spain by the will of God. The problem lay in how to impose the will of God upon a nation that had fallen prey to leftist and atheist ideas. A 3-year war allowed Franco and his generals to pursue the task of cleaning Spain in a painstaking way: a rapid victory would have made that more complicated. It is often argued that Franco's decision not to capture the capital of Madrid two months after the beginning of the war was a bold and smart political move. The capture of Madrid, which was feasible, would have probably put an end to the conflict. Yet Franco's leadership was not yet well established by then and the purges needed more time to be completed. Franco decided to free the old imperial capital, Toledo, from the Republican siege: this provided him with a powerful symbolic capital, which eventually made him paramount chief of the rebel armies, and extended the war for 32 more months, as the Republicans obtained precious time to defend Madrid (Preston 2007:131–133). Franco did not capture the capital for the entire duration of the war, but this allowed him and his acolytes to occupy the country systematically. Franco's generals perceived their war as a colonial war of occupation. Concentration camps served to jail the tens of thousands of enemies or potential enemies captured as they proceeded to occupy the country: they also helped classify and reeducate the Reds, in order to turn them into good, Catholic Spaniards.

Detention centers and concentration camps were also established by different factions within the Republican side, as well, and disciplinary programs were enforced in them (Beevor 2001:192–193). Some Francoist concentration camps, such as Albatera (Valencia), were in fact set up on the premises of Republican camps. But they were not part of a systematic, state-sponsored technology of repression as with the other side. The most important (and brutal) of the places of punishment created in the zone controlled by the Republic were the *checas*—centers of detention and torture in the hands of anarchists and communists, which started in Madrid and Barcelona from the beginning of the war (Villarroya and Solé i Sabaté 1996).

From Camps to Prisons: The Institutional Typology of Franco's Internment Centers

To understand the varied typology of internment camps deployed by the new fascist regime, it is necessary to take into account the transformations undergone by the repressive strategies from July 17, 1936, to the late 1940s. Rodrigo (2008) distinguishes three different phases of violence and repression: one of parastatal violence, linked to the failed military coup (July–October 1936) that led to the war, one related to the war itself (November 1936–April 1939), and one which started with the end of hostilities (April 1939 onward). Each of these phases was characterized by different practices and places of repression. During the first phase, concentration camps were scarce, as many prisoners of war were shot on the spot or herded into improvised detention centers. Extermination prevailed: around 80–85% of the 100,000 people murdered by fascist militiamen or the rebel army during the war were killed in the first 6 months of the conflict (Rodrigo 2008:43). Concentration camps and the first forced labor camps marked the second period: war needs demanded a method of dealing with the hundreds of thousands of prisoners captured during the Francoist advance, especially from late 1937 onward. Finally, labor camps and conventional prisons prevailed during the third phase, that of the consolidation of the new state. The idea of atonement through work was prevalent in this period, which saw the closing of most concentration camps. Here I will focus on the second and third phases of repression, where internment camps were most widely used.

The organization of the concentration camp system in Francoist Spain was implemented between March and July 1937. During that period a series of orders and decrees were enacted that helped rationalize and maximize the repressive machine. On March 11, 1937, the General Order of Classification was passed that distinguished four categories of people among the prisoners of war, each marked by a letter: "A" for soldiers forcibly recruited by the Republican army, but who sympathized with the fascists; "B" for volunteers in the Republican army; "C" for union and political leaders of the Republic; and "D" for common criminals (Rodrigo 2005:31). A subcategory was later added: "Ad" (*afecto dudoso*) for soldiers that had been forcibly recruited by the Republic, but whose support to the new fascist regime was under suspicion. Those under the category "A" had to join the Francoist army. Officers fighting for the Republic ("Bs"), and politicians and unionists ("Cs") were often executed; alternatively, they were imprisoned in concentration camps and other detention centers. "Ds" ended up in jail. Those categorized as "Ad" or "B" were usually incorporated into forced labor punishment squads (*batallones de trabajadores*). The circumstances of these battalions were regulated by a decree of May 1937 (Rodrigo 2005:56). Inmates were forced to dig trenches, build pillboxes, pave roads, or work in the iron mines of the Basque Country. Ironically, the forced labor was justified as the Prisoner of War's (PoW) "right to work." In July of that same year, the Inspection of PoW Concentration Camps was created (Rodrigo 2008:117).

By the autumn of 1937 there were already 70,000 people in concentration camps, many of them soldiers captured during the conquest of northern Spain that year (Rodrigo 2008:119) and 107,000 prisoners from the Republican Army had been examined by the Committee of Classification. Thirty-four thousand people were incorporated into forced labor battalions (Rodrigo 2008:120). The number of prisoners increased exponentially as the rebel army advanced toward the Mediterranean. Thus, by the end of the war, concentration camps held over 277,000 prisoners, and 90,000 soldiers were serving in *Batallones de Trabajadores* (Rodrigo 2008:125). The ambitious program of purging and brainwashing that the ideologues of concentration camps intended to impose was thwarted by the evolution of the war. With thousands of soldiers being captured in every campaign, practical needs overcame any ideological considerations. Nevertheless, reeducation programs continued unabated in a simplified form: compulsory masses, patriotic songs, parades, political indoctrination through lectures and meetings, and fascist salutes were common in internment camps throughout the war and after. In total, 188 concentration camps were opened in Spain between 1936 and 1947 (Rodrigo 2005:308).

Except from the absence of a systematic policy of extermination, daily life in Spanish concentration camps was not much different from those of Nazi Germany. Men and women (and sometimes children) often arrived to concentration camps in cattle wagons; many camps had no substantial buildings and prisoners were exposed to extreme weather conditions (Núñez Díaz-Balart 2005:81). Hunger and thirst prevailed. Thirst, in particular, is often mentioned by former inmates as one of the worst sufferings (Rodrigo 2005:149–150). Hunger is omnipresent in memories written by former inmates (e.g. Guzmán 2001) and deaths from starvation were common, as well as from exhaustion due to heavy work. The lack of hygiene favored outbreaks of all sorts of diseases, some of which were fairly controlled before the war, such as malaria and tuberculosis. In the penitentiary of Valdenoceda, for example, 61.6% of deaths in the prison were as a result of tuberculosis (Ríos et al. 2008:149). Arbitrary killings and tortures occurred frequently. All miseries endured by the prisoners were part of a strategy of humiliation and punishment of the vanquished, who were thoroughly deprived of their human dignity (Rodrigo 2005:147).

The dual typology of internment centers (concentration camps and forced labor camps) became more complicated during the postwar period. Concentration camps were gradually closed, but some of them were still active as late as 1947, such as Miranda de Ebro (Burgos), one of Spain's most important camps, which was reused during the Second World War to host exiles, refugees, and prisoners of war coming from Europe (Pallarés and Espinosa de los Monteros 2005). However, concentration camps became unnecessary as inmates were executed, sentenced to prison terms or forced labor, or simply released. Those sentenced to forced labor could end up in penal detachments (*destacamentos penales*), military penal colonies (*colonias penales militarizadas*), or disciplinary battalions of workers (*batallones disciplinarios de trabajadores*) (Lafuente 2003:57). The vanquished in the war most often passed through different institutions during several years, in what was derisively known as "penal tourism" (Bravo 2007:55). The prison tour was certainly one of the means used by Francoism to break the prisoner's will and capacity for resistance. They also gave the inmates an idea of the character of this new Spain, dominated by surveillance and control.

Penal colonies were created in September 1939 and the main task of the inmates was to build dams and canals. Colonies were established alongside the Guadiana, Tajo, Guadalquivir, and other rivers. Six groups of penal colonies with 5,000 prisoners were set up between 1939 and 1942 (Gutiérrez Casalá 2003:21). The detachments absorbed the greater number of inmates, numbering 16,000 people in the mid-1940s, distributed in 121 camps (Olaizola Elordi 2006:12). They worked on diverse projects: from large public works, such as railways, roads, hospitals, and the reconstruction of whole villages, to private businesses, such as building houses or producing concrete. Many entrepreneurs became rich thanks to this cheap labor: businessmen had to pay to the state the whole salary due to the prisoner, but the inmate only received a tiny fraction of it. Often, the relatives of the prisoner depended on this meager pay. Political prisoners made for extremely good workers, because the redemption of their sentence depended on it, as did their relatives' survival. Many of them were highly skilled workers, such as architects, engineers, and medical doctors. Penal detachments were long-lived: the last one was only closed in 1970 (Lafuente 2003:235). Finally, the battalions of workers (*Batallones de Trabajadores*) already existed during the war, as we have seen, and they changed little from a legal and disciplinary point of view after the conflict. The main difference was that prisoners were no longer involved in building military infrastructures.

Those who joined the penal colonies, detachments, or battalions had been previously sentenced in court for "supporting the rebellion." The truth was exactly the opposite, but the fascists considered the men and women who did not adhere to their cause as rebels. With twisted logic, they criminalized those who maintained their loyalty to the legal government at the time of the coup (Lafuente 2003:27–30). Sentences were mostly 20 or 30 years in prison. Documents from the time indicate the kind of "crimes" committed by those sent to forced labor: "member of the Young Socialists," "member of the General Union of Workers," "deputy mayor [with the leftist Popular Front]," "pilot of the Republican air force trained in Russia," "member of the local revolutionary committee" (Gutiérrez Casalá 2003:54–55).

Yet those long prison terms could not have possibly been applied, as a large percentage of the Spanish population would have remained in jail which would have led to crippling social and economic results. Therefore, in June 1939 a decree was passed that established the "redemption of sentences through work." The use of the word "redemption," instead of "reduction" was not accidental. The theoretical foundations of the new penitentiary regime were based on Catholic ideas of sin, atonement, and forgiveness that superseded the legal concepts of crime, sentence, and amnesty (Gómez Bravo 2007:15, 20). This particular penal system thrived during the days of the Second World War. From the late 1940s onward, forced labor declined in importance, and prisons became the most important technology of punishment, remaining so until the end of the dictatorship in 1975.

The Material Culture of Totalitarianism

I have briefly described the evolution and characteristics of the penal system in Spain during the Spanish Civil War and after. The institutional typology of repressive centers, however, did not coincide with a material typology. That is, there was no particular model of concentration camp, different from a penal colony or a penal detachment. The circumstances of the war and postwar period explain the variety of buildings and spaces transformed into internment centers. Some concentration camps were newly created. Others were little more than a fence of barbed wire where prisoners had, at best, a piece of canvas to cover themselves at night. Most internment camps, however, reused older buildings: bullrings, seminaries, monasteries, convents, castles, schools, and factories. This typology is likely not fortuitous. There might be other reasons—beyond practical ones—behind the recurrent use of certain types of buildings.

I argue that the use of religious buildings (Fig. 4.1), for example, served a particular purpose, even if this purpose was not openly stated. The Spanish Civil War was presented as a "National Crusade" (*Cruzada Nacional*) by the Francoist side and it received strong support from the Catholic Church, which resented the killing of almost 7,000 priests and monks by anarchists and communists, as well as the secularist policies of the Republic, which deprived the Church of much of its social power and influence. The re-education of the Republican prisoners not only included the attempt to impose right-wing, imperialistic, and ultranationalist ideas,

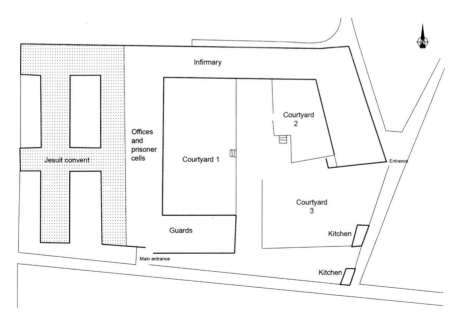

Fig. 4.1 Layout of the concentration camp of Camposancos (Pontevedra), established on the premises of a Jesuit school. Drawn by the author based on original plan with no scale

but also religious beliefs (Rodrigo 2005:128–138). What better setting than monasteries, seminaries, and convents to achieve these purposes, or at least, to make the prisoners feel the punishment of God? Priests were always present in internment camps to celebrate mass, hear confessions, and catechize. Some of the masses became grand performances of power to which the ecclesiastical setting certainly contributed (Rodrigo 2005:137).

Concurrently, the attempt to make punishment a public performance might be behind the choice of certain buildings and scenarios. It was a return to the economy of punishment of the *Ancien Regime*, which provoked "an effect of terror through the spectacle of power wreaking havoc on the culprit" (Foucault 1975:70). Typical of internment camps in Spain were prisoner parades: they marched in formation through villages and towns to attend mass or to go to work. The queues of prisoners flanked by armed guards became part of the spectacle of Francoist power, whose didactic purposes are obvious. Fermín Maguire and Ayán (2008) remind us that monasteries, bullrings, factories, and schools were among the most prominent structures in Spanish cities and villages. They were landmarks in locals' cognitive maps that became reinscribed indelibly as places of punishment. The participation of political prisoners in the construction and reconstruction of important infrastructures, including whole towns, provided "a thousand small theaters of punishment" (Foucault 1975:133), continuously delivering their political lessons.

Schools and bullrings, on the other hand, unconsciously helped to give material support to ideas of the enemy that were widespread among the fascists: the Reds were either like children who had been hoodwinked by Soviet agents (Rodrigo 2005:131) or like animals, moved by basic instincts. Herded in those places, dirty and weakened by famine, the stereotypes were naturally reinforced. An architect in charge of forced workers later commented: "It is not that they had the conscience of being criminals... They were so primitive, so primitive, that they did things as an animal would, without any consequence of what they were doing. This was due to the war and their low intellectual state, of course..." (Lafuente 2003:122). We have both themes here: the Reds were like primitives (and therefore, like children, following colonial logic) and animals at the same time. The places used as concentration and forced labor camps did not just serve to humiliate, punish, and re-educate the vanquished, they were also a powerful, yet unconscious, means of reinforcing political clichés: so unconscious, in fact, that those who created them were not fully aware of their role in depriving the prisoners of their humanity. Given that internment camps were all over the country, a generation of Spaniards grew accustomed to look at Reds as filthy and primitive.

The use of factories (Fig. 4.2) might be related to the reification of the enemy, typical of totalitarian regimes. As Fermín Maguire and Ayán (2008) remark:

> Prisoners were shaved, made to wear uniforms, transported in trains and ships and stored in factories; thus becoming literally presented and treated as cattle by and through industrial material culture. The Spanish Civil War graphically and tragically portrayed the dangers of social transformations detected by Weber or Marx: in modern society and under logistical imperatives people can be seen as commodities.

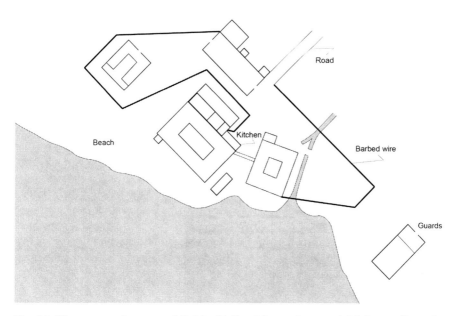

Fig. 4.2 The concentration camp of Cedeira (A Coruña) reused a canned fish factory. Drawn by the author based on a plan from the period with no scale

There is another unconscious reason for turning factories, schools, and convents into concentration camps. They are all inherently disciplinary spaces that share the same logic of control, surveillance, and modification of bodily practices (Foucault 1975; Fermín Maguire and Ayán 2008). Not surprisingly, many eighteenth- and nineteenth-century proposals for penitentiaries, schools, and factories drew upon the model of the monastery.

The heterogeneity of buildings used for internment purposes reminiscent of the *Ancien Regime*, the prevalence of improvisation, and the overwhelming relevance of the Church with its concepts of sin and redemption are premodern elements in the fascist technology of punishment. Equally archaic was the layout of the prisons founded after the end of the war (Johnston 1961:319–321): they followed the mid-nineteenth-century Panopticon model, which was quite outdated by the 1930s, but fit well with the notion of permanent and total surveillance espoused by the new fascist regime. One exemplar is the prison of Carabanchel in Madrid, which was built by its own inmates. Yet this is an archaism coalesced with highly modernist principles: classification, for example, is typical of social engineering aimed at making a whole society legible (Scott 1999). Likewise, the totalitarian magnitude of incarceration by the end of the war could only be achieved with modern means such as railways, a well-organized bureaucracy, and a modern mind.

Material culture was central to the totalitarian project: that the country was turned into an "immense prison" (Molinero et al. 2003) was more than a metaphor. By using every place at their disposal as a concentration camp, the new regime achieved their fascist dream: transforming every corner of Spain into a space of control. The socialization of surveillance that characterizes the end of the civil war—with half of Spain informing on the other half—has its material realization in the spread of penal institutions. With tens of thousands of Spaniards turned into police informants (Casanova 2004:28–33) and hundreds of premises made into detention centers, every neighbor could be a spy and every building a prison.

The layout of some internment centers was also typically modern: Miranda de Ebro, one of the central concentration camps, adopted a typical camp configuration, with rows of parallel blocks surrounded by barbed wire and sentry boxes (Fig. 4.3). It occupied 42 hectares and was designed for 1,500 prisoners, but the figures soon doubled. Space was similarly organized in Castuera (Extremadura). In its 72 hectares, there were around 80 blocks for prisoners arranged in streets. The camp was surrounded by a ditch and a fence of barbed wire 4 meters high (López Rodríguez 2006). The model was not exclusive to concentration camps: it also appears in some penal colonies, such as those established in Montijo (Extremadura) (Fig. 4.4). Orders were dispatched for the construction of concentration camps following this system, but they were only fulfilled in particular cases. Yet even in these

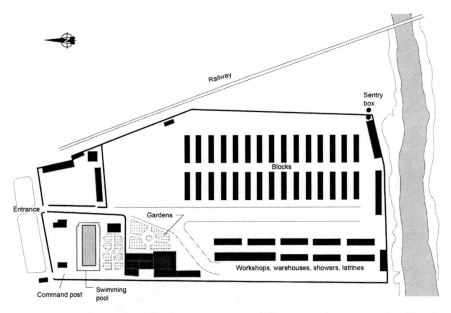

Fig. 4.3 The concentration camp of Miranda de Ebro (Burgos), one of the most important in Francoist Spain, was created *ex novo* following a regular pattern. Like Castuera (Cáceres) and other large camps, it was built next to a railway for the rapid processing of prisoners (arrival, classification, and eventual transfer to other places). Drawn by the author

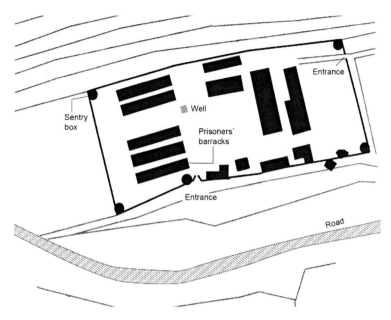

Fig. 4.4 Penal colony of Montijo (Badajoz). Drawn by the author after Gutiérrez Casalá (2003)

high modernist spaces of punishment there was place for the archaic: the camp of Castuera was presided over by a large cross, a permanent reminder of the National Crusade in which the Reds had been defeated (Fig. 4.5).

There is a long-running debate in Spain on the nature of General Franco's regime in the 1930s and 1940s, some labeling it as authoritarian and dictatorial, others as fascist and totalitarian—following Juan Linz's famous definitions (Linz 2000). The problem is with the concept of "fascism" itself, which, according to Payne (1996:3), "remains probably the vaguest of the major political terms" due to its lack of any explicit political reference, as with liberalism or communism. Francoism certainly shared most of the key elements of fascist totalitarianism as pointed out by Payne (1996:7): antiliberalism, anticommunism, male dominance, personal style of command, national syndicalist economy, imperialism, positive evaluation of war, and nationalist authoritarian state. What Francoism clearly lacked was a secularist attitude. At any rate, there is consensus among historians now, that Francoism was fascist at least between 1936 and 1943 (Thomàs 2001). The turn of the tide during the Second World War led to political, juridical, and rhetorical changes in the regime. If we look to material culture, we see that the new state had adopted more than a "fascist hue" (Trevor-Roper 1981:36): the extension of internment camps, the way they took hold of the whole country, and the classification system which they served would be good criteria to label the Franco regime as fascist, at the minimum, until 1943–1944.

The camps and prisons were just one part of the totalitarian material culture that was inherent to the foundation of the dictatorship. Military camps, fortified

Fig. 4.5 Concrete base of the cross that towered upon the concentration camp of Castuera (Cáceres). Photograph by Kiko Esperilla (www.kikoesperilla.blogspot.com)

police headquarters, schools, social housing and monuments, and memorials were all part of a transformation of the country along totalitarian lines (González-Ruibal 2007:218). Some historians argue that Spain was not fascist because of the aforementioned mixture of hypertraditionalist and modernist elements that was obvious in every aspect of the regime, from the idea of the state to conceptions of morality. However, the perfect totalitarian project was only fulfilled by Nazi Germany: "Only in Germany was fascism both revolutionary and totalitarian in deed as well as in word," reminds Ferguson (2007:232)—and even there, traditionalism (an idealized countryside, for example) played as vital a role as modernism in the configuration of the regime. Mussolini's Italy was much more similar to Spain than to Germany. Referring to Italian fascism, Ben-Ghiat (2003:17) writes that "with an impossible heterogeneous coalition of supporters, which included Nationalists, monarchists, national syndicalists, squadrists, and conservative clericals, Mussolini did not really intend to clarify his movement's ideological identity."

Materiality, again, may be a useful element here. If we focus on internment centers, we see that the situation in Italy was not much different from Spain. Unlike Hitler, Mussolini did not rush to create new spaces of punishment: many concentration camps reused older buildings, with the difference that camps created *ex novo* were very few in Italy before the outbreak of the Second World War. Not many camps followed the gridded pattern that we find in Miranda de Ebro and Castuera. Among these, the camp of Ferramonti (Calabria) stands out. Ferramonti had 92 blocks aligned in parallel rows and surrounded by a fence of barbed wire with sentry boxes (Capogreco 1987:18). It had an average of 2,000 inmates (including Jews, partisans, political prisoners) and a maximum of 2,700 in 1943. PoW camps had more inmates, but rarely over 3,000.

Many Spanish camps exceeded the above-mentioned figures (Rodrigo 2005:86–87): Burgo de Osma was built for 3,500 inmates, San Pedro de Cardeña for 3,000, and Aranda de Duero for 4,000 (all in Burgos province). The British and French prisoners alone in Miranda de Ebro during the Second World War accounted for 3,000 of the inmates (Pallarés and Espinosa 2005:172). In April 1938, the camp held 18,406 prisoners (Rodrigo 2005:87). The camp of Albatera (Valencia) reached 30,000 prisoners after the end of the conflict (Rodrigo 2005: 202). As opposed to the 188 concentration camps in Spain, Italy had a maximum of 113 concentration camps in the peninsula and 22 in the occupied territories, despite having a greater population and their involvement in the international war (Galluccio 2002).

In the case of Spain, it is difficult to distinguish a concentration camp for political prisoners from a PoW camp, since the enemy was above all a political foe. Unlike in Germany, where life in the PoW camps was incomparably better than in concentration camps (except for Russian PoWs), in Spain there is no difference that can be drawn and therefore I have invariably used the word "concentration camp" for referring to PoW camps. As had occurred in Spain, Italy developed a typology of internment centers which did not have a perfect material correlate, as most camps reused older buildings: *colonie di confine* (penal colonies for banishing political opponents) and *campi di lavoro coatto* (forced labor camps). Forced labor camps did not have the preeminence that they enjoyed in Spain. In that sense, Spain's technologies of punishment were more akin to those of Nazi Germany, where slave labor played a paramount role in the economy of the new state. A large part of the state infrastructure constructed in Spain during the 1940s and early 1950s (and still in use today) was built by forced labor. The new cultural landscape of Francoism, then, was materially produced by slaves.

A Closer Look at the Camps: Ambiguous Domination/Ambiguous Resistance

Archaeological studies on internment centers are scarce in Spain, even if we use a flexible concept of archaeology (Ballesta and Rodríguez Gallardo 2008; Falquina et al. 2008; Fermín Maguire and Ayán 2008; López Rodríguez and León Cáceres 2008; Ríos et al. 2008). However, the potential that such an approach offers toward understanding the microphysics of fascist power is significant. One possible area of investigation is that of the unmarked graves and cemeteries that surrounded internment camps and prisons. A few have already been excavated: Valdenoceda, San Pedro de Cardeña, and Fuerte de San Cristóbal—but the results have not yet been fully published (Junquera 2007; Ríos et al. 2008). Forensic studies might offer details on the many sufferings of inmates, including starvation, diseases, and beatings. They may also clarify the circumstances of death of some prisoners, whose unlawful killing in prison was often concealed from the family (Ríos et al. 2008:150).

The simple study of the plans of internment centers may be illustrative of the way power and surveillance were enforced in them. The central contribution of archaeology might lie in the exploration of the mechanisms of domination and resistance, which were often subtle, and rarely verbalized. For an archaeological example, I will rely mostly on the work of my research team in Bustarviejo, a penal detachment near Madrid (Falquina et al. 2008).

In all cases, the spaces where the prisoners slept were common dormitories. This is a characteristic shared by concentration camps elsewhere in Europe during the Second World War. The rigid structure and repetition served to undermine the individuality of the inmates. It is a return to *Ancien Regime* practices, after the individualizing trends of nineteenth-century prisons (Foucault 1975). Prisoners were not perceived as individuals by the Francoist regime, but as an amorphous mass, and were treated as such. In the case of Spain, bunks—a typical image from Nazi camps—were mostly absent. We were able to prove their absence through archaeological means at Bustarviejo camp (Falquina et al. 2008), and our inference was later corroborated by oral testimonies. There are data—oral sources and rare drawings—of prisoners sleeping on the floor in other concentration camps and penitentiaries (e.g. Acuña 2007:210–211; Costa and Santos 2007:67–68). Dormitories were often endowed with a continuous shelf—one of which has been preserved in Bustarviejo—where the prisoners put their few personal belongings. The absence of bunks or cots is pragmatic: during the day, the dormitory can be put to other uses. Yet it also helps to dissolve even further the concept of the individual self: open rooms with no furniture resemble animal stalls more than human living quarters. It is not by chance that the prison bedrooms of Bustarviejo and Valdenoceda were later used as cowsheds. The latrines of the camp have also been identified: a series of holes in a concrete platform—a setup that prevented any privacy. Prisoners usually had to wash themselves in troughs in open air, where they also washed their clothes. This can be seen in Bustarviejo and the concentration camp of Rianxo (Fig. 4.6). The lack of separation of different daily activities also aimed at breaking the inmates' dignity and sense of self.

The dissolution of the prisoners' individuality did not end in life, as camp cemeteries were either simple mass graves (e.g. at Castuera) or unmarked individual tombs (e.g. at Valdenoceda). The case of the fortress of San Cristóbal is intriguing, because although the graves were anonymous, somebody put a glass bottle between the prisoners' legs with a document inside telling his circumstances of death (Junquera 2007). Undoubtedly, the officer who did that thought that sometime in the future the relatives could want to recover the corpses, as in fact it has happened. Unfortunately, the cork of all the bottles but one decayed and the papers had disintegrated.

Irrespective of the layout of the camps, some elements are always present: the courtyard, which was used for indoctrination, masses, and parades; the sentry boxes, which instilled the sense of always being observed, the location of the dormitories. These were always diametrically opposed to the entrance, where the quarters occupied by the prison guards stood (Fig. 4.7). The guards' rooms created a barrier between the prisoner and the outside. Thus, when the inmates went out of

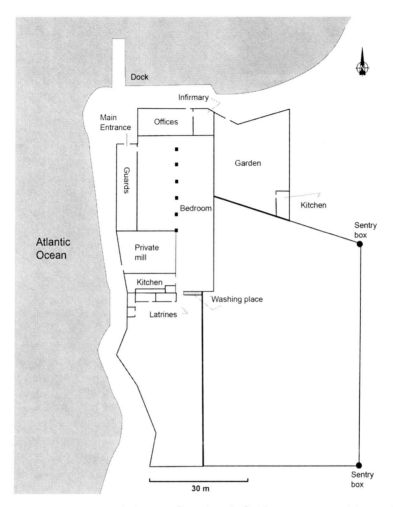

Fig. 4.6 Concentration camp of Rianxo (A Coruña). As in Cedeira, the camp reused the premises of a canned fish factory. The sea fulfilled the role played by the railway in other camps. Drawn by the author based on original plans and satellite images

their blocks, the first thing they saw was their guardians' rooms. In Bustarviejo, the windows in the guards' rooms are bigger and lower, so that they can observe and control the prisoners' quarters. The prisoners' room, in contrast, had narrow elevated openings, which prevented virtually all visibility (Falquina et al. 2008:185). The kitchens always occupied a marginal position in the compound, probably for practical reasons such as preventing the prisoners from stealing food.

Thus far I have focused on the strategies of domination and dehumanization of the prisoner. Was there room for resistance in the totalitarian technology of incarceration deployed by the Francoist regime? I argue that the concept of resistance has been trivialized and exaggerated in recent times. There is a far too optimistic notion

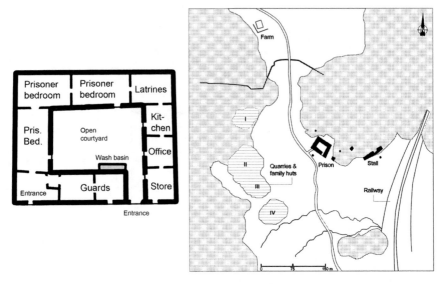

Fig. 4.7 Penal detachment of Bustarviejo (Madrid). *Left*: plan of the main building. *Right*: general map with the location of the railway built by the inmates, the quarries, and the areas where the prisoners' relatives lived. Drawn by the author

of the agency of the subaltern. This ascribing of agency purportedly aims to give them voice, but may actually betray the iniquities of their situation. By granting too much capacity for resistance to the oppressed, either practical or moral, we run the risk of downplaying their suffering and exonerating the brutality of the repressive instances.

The particular context of totalitarianism is an interesting one to put resistance in its right place. I will try to show here that many practices that could be deemed elements of resistance may in fact turn out to be strategies at the service of power. My examples come from two places: the forced labor camp of Bustarviejo (Falquina et al. 2008) and the concentration camp of Camposancos (Pontevedra) (Ballesta and Rodríguez Gallardo 2008).

The concentration camp of Camposancos was in use between the fall of the northern front in October 1937 and the end of the war in 1939. The camp reused an old school of the Jesuit Order that had been abandoned in 1932 after the expulsion of the Jesuits from Spain. Many inmates were killed by firing squad in 1938 and others were transferred to other prisons and camps. The old building has miraculously preserved an outstanding collection of graffiti from the time it was a concentration camp, most of it created by the prisoners. The situation, although exceptional, is not unique. Graffiti have also survived in the nearby concentration camp of Oia, also located in a religious building (a Cistercian monastery), and in the fortress of San Cristóbal (Navarre region).

Those from Camposancos are the only ones thus far published (Ballesta and Rodríguez Gallardo 2008). Both words and images have been documented. Among the images, there are several war scenes, notably aerial bombings: the reflection of a trauma caused by industrial war. Ballesta and Rodríguez Gallardo interpret the words on the walls as an impulse of the self that forces the prisoner to leave a trace of his presence. This was felt as an especially pressing need in Camposancos given the high rates of execution and death by disease that marked the carceral experience: "To leave the name as a trace was regarded by the inmates as a denunciation of a confinement dominated by infrahuman conditions" (Ballesta and Rodríguez Gallardo 2008:205). Writing the name was also a way of reasserting the self in the circumstances of dehumanization and de-individualization.

Yet the walls were not a simple space of resistance: they were rather an ambiguous arena where the dominators and the dominated struggled to achieve control: the existence of graffiti made by prison guards interspersed between the prisoners' proves that the inmates' writing was being monitored, even if in an informal way. But most importantly, the very fact that the graffiti were allowed in such a regimented institution, as Ballesta and Rodríguez Gallardo point out, cast doubt on their being mere "weapons of the weak." They further suggest that the graffiti were actually useful for controlling purposes: "What better surveillance than supervising the personal writing produced by the inmates, for the most part small biographical fragments observed with interest by the guards" (Ballesta and Rodríguez Gallardo 2008:210). Graffiti, then, allowed the prisoners to leave a physical trace of their predicament, before being wiped out of history—but at the same time rendered them more transparent and legible before power.

Bustarviejo camp offers another case of ambiguous domination and resistance. One of the important finds of the project was the identification of the huts where the relatives of the inmates lived. In all, over 40 structures surrounding the prisoners' block were located (Falquina et al. 2008). The existence of women and children living around some penal detachments was already known from oral testimonies. These testimonies were mostly gathered among the inmates working in the fascist monument of the Valley of the Fallen in Madrid, and their relatives (Lafuente 2003:126–128). However, the nature and size of those shantytowns remained unknown. Archaeology has proven to be crucial in bringing to light an important historical phenomenon: The presence of relatives can be explained for their dependence on the minuscule salary that the forced workers received. This was the only income for many Republican families in the postwar period. Therefore, their fate was inextricably bound to that of the imprisoned paterfamilias. Looking at the tiny shacks where the relatives resided (Fig. 4.8), one can obtain a fair idea of the living conditions of thousands of Spaniards after the war. The case of Bustarviejo illustrates the hardships endured by the inmates' families especially well: located in the Madrid sierra, the area of the camp was covered with snow part of the year and the huts were built over the debris of the quarries on a steep slope, crisscrossed by river torrents.

We can interpret the presence of the families as an element of resistance, a means of alleviating the process of brutalization and dehumanization of the inmates. The possibility of visiting their wives and children might have had very important psychological benefits for the prisoners. Nevertheless, as with the graffiti, the situation

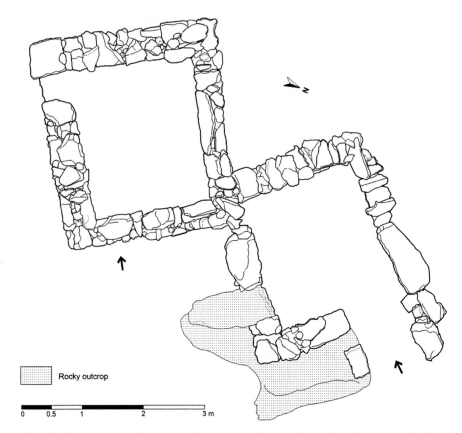

Fig. 4.8 Two family huts built around the prisoners' block in Bustarviejo. The standardized size (2 meters × 2 meters) of most structures leads us to think that their construction was regulated by the camp authorities. Drawn by the author

is ambiguous and complex. One of the things that grabbed our attention when we started our research was the scarce elements of surveillance and control in the camp. There are four sentry boxes in all which, instead of facing into the camp, are looking outward. This has an explanation: the detachment was in use between 1944 and 1952, coinciding with the heyday and decline of the *maquis*, the anti-Francoist guerrilla, which was very active in the Madrid sierras. Surveillance was directed toward the potential dangers coming from the outside, rather than the inside. Unlike in the concentration camps of Castuera, Miranda, and Albatera, there were no fences of barbed wire or ditches to prevent the 300 inmates of Bustarviejo from escaping. The same has been observed in other forced labor camps in the vicinity, such as Garganta de Montes and elsewhere in the Valley of the Fallen (Lafuente 2003:126).

How then was surveillance effected? It was performed in the most insidious and totalitarian way: it was the relatives that unwittingly surveilled the inmates. If a prisoner escaped, what would be the fate of his family? If he was caught and condemned to a long prison term, how would his family survive? It was much better to pay one's dues for a few years and start a new life reconciled with the new state. This was totalitarianism at its most efficient, since control did not lie in a specialized group alone (soldiers, guards, policemen, or spies), but in society as a whole. The surveillance of Bustarviejo was subtle: it is not that the relatives blatantly informed against the inmate, but that their very presence discouraged all attempt of resistance to the system. It is probably not by chance that the family huts are all located in elevated positions, visible from anywhere in the camp. It is not by chance either that during the great escape of the Fuerte de San Cristóbal (Navarre) in May 1938, hundreds of prisoners returned voluntarily to their cells or remained in them (Carratalá 2007:188), despite the terrible conditions of imprisonment in the fort. The doors were opened and the soldiers were overpowered—yet only 30% of the almost 2,500 inmates truly tried to run away.

Conclusion

In this chapter I have described the evolution and typology of internment camps in Spain during the 1930s and 1940s from both a material and an institutional point of view. I have tried to show the magnitude of the Spanish *univers concentrationnaire*, which is less well known than that of contemporaneous dictatorships. Concentration and forced labor camps were more brutal than their counterparts in other countries, such as fascist Italy or Salazarist Portugal. Although they certainly did not attain the extreme degree of violence of the Nazi *lager* and the Soviet *gulag* in their aspirations at wholly transforming the country, they were probably closer to ideal totalitarian models. One of the main characteristics of General Franco's camps was the mixture of highly modern elements and preindustrial ones. Modern traits include classification, which amounted to an act of social engineering at a mass scale; the gridded layouts of some camps; the dehumanization of the enemy; the relevance of bureaucracy and the mechanisms for annihilating the prisoners' identity. Archaic traits include the reuse of older buildings, the presence of religious elements, and the concepts of sin and atonement that guided the technology of punishment. This contradictory reality did not preclude early Francoism from being a fascist regime: the same contradictions and mixtures can be found in Italian fascism. They are, in fact, at the political heart of both regimes. They can be seen in their political postulates and practices, in their social and moral ideals, and in their material culture.

The archaeology of modern internment camps is useful for exploring the relationships between modernity, tradition, and totalitarianism. Yet one of the main contributions of this kind of archaeology might lie in interrogating domination and resistance through material culture. I have tried to show that the prevalent concepts of resistance are far too optimistic, and that power, especially with the advent of modernity, is much more insidious than many social scientists readily admit. I propose to look for the subtle and ambiguous mechanisms of control and resistance that allow us to more fully understand modern disciplinary institutions and technologies of punishment.

Acknowledgments Many of the ideas of this chapter have arisen from discussions with members of the Bustarviejo Project: Alicia Quintero Maqua, Carlos Marín, Álvaro Falquina, Jorge Rolland, and Pedro Fermín Maguire. I am grateful to Kiko Esperilla for kindly providing a photograph of the concentration camp of Castuera. Thanks are also due to the editors of the volume for the invitation to participate in this book and for organizing a thought-provoking session at the Sixth World Archaeological Congress.

References

Acuña, X. 2007 *Memorial da Liberdade. Represión e Resistencia en Galiza 1936–1977*. Xunta de Galicia, Santiago de Compostela.

Ballesta, J. and A. Rodríguez Gallardo 2008 Camposancos: Una "Imprenta" de los Presos del Franquismo. *Complutum* 19(2): 197–211.

Bauman, Z. 1989 *Modernity and the Holocaust*. Polity Press, Cambridge.

Beevor, A. 2001 *The Spanish Civil War*. Penguin, London.

Ben-Ghiat, R. 2003 *Fascist Modernities: Italy, 1922–1945*. University of California Press, Berkeley.

Capogreco, C. 1987 *Ferramonti: La Vita e gli Uomini del Più Grande Campo d'Internamento Fascista, 1940–1945*. Giuntina, Florence.

Carratalá, E. 2007 *Memorias de un Piojo Republicano (Cautivo en los Penales Franquistas de Burgos, Fuerte de San Cristóbal, Isla de San Simón, Astorga y Cárcel Modelo de Barcelona)*. Pamiela, Pamplona.

Casanova, J. 2004 Una Dictadura De Cuarenta Años. In *Matar, Morir, Sobrevivir. La Violencia en la Dictadura de Franco*, edited by J. Espinosa, pp. 3–50. Crítica, Barcelona.

Costa, X. and X. Santos 2007 *Galiza Na Guerra Civil. Campos de Concentración de Muros, Padrón, A Pobra e Rianxo*. Concellos de Rianxo e A Pobra do Caramiñal, Rianxo/A Pobra do Caramiñal.

Everdell, W. 1997 *The First Moderns: Profiles in the Origins of Twentieth-Century Thought*. University of Chicago Press, Chicago.

Falquina, A., P. Fermín, A. González-Ruibal, C. Martín, A. Quintero, and J. Rolland 2008 Arqueología de los destacamentos penales franquistas en el ferrocarril Madrid-Burgos. El caso de Bustarviejo. *Complutum* 19(2): 175–195.

Fermín Maguire, P. and X. Ayán 2008 The Archaeology of Concentration Camps in Galicia (Spain). Paper Presented at the 6th Conference of the World Archaeological Congress, Dublin, Ireland. 29 June–4 July, 2009.

Foucault, M. 1975 *Surveiller et Punir*. Gallimard, Paris.

Ferguson, N. 2007 *War of the World: History's Age of Hatred*. Penguin, London.

Galluccio, F. 2002 *I Lager In Italia: La Memoria Sepolta nei Duecento Luoghi di Deportazione Fascisti*. Libere Edizioni, Civezzano.

Gómez Bravo, G. 2007 *La Redención de Penas. La Formación del Sistema Penitenciario Franquista (1936–1950)*. Catarata, Madrid.

González-Ruibal, A. 2007 Making Things Public: Archaeologies of the Spanish Civil War. *Public Archaeology* 6(4): 259–282.

Gutiérrez Casalá, J. 2003 *Colonias Penitenciarias Militarizadas de Montijo*. Editora Regional De Extremadura, Mérida.

Guzmán, E. 2001 *El Año de La Victoria*. Vosa, Madrid.

Izquierdo Canosa, R. 1998 *La Reconcentración 1896–1897*. Verde Olivo, La Habana.

Johnston, N. 1961 Recent Trends in Correctional Architecture. *The British Journal of Criminology* 1(4): 317–338.

Junquera, N. 2007 La Fuga De Los 221 Muertos. *El País*, October 21 2007. http://www.elpais.com/articulo/reportajes/fuga/221/muertos/elpepusocdmg/20071021elpdmgrep_3/Tes

Lafuente, I. 2003 *Esclavos por la Patria. La Explotación de los Presos bajo el Franquismo*. Booket, Madrid.

Lindqvist, S. 1996 *Exterminate All the Brutes. One Man's Odyssey into the Heart of Darkness and the Origins of European Genocide*. Free Press, New York.

Linz, J. 2000 *Totalitarian and Authoritarian Regimes*. Lynne Riener, Boulder.

López Rodríguez, A. 2006 *Cruz, Bandera y Caudillo: El Campo de Concentración de Castuera*. Ceder La Serena, Badajoz.

López Rodríguez, A. and G. León Cáceres 2008 La Recuperación de la Memoria de la Guerra Civil y de la Represión de la Dictadura Franquista en Extremadura: La Experiencia de la Asociación Memorial Campo De Concentración de Castuera. *Entelequia* 7: 173–186.

Molinero, C., M. Sala, and J. Sobrequés (eds.) 2003 *Una Inmensa Prisión: Los Campos de concentración y las Prisiones durante la Guerra Civil y el Franquismo*. Crítica, Barcelona.

Núñez Díaz-Balart, M. 2005 El Dolor como Terapia: La Médula común de los Campos de Concentración Nazis y Franquistas. *Ayer* 57(1): 81–102.

Olaizola Elordi, J. 2006 Trabajo Forzado y Ferrocarril. Destacamentos Penales y Construcción de Infraestructuras Ferroviarias. Paper presented at the IV Congreso de Historia Ferroviaria. Málaga, 20–22 September, 2006.

Pallarés, C. and J. Espinosa de los Monteros 2005 Miranda, Mosaico de Nacionalidades: Franceses, Británicos y Alemanes. *Ayer* 57(1): 153–187.

Payne, S. 1996 *A History of Fascism 1914–1945*. Routledge, London.

Preston, P. 2007 *The Spanish Civil War. Reaction, Revolution, and Revenge*. Norton, New York.

Ríos Frutos L., B. Martínez Silva, A. García-Rubio, and J. Jiménez 2008 Muertes en Cautiverio en el Primer Franquismo: Exhumación del Cementerio del Penal de Valdenoceda (1938–1943). *Complutum* 19(2): 139–160.

Rodrigo, J. 2005 *Cautivos: Campos de Concentración en la España Franquista (1936–1947)*. Crítica, Barcelona.

Rodrigo, J. 2008 *Hasta la Raíz: Violencia durante la Guerra Civil y la Dictadura Franquista*. Alianza, Madrid.

Scott, J. 1999 *Seeing Like a State: How Certain Schemes to Improve the Human Condition Have Failed*. Yale University Press, Yale.

Sevillano, F. 2007 *Rojos. La Representación del Enemigo en la Guerra Civil*. Alianza, Madrid.

Thomàs, J. 2001 *La Falange de Franco: Fascismo y Fascistización en el Régimen Franquista (1937–1945)*. Plaza y Janés, Barcelona.

Trevor-Roper, H. 1981 The Phenomenon of Fascism. In *Fascism in Europe*, edited by S. Woolf, pp. 19–38. Taylor & Francis, London.

Villarroya, J. and J. Solé I Sabaté 1996 Las Checas. In *La Guerra Civil Española, Volume 9 (La Batalla De Madrid)*, edited by M. Tuñón De Lara, pp. 101–106. Folio, Madrid.

Zimmerer, J. 2004 Colonialism and the Holocaust. Towards an Archaeology of Genocide. In *Genocide and Settler Society: Frontier Violence and Stolen Indigenous Children in Australian History*, edited by A. Moses, pp. 49–76. Berghahn, New York.

Zimmerer, J. 2005 The Birth of the Ostland Out of the Spirit of Colonialism: A Postcolonial Perspective on the Nazi Policy of Conquest and Extermination. *Patterns of Prejudice* 39(2): 197–219.

Chapter 5
The Things of Auschwitz

Adrian Myers

Abstract Like any other factory, the death factory of Auschwitz consumed primary materials and produced secondary products. Unique to Auschwitz, though, is that the primary material was human life; and not just the life of the breathing human body, but also the material possessions associated with that life. The detritus of this most efficient genocide—including clothing, jewelry, food, and corpses—was appropriated and put to new uses by the *Schutzstaffel* (SS) and the prisoners. Others have recognized the various postwar material cultural outcomes of the camp: the writing, the film, the theater, the art, the tourism. This chapter, however, demonstrates that the material culture of Auschwitz is not a phenomenon exclusive to the postwar era. Inside the camp during the war, despite the landscape of death and deprivation, intimate interaction between humans and material culture continued; and, as we move into a new era of study, understanding that interaction will play an important role in our continued probing of wartime Auschwitz.

Introduction

About 50 kilometers west of Kraków in southern Poland lies the town of Oświęcim. Though it has a tumultuous history going back as far as the thirteenth century, awareness of the town by the outside world is due to a series of events set in motion only in the first half of the twentieth century. The town itself draws little attention from the thousands of tour buses that pass through each year. The object of attention, the central object of attention of the entire region, is of course *Konzentrationslager Auschwitz* (Auschwitz concentration camp).

The remains of Auschwitz are well known even to many who have never set foot in it (Figs. 5.1 and 5.2). The mocking *Arbeit Macht Frei* (Work Brings Freedom)

A. Myers (✉)
Stanford Archaeology Center, Stanford University, Stanford, CA, USA
e-mail: adrianmyers@stanford.edu

A. Myers, G. Moshenska (eds.), *Archaeologies of Internment*, One World Archaeology,   75
DOI 10.1007/978-1-4419-9666-4_5, © Springer Science+Business Media, LLC 2011

Fig. 5.1 Auschwitz I in 2004. Photograph by Adrian Myers

wrought iron gate, the dead-end train tracks, the piles of shoes, the barbed wire fences, and the plain wooden block houses of Auschwitz II-Birkenau (Fig. 5.3) are among the most recognizable images in photographic history. The creation of concentration camp Auschwitz altered forever the status of the previously inconspicuous name of Oświęcim. That some 800 years of ordinary history have been overshadowed by the short period of the Nazis' appropriation of the town testifies to the powerful and far-reaching repercussions of that time and place (Van Pelt and Dwork 1996).

Significant historical events impact the material culture of their own era as well as that of later eras. The relatively short period of life and death in concentration camp Auschwitz is no exception. A scholarly book on the long-term history of the town and the camp and the existence of sustained academic discussion are evidence of the continuing influence of wartime Auschwitz. While perhaps not using the distinctively archaeological trope of material culture, many others, from diverse fields, have dealt with just that in their writings on Auschwitz. Scholars, journalists, and others have produced an imposing corpus of work, examining various material outcomes of the camp: film, television, radio, museums and memorials, painting and sculpture, and tourism. Each focus of interest contributes not only to the discussion

Fig. 5.2 Auschwitz I in 2004. Photograph by Adrian Myers

of the materiality of the camp, but itself adds to that materiality as well, the tangible legacy of Auschwitz.

Dealing with the relationship between Auschwitz and its material culture is challenging. Historians, artists, cultural critics, and others continuously grapple with, and in so doing perpetuate, the material cultural legacy of the camp; but no one has so far focused specifically on the role of material goods inside the camp during the years it was actually in use. Inside concentration camp Auschwitz during the war, despite the landscape of death and deprivation, a complex interaction between people and material culture persisted.

Ordinary Men

The utter incomprehensibility of Auschwitz has led some to believe it to be a historic anomaly, a terrible aberration from the upward progress of modern society (Bauman 1989:6–12). Typically we imagine the perpetrators of Auschwitz to be very different from ourselves: Surely Auschwitz was only possible because of a deviant, evil group of people. Sound scholarship has established, however, not only the fact that

Fig. 5.3 Wooden block house at Auschwitz II-Birkenau in 2004. Photograph by Adrian Myers

"ordinary men" can exhibit genocidal behavior (Browning 1998), but also that, far from being an aberration from the progress of modernity, the Holocaust might even be an entirely logical facet of modernity. In the words of Bauman:

> We suspect (even if we refuse to admit it) that the Holocaust could merely have uncovered another face of the same modern society whose other, more familiar face, we so admire. And that the two faces are perfectly comfortably attached to the same body. What we perhaps fear most, is that each of the two faces can no more exist without the other than can the two sides of a coin. (1989:7)

If we are to continue our attempts to understand Auschwitz, then there must be a fundamental recognition that the past actors of the camp—be they guards, prisoners, civilians, or others—are not intrinsically different from ourselves. As Agamben suggests, "many testimonies—both of executioners and victims—come from ordinary people, the 'obscure' people who clearly comprised the great majority of camp inhabitants" (Agamben 2002:13). The stories of Auschwitz are stories of people like us, in nearly unimaginable circumstances. Accepting this fact is the first step toward the archaeologist's goal of understanding the past from the perspective of those who lived it.

Deprivation and Abundance

Schiffer states that "human life consists of ceaseless and varied interactions among people and myriad kinds of things," and that "never during a person's lifetime are they not being intimate with artifacts" (Schiffer 1999:2–3, italics removed). While

Fig. 5.4 Remains of *Kanada* sorting warehouses at Auschwitz II-Birkenau in 2004. Photograph by Adrian Myers

perhaps counterintuitive, these statements remain truthful even for those incarcerated inside wartime concentration camp Auschwitz. For most inmates, material possessions were certainly severely limited; however, even the least fortunate of the camp possessed and interacted with objects daily. Others, those highest in the socioeconomic hierarchy that dominated prisoners' lives, had more possessions, including luxury goods, in the camp than in their previous lives (Sofsky 1999; Myers 2008).

Including the words "Auschwitz" and "superabundance" in the same sentence seems incongruous until one considers the surreal story of Auschwitz's *Kanada* warehouses, the area of the camp used to sort the belongings of those recently murdered (Fig. 5.4). Like any other factory, the death factory of Auschwitz consumed primary materials and produced secondary products. Unique to Auschwitz, though, is that the primary material consumed was human life: the breathing, human body, and associated material possessions. The particularities of Auschwitz bred a system of inequality, an odd dichotomy of simultaneous scarcity and plenty. While most prisoners had only a few meager possessions, some lived in relative luxury. While most block houses were barren except for bunks and a small wood stove, others were, quite literally, filled to the ceilings with material goods.

The Primacy of Spoons

The average prisoner in Auschwitz did not own much; however, each prisoner did possess a few items crucial to survival. So critical was this small kit that those who did not acquire the elements soon after arrival, and those who lost them or had them stolen, usually perished. Shortly after entering the camp, each prisoner was stripped naked and shaved. As survivor Victor Frankl states, at this point "all we possessed, literally, was our naked existence" (Frankl 1969:13). Owning nothing, no corporeal thing other than their bodies, the new prisoners would now begin a process of acquisition. The SS issued each prisoner a filthy, tattered, zebra-striped costume, a "uniform of rags" (Frankl 1969:19). The prisoners' new clothing, though pathetic and demeaning, nevertheless offered a basic level of protection from something much more dangerous, the "extremity" of nakedness (Des Pres 1976:7). As survivor Primo Levi suggests, "Clothes, even the foul clothes distributed, even the crude clogs with their wooden soles, are a tenuous but indispensable defense" (Levi 1988:113). The prisoners were thrown into a hell on earth, but they had at least received a chance at life and, in the coming hours and days were forced to learn quickly what other acquisitions were necessary.

The high status of the prisoner's bowl and spoon demonstrates the primacy of material objects in the camps. Without a bowl, a prisoner had no way to receive his daily ration. Although sometimes the inmates used their caps instead of bowls, this system had obvious problems when it came to the distribution of soup, the standard daily fare. A bowl was a precious thing. A spoon was also a critical piece of hardware, for "Without a spoon, the daily soup could not be consumed in any other way than by lapping it up, as dogs do." It was only "after many days of apprenticeship [that] one discovered that there were spoons in the camp but that one had to buy them on the black market with soup or bread" (Levi 1988:112, 114). When one inmate's father realized he was being sent to the gas chamber, he gave his son his "inheritance": a knife and a spoon (Wiesel 1982:71). It is one more absurdity of the concentration camps that when Auschwitz was liberated, tens of thousands of spoons were found in storage.

Informal Economy

The bowl and the spoon were critical first acquisitions, but all prisoners were wise to make further use of exchange on the camp black market. Ubiquitous in the camps, the black market provided other aids in the struggle for survival. Shoes were of much consequence in the camp, for "Death begins with the shoes; for most of us, they show themselves to be instruments of torture, which after a few hours of marching cause painful sores which become infected." The prisoner with a bad pair of shoes "arrives last everywhere, and everywhere he receives blows" (Levi 1986:21–22). Infected feet, and the beating that came to whoever was the slowest marcher, was certainly enough to kill.

An indecipherable web of conflicting regulations dominated the prisoners' daily lives. For instance, the rules generally forbade a prisoner any food aside from his official daily ration, but the caloric value of that ration was so low that he would starve on it alone. Prisoners had to have greased boots, but grease was rarely distributed. A prisoner was forced to work on his knees all day, yet if he had a hole in his trousers at an inspection he might be shot. Trousers one size too large could be a death sentence: if he had oversize trousers the prisoner had to use his hands to hold them up; but how could he work with a single hand? The problems were many and complicated, and highlight the dire need for material items. Each of the above scenarios could be solved by the black market.

De Cunzo reminds us that "Material culture is used to accomplish and thwart institutional goals" (De Cunzo 2006:167). In the inmate's struggle against the SS captors, everything had value. A scrap of paper, cloth, metal, wire, or string was, if not of immediate use to the owner, useful to another and hence held trade value. Levi states:

> We have learnt that everything is useful: the wire to tie up our shoes, the rags to wrap around our feet, waste paper to (illegally) pad out our jacket against the cold ... I have already learnt not to let myself be robbed, and in fact if I find a spoon lying around, a piece of string, a button which I can acquire without danger of punishment, I pocket them and consider them mine by full right (Levi 1986:21–23).

The prisoners became "expert scavengers, forever on the lookout for anything at all" to use for themselves or "with which to transact 'business'" (Des Pres 1976:114). An anecdote from Buchenwald camp demonstrates how the resourcefulness of the prisoners sometimes allowed them privileges denied even to free Germans. Some of the Reich's millions of banned books found their way into the camp as toilet paper. Survivor Eugen Kogon details how the prisoners retrieved what was of value: "It was even possible to conduct salvage right there in the privies, though the collector had to provide an immediate substitute, to quell any incipient revolt from his fellows. This was not easy, for paper was extremely scarce." Once the precious books were saved from their unmentionable fate, "What an experience it was to sit quietly ... delving into the pages of Plato's dialogues, Galsworthy's *Swan Song*, or the works of Heine, Klabund, Mehring!" (Kogon 1998:140).

An intimate relationship existed between the prisoners and their possessions. Every inmate motivated to survive scavenged, traded, and stole; but the most industrious put any special skills to use and produced saleable goods. Many in the camp "were made to exercise their own trade," such as "tailors, cobblers, carpenters, blacksmiths, bricklayers" (Levi 1988:122). Whenever and wherever possible, these Auschwitz artisans used scavenged and stolen materials to fashion useful tools and other goods both to use for themselves and to sell on the camp black market. There are parallels here with other historical moments: De Cunzo writes of American Civil War prisoners who "crafted commodities and gifts" (De Cunzo 2006:175), and Saunders discusses First World War civilian internees and the "objects they made" (Saunders 2004:14; see also Chapter 3 by Mytum, this volume).

The Ramp

The common experience of life in Auschwitz was one of hunger, filth, and extreme material scarcity. The vast majority of prisoners, aided by their few but crucial personal possessions, expended every modicum of energy in the search for food. These inmates relied on both the severely inadequate official ration and any other food-stuffs they could get their hands on. While most areas of the camp were places of scarcity, it is not accurate to describe the camp on the whole as a place of scarcity. For certain prisoners the camp experience was not one of scarcity of material goods at all, but rather one of superabundance. These were the prisoners who worked with the daily arrival of new people and their possessions. One such worker stated, "I found that the longer I survived, the nearer I drew to the hard core who had learned not only to live, but to prosper" (Vrba 1997:133). While only a select few prison-ers dealt firsthand with the mountains of goods repossessed from incoming victims, through an efficient and complex network of graft and trading, the commodities quickly spread through the whole camp.

At one time the rails at the most infamous train station in the world came to a stop in front of an expansive wooden disembarkation platform, just inside the barbed wire of the Auschwitz sub-camp, Birkenau (Figs. 5.3, 5.4, 5.5 and 5.6). Known as the *Judenrampe* or simply *the ramp*, here incoming prisoners and future victims left the trains and entered the camp. The arriving cattle cars were over-flowing with people inhumanly crammed, both living and dead, and all of their transportable worldly possessions: "Everything that had been their past and was to start their future" (Borowski 1976:37). They had stuffed their suitcases, filled their pockets, and stitched into their clothes material goods, including emotionally impor-tant mementoes and items thought to be useful in their unknown future. In the words of Levi, "The climax came suddenly. The door opened with a crash, and the dark echoed with outlandish orders in that curt, barbaric barking of Germans in command

Fig. 5.5 Auschwitz II-Birkenau in 2004. Photograph by Adrian Myers

Fig. 5.6 Auschwitz
II-Birkenau in 2004.
Photograph by Adrian Myers

which seems to give vent to a millennial anger. A vast platform appeared before us,
lit up by reflectors" (Levi 1986:9).

At the ramp, a special group of experienced prisoners was assigned to empty
out the wagons and separate the women from the children, the fit from the weak,
and each of these from their packages, bags, and suitcases. Once the human cargo
was out of the way, the ramp workers began the work of clearing the cars of the
detritus inside. They climbed in the wagons and emptied out the luggage. The cars,
ramp, and ground were in complete disarray, swelling with piles of goods of every
kind:

> The heaps grow. Suitcases, bundles, blankets, coats, handbags that open as they fall, spilling
> coins, gold, watches; mountains of bread pile up at the exits, heaps of marmalade, jams,
> masses of meat, sausages; sugar spills on the gravel ... suits, shirts, books drop out on
> the ground ... I pick up a small, heavy package. I unwrap it—gold, about two handfuls,
> bracelets, rings, brooches, diamonds ... 'Gib Hier,' an SS man says calmly, holding up his
> briefcase already full of gold and colorful foreign currency. (Borowski 1976:38–42)

The ramp *kommando* worked swiftly to unload the belongings left in the train, but
worked just as hard watching for opportunities to eat and smuggle. The SS allowed

them to eat as much as they wanted; however, they were forbidden to keep anything of value to the Reich. One SS man warned, "Whoever takes gold, or anything else besides food, will be shot for stealing Reich property . . . Verstanden?" (Borowski 1976:36–37).

Despite the harshest penalties, the workers concealed food and articles of every kind in their clothing: The men "weighed down under a load of bread, marmalade and sugar, and smelling of perfume and fresh linen, line up to go" (Borowski 1976:49). The men of the ramp became expert smugglers and traders, and they lived in relative luxury. A new arrival described their healthy demeanor: "The sight of the red cheeks and round faces of those prisoners was a great encouragement. Little did we know then that they formed a specially chosen elite, who for years had been the receiving squad for new transports as they rolled into the station day after day" (Frankl 1969:8). Smuggling from the ramp had immediate effects on the whole camp, for the ramp men stole more than they could eat themselves. For several days the entire camp will live off this transport, and will talk of "Sosnowiec-Bêdzin. . . a good, rich, transport" (Borowski 1976:49).

The Kanadakommando

Assignment to the ramps meant a sure supply of food and trade goods; but the apex of superabundance in the camp was certainly among the *Kanadakommando*. The group worked in a special area of Birkenau, a fenced-off row of blocks next to the crematoria. "Thirty barracks, filled to the rafters with possessions taken from the victims who had been gassed" (Sofsky 1999:51). Anyone who worked there could steal food and trade goods that gave them a significant advantage in the struggle for life. Officially called the *Effektenkammer*, the prisoners renamed the area *Kanada*, as it "represented life, luxury, and salvation; it was a Garden of Eden in Hell" (Abella and Troper 2000:xxi). Survivor Rudolph Vrba states that it was "where hundreds of prisoners worked frantically to sort, segregate and classify the clothes and the food and the valuables of those whose bodies were still burning, whose ashes would soon be used as fertilizer" (Vrba 1997:127).

The workers' task was to organize the possessions of those recently murdered in the gas chambers, separating valuables such as gold and jewels from everyday items such as clothes and cooking utensils. The former went to the *Reichsbank* in Berlin and the latter were sold or given to war-ravaged German civilians in need. Before loading the shipments, however, the prisoners and the SS alike stole prodigious amounts of food, valuables, and everyday items for personal use and trade. The phenomenon reminds us "that goods have both a use and an exchange value that extends well beyond the first cycle" (Gregson and Crewe 2003:2). "An immense amount of property was stolen by members of the SS and by the police, and also by prisoners, civilian employees and railway personnel" (Höss 1959:194). The endless stream of arriving suitcases was a constant reminder of what was occurring very nearby.

The Sonderkommando

The modern industrial methods employed to process the belongings of those gassed mimicked the industrial methods employed in the processing of the human bodies themselves. The assembly line of *Kanada* sorters worked in tandem with a second group of prisoner workers just meters away in the crematorium complex, who labored daily facilitating the most efficient genocidal process in history. It was here that the persistent stench of burning corpses that hung over the camp and its environs originated (Classen et al. 1994:172–175). These crematorium workers dealt directly with intimate "material cultures of death" (Hallam and Hockey 2001:9), what was left after the disembarkation process: clothing, jewelry, and other small possessions, and the body itself. Extermination camp Auschwitz was the product of a technologically advanced, fundamentally modern society. For the first time in history, the killing of humans occurred on such a scale that bureaucrats and engineers had to be employed just to deal with the corpses.

Sonderkommando, or Special Command, is the euphemism the SS used to denote the squad of mostly Jewish concentration camp prisoners whose job it was to operate the crematoria, most famously at Auschwitz II-Birkenau, but also at the other extermination camps (Greif 2005; Levi 1988:50). These men were assigned the task of ushering the victims underground, convincing and forcing them to disrobe and enter the gas chambers, and, finally, clearing and disposing of the bodies. After searching the corpses for hidden valuables, the workers burned them in the crematoria and buried the ashes. The SS had a second name for these men—they were designated *Geheimnisträger*, the bearers of secrets.

Since these workers were privy to the details of National Socialism's biggest secret, an assignment on the squad was tantamount to a death sentence. At Auschwitz, about a dozen squads followed one after the other, each operating only for a few months. "As its initiation, the next squad burnt the corpses of its predecessors" (Levi 1988:50). The early Sonderkommando was not one cohesive group of prisoners; instead, there were numerous *kommandos*, all with different names and functions. There were the corpse-haulers, the stokers, the pit-diggers, and others. The process slowly became more and more efficient, culminating in the expert system in place during the busiest periods of mass killing. At its most efficient stage, the death process was similar to the process of a factory assembly line, with its success dependent on a highly organized division of labor. At periods of peak processing, the Sonderkommando worked in shifts and the crematoria fires burned 24 hours a day.

The Sonderkommando labored at the crematoria, and, like the SS before them, those working the crematoria used deception to ensure the unhampered flow of humans. Rudolf Höss, the unapologetic *kommandant* of Auschwitz, tells us, "It was most important that the whole business of arriving and undressing should take place in an atmosphere of the greatest possible calm" (Höss 1959:148). Standing in the anteroom to the gas chamber, the Sonderkommando men avoided eye contact but in reassuring tones repeated, "*Bitte, ziehen Sie sich doch aus*! [Please be so kind as to undress!]" (Greif 2005:12). To avoid chaotic scenes, and to avoid the wrath of the SS, the weary and stuporous workers did not warn the victims of their impending doom. Borowski emphatically states that, "It is the camp law: people going to their death must be deceived to the very end. This is the only permissible form of charity" (Borowski 1976:37). The Sonderkommando prisoners had entered Levi's "Grey Zone": that shadowy place "where the oppressed becomes oppressor and the executioner in turn appears as victim" (Levi 1986, 1988; Agamben 2002:21).

The highly organized industrial labor of the Sonderkommando consumed the material of human life and through its consumption produced other materials and products. The clothes and other possessions, once stripped from the corpses, were sent to *Kanada* for recycling and reuse. The corpses themselves were searched for hidden valuables. Benjamin Jacobs, a dentist at Auschwitz, remembers entering the killing center to pull gold teeth from the dead (Jacobs 1995:147). The SS shaved the hair from the bodies and added this to their stock of war materials, hair being useful to make coarse fabrics, insulation and mattress stuffing (Agamben 2002:25). As Schofield et al. remind us, the corpses of war, even those stripped and ravaged by genocide—in this case even reduced to dust—are themselves a form of "matériel culture" (Schofield et al. 2002:1).

Conclusion

The concentration camps of the Third Reich have engendered some of the most difficult debates in the study of history and human nature. Sixty-five years after the end of the Nazi era, Auschwitz continues to be widely studied across the academic disciplines. This ongoing creation of new material culture of the camp inevitably influences consecutive generations of academics and laypeople. Auschwitz is "caught in the double hermeneutic whereby we cannot study without changing the object of our study" (Buchli and Lucas 2001:9). While this proliferation of postwar writing, film, theater, and art plays an important role in the ongoing discussion of Auschwitz, materiality in the daily life of the camp during the war should be of interest as well. Despite the most extreme conditions, interaction between humans and material goods continued, and indeed thrived, in Auschwitz during those years. In certain situations, material goods were even found in abundance unknown to most in their prewar lives.

Fletcher states that "material possesses inertia, allowing it to continue its impact long after the actions have passed into memory or been forgotten" (Fletcher 2002:304). Consider the humble yet emotive everyday objects that have been excavated at concentration camps (Gilead et al. 2009). At the site of Auschwitz today, in a brick barrack one can see piles of shoes and bundles of human hair behind glass, and the steps of the ruined crematoria at Birkenau have become "foci of gift giving": Here we find carefully placed candles, pebbles, and other small offerings of remembrance (Hallam and Hockey 2001:149).

With the end of the age of living survivors of the Auschwitz of 1939–1945, the end of oral history and of firsthand experience, we are entering a new era of research, one led by the particular inquisitive strengths and attitudes of archaeology. We are on the "the cusp upon which history becomes archaeology" (Saunders 2004:5). The theory and methods of historical archaeology, a discipline devoted to the interaction of texts and objects—two manifestations of material culture—offer one way forward in the pursuit of better understanding of concentration camp Auschwitz.

Acknowledgments   This chapter is a revised version of an article that originally appeared in *Papers from the Institute of Archaeology* (Myers 2007). Thanks are due to the editors of that journal. For commenting on drafts, many thanks are due to Gabriel Moshenska, Christopher Friedrichs, David Robinson, Paul Myers, Kathy LaVergne, and two anonymous referees. Responsibility for the interpretation presented is the author's alone.

References

Abella, I. and H. Troper 2000 *None Is Too Many: Canada and the Jews of Europe 1933–1948*. Key Porter, Toronto.

Agamben, G. 2002 *Remnants of Auschwitz: The Witness and the Archive*. Zone Books, New York.

Bauman, Z. 1989 *Modernity and the Holocaust*. Blackwell, Oxford.

Borowski, T. 1976 *This Way for the Gas, Ladies and Gentlemen*. Penguin, New York.

Browning, C. 1998 *Ordinary Men: Reserve Police Battalion 101 and the Final Solution in Poland*. Harper Perennial, New York.

Buchli, V. and G. Lucas (eds.) 2001 *Archaeologies of the Contemporary Past*. Routledge, London.

Classen, C., D. Howes, and A. Synott 1994 *Aroma: The Cultural History of Smell*. Routledge, New York.

De Cunzo, L. 2006 Exploring the Institution: Reform, Confinement, Social Change. In *Historical Archaeology*, edited by M. Hall and S. Silliman, pp. 167–189. Blackwell, Oxford.

Des Pres, T. 1976 *The Survivor: An Anatomy of Life in the Death Camps*. Oxford University Press, New York.

Fletcher, R. 2002 The Hammering of Society: Non-Correspondence and Modernity. In *Matériel Culture: The Archaeology of Twentieth Century Conflict*, edited by J. Schofield, W. Johnson, and C. Beck, pp. 303–311. Routledge, London.

Frankl, V. 1969 *Man's Search for Meaning: An Introduction to Logotherapy*. Beacon, Boston.

Gilead, I., Y. Haimi, and W. Mazurek 2009 Excavating Nazi Extermination Centres. *Present Pasts* 1: 10–39.

Gregson, N. and L. Crewe 2003 *Second-Hand Cultures*. Berg, Oxford.

Greif, G. 2005 *We Wept Without Tears: Testimonies of the Jewish Sonderkommando from Auschwitz*. Yale University Press, New Haven.

Hallam, E. and J. Hockey 2001 *Death, Memory, and Material Culture*. Berg, Oxford.

Höss, R. 1959 *Commandant of Auschwitz; The Autobiography of Rudolf Hoess*. Weidenfeld and Nicolson, London.

Jacobs, B. 1995 *The Dentist of Auschwitz*. The University Press of Kentucky, Lexington.

Kogon, E. 1998 *The Theory and Practice of Hell: The German Concentration Camps and the System Behind Them*. Berkley, New York.

Levi, P. 1986 *If This Is a Man: Remembering Auschwitz*. Summit, New York.

Levi, P. 1988 *The Drowned and the Saved*. Summit, New York.

Myers, A. 2007 Portable Material Culture and Death Factory Auschwitz. *Papers from the Institute of Archaeology* 19: 57–69.

Myers, A. 2008 Between Memory and Materiality: An Archaeological Approach to Studying The Nazi Concentration Camps. *Conflict Archaeology* 4(1): 231–245.

Saunders, N. (ed.) 2004 *Matters of Conflict: Material Culture, Memory and the First World War*. Routledge, Oxford.

Schiffer, M. 1999 *The Material Life of Human Beings*. Routledge, London.
Schofield, J., W. Johnson, and C. Beck (eds.) 2002 *Matériel Culture: The Archaeology of Twentieth Century Conflict*. Routledge, London.
Sofsky, W. 1999 *The Order of Terror: The Concentration Camp*. Princeton University Press, Princeton.
Van Pelt, R. and D. Dwork 1996 *Auschwitz, 1270 to the Present*. Yale University Press, New Haven.
Vrba, R. 1997 *I Cannot Forgive*. Regent College, Vancouver.
Wiesel, E. 1982 *Night*. Bantam, New York.

Chapter 6
Gordon Hirabayashi, the Tucsonians, and the U.S. Constitution: Negotiating Reconciliation in a Landscape of Exile

Mary Farrell and Jeff Burton

Abstract A recent archaeological survey at the Catalina Prison Camp, a mid-twentieth-century labor camp in the mountains of Arizona, found few significant features or artifacts, and an archival search also suggested little of note. It was only through public outreach that the site's relationship to one of the more shameful events in American history was revealed: individuals who nonviolently protested the internment of Japanese Americans during the Second World War were imprisoned there. This paper discusses the way in which the archaeological site played a role in the recognition, remembrance, and redefinition of this history, and in the reconciliation of disparate struggles for civil rights.

Introduction: The Construction of the Catalina Highway

Our story begins in the early 1980s, when the US Federal Highways Administration began a decades-long process of widening the Catalina Highway, near Tucson, in southern Arizona. By some accounts this twisty mountain road, completed in 1951, was the most dangerous stretch of asphalt in Arizona (Taylor 1995) and perhaps in the country (Ibas 2008). In 1986 the Federal Highway Administration proposed reusing an area known as the "old prison camp" along the Mt. Lemmon Highway as a staging area for the new highway construction (Farrell 1986). The first step in meeting federal requirements regarding historic properties was to determine just what the "old prison camp" was, and whether the site was eligible for the National Register of Historic Places (National Register).

M. Farrell (✉)
Coronado National Forest, Tucson, AZ, USA
e-mail: mollyofarrell@gmail.com

J. Burton
Manzanar National Historic Site, Independence, CA, USA
e-mail: jeff_burton@nps.gov

A. Myers, G. Moshenska (eds.), *Archaeologies of Internment*, One World Archaeology,
DOI 10.1007/978-1-4419-9666-4_6, © Springer Science+Business Media, LLC 2011

It was at least known that the prison camp housed prisoners who built the Catalina Highway. The most detailed information about the original road and the prison camp was provided by the *Final Construction Report: Arizona Forest Highway Project 33, Catalina Highway* (McLain 1951). Tellingly, the construction report begins not with miles of road completed or tons of asphalt laid, but with a description of the weather in Tucson. Located in the Sonoran Desert at an elevation of about 2,400 feet above sea level, temperatures in Tucson commonly exceed 100 degrees Fahrenheit in the summer. The report then goes on to describe the temperatures in the Santa Catalina Mountains, located to the north of Tucson. With some peaks over 10,000 feet, and with over 50 square miles above 6,000 feet, the higher parts of the mountains are typically 20–30 degrees cooler than the valley floor.

Herein lies the reason the Catalina Highway was constructed. In a time before air-conditioning, Tucsonans[1] either suffered through the heat, or moved to the mountains in the summer. Trails went up the Santa Catalina Mountains from the south; a mining road provided vehicle access to the high elevations of the mountains from the northeast. But it took at least two and a half hours to drive the 70 miles from Tucson to the recreational areas near the summit. Part of the route was the "Control Road," where traffic could travel a particularly narrow stretch of the road only in one direction at a time. The trip could be increased by up to one and a half hours if you had to wait for the traffic flow to change direction. The trip up the mountain was long and arduous, and generally only the wealthy and adventurous could go.

City planners in the 1920s and 1930s believed they could get a lot more people to come live in Tucson if it were easier to leave Tucson in the summer. As the *Final Construction Report* states, "[t]he principal function of Forest Highway No. 33, also known as Catalina Forest Highway, General Hitchcock Highway and Mt. Lemmon Road, is to provide direct and easy access to this 'cool island' for the 136,000 population of the Metropolitan Area of Tucson. ..." (McLain 1951:2). The report also summarizes some of the engineering challenges involved in building a road suitable for automobiles, given the steep rock escarpment on the side of the mountain that faces Tucson. The canyons that provided foot or horse access were steep and narrow. Several routes had to be considered and surveyed to find an alignment that would permit construction of the 6% grade considered necessary for vehicles.

The report, however, only hints at the political maneuvering needed to secure funding and approval, which may have been even more ambitious and tortuous than the road itself (Gillespie 2009). Tucsonans approved $100,000 in a bond election to build the road in 1915, but the engineering survey determined that the cost would be three times that amount. County bond elections were held again in 1928 and 1930

---

[1]"Tucsonan" is standard for a resident of Tucson, and is used when talking about the general population of the city. The resisters weren't part of the Tucson community, and came up with their own term, "Tucsonian."

to fund the road, but both were defeated. By 1932, building a road in such steep, rugged country was expected to cost over $1,000,000.

A review of correspondence and newspaper clippings in Forest Service files (Gillespie 2009) describes how the prohibitive costs and political resistance were overcome. Road promoters suggested that costs could be reduced considerably by using the free labor of convicts. The idea of rehabilitating prisoners through labor was part of a progressive prison reform movement, and was supported by President Herbert Hoover. But it was the antithesis of President Franklin D. Roosevelt's New Deal, in which funding for public works projects would be used to provide paid employment for some of the millions of people out of work during the Great Depression. Only through intensive and last-minute lobbying was the use of prisoners to build the Catalina Highway authorized. In fact, the project was not approved until March 3, 1933, Hoover's last day in office.

Work started in June 1933 with about 60 prisoners and five guards. The first temporary prison camp was set up at an existing Boy Scout Camp, with the Boy Scouts agreeing to camp elsewhere that summer (McLain 1951:19). The *Final Construction Report* listed the kinds of offenses that the prisoners had been convicted of:

> Violation of immigration and narcotic laws, sale of liquor to Indians, failure to pay income tax, driving stolen automobiles across State lines, robbery of post offices and banks and murder of Federal agents. During World War II many draft evaders and conscientious objectors were inmates of the Prison Camp. (McLain 1951:np)

During the 18 years of road work, over 8,000 inmates were incarcerated at the Catalina Prison Camp (McLain 1951:np).

The Permanent Prison

Vail Corral was selected as the permanent site for the prison camp early in the project because flat land was available for construction, nearby springs could provide water, and the mid-range elevation would be suitable for year-round habitation (Fig. 6.1). The site was located near the proposed highway alignment, but the camp was not built until road construction had advanced enough to make it accessible by vehicle. Developments at the site included a well, a reservoir, and a septic system, as well as "an administration building, two barracks, kitchen and mess hall, power and steam heating plant, laundry, a small manual training shop and garage" all built of wood (McLain 1951:62). Because of a housing shortage that developed in Tucson, the Prison Bureau built several substantial granite masonry cabins for the officers and guards on a hillside near the camp. Prisoners and guards moved to the prison camp in February 1939. The prison camp had no fences or guard towers: white-painted rocks marked the boundary, beyond which prisoners were not supposed to go (Figs. 6.2 and 6.3).

Although the administration considered the new accommodations much better than the temporary prison camp, the inmates may not have been as content. The *Final Construction Report* notes that "[t]here was a period of unrest in the prison camp which detracted from road progress. Two inmates escaped and four requested

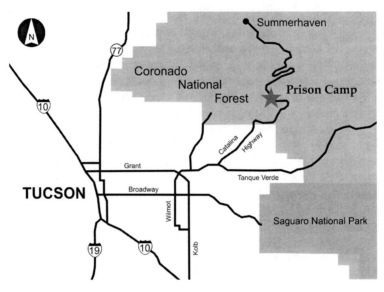

Fig. 6.1 Prison camp location. Drawn by Jeff Burton

transfer back to Terminal Island Penitentiary" (McLain 1951:67). Construction at the camp itself continued, and by November 1939 the barracks had electric lights and steam heat, and a ball field (Fig. 6.4). Construction at camp apparently continued even longer, as the *Final Construction Report* noted that in April 1940, "only 42 inmates were on road and shop work due to cabin construction in camp" (McLain 1951:70). The total number of inmates varied, with the all-time high at 292 and the low at 70. At times the number of inmates had to be reduced because there was not

Fig. 6.2 Catalina Prison Camp ca. 1945. Courtesy of the Coronado National Forest

Fig. 6.3 Drawing of the prison camp from the *Road Runner*, the prison newsletter. Courtesy of the Coronado National Forest

Fig. 6.4 "Prison camp ball field in Vail Corral," from the *Final Construction Report*. Courtesy of the Coronado National Forest

enough water available to sustain the maximum possible population. The ending of the war was also a factor: in January 1946, "the force was reduced to about 70 by the release of a large percentage of the very capable conscientious objectors" (McLain 1951:89).

What the Prisoners Accomplished

On-the-job training included "rock drill operation, caterpillar tractor operations, diesel power air compressor operations, blacksmithing, surveying, machinists and mechanics for all types of road grading machinery" related to the highway construction (Mead n.d.:2) (Fig. 6.5). Camp maintenance work generated training in cooking, clerical work, plumbing, electrical wiring, automobile mechanics, welding, carpentry, and infirmary care. Although the primary goal was clearly cheap labor for highway construction, the camp administration also hoped that through training, inmates would be better equipped to find honest employment upon their release (Mead n.d.:3).

As the Catalina Highway neared completion, prisoners also worked on shorter Forest Development roads that provided access from the new highway to recreation and administrative sites. When the final inspection was made on February 28, 1951, the prisoners had built "25 miles of bituminous surfaced Forest Highway (F.H.) at a cost of less than a million dollars of F.H. funds, plus the construction of nearly 18 miles of gravel surfaced Forest Development and County roads at an average cost of $4,000 per mile" (McLain 1951:112–113).

Fig. 6.5 "Catnip Canyon Crossing, Mile 8.8," from the *Final Construction Report*. Courtesy of the Coronado National Forest

Fig. 6.6 Catalina Prison Camp today. Photograph by Jim McDonald

Rising from 2,800 feet elevation at the base of the mountains to over 8,000 feet, the road winds through groves of saguaro cactus, desert grassland, oak woodland, ponderosa pine forest, and spruce and fir. According to the Coronado National Forest (2009),

> Because the road starts in the Lower Sonoran vegetative life zone and climbs to the high forests of the Canadian zone, it offers the biological equivalent of driving from the deserts of Mexico to the forests of Canada in a short stretch of 27 miles. Here, you'll find plants and animals and geology that exhibit some of the most wide-ranging natural diversity to be found in any area of comparable size in the continental US.

In 1965 the prison camp was converted to a juvenile prison or youth camp for 17–22-year-olds. The young inmates worked on fire suppression, cleaned and maintained campgrounds and picnic areas, and undertook various construction projects. In 1967 the US Bureau of Prisons turned control of the facility over to the State of Arizona, and later the site functioned as a "rehabilitation camp" for American Indian youth until 1972 (Mead n.d.:4). The buildings were removed in the early 1970s (Fig. 6.6). Like many of the flat areas in the Catalina Mountains with easy road access, the site was subsequently used by the public as an unofficial camping area.

A Million Visitors a Year

The advent of the widespread use of air conditioning after the Second World War brought more people to Tucson than the highway promoters ever envisioned. Between 1950 and 1960 the population of Tucson more than tripled (US Census).

But the ability to picnic and camp in the cool pines when the city was swelter-
ing in 100-degree heat remained popular, and by the 1970s the Catalina Highway
drew over one million visitors a year. In the 1980s it was determined that the highway needed widening and improvement. To meet the requirements of the National
Historic Preservation Act of 1966, an archaeological survey of the road corridor was
conducted (Phillips et al. 1983). Although portions of the prison camp were within
the surveyed area, it was seemingly considered too recent to be noted as an archaeological site. The "old Federal honor camp" is mentioned in the report, but only as
the location of one of the Native American sites recorded.

By the time the federal engineers proposed using the old prison camp as a staging
area for the road widening project in 1986, the site almost met the 50-year minimum age for listing on the National Register. An archaeological survey of the area
revealed concrete slabs and rock retaining walls (Figs. 6.7 and 6.8) (Farrell 1986).
Consistent with the minimal security described in the *Final Construction Report*,
the site did not have any features that might be considered characteristic of prisons;
there were no substantial walls or guard towers. In fact, the old prison camp looked
like many other abandoned and razed administrative sites.

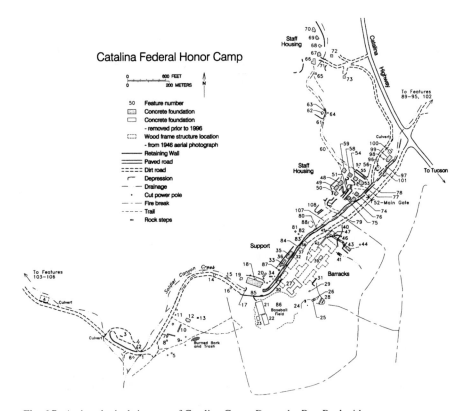

Fig. 6.7 Archaeological site map of Catalina Camp. Drawn by Ron Beckwith

Fig. 6.8 Stairway in guards' residence area. Photograph by Jeff Burton

Was the prison camp eligible for the National Register? The criteria for eligibility are specified in Title 36 of the Code of Federal Regulations, Section 60.4:

The quality of significance in American history, architecture, archeology, engineering, and culture is present in districts, sites, buildings, structures, and objects that possess integrity of location, design, setting, materials, workmanship, feeling, and association and:

a. That are associated with events that have made a significant contribution to the broad patterns of our history; or
b. That are associated with the lives of persons significant in our past; or
c. That embody the distinctive characteristics of a type, period, or method of construction, or that represent the work of a master, or that possess high artistic values, or that represent a significant and distinguishable entity whose components may lack individual distinction; or
d. That have yielded, or may be likely to yield, information important in prehistory or history.

The prison camp had been associated with construction of the Catalina Highway, important at least at the local or county level of significance (criterion a). The site had integrity of location and setting. But because the buildings and other structures had been removed, the site lacked sufficient integrity of design, materials, workmanship, and feeling. Even the integrity of association was less than ideal: by 1986 the reconstruction was in full swing, so many of the road features that the prisoners built had already been removed or modified. In addition, although the prison camp had been associated with 12 years of the 18-year highway construction project, when the highway was completed the camp was used for other purposes for over 20 years.

We had no evidence that the prison camp had been "associated with the lives of persons significant in our past" (criterion b). The site certainly did not meet the National Register criterion for sites that "embody the distinctive characteristics of a type, period, or method of construction, or that represent the work of a master, or that possess high artistic values" (criterion c). Neither did the site appear to fit the criterion for sites that "have yielded or may be likely to yield, information important in prehistory or history" (criterion d). The *Final Construction Report* provided thorough documentation, and it seemed that a federal prison would likely have other archival information available, if new research questions ever arose.

In consultation with the State Historic Preservation Officer, the Forest Service determined that the prison camp was not eligible for the National Register. It could be modified without further compliance with the National Historic Preservation Act. The Forest Service decided to allow Federal Highways to use the site as a staging area for the Catalina Highway widening project. After the highway project was completed, the site would be returned to public use as a campground and picnic area.

A decade later, however, we discovered that the prison camp had indeed been associated with historical events of national importance, that is, the Second World War internment of Japanese Americans.

Wartime Hysteria and Racial Prejudice

After the Japanese Imperial Navy attacked Pearl Harbor on December 7, 1941, nervous officials were afraid that Americans of Japanese heritage would conduct espionage and sabotage along the West Coast of America. In 1942, almost 120,000 Japanese Americans were forced from their homes in California, western Oregon, Washington, and southern Arizona in the single largest forced relocation in US history. Most of these men, women, and children—two-thirds of whom were US citizens—spent the war years in one of ten large, dusty, and hastily constructed relocation centers located in remote parts of the country, and surrounded by barbed wire and guard towers. Others, mostly immigrants who had not been allowed to apply for citizenship because of their race, were confined in Department of Justice camps. All were held without trial; none of those incarcerated was ever charged with (let alone convicted of) espionage or sabotage. During the internment, they lost homes, farms, fishing boats, and businesses.

At the start of the relocation, three Japanese Americans contested the government's action in court in separate cases. All three lost. Two of the plaintiffs ended up in the internment camps; one, Gordon Hirabayashi, went to federal prison. When the Second World War started, Gordon Hirabayashi was a senior at the University

Fig. 6.9 Gordon Hirabayashi
as a student. Courtesy of the
Wing Luke Asian Museum

of Washington and lived just off campus in an international students' dormitory
(Fig. 6.9). When the deadline for forced removal came, instead of boarding the bus
for an internment camp, Hirabayashi reported to the Federal Bureau of Investigation
(FBI) office to turn himself in. He reasoned that as an American citizen, he would
be violating the U.S. Constitution if he obeyed an order based solely on race or
ancestry (Hirabayashi personal communication 1999).

Hirabayashi was the only person known to have directly challenged the government's roundup by openly refusing to comply with the relocation orders.
Hirabayashi's case went to the US Supreme Court, but he was convicted, with the
reasoning that military necessity trumped civil rights. The lower court had sentenced
Hirabayashi to 30 days in jail for violating curfew, and 30 days for refusing to
participate in the forced removal and internment of Japanese Americans. Having
heard from prison cohorts that at least a 90-day sentence was required to be sent
to a less restrictive, outdoor location, Hirabayashi asked if his sentence could be
increased. The court extended both sentences to 90 days for each offense, to be
served concurrently. A prison in Tucson was the nearest and thus named the location
for his internment. However, the government would not provide transportation—he
would have to get there himself (Hirabayashi personal communication 1999; Irons
1983:87).

Hirabayashi hitchhiked over 1,500 miles from Seattle to Tucson to serve his sentence. The trip took him 2 weeks; he often slept in ditches at the side of the road.
On the way, he visited his family, who had obtained furloughs from the Tule Lake

internment camp to work at an Idaho beet farm. When Hirabayashi arrived at the US Marshal's Office in Tucson in August 1943, the officers could not find his papers and told him to go home. Hirabayashi explained that he had gone through a lot of trouble to get to prison, and "in due course, somewhere down the line, you're going to find my name, and then I'll have to come back again. So you might as well check around to see what's happened to the orders" (Erickson 1998a). The prison officials looked for his papers while Hirabayashi went to a movie. By the time he returned they had found the paperwork, and took him to the prison camp.

Justice Delayed and the Site Rediscovered

Forty years after Hirabayashi's original conviction, historians discovered that the Justice Department had withheld evidence that showed that the forced removal and internment of Japanese Americans was unnecessary. In the 1980s, Hirabayashi's case was reopened. He wrote at the time: "it is not just a Japanese American case. It is an American case, with principles that affect fundamental human rights of all Americans" (Hirabayashi 1985:7). In 1987, his conviction was overturned. A federal commission determined that the internment was motivated by racial prejudice, wartime hysteria, and failed political leadership. In 1988 President Ronald Reagan signed the Civil Liberties Act, which acknowledged the injustice and apologized for the internment.

Hirabayashi was celebrated as a hero. He was interviewed by the media, was the subject of a play, and his likeness was cast in bronze in a memorial in California. But even though the events were now famous, there was no connection to place. It was not until 1998, at a conference at which he was the guest of honor, that we had a chance to ask him: where exactly was the prison in Tucson? Hirabayashi described the work the prisoners did: building a highway north of Tucson. He described the surroundings, in the mountains. And he discussed the irony that the federal prison camp had no fences and few guards, so the convicted inmates had more freedom than his own family did in their "relocation center," when they had never been accused nor convicted of any crime. Hirayabashi, clearly, was describing the Catalina Prison Camp.

With the new information that the renowned civil rights hero Gordon Hirabayashi did time there, it appeared that the Catalina Prison Camp site might be eligible for the National Register under criterion b, after all. We proposed that the new campground being constructed at the old prison site be named for him. We thought it would be a way for the public to learn about the internment, and about Hirabayashi's stand for constitutional rights. We envisioned some kind of interpretive sign that would talk about the prison, the road, and the small but important link to the Japanese American relocation. For the million-plus visitors who drive up Mount Lemmon every year, even the campground sign along the highway could be intriguing, juxtaposing a typically American name like Gordon and a typically Japanese name like Hirabayashi.

The names of natural features, such as mountain peaks and rivers, cannot be changed without going through the US Board of Geographic Names, created in 1890 to maintain uniform geographic name usage throughout the federal government. However, the Forest Service has the authority to name constructed features such as administrative sites or campgrounds. Nevertheless, there was disagreement within the Forest Service about whether a campground should be named for a former prisoner. Some argued that it would be more appropriate to have a courthouse or law school named after Hirabayashi, since his legal stand was what was important, not his imprisonment. Others noted that he spent only 3 months at the Catalina Prison Camp, and although he had been convicted by a lower court of refusing to obey the relocation orders, the charge upheld by the Supreme Court was curfew violation, hardly an exciting or romantic crime to be forever memorialized.

The Forest Service asked the public what they thought of the idea of naming the new campground for Hirabayashi. The responses were overwhelmingly in favor, but there were a few objections. One person erroneously labeled Hirabayashi an ignoble "draft dodger" not worthy of any recognition or honor. Another thought that "Gordon Hirabayashi Recreation Site" would be "too weird" a name, perhaps indicating that such a Japanese-sounding surname still sounded un-American. Another comment suggested that there had been no good reason for Hirabayashi to protest the internment, reasoning that Japanese Americans were incarcerated for their own good; they might "have eventually been victims of violent lynch mobs" if they had been left in their communities for the duration of the Second World War. A few of the comments betrayed ignorance of the fact that the majority of Japanese Americans interned were American citizens, by comparing favorably the United States' treatment of its own citizens with Japan's treatment of enemy aliens. In fact, it appeared that all the objections to the name change were based on misconceptions, which only reinforced our resolve to use the old prison camp site as an aid to education.

The Other Resisters

The most surprising, and most important, comment we received noted that other young Japanese American men protesting the internment had been imprisoned at the prison camp during the Second World War. The young men were inspired by Hirabayashi's actions and mirrored his in motive and intent. The protagonists, like Hirabayashi, ended up convicted and imprisoned. However, their stories had been kept virtually secret for almost 60 years. While Hirabayashi was celebrated as a hero, the other Japanese American prisoners at the Catalina Prison Camp were ostracized from their communities. Part of the reason that their stories had been hidden is that they contradicted a narrative that was more cohesive and convenient.

Traditionally, the story goes that Japanese Americans passively accepted the relocation as a way to prove their loyalty to the United States. Aside from Hirabayashi and the two others who took their cases to court, the Japanese Americans boarded the buses, trains, and trucks for the relocation centers willingly, and once there, made the best of the situation. Once released, the Japanese Americans returned to the West Coast or made homes elsewhere, cheerfully rebuilding their lives and successfully recovering from the loss of billions of dollars' worth of homes, farms, and businesses. The meek acceptance of government decisions was touted as a virtue and proof of loyalty; such passivity may even be tacitly encouraged in minorities today.

The truth is more complicated: Japanese Americans had been conflicted on the best way to respond to the United States' prejudice and racism. Many actively sought justice by whatever means available. Some of the most optimistic and idealistic young men in the internment camps protested the relocation by conscientiously violating the Selective Service rules. In January 1942, Japanese Americans had been barred from military service, classified as unsuitable because of their race. A year later, the military ordered the creation of a segregated combat team for Japanese American citizens, publicly supported by President Roosevelt in February of 1943. In January 1944, the draft was reinstated for all Japanese Americans (Muller 2001:41–48). Some volunteered for the military as soon as they were eligible; many more accepted the draft call and served in the military with distinction. However, about 300 internees refused to be drafted until their constitutional rights as citizens were restored. The resisters did not object to the draft in itself, nor were they against military service. Many, in fact, had tried to enlist at the start of the war but were rejected because of their race. The resisters simply hoped that by defying the draft they would clarify their citizenship status in the only legal forum they had, a draft board hearing.

Yosh Kuromiya, one of over 60 Heart Mountain resisters, explains the draft resistance as a fourth option to the three more common reactions to confinement (Kuromiya 2002:79). Exemplifying one reaction, some "believed in cooperation and sacrifice without question as a means of regaining the trust and acceptance of our government and the public at large"; others became the "so-called 'dissidents'... who had become disenchanted with the government's professed 'ideals and good intentions'....They held in common, a righteous anger and resentment resulting from years of racial injustice and had apparently given up all hope of ever attaining equity." Of the third group, Kuromiya writes: "The vast majority, however, for various personal reasons, vacillated somewhere between the two extremes... [They remained] ineffective victims." Draft resistance, Kuromiya (2002:80) reflects, "provided a fourth option; one which demanded absolute faith in the principles of the U.S. Constitution while challenging, in the courts, government policies which were blatantly in violation of those principles."

As a protest, draft resistance had little effect; most of the resisters were convicted of draft evasion and served 2–3 years in federal prisons. Some 45 Japanese American draft resisters were sent to the Catalina Prison Camp to serve their sentences. The majority were from the Granada/Amache Relocation Center in Colorado; others were from the Poston Relocation Center in Arizona, and the Topaz Relocation Center in Utah (Burton et al. 2002:411–414). One, whose family had escaped internment by moving to Colorado, was inspired by Gordon Hirabayashi's stand for civil rights to resist the draft in support of his incarcerated fellow citizens. Kenji Taguma, who had alerted us to this piece of history, gave us the names and telephone numbers of some of the resisters, including his father, Noburu Taguma. Mr. Taguma was one of about 15 Japanese Americans who arrived in Tucson by train late at night in April 1944. While Hirabayashi had hitchhiked, these young men were transported in leg irons and chains. Still in chains, they were herded into the back of a big truck. As the truck climbed the mountain, Taguma could see that there were steep cliffs off the edge of the road, and thought "If this truck turns over, we've got no way to escape [death or injury], with legs chained and handcuffed" (Erickson 1998b).

The resisters were keenly aware of the irony that they, convicted of felonies, had greater freedom than their clearly innocent families did back in the internment camps, where guard towers and fences were the norm. In an interview, resister Ken Yoshida stated that:

> prison, compared with life in a concentration camp like Topaz, was 'paradise'. For two years, Yoshida had lived in a place euphemistically called the 'Central Utah Relocation Center', otherwise known as Topaz, where detainees suffered from low quality food, inadequate nutrition, and poorly constructed housing. They suffered from extreme heat and dust storms in the summer and freezing temperatures and snow in the winter. After he was convicted of violating Selective Service laws, Yoshida was sent to a work camp in the mountains just east of Tucson, Arizona where he and the other inmates labored to build a highway to the top of Mt. Lemmon. This was a prison with no fence and no wall. The only barrier between prisoners and the outside world was a line of painted rocks marking the perimeter of the property. Prison was a place where Yoshida enjoyed good food, worked seven to eight hours a day, learned new skills, enjoyed recreation, and made life long friends. He called it 'summer camp'. (Lyon 2006:158–159)

Before and during their trials, the resisters were pressured by the government and by the Japanese-American Citizens League (JACL) to relinquish their stand against being drafted and join the military before their civil rights were restored. The JACL, formed shortly before the war, promoted the idea that the only way to combat racism against American citizens of Japanese ancestry was to promote a kind of hyper-patriotism, which included proving their loyalty by going quietly to the relocation centers and by joining the military. Even at the Catalina Prison Camp, resister Harry Yoshikawa noted, the administration would call them in once a month, one at a time, and offer to erase their prison conviction from their records if they would join the military. But all the resisters offered to go to war only if the government restored their civil rights and released their families from the internment camps. "We used to tell them, 'send me home and give me back all of what I had; then I'll go'" (Lyon 2006:158–159).

Given the obvious parallels between Hirabayashi's stand for civil rights and the resisters', we then proposed that the resisters be included in the campground dedication celebration. However, it soon became clear why the resisters' stories were even less well known than that of the relocation in general. The resisters, although they had been pardoned by President Harry Truman in 1947, had never been pardoned by their own community. Draft resistance was considered "un-American," and the resisters were condemned and ostracized. Many considered them traitors or cowards. During the Second World War the JACL had declared that resisters should be charged with sedition, and tried to use intimidation and threats to force resisters to change their minds.

The resisters' punishment continued after their release from prison: they were shunned by their own Japanese American community. Four of the Tucson resisters tried to return to Amache relocation center, to rejoin their families. However, as convicted felons, they were not allowed into the camp. So they would sneak under the fence to check on their families. They rented a house nearby, and got jobs. But one was fired when it was discovered he had been a resister, and their house was burned by vandals (Lyon 2006:180–182). After the war another resister tried to return with his family to their farm in California, but they were told by their Japanese American neighbors they had better move: "You have no right to come back over here" (Lyon 2006:187).

United by their prison experience and by their post-prison treatment, the prison camp resisters formed a tight bond. The "Tucsonians" (Fig. 6.10), as they called themselves, held reunions in the years following their release, and continued to believe they had done the right thing by following their consciences. But many resisters never told their neighbors, friends, or even family about their wartime records. Their silence contributed to the postwar myth that Japanese Americans did nothing to oppose their own incarceration. So although there was much support for honoring Dr. Hirabayashi, there was much less enthusiasm for honoring the resisters. Some still considered them cowards or traitors.

Fig. 6.10 The "Tucsonians" reunion, 1947. Courtesy of the Coronado National Forest

The Road to Reconciliation

The prison camp site itself played a role in reconciling the widespread admiration for Hirabayashi with the widespread scorn for the resisters. First, the fact that the resisters and Hirabayashi were imprisoned at the same place forced recognition of the similarities of their situations. Second, the dedication ceremony, held at the site in 1999, focused on the true patriotism of upholding constitutional ideals. A student from the University of Arizona sang *America the Beautiful*. An honor guard of veterans gave military credence (Fig. 6.11). A taiko drum performance highlighted the Japanese heritage. Two sons of resisters gave speeches about the pride they felt for their fathers. Jim Kolbe, a member of the US House of Representatives, spoke eloquently about the heroism of standing up for civil rights and the need for civil disobedience:

> Acts of peaceful civil disobedience have time and again been the springboard for dramatic change, both in the short history of this great nation and in the longer history of others. The actions are invariably simple: a woman does not give up the seat on a bus. A man insists on dining where laws say he may not. A wheelchair-bound man insists that he, too, is capable of performing a task. A woman insists her discharge of duty is on par with a man's. (Kolbe 1999)

Third, and perhaps most importantly, Gordon Hirabayashi himself paid tribute to the resisters, delighted to share the stage with them, seeing them as kindred spirits, and in fact refusing to be honored without them (Fig. 6.12).

Fig. 6.11 Recreation area dedication ceremony, 1999, Color Guard, Ira H. Hayes American Legion Post 84, Sacaton, Arizona. Photograph by Jeff Burton

Fig. 6.12 Recreation area dedication ceremony, 1999. *Left* to *right*, Tucsonians Joe Norikane, Hideo Takeuchi, and Ken Yoshida; Coronado National Forest Supervisor John McGee; Gordon Hirabayashi; Congressman Jim Kolbe; Tucsonian Harry Yoshikawa; Takashi Hoshizaki; Tucsonian Noboru Taguma; and Yosh Kuromiya. Photograph by Jeff Burton

The ceremony received a lot of media attention, featured in television spots and newspaper articles, and was attended by leaders in the Japanese American community as well as the general public. The JACL, which had vilified the resisters during the war, was represented by several state and local chapters as well as by their national president. Visits to the site triggered memories, so that the forum provided by the place allowed more details of the prison camp history to come out. For example, Hirabayashi told a story about being welcomed to the prison camp by Hopi Indians, who washed his hair with yucca root shampoo at their ramada, built on a ridge adjacent to the camp. One of the authors went to the Hopi Tribe's reservation in northeastern Arizona, and learned that six young Hopi men were found guilty of failing to register for the draft. Following the Hopi Way, the six were forbidden by their particular status in Hopi religion and culture from joining the military. According to a Hopi archivist and historian, "They were found guilty because they were unable to demonstrate church membership and attachment to an American concept of theology because the United States Government didn't recognize the Hopi religion as being a legitimate religious practice" (Koyiyumptewa 2001).

The events, interviews, and revelations surrounding the dedication resulted in two doctoral dissertations and one master's thesis. The stories were incorporated into the interpretive information developed for a more permanent display at the site, and a second ceremony was held in 2001, at the unveiling of the interpretive kiosk. One of the Hopi Indians who had been imprisoned at the camp for adhering to the Hopi Way was able to attend (Fig. 6.13). Less than 3 years after the first dedication, the same JACL that had labeled the resisters as traitors during the war offered an official apology in a public ceremony. Their resolution states, in part: "the Constitution of the U.S. extends to its citizens the right to protest unfair treatment," and "There is

Fig. 6.13 Interpretive kiosk dedication, 2001, *left* to *right*, Hopi conscientious objector Roger Nasavaema; Tucsonian Ken Yoshida; Gordon Hirabayashi, and Tucsonians Sus Yenokida, Harry Yoshikawa, and Noboru Taguma. Photograph by Jeff Burton

Fig. 6.14 Entrance sign. Photograph by Jeff Burton

no easy and 'correct' response, emotionally or politically, to a civil rights violation as massive and destructive as the evacuation and internment" (JACL 2002).

Resisters have told us that they believed this journey to community acceptance and respect began with the ceremony at the Gordon Hirabayashi recreation site (Fig. 6.14). Some of the resisters have returned over the years and even camped at the site. The kiosk at the campground tells the story. School groups visit the old prison camp to learn about the relocation, and to discuss how individual citizens must uphold the constitution. As Tetsuden Kashima has written about the Japanese American relocation as a whole, "Examination of this tragic era in our nation's history is necessary, not for purposes of self-mortification but rather to ensure that our eyes and actions move toward the highest principles. We can do this only by knowing the reality of our nation's past" (Kashima 2002:xi–xii).

Conclusion

The Coronado National Forest is now reevaluating the National Register eligibility of the site. The prison camp site has more historic significance than originally thought, because of its association with Gordon Hirabayashi and the Japanese American internment. Thus, it may be eligible for the National Register of Historic Places under criteria (a) and (b). Additionally, its relative integrity may be better than originally determined: Although in 1986 the physical traces of the prison camp seemed unremarkable, the connections discovered provide a new context for comparison. Many of the other Department of Justice facilities where Japanese American draft resisters were held, such as Leavenworth Federal Penitentiary in Kansas or the McNeil Island Federal Penitentiary in Washington, are still used as prisons, and are thus not accessible to the public. With concrete foundations, retaining walls, and rock steps, the Catalina Prison Camp has relatively good integrity compared with many of the former relocation centers, where subsequent farming resulted in the removal or destruction of many archaeological features (Burton et al. 2002). Volunteer archaeologists investigating the prison camp have recently discovered a rock ring and depression that may even be the remains of the structure where the Hopis welcomed Hirabayashi to the prison site.

We would further argue that the site might be eligible for the National Register under criterion (d) in that it has yielded information important in history. The archival record, although ostensibly extensive, failed to tell some of the camp's most significant history. The prison camp itself helped us examine that history more closely, not through analysis of features and artifacts, but through the stories it elicited. More important than the physical remains of buildings and pathways is the setting itself, and the remembrance, honoring, and healing that have occurred there. As one of the students who did her doctoral dissertation on the stories that emerged around the prison camp said, "The voices of the resisters added a new dimension to our understanding of resistance and the importance of seemingly marginal sites in the landscape of internment" (Branton 2000).

The story of Hirabayashi and the resisters is ultimately a story of hope. Hirabayashi has said:

> The passage of the Civil Liberties Act of 1988 demonstrated the resilience of the U.S. Constitution. This is a great Constitution, but we badly failed it in World War Two. We failed to uphold it. If it doesn't serve you during a crisis, what good is it? We faltered once, but to show how good our Constitution is, we were able to recover and we were able to apologize and acknowledge an error, and we're going to be stronger for it. (Hirabayashi, personal communication 1999)

Our hope is that the Gordon Hirabayashi Recreation Site provides a space where visitors can learn how fragile civil rights can be, and how important it is for individuals to stand up for our Constitution even in difficult times. With today's political climate and the new fears of terrorism, the questions raised by Hirabayashi and the resisters still demand answers. What are the responsibilities and rights of citizens? Do some citizens have to prove their loyalty before they are allowed the rights of citizenship? When can the government abrogate civil rights? Is the present-day practice of racial profiling different from the wholesale incarceration of Americans of Japanese ancestry during the Second World War? As archaeologists, we are humbled, honored, and intrigued that an archaeological site can play a role in this discourse.

Acknowledgments Not only for the information but also for the inspiration they have provided, we owe many thanks to Dr. Hirabayashi, the resisters, their families and supporters, especially: the late Joe Norikane, Tee Norikane, Joey Norikane, Ken Yoshida, the late Kay Yoshida, Noboru Taguma, Kenji Taguma, the late Hideo Takeuchi, Susumu Yenokida, Harry Yoshikawa, Takashi Hoshizaki, Yosh Kuromiya, and Frank Emi. Many others were instrumental in helping us learn about and celebrate the story of the resisters, including Ross Hopkins, Rose Ochi, Martha Nakagawa, Jim Erickson, Cherstin Lyon, Bill Gillespie, Pete Taylor, and Nicole Branton.

References

Branton, N. 2000 The Gordon Hirabayashi Recreation Site: Multiple Voices in the Interpretation of Japanese-American Relocation. Paper Presented at the 27th Annual Great Basin Anthropological Conference, Ogden, Utah.

Branton, N. 2006 *Drawing the Line: Places of Power in the Japanese-American Internment Eventscape*. Ph.D. Dissertation, University of Arizona, Tucson, Arizona.

Burton, J., M. Farrell, F. Lord, and R. Lord 2002 *Confinement and Ethnicity: An Overview of World War II Japanese-American Relocation Sites*. University of Washington Press, Seattle.

Coronado National Forest 2009 Scenic Drives: Catalina Highway. http://www.fs.fed.us/r3/coronado/forest/recreation/scenic_drives/catalina_hwy.shtml (Accessed 18 April 2010)

Erickson, J. 1998a WWII Internees' Lives in Catalina's Examined: Renowned Japanese-American Looks Back. *Arizona Daily Star*, 30 August.

Erickson, J. 1998b 45 Japanese-Americans Lent Muscles to Build Highway. *Arizona Daily Star*, 31 August.

Farrell, M. 1986 *A Cultural Resources Investigation of the Proposed Mt. Lemmon Highway Staging Ground (Report 1986-05-037)*. Coronado National Forest, Tucson.

Gillespie, W. 2009 *The Roads to Mount Lemmon*. Report on File at the Coronado National Forest, Tucson.

Hirabayashi, G. 1985 *Good Times, Bad Times: Idealism Is Realism*. Canadian Quaker Pamphlet No. 22. Argenta Friends Press, Argenta.

Ibas, M. 2008 Mount Lemmon Time Trial, 28 August 2008. http://www.masonibas.com/mionline/ (Accessed 18 April 2010)

Irons, P. 1983 *Justice at War: The Story of the Japanese-American Internment Cases*. Oxford University Press, New York.

JACL (Japanese-American Citizens' League) 2002 *Nisei Resisters of Conscience of World War II Recognition and Reconciliation Ceremony Program Notes*. 11 May, San Francisco.

Kashima, T. 2002 Foreword. In *Confinement and Ethnicity: An Overview of World War II Japanese-American Relocation Sites*, by J. Burton, M. Farrell, F. Lord, and R. Lord, pp. ix–xii. University of Washington Press, Seattle.

Kolbe, J. 1999 *Open Letter*. House of Representatives, US Congress, Washington, DC, 5 November.

Koyiyumptewa, K. 2001 *The Hopi Conscientious Objector*. Hopi Cultural Preservation Office, 25 August, Kykotsmovi, Arizona.

Kuromiya, Y. 2002 The Fourth Option. In *A Matter of Conscience: Essays on the World War II Heart Mountain Draft Resistance Movement*, edited by M. Mackey, pp. 77–80. Western History Publications, Powell.

Lyon, C. 2006 *Prisons and Patriots: The "Tucsonian" Draft Resisters and Citizenship During World War II*. Ph.D. Dissertation, University of Arizona, Tucson, Arizona.

McLain, G. 1951 Final Construction Report Arizona Forest Highway Project 33 Catalina Highway, Coronado National Forest, Pima County, Arizona, US Department of Commerce, Bureau of Public Roads Division Seven.

Mead, C. n.d. *Federal Prison Camp*. Report on File at Coronado National Forest, Tucson, Arizona.

Muller, E. 2001 *Free to Die for Their Country*. University of Chicago Press, Chicago.

National Register of Historic Places, www.nps.gov/history/nr/listing.htm and www.nps.gov/nr/regulations.htm (Accessed 7 August 2009).

Phillips, D., P. Castalia, and G. Bronitsky 1983 Cultural Resources Survey and Evaluation of Forest Highway 39, Santa Catalina Mountains, Pima County, Arizona (Report 1984-05-021). Prepared for the Federal Highway Administration, Central District, Federal Division, Denver, Colorado. On File at Coronado National Forest, Tucson, Arizona.

Taylor, M. 1995 Arizona's General Hitchcock Highway: Balancing Safety and the Environment. *Public Roads*, Spring.

Chapter 7
Control or Repression: Contrasting a Prisoner of War Camp and a Work Camp from World War Two

Iain Banks

Abstract There are clear signs of control and repression in the architecture and layout of most internment camps, but internment camps were not the only form of institutional accommodation present in the United Kingdom during the Second World War. Comparison of a prisoner of war camp and a forestry work camp, both in Scotland, reveals similarities and differences between the two. The similarities highlight issues of control and authority, while the differences reveal issues of repression and punishment. The comparison also reveals much about official mind-set in the United Kingdom during the Second World War.

Introduction

As part of development control work in Scotland, Glasgow University Archaeological Research Division (GUARD) was involved in the recording of two sites from the Second World War, both of which provided accommodation for groups of young male foreigners. The two sites were very different in nature, however. The first was Deaconsbank, a prisoner of war (PoW) camp near Hamilton, South Lanarkshire (Swan and Scott 2005), while the second was a Newfoundland Overseas Forestry Unit (NOFU) work camp at Strathmashie, Invernessshire (Sneddon 2007). GUARD undertook the work on the two sites as separate projects, and there was no thought of combining or comparing the two projects at that time. In retrospect, however, it seemed reasonable to contrast the two sites, as they date from the same historical period, relate to the same historical events, and represent the accommodation of groups of young alien males within the Scottish landscape. Similarities and differences between the sites are a reflection of the attitudes to the two differently classified populations: similarities arise from the fact that both populations represent young, single males far from home (and

I. Banks (✉)

Centre for Battlefield Archaeology, University of Glasgow, Glasgow, Scotland, UK

e-mail: iain.banks@glasgow.ac.uk

A. Myers, G. Moshenska (eds.), *Archaeologies of Internment*, One World Archaeology, DOI 10.1007/978-1-4419-9666-4_7, © Springer Science+Business Media, LLC 2011

therefore needing some level of control and policing), while differences arise from the fact that the PoWs were "enemies" (creating a constant threat of future violence), and the foresters represented workers brought to Britain to support the war effort and replace the men who had gone off to war.

The study of confinement and repression through archaeology is relatively recent, particularly in Britain. In America and continental Europe, there have been projects to record and excavate PoW camps from the American Civil War and Second World War (e.g. Thoms 2000, 2004; Prentice and Prentice 2000; Buchner and Albertson 2005; Doyle et al. 2007), while there have been some recent attempts to look at the archaeology of concentration and labor camps (Aparicio et al. 2008; Kola 2000; Myers 2008). In Britain, the Long Kesh/Maze internment camp has recently been the subject of investigation and analysis (McAtackney 2005a, b; Purbrick 2006). Very little has been published on the camps of the First and Second World Wars on mainland Britain. This volume partly redresses this, but the situation until recently was symptomatic of a lack of interest in the physical remains of the camps since the end of the war. English Heritage did undertake a specific study of PoW camps in England (Thomas 2003a, b), and the *Defence of Britain* project (Lowry 1998) recorded some examples.

Imprisonment and Prisoners of War

We are used to incarceration as a way of dealing with problematic individuals and groups. Those guilty of crimes are routinely sent to prison, to the point that there are serious concerns in both Britain and America that the prison populations are too high. Prison overcrowding has been a problem for decades. We are also used to mass incarceration, with detention centers for asylum seekers in Britain frequently in the news, internment camps for enemy aliens in the World Wars, such as the Isle of Man sites (Chapter 3 by Mytum, this volume), going back to the invention of the concentration camps in the late nineteenth century (Chapter 1 by Moshenska and Myers, this volume). Alongside images of the death camps in the Nazi empire, we also have more recent examples such as the camp at Omarska in Prijedor, Bosnia, and the images of its abused prisoners that were beamed around the world. We have become used to PoW camps themselves, being a well-known phenomenon in all of the wars of the twentieth century, including from the iconic images of *The Great Escape* and of Colditz. More recently, Hollywood has also presented us with images of Vietnamese prisoner of war camps in *The Deerhunter* and *Rambo*.

The traditional approach to those who lost a battle or surrendered was to keep the nobility for ransom and to either kill or exchange the soldiery. In many cases, the rout at the end of a battle led to slaughter as the fleeing men were hunted down; those who escaped made their way home as best they could or became outlaws. On other occasions, such as when the Scots surrendered at Pinkie in 1547, they were marched away and held in poor conditions until many died (Cooper 2008:17). The men captured at Dunbar in 1650 were taken to Durham and imprisoned in the cathedral, where many died of disease and neglect (Grainger 1997:55, 57).

The Napoleonic wars were the first time that captured troops were routinely held for the duration of the conflict, where preventing the men from returning home was an important strategic aim (Daly 2004). Later in the nineteenth century, large prison camps accommodated captured men and officers in the American Civil War, which has generated some archaeological interest (Prentice and Prentice 2000; Thoms 2004; Bush 2009). In the Franco-Prussian War of 1870–1871, thousands of French prisoners were held in camps of up to 25,000 men, which had a role in the epidemic of smallpox that killed 500,000 people in France and Germany at that time (Smallman-Raynor and Cliff 2002).

One factor that should be considered in approaches to prison camps is how far developments in understanding of the spread of disease and the need for sanitation affected attitudes toward prison camps. A concentration of men in a large camp with primitive sanitation was a potential source of epidemics, and this must have created a certain level of fear and concern about such camps in wartime. It was a very real threat to public health at a time when there were already considerable strains on populations because of the difficulties of wartime conditions. This probably explains why many of the prison camps in Britain had relatively efficient sanitation systems. Whether the local populations were aware of the threat, rather than the threat of having a large number of enemy soldiers incarcerated nearby, is moot; it will undoubtedly have been a concern for the administrative authorities.

The development of the military incarceration of large populations of men took place at the same time as completely different developments in the field of criminal incarceration (Casella 2007). In judicial confinement, the trend was toward reformation of the moral character of the individual through the architecture of the prison; this was a process that was necessarily focused upon the individual and where the individual experience of incarceration, the loss of anonymity and privacy, and of constant surveillance were key aspects of the new, scientific approach to punishment. This was, of course, impossible for camps of up to 25,000 men such as Magdeburg in Prussia in the Franco-Prussian War (Smallman-Raynor and Cliff 2002:250). The differences between the two forms of incarceration are quite clear: The judicial approach was underpinned by notions of improving human nature and reforming anti-social elements of society, and the military approach was underpinned by the necessity of controlling large numbers of enemy combatants and removing them from the resources of the enemy. There was no need to address the character of the inmates and there was no need to deal with them as individuals. PoWs were a population unit to be bounded and controlled, which required significant resources to sustain.

Second World War PoW Camps in Britain

The history of PoW camps in Britain is under-researched. It is a topic that has barely penetrated the public consciousness, and there are many in Britain today that have no idea that Britain had enemy soldiers incarcerated on British soil. The public perception of PoW camps is largely shaped by films such as *The Great Escape*, and to a lesser extent, *The Wooden Horse*. Members of a particular British generation will have grown up with an intimate knowledge of life in Colditz Castle, courtesy of BBC TV, but there is little in popular media that covers the topic of the men who were held prisoner in Britain. Michael Radford's 1983 film *Another Time Another Place* told the story of an Italian prisoner in Scotland, while the *Broken Souls* episode of the program *Foyle's War* has a German PoW working on a local British farm. Beyond this, there is little to remind the general public of the presence, in Britain, of over half a million enemy prisoners during the war other than the restored Harperley Camp in County Durham that is now a visitor attraction.

There were very few Axis prisoners held in Britain until 1942–1943. There were particularly few German prisoners, and those that were held in Britain tended to be *Luftwaffe* or *Kriegsmarine* (German air force and navy). In 1940, there were 257 German prisoners being held in Britain (Moore 1996:19). The war was going badly for Britain in July 1940: the Phoney War was over; Holland, Belgium, and France had fallen; the Germans had taken Norway; and the Battle of Britain had begun. In 1939, Rule 18B of the Emergency Powers Act (1939), commonly known as "Defence Regulation 18B," allowed for the detention of suspected Nazi sympathizers with the suspension of *habeas corpus*. Initially, it was little used, and there were only a handful of arrests in 1939. However, as the disasters of 1940 unfolded, public opinion not only hardened against potential Nazi sympathizers, but was also underpinned by a fear of invasion and internal attack by the fifth column. As fears of far-right collaborators grew in both the public and the state's mind, Defence Regulation 18B was enacted far more vigorously. Leading British fascists, such as Oswald Mosley, were imprisoned, with up to 1,000 British citizens incarcerated, while 74,000 foreign citizens (mainly Germans, Austrians, and Italians) were rounded up and held in camps. Ironically, many of these were Jews and others who had fled to Britain to escape Nazi persecution.

This climate of fear meant that there was a very strong reaction against having enemy soldiers held on British soil. It was considered that they would form a reserve army for the Nazis in the event of invasion, and that it was far too dangerous to hold them in Britain. The fear of paratroopers, reflected in the parodies of the BBC TV comedy *Dad's Army*, was another factor, with the notion that airborne troops would be able to free the prisoners and thus release an army behind the lines. As a result, during the dark years of 1940, 1941, and 1942, many enemy prisoners were sent to Canada, Australia, and the United States (Waters 2004; Waiser 1995).

The impact of sending hundreds of thousands of young men away to fight was being felt in agriculture and industry. Despite the fact that some jobs were considered "reserved" and therefore people in those jobs were not eligible for conscription, the manpower needs of the armed forces meant that there were major labor shortages. As early as November 1939, in an attempt to deal with the labor shortages, the Newfoundland [Canada] Commissioner for Natural Resources made a radio appeal for men to go to Britain as loggers. The Newfoundlanders were only one of a range of groups that heeded this call: Australians, New Zealanders, Canadians and British Hondurans all came to help with the labor shortage. The use of women in the workplace reduced the scale of the problem, but there was still a desperate need for labor that worsened as Britain began to prepare its assault on Fortress Europe.

The prisoner of war population was another potential solution to the labor crisis. In February 1942, the decision was made to use Italian PoWs to work in nonmilitary roles, and 28,000 men were brought to Britain (Hellen 1999:193–194). In contrast, because fear of German invasion meant that German PoWs were still considered too dangerous to hold in Britain, the same period (between December 1941 and March 1942) saw the population of German PoWs in Britain fall from 1,850 to 1,150, reaching its lowest level at 200 by June 1942 (Hellen 1999:193; Wolff 1974). This reflects the policy of moving German prisoners out of Britain, to more secure locations abroad. Meanwhile, the Italians were accommodated in camps scattered across Britain in 53 work camps, five PoW camps, and a military hospital. These prisoners were used in agriculture and forestry work throughout Britain and were a relatively common sight during the second half of the war.

With the change in fortune that began in 1942 and 1943, however, the fear of invasion of Britain began to recede. Germany was fully engaged on the Eastern Front, losing hundreds of thousands of troops to winter and in battles such as those at Stalingrad and Leningrad, and was losing ground in North Africa. The British authorities were able to concentrate more on preparations for invading occupied Europe, rather than preparing for an invasion. This allowed a change in attitude to German PoWs, who became potentially useful rather than potentially dangerous. There was no immediate change in policy, but the reduction of the threat of invasion meant that the German prisoners could also be considered as potential workers rather than a potential fifth column.

On September 3, 1943, Mussolini's successor, General Badoglio, signed an armistice with the Allies. The Wehrmacht promptly seized control of Italy but the Italian military personnel held in Allied captivity were no longer considered enemy combatants. They were treated as allies and moved to better accommodations, leaving many of the work camps and prison camps that they had previously occupied. The camps were not to stand empty for long. After D-Day (June 6, 1944), the numbers of German prisoners increased significantly: in December 1943 there were 1,100; in June 1944, 7,600; in September 1944, 90,000; and in December 1944, 144,450 (Hellen 1999:193). As well as reflecting the reduced fear of invasion, the rise in numbers was the result of the government decision taken in October 1944 to use some of the German troops for agricultural and forestry work (Hellen 1999:194).

The fearful attitude toward the German prisoners before 1944 seems strange when considered in light of the fact that 65,497 German prisoners had been used for labor during the First World War (Hellen 1999:197) and despite some public hostility had not created any serious problems for the authorities. In February 1940, there was a question in parliament about the possibility of using prisoners to plug the labor gaps as had been the case in the previous conflict, which was rejected as a possibility by the Minister for War. By 1943 there were tens of thousands of Italian prisoners working across Britain, while the ministerial response to questions about the use of German prisoners remained as negative as in 1940. This indicates that the Germans were seen as being different to the Italians, and also that they were different in some way to their fathers who had been imprisoned in 1914–1918.

Prisoner of War Camp Design

The 1929 Geneva Convention stipulated the nature of facilities to detain enemy combatants once they had surrendered. Under Article 10, the facilities used by the prisoners had to be of the same standard as those available to the holding power's own troops in a normal army camp:

> Prisoners of war shall be lodged in buildings or huts which afford all possible safeguards as regards hygiene and salubrity. The premises must be entirely free of damp, and adequately heated and lighted ... As regards dormitories, their total area, minimum cubic air space, fittings and bedding material, the conditions shall be the same as for the depot troops of the detaining power (Article 10, *Convention relative to the Treatment of Prisoners of War, Geneva, 27 July 1929*).

This was accompanied by similar requirements with regard to food (Article 11), clothing (Article 12), and sanitation (Article 13). Prisoners were to be accommodated in enclosed compounds, where access was only possible through the guards' facilities. The barrack blocks for the prisoners would be on a grid pattern, with all the same basic facilities as the guards. This had the advantage of complying with the Geneva Convention and at the same time reducing the occasions on which prisoners had any reason to leave their compound. This meant that leisure facilities (such as a parade ground, theatre, and library) were on site within the enclosure, reducing the security risk of allowing prisoners to leave the compound. Medical facilities, barbers, and a shop selling local produce were all to be within the compound.

A distinction was made between the detention section and the garrison section. The area of detention was called "inside the wire," while the surrounding guard facilities were collectively "outside the wire." While the facilities were essentially the same, there were specific differences between the two areas. There was to be an exclusion zone of 60 feet (approximately 18 meters) between the wire of the enclosure and any of the structures to ensure that no prisoner could approach the enclosure fence without being seen and challenged (Swan and Scott 2005:11). There were to be wide passages between the buildings to ensure that there was visibility at all times, while the grid pattern of the huts was intended to keep this element of visibility.

The facilities for the guards also underline the differences between inside and outside the wire: there were motor pools and workshops for the camp vehicles that were used to move around outside the camp, something that the prisoners could only do under escort and under the direction of their captors. There would have been quartermaster's stores in the garrison area, which was the source of replacement materials for the prisoners; under Article 12, they were entitled to replacement clothes and footwear as their own wore out. The quartermaster's stores were a cornucopia of the things that made life in detention easier and more bearable, but were kept at a distance and outside the compound so that access to those stores by prisoners could be rigidly controlled. Completing the sense of separation was the placing of the reception station, which would process arriving prisoners inside the wire rather than at the entrance to the camp. This meant that prisoners arriving at the camp would have been fully inside, away from the outside world, before they were incorporated into the camp. Henceforth, their entire world would be the camp, unless the authorities determined otherwise. The guards' area was off limits as much as the rest of the world.

Deaconsbank/Camp 660

The Deaconsbank camp, also known as Camp 660, conformed to the above pattern to some degree. The following is taken from the report on the archaeological survey of the camp (Swan and Scott 2005:9–10). The buildings were of both semi-circular and pitched roof profile, of both Nissen and Jane hut types. The entrance to the compound was through a point adjacent to the bungalow to the west of the site, where a brick-and-ash road survives today. The huts immediately adjacent to the entrance are 16 and 24 foot span metal Nissen huts. These could have been used as a messing facility for the compound, with the three huts opposite utilized as the reception station. The smaller huts to the south of the bungalow could not be identified, but may have been used as shops ancillary to the camp. The huts visible along the west boundary are located within the exclusion zone, and were probably constructed later; the aerial photograph dates to 1946, when the war was over and the inmates had changed in status to become displaced persons rather than enemy combatants (Fig. 7.1). The precise use for these huts is unclear, but they may well have been for accommodation.

Accommodation huts on the west boundary, based on the aerial photograph, were about 55 feet from the boundary fence, as would be expected from the pattern required by the Ministry of Works. The huts built for accommodation on standard camps would be intended to accommodate up to 35 men, but were of 10 bays in length—about 60 feet. The huts on this camp were smaller in length, of approximately six bays, and correspondingly may have accommodated 20 men (Fig. 7.2). The accommodation levels in the camp reached 600 in October 1946, which would have required around 30 accommodation huts.

The accommodation huts were provided with lavatory facilities in two huts along the east boundary. These had slab urinals and toilet compartments, providing a reasonable level of amenity. Showers were generally provided in two huts in tandem, and located along the north boundary of the compound. The shower compartments are located in the center of the huts, back-to-back, taking advantage of the highest point of the huts. These facilities contrast with those provided for German PoWs at Happendon Camp in South Lanarkshire, where the toilet facilities were comparatively basic, with toilet compartments formed by low separating walls within the huts and waste being deposited into large-bore open pipes, with toilet seats being

Fig. 7.1 Aerial photograph
of Deaconsbank Camp in
1946. Courtesy of the Royal
Commission on the Ancient
and Historical Monuments of
Scotland

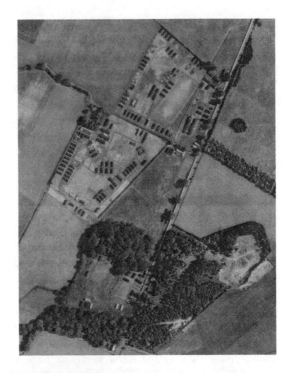

Fig. 7.2 Macoul Camp in winter 1944/1945. Courtesy of Mr & Mrs Park

formed by timber rims on the outlets of the waste pipes. Showers were created within the curved profile of the sides, and were probably uncomfortable to use. A Red Cross report on a visit made in November 1945 describes the sanitary facilities as "good (showers with hot and cold running water and flushing toilets)"; this was after the war but is accurate for the facilities during the war as well.

The Geneva Convention prescribed that accommodation for prisoners was to be of an equivalent standard as that which was provided for the guards. It can be seen in the Ministry of Works drawings that this was generally the case, although the guards' accommodation had a greater degree of privacy, with doors to lavatory compartments as an example. Within the compound was a landscaped area bounded by a dressed stone wall. This lay south of, and adjacent to, the reception station. This may have been the offices of the camp staff, while it is also possible that the theatre and hut set aside for religious worship were in this area. The Red Cross report lists how the 59 huts were used (Table 7.1).

Table 7.1 Facilities at Deaconsbank PoW Camp	Dormitories (on average 20 men per hut)	26
	Classrooms	2
	Theatre	1
	Chapel	1
	Canteen	1
	Refectory	1
	Infirmary	3
	Showers	3
	Wash-hand basins	3
	Latrines	2
	Large kitchen with bakery	1
	Stores with provisions	2
	Bread storehouse	1
	Hut for teachers and interpreters	1
	Artists' workshop	1
	Tool storehouse	1
	Office	1
	Hairdresser	1
	Craft workshop	3
	Carpentry	1
	Quarter-master's hut	1

Newfoundland Overseas Forestry Unit (NOFU)

While there were thousands of foreign young men being held and accommodated in Britain as PoWs, there were also thousands of foreign young men being accommodated in Britain as workers in essential industries. One area of particular concern was forestry, because of the importance of timber in all aspects of the industrial and military prosecution of the war. There was a parallel incomer population of workers, the substantive difference being the classification of these young men as "allies" rather than "enemies."

Background

On November 9, 1939, the Office of the Secretary of State for the Dominions sent a telegram to the Commission Governor of Newfoundland, Sir Humphrey Walwyn, on the problems within the timber industry:

> Pit prop supply position will be very difficult in this country from the early new year until the end of June when anticipated supplies from Newfoundland and North America should begin to arrive in quantities.

The telegram noted the labor shortages being experienced and enquired

> ....whether 2,000 suitable men could be supplied from Newfoundland for this work at the earliest possible date either for the period say of six months or preferably for the duration of the war. (Curran 1987:105)

On November 11, Walwyn promised an initial shipment of 200 men leaving in December, with a further 1,800 leaving as soon as possible afterward. Subsequently, on November 18, the Newfoundland Forestry Act 47 was passed, creating the Newfoundland Overseas Forestry Unit under the Commissioner for Natural Resources. The unit was recruited as a civilian force as this would avoid the lengthier procedures of training and enrolling a military group. It was led by Chief Forestry Officer, Lt. Col. Jack Turner. The first group of 350 men left Newfoundland on the RMS *Antonio* on December 13; they arrived in Liverpool 5 days later (Sneddon 2007:235). By early 1940, the full contingent of NOFU was in the forests, primarily in Scotland.

During the years that NOFU was in operation, over 3,400 men left Newfoundland to work as foresters, mainly in the early years of the war. The number and speed with which the men were mobilized proved critical in filling the vacuum in timber supply during the initial phases of the war effort. Military units—for example, the Canadian Forestry Corps—were not efficiently harvesting timber until 1941 (Wonders 1987). The NOFU operated under eight districts (A–H), with at least 71 camps and related sawmills (see Sneddon 2007). One problem they faced through the rapid mobilization was a total lack of preparation at their destination; there was a severe deficiency in accommodation and necessary equipment. The initial group were temporarily housed in camps within the border regions of England and Scotland, while the next group were housed in three camps in Argyll. They were then dispersed to logging camps throughout Scotland, the majority of which had yet to be constructed. The initial task for the unit was to build their own camps, while temporary accommodation was provided through local halls and barns.

A typical camp of the NOFU would consist of bunkhouses, a cook house, a dining hall, a recreation hut/canteen and the fore peak, where the camp foreman, his clerk, and the tallymen would work. Further buildings would include sheds to house horses, tractors, and other machinery. Most of the buildings would have been constructed with either plain wood sections/planks or logs caulked with moss, and sometimes protected at the base by an outer wall of earth (Sneddon 2007:237). It took the Newfoundlanders 3–4 days to build a log cabin to sleep twenty men, and approximately a week to build a dining room and kitchen combined. This would provide accommodation for 150 men within roughly 1 month. In addition to the camps, there was also a requirement for offices, sawmills, and a network of roads to transport the felled timber, which was moved by tractors, horses, and light-gauge railways.

In 2005, as part of a project to map the archaeological sites in Strathmashie Forest to inform a heritage trail, a combination of terrestrial survey and trial excavation was carried out by GUARD on a series of NOFU sites within the area. The results of this work have been published elsewhere (Sneddon 2007), and the results of one particular camp, Macoul, are discussed here. Three other camps were studied in the original project and the details of those camps can be found in Sneddon's 2007 article.

Macoul NOFU Camp, Strathmashie Forest

The only camp known to have been photographed while in use was Macoul camp on the Ardverikie Estate (Figs. 7.3 and 7.4). The camp was located southeast facing grassy slopes continuing down to the A86. The site was bound on the north

Fig. 7.3 Macoul Camp in c 1942. Courtesy of Laggan Heritage

Fig. 7.4 Macoul Camp in 2005. Courtesy of GUARD

and northwestern sides by a disused field dyke, beyond which the ground became steeper and rougher. Today, 12 platforms lie either side of a track that runs southwest through the site. This was possibly the main entrance into the camp. The platforms varied between squares and rectangles, with some showing clear signs of a concrete base. These were the bases for timber structures including bunk houses and cook house toilets.

The number of concrete bases at Macoul is unusual in comparison to the other Strathmashie camps. The excavator noted that at most camps concrete was only used for the larger buildings such as the cookhouse and the washrooms (Sneddon 2007:255). He suggested that this was a reflection of the sloping ground on which the camp stood. More typically, the bunkhouses would have been raised wooden floors. Despite this, the huts seem to have been quite comfortable. An article on a camp near Ballater in Aberdeenshire reported:

> There are log huts built by the Newfoundlanders, set in a forest clearing and exposed to the bitter weather on mountain sides, which for warmth and comfort surpass anything suburban builders have produced. Moss gathered from the forest is used to stuff between the rough hewn logs and keep the huts draught proof, and spending a few minutes inside them from the bitter weather one realizes that English and Scots alike have not yet learned how to keep themselves warm. (Passingham 1941)

Macoul is laid out along the road, and accordingly consists of huts lying along the central path, aligned along its axis.

The men were incorporated into the life of the community, and there are records of several marrying local girls. They were members of the library, took part in community events, socialized with the local community, and generally were treated well. Naturally, this free license occasionally meant that things could go wrong; there are several instances in the local papers of NOFU men being in court as a result of disturbances following drinking sessions. However, the press coverage is always reasonably sympathetic, and the young men of NOFU are consistently seen as being there for the benefit of the locals. There is no hint of there being a feeling that the men were a problem or a burden on the community. There is certainly none of the same reaction as there was to the German prisoners. One of the most striking differences is that the NOFU men were frequently involved in the local Home Guard units, and 3rd Inverness Battalions of the Home Guard was entirely comprised of NOFU men, making it the only unit to consist entirely of non-British men. For obvious reasons, neither the German nor the Italian prisoners were ever assimilated to that extent.

Structural Differences between Deaconsbank and Macoul

There was little difference between the huts that were used for accommodation for the PoWs and for the NOFU men. The PoWs at Deaconsbank lived in Nissen huts that were roughly the same dimensions as those at Macoul, although the latter were built from wood and were probably warmer. Both had electric lighting, and both sets of accommodation were heated by stoves in the huts. In many ways, the facilities available to the PoWs were superior to those of the foresters: the prisoners had classrooms, a theatre, a chapel, three infirmaries, an artists' workshop, and a hairdresser, while the foresters would have had to wait for an opportunity to get to Newtonmore for a haircut. The NOFU camps were very much workstations, and there was no need to provide a full range of facilities on site because the foresters had the option of being able to travel to those facilities. Facilities for the PoWs had to be inside the wire, whenever possible.

If the buildings themselves were essentially similar, there were differences in the layout of those buildings. All of the huts at Deaconsbank were built perpendicular to pathways, whereas at Macoul, the buildings lay along the axis of the central roadway. Elsewhere, the foresters' camps had a variety of orientations (e.g. Kildrummy, Fig. 7.5), indicating that there was no determining principle guiding the layout. In PoW camps, the practice was to position the buildings at right angles to the pathways, creating long lines of sight. Lines of sight were crucial for the guards of the PoW camp. They had to be able to observe the movement and location of the prisoners to be able to detect escape attempts or other outbreaks of trouble.

There is no record of violent incidents at Deaconsbank, but there are well-known incidents elsewhere that involved prisoner on prisoner violence. There were particular problems in many American camps because there was little attempt to isolate the hardcore Nazis from others. The Nazi party members were able to take control of life within the camp and attacked people considered to be enemies. This included incidents of murder, such as the case of Karl Lehmann, murdered by Nazi PoWs at Medicine Hat, in Canada, in September 1944, for saying that Germany would lose the war (Kilford 2004:175), or Hugo Krauss, murdered in December 1943 at Camp Hearne in Texas (Waters 2004:124–131).

Fig. 7.5 Kildrummy Camp circa 1941. Courtesy of Cliff Pike

The central difference between the two camps is the level of restrictive enclosure. At Macoul, there was a simple wire fence. However, this was a standard wire fence designed to stop livestock wandering, and certainly not designed to restrict the passage of humans. There is a similarity in that the fences of both camps define the area of the camp, that which was "inside" and that which was "outside." However, the difference can be seen in the psychologies at work. At Deaconsbank, the wire of the enclosures, just at any other PoW camp during the Second World War, was forbidden to the prisoners. To cross the line into the restricted area leading to the fence was to step into mortal danger. All prisoners knew that the exclusion zone was forbidden and that they could be shot on sight by entering it. There are examples of prisoners, presumably suffering from depression or post-traumatic stress, deliberately walking into the exclusion zone, ignoring warnings, in order to provoke the guards into shooting them.

The difference arises in the implications of those designations. For the foresters, outside represented work, community, really just an extension of inside. For the PoWs, outside could represent freedom, work (but only when escorted to their duties, and therefore symbolically still inside), but it also represented enemy territory and potential physical danger. Even the most self-confident of prisoners would have known that to be outside the wire without permission meant that they would be hunted and potentially killed. The psychological effect of being incarcerated while not knowing what was happening to their families; while having the psychological blow of having been defeated and captured; and where frequently life inside the camp could be dangerous because of the internal Nazi organization; all of this could create a very negative and depressed state of mind. Some prisoners thrived, however, and there are several accounts available where the prisoners describe the relief of knowing that they were now out of the war and no longer in danger (for an example from the United States, see Waters 2004).

Fear, Control, and Repression

The architecture and design of the PoW camp was focused on the control and supervision of the inmates; for the forestry camp, the overriding principle was utility and convenience of access. There is nothing about the layout of the forestry camp to suggest an attempt at controlling the activities of the young men living there. They were active in the local community, as various newspaper reports indicate, participating in community events, getting into fights, marrying local girls, and being arrested. The inmates of Deaconsbank had far less impact on the local community; they worked on farms and in factories, but they had no interaction with the local community and were under constant supervision. As a result, the local newspapers have little to say about them.

The main incident that caused comment was the accidental death of an Italian prisoner on January 3, 1945, who was knocked down on the road in the blackout coming back from work (Swan and Scott 2005:13). The irony is that, as an Italian, he was under a looser regime and was not under guard; otherwise, he might have lived. The regime for the Germans was much stricter: WO/32/11687 stated that a ratio of 15% guards was needed for German PoWs, in contrast to the 5% required for the Italians; the camps were also considered to require additional secure boundaries. Even in the period after the war, the Germans were still considered a potential threat because of the unreconstructed Nazis—this meant that German prisoners of war continued to be detained in Britain under armed guard until 1947 in some cases.

It is undoubtedly the case that German PoWs were considered dangerous and engendered a degree of nervousness in the British population. The architecture of the camps reflects this; they were isolated as far as possible from British life, with the interior of the camp providing everything that they might need. This included good sanitation to reduce the risk of disease that had always characterized prison camps of an earlier era. The camps were located away from population centers and away from coasts and major lines of communication. The layout was designed to ensure that the guards could observe what the prisoners were doing and to be able to control their activities. However, there was no attempt to repress the prisoners, to break them down, or to change them other than through education. There was no attempt to limit their sensory experiences beyond the fact of their incarceration, or to overload them. This contrasts with more recent approaches used in Stammheim Prison, or Camp Delta at Guantánamo Bay, which ironically echoes back to Jeremy Bentham's prison designs and the belief of nineteenth-century reformers that they could change the character of inmates through the architecture of the prisons (Casella 2007; Myers 2010). In contrast, the PoW camp was designed to detain and control the inmates. There was no attempt to alter them through the environment in which they lived. Efforts of reform were limited to education and denazification.

Deaconsbank and Macoul Camp were both designed to accommodate an alien population, and to do so hygienically and without risk of disease. Neither was designed to change the inmates or alter their behavior: there was no attempt at blatant repression. The difference is in control. The prison camp controlled the lives of the inmates, determining where they could move and when; it also acted to remove them from the world and replace the outside world with a self-contained environment. The forestry camp was purely accommodation and work, and the lack of facilities on site ensured that the denizens remained a part of the world outside and were never isolated from it. The key differences between the types of accommodation are the control mechanisms and the level of facilities; the PoW camp has high levels of both in its role of control.

Conclusion

The two sites are very different, one being a prison and the other more of a home. The lives of the inmates were very different too, despite the fact that both groups were involved in manual labor on behalf of the British war effort. Life for the German prisoners was restricted, controlled, and regulated. Apart from work, their lives were entirely encompassed by the wire of the fence. The foresters had no such boundaries and were fully engaged with the communities around them—they were accepted in a way that the Germans were not. Both sites had fences around them, but the purpose of the fences was very different. In both camps, the fence was a demarcation between inside and outside, but for the PoWs, it also represented the difference between freedom and restriction, and to a lesser extent, life and death. Crossing the barrier could result in them being shot, while being inside meant that they were no longer part of the war.

Despite the fact that the treatment of the German PoWs was clearly governed at least partially by fear on the part of the British, it does not appear that the architecture reflects that fear. The camps that accommodated the Germans were largely those previously occupied by Italians, so they tended not to have been purpose built for them. Consequently, the design and layout was more practical than repressive. Where the fear factor was expressed was in the far higher ratio of guards for the Germans, the segregation of prisoners according to perceptions of how ardent their Nazism was, and the active attempts to change their ideological outlook through denazification. For all the prisoners, German and Italian alike, the architecture of the camp was designed to keep them under control, to ensure that the guards would be able to control any problems that arose. It was not designed as punishment, as a tool of repression. The requirements of the Geneva Convention were paramount in a way that the current inmates at Guantánamo Bay would surely envy.

Acknowledgments I thank Bob Scott, Dave Sneddon, Dave Swan, and Bob Will for the work that they put into the original projects and for the amount of information that they provided for this paper. I would also like to thank the staff of the National Archives at Kew Gardens for their assistance with the documentary research, and to Adrian Myers and Gabriel Moshenska for organizing the World Archaeology Congress session at which the original paper was presented. I would also like to thank Tony Pollard for his encouragement.

References

Aparicio, A., P. Maguire, A. Gonzalez-Ruibal, C. Suárez, A. Maqua, and J. Calvo 2008 Arquelogía de los Destacamentos Penales Franquistas an el Ferrocarril Madrid-Burgos: El caso de Bustarviejo. *Complutum* 19: 175–195.

Buchner, C. and E. Albertson 2005 An Example of PoW Camp Archaeology in Arkansas. *Arkansas Archaeological Society Field Notes* 1(324): 9–13.

Bush, D. 2009 Maintaining or Mixing Southern Culture in a Northern Prison: Johnson's Island Military Prison. In *The Archaeology of Institutional Life*, edited by A. Beisaw and J. Gibb, pp. 153–171. University of Alabama Press, Tuscaloosa.

Casella, E. 2007 *The Archaeology of Institutional Confinement*. University Press of Florida, Gainesville.

Cooper, J. 2008 *Scottish Renaissance Armies, 1513–1550*. Osprey Publishing, Oxford.

Curran, T. 1987 *They Also Served: The Newfoundland Overseas Forestry Unit, 1939–1946*. Jepherson Press, Newfoundland.

Daly, G. 2004 Napoleon's Lost Legions: French Prisoners of War in Britain, 1803–1814. *History* 89: 361–380.

Doyle, P., L.E. Babits, and J. Pringle (2007) "For You the War Is Over": Finding the Great Escape Tunnel at Stalag Luft III. In *Fields of Conflict Battlefield: Archaeology from the Roman Empire to the Korean War*, edited by D. Scott, L. Babits, and C. Hecker, pp. 398–416. Praeger Security International, Westport.

Grainger, J. 1997 *Cromwell Against the Scots: The Last Anglo-Scottish War, 1650–1652*. Tuckwell Press, East Linton.

Hellen, I. 1999 Temporary Settlements and Transient Populations: The Legacy of Britain's Prisoner of War Camps, 1940–1948. *Erdkunde* 53: 191–219.

Kilford, C. 2004 *On the Way! The Military History of Lethbridge, Alberta (1914 1945) and The Untold Story of Ottawa's Plan to De-Nazify and Democratise German Prisoners of War Held in Lethbridge and Canada During the Second World War*. Trafford Publishing, Bloomington.

Kola, A. 2000 *Belzec: The Nazi Camp for Jews in the Light of Archaeological Sources. Excavations 1997–1999*. United States Holocaust Memorial Museum, Washington.

Lowry, B. 1998 *20th Century Defences in Britain: An Introductory Guide. Handbook of the Defence of Britain Project*. Council for British Archaeology, York.

McAtackney, L. 2005a Long Kesh: An Archaeological Opportunity. *British Archaeology* 84: 11–15.

McAtackney, L. 2005b What Can Archaeology Tell us About the Maze Site? *Archaeology Ireland* 19: 22–24.

Moore, B. 1996 Axis Prisoners of War in Britain During the Second World War. In *Prisoners of War and Their Captors in WWII*, edited by B. Moore and K. Federovich, Berg, Oxford.

Myers, A. 2008 Between Memory and Materiality: An Archaeological Approach to Studying the Nazi Concentration Camps. *Journal of Conflict Archaeology* 4: 231–245.

Myers, A. 2010 Camp Delta, Google Earth and the Ethics of Remote Sensing in Archaeology. *World Archaeology* 4(3): 455–467.

Passingham, W.J. 1941 We Visit a Scottish Lumber Camp. *Illustrated London News*, Feb 8 1941.

Prentice, G. and M. Prentice 2000 Far from the Battlefield: Archaeology at Andersonville. In *Archaeological Perspectives on the American Civil War*, edited by C. Geier and S. Potter, pp. 166–187. University of Florida Press, Gainesville.

Purbrick, L. 2006 Long Kesh/Maze, Northern Ireland: Public Debate as Historical Interpretation. In *Re-mapping the Field: New Approaches in Conflict Archaeology*, edited by J. Schofield, A. Klausmeier, and L. Purbrick, pp. 72–80. Westkreuz-Verlag, Berlin/Bonn.

Smallman-Raynor, M. and A.D. Cliff 2002 The Geographical Transmission of Smallpox in the Franco-Prussian War: Prisoner of War Camps and Their Impact upon Epidemic Diffusion Processes in the Civil Settlement System of Prussia, 1870–1871. *Medical History* 46: 241–264.

Sneddon, D. 2007 Newfoundlanders in a Highland Forest During WWII. *Journal of Conflict Archaeology* 3: 235–268.

Swan, D. and R. Scott 2005 *Deaconsbank*. GUARD Report 1772. University of Glasgow, Glasgow.

Thomas, R. 2003a PoW Camps: What Survives and Where. *Conservation Bulletin* 44: 18–21.

Thomas, R. 2003b *Prisoner of War Camps (1939–1948)*. Project Report, Twentieth Century Military Recording Project. English Heritage, London.

Thoms, A. (ed.) 2000 *Uncovering Camp Ford: Archaeological Interpretations of a Confederate Prisoner-of-War Camp in East Texas*. Centre for Ecological Archaeology, Texas A&M University, College Station.

Thoms, A. 2004 Sand Blows Desperately: Landuse History and Site Integrity at Camp Ford, a Confederate POW Camp in East Texas. *Historical Archaeology* 38(4): 72–92.

Waiser, B. 1995 *Park Prisoners: The Untold Story of Western Canada's National Parks, 1915–1946*. Fifth House, Saskatoon.

Waters, M. 2004 *Lone Star Stalag: German Prisoners of War at Camp Hearne*. Texas A&M University Press, College Station.

Wolff, H. 1974 Die Deutsche Kriegsgefangenen in Britischer Hand. In *Zur Geschichte der Deutsche Kriegsgefangenen des Zweiten Weltkrieges*, edited by E. Maschke. Volume XI/I. Verlag Ernst und Werner Gieseking, Bielefeld.

Wonders, W.C. 1987 The Canadian Forestry Corps in Scotland During World War II. *Scottish Geographical Journal* 103(1): 21–31.

Chapter 8
Engraving and Embroidering Emotions Upon the Material Culture of Internment

Gillian Carr

Abstract During the German occupation of the Channel Islands during the Second World War, around 2,200 Channel Islanders were deported to civilian internment camps in Germany and Austria. This chapter explores the range of objects and artworks that these internees made out of scavenged materials. The items represent experiences of deportation and internment, and through them, internees expressed their emotions, frustrations, homesickness, and boredom.

Abbreviations

BRCMA British Red Cross Museum and Archive
ICRC International Committee of the Red Cross
JA Jersey Archives

Introduction

During the Second World War, about 2,200 Channel Islanders were deported from their homes to civilian internment camps in Germany in retaliation for British deportation and internment of Germans working in Iran. The emotional lives of these deported islanders are partially accessible through the diaries, memoirs, and letters of their period of incarceration. Though writing was an important part of daily life for many, it was not their only way of passing the time behind barbed wire.

One of the chief problems of incarcerated life was boredom, and this soon led to depression and a variety of psychological problems for some. However, soon after the first Red Cross parcels started to arrive from December 1942 onwards, the Channel Islanders started to recycle the contents of their parcels to make a variety of items to pass the time. The cardboard parcels themselves were used for shoe soles, and the parcel string was plaited and crocheted to make hats and handbags,

G. Carr (✉)
Institute of Continuing Education, University of Cambridge, Cambridge, UK
e-mail: gcc20@cam.ac.uk

A. Myers, G. Moshenska (eds.), *Archaeologies of Internment*, One World Archaeology,   129
DOI 10.1007/978-1-4419-9666-4_8, © Springer Science+Business Media, LLC 2011

and a variety of other fashion accessories. Food tins were engraved, or flattened and turned into plates and trays, and the coloured strips of cellophane used as packing material was woven into the parcel string handbags to add designs. The packing crates themselves were used to make everything from chess sets to armchairs, dolls houses and deck chairs. This chapter explores the range of objects and artwork made by the Channel Islander internees during their incarceration. These items speak of the individual and communal experiences of deportation and internment. They also eloquently reflect and embody the emotions experienced during this period, and were made using only the raw materials of the Red Cross food parcels and what art materials were passed on to the internees through the YMCA.

Recyclia and Internment Material Culture

The study of civilian internment material culture and art is now well established (Archer 2004:156–165; Becker 2004; Cresswell 1994, 2005; Dusselier 2008; Hinrichsen 1993; Müller-Härlin 2005). For the Channel Island deportees, items made by men, women and children of all ages and social backgrounds survive. Every item is unique, each with its own biography, and we can sometimes learn of these through oral testimony, letters, diaries and memoirs. They are potent items that convey the psychological conditions of civilians in internment camps.

The arts and crafts made in the internment camps discussed here can be conceptually categorised as trench art (Saunders 2003:11). As the recycled contents of PoW Red Cross parcels, they are very much associated temporally and spatially with armed conflict. Most trench art is, by definition, "recyclia" (Saunders 2003:183–186), and this chapter describes how tins, string, paper, cardboard and cellophane were recycled to make new things. The PoWs turned the waste packaging of food intended to preserve physical health into new items, which in turn preserved mental and emotional health. The very act of making new objects was therapeutic, and the majority of items made were able to calm frayed nerves by consuming time and distracting internees from their circumstances. When Britain sent food parcels to her subjects interned abroad, those subjects were able to use the food packaging to recreate the world they had lost or left behind. Dusselier (2008) has interpreted these kinds of objects as "artefacts of loss", as they represented or replaced items that could not be carried by the PoWs into internment.

Close inspection of items of PoW recyclia enables us to perceive the raw materials, and thus sometimes the original objects, from which the recycled items were made. This double vision allows former internees in the Channel Islands to perceive these objects as dual memory objects, prompting recollections of both their relationship with the recycled, finished object, and the materials out of which they were made. These artefacts, so redolent with memory and emotion, are rarely put on display: they are, instead, kept in cupboards and attics, and seldom brought out for handling. While this has preserved them well, it has also meant that the relatives of internees are not well acquainted with either the items or their meanings. This has resulted in the consequent loss of value of these objects within families—many items have been thrown away over the years; others have been purchased by collectors, or given to Island archives and museums, and have lost their associated stories.

Historical Background

The occupation of the Channel Islands and the subsequent deportation of many of its citizens is little known outside the islands themselves. In the spring and early summer of 1940, German forces rapidly invaded and occupied much of Western Europe. Norway, Denmark, Holland, Belgium, Luxemburg and France fell. By June, the British Channel Islands, which lie within sight of the French coast in the Bay of St. Malo, were within easy striking distance. From the middle of that month, panic and chaos reigned as tens of thousands of islanders evacuated. This atmosphere was exacerbated by the arrival, in the islands, of French refugees and wounded soldiers fleeing Dunkirk. The ensuing demilitarisation left the islanders vulnerable, and the sight and sound of explosions from the direction of Cherbourg added to their fears. On 28 June 1940 St. Peter Port and St. Helier, the capitals of Guernsey and Jersey, respectively, were bombed and within a few days the Channel Islands were occupied by the Germans. They were the only British soil captured by the Germans, and provided a propaganda coup for the Nazis.

For the first couple of years, despite the growing rationing of food, fuel and raw materials, and the increasing hunger of islanders, most people saw the behaviour of the occupiers as "correct". This perspective changed in the second half of 1942 due to three events: the confiscation of radio sets in June; the arrival, from August, of thousands of slave labourers working for the Organisation Todt (OT), who were treated with great cruelty; and the announcement of deportation to Germany for English-born island men aged between 16 and 70, along with their families (Willmot 2005). This category of people was targeted as a reprisal for the British deportation and internment in Australia of around 500 German technicians and engineers who were working in neutral Iran (Harris 1979:2). Germany was an important trading partner of Iran and there were German civilian communities within the country. The British were worried that these German residents might seize or sabotage the valuable oil fields to prevent the Allies from using them. In August 1941, the British and Russians jointly invaded the country (Remfrey 2002:5).

There were two waves of civilian deportations from the Channel Islands, in September 1942 and then February 1943. The second wave included Jews, Freemasons, former officers who had served in the First World War, and those who had upset the German administration in some way and had spent time in prison for offences against the occupying authorities. A group of people from Sark were also included in the second wave of deportations because the Germans suspected that the British commando raid, which had taken place on the island several months previously, had received local help.

The deported islanders were put aboard overcrowded boats and shipped to mainland France. Many had been forced to sell or give away their houses, pets and possessions. Once in St. Malo, they were loaded onto trains. They travelled for several days with only the clothes they stood in, and a suitcase of items such as utensils, clothes and blankets, which had been stipulated in the instructions in the deportation order (Harris 1979:9–14). For those deported in February 1943, during the train journey from St. Malo, men under 65 years old were placed in the front of the train, and the older men, women and children were placed in the rear. Without warning, the train was decoupled. The younger men were taken to Laufen Camp, and the women and older men went to the vast transit camp of Compiègne, just outside Paris (Harris 1979:33), which was already packed with thousands of French Jews on their way to death camps in the East. The islanders lived for 3 months in this sad camp before being sent to Biberach. The younger men with relatives in this family camp joined them in August of 1943 amid much celebration. The majority of the 2,200 deportees from the Channel Islands were eventually spread between four camps in southern Germany: Biberach (mostly Guernsey families), Schloss Wurzach (for Jersey families), Schloss Laufen (for single men) and Liebenau (for single women).

Communal Living

Despite living in small and close-knit communities in the Channel Islands, nothing could prepare the deportees for life within internment camps in southern Germany. A letter from Yvonne Sinclair in Biberach, written in June 1944, and published in the *Channel Islands Monthly Review* (CIMR) describes the camp thus:

> Imagine long white buildings with two rings of high barbed wire, gravel, 1,000 odd people all of different classes, mix them up and there you have us. No quiet, no peace ever, nowhere to go to be alone, no privacy of any sort. When it's over we want to hide away from everyone for a while. (Sinclair 1944:71)

Communal living took some getting used to. In her diary entry for 18 June 1943, Joan Coles wrote that it was

> Nine months ago today since we left Jersey. I have come to the conclusion that communal living, as a system, is impossible. Perhaps it is the conditions under which we are forced to live, but there seems to be so much unrest and bad feeling amongst both men and women, that feuds are very constantly occurring. Even the children have got right out of hand, in spite of daily schooling. The feeling of fellowship in distress seems to have vanished and, sad to relate, I have become ashamed of the conduct of my fellow countrymen. (Coles 1985).

Some internees found themselves quickly adapting to institutional life. As Eileen and Ron Harris wrote from Biberach camp on 17 November 1943,

> the only snag is being surrounded by barbed wire, but strangely enough the body and mind seen to grow accustomed to any kind of restraint in time. I sometimes think that in order to feel at home when the happy days of peace arrive, it will be necessary to seek accommodation at Colney Hatch or Pentonville. (BRCMA 2378)

Some people were able to adjust to their circumstances, but the incessant noise and chatter of communal, overcrowded rooms and lack of privacy were more problematic for others. One of the most popular types of artefacts to be made from the raw materials of the Red Cross parcel was the trinket box. As a private possession for storing personal items, this seemed to form a kind of material antidote to communal life lived perpetually under the gaze of other people. These boxes were most commonly made from small Red Cross food tins. The colourful cellophane strips that were found within British parcels, used as packing material to protect the tins from getting dented, were crocheted by internee Nellie Faulder to form a decorative sleeve that covered the tin (Fig. 8.1). Boxes were made out of wood, and needlework, knitting, crocheting or plaiting using string or cellophane. Parcel-string baskets were made by Bill Grimshaw in Wurzach camp, who adapted a traditional basket-weaving technique used by fishermen in the Channel Islands to make crab pots.

Fig. 8.1 Trinket box made by Nellie May Faulder. Courtesy of Jersey Heritage Collections

In his many greetings cards, camp artist Thomas Webber often reused and reworked rhyming couplets. A recurring theme described the need to remain cheerful and to show the Germans that they knew no fear, as exemplified by the following stanza: *We hide our tears, we tried to smile / Although it's hard, dear, to bear the trial.* The same sentiments are revealed in a Laufen version of Rudyard Kipling's poem, *If*, composed by a man known only to us today by his initials S.G.S. It contained the verse: *If you can do a coal fatigue / And shovel with a smile, / And scrub the stairs, or peel the spuds / A-grinning all the while*, ending with *If you can do these things I've named / And still come smiling through, / Then you're a blessed marvel, lad – / I'll give my place to you!* A poem about Dorsten Camp contains the lines: *We've learned a lot since in this spot / About our fellow creatures; / We close our eyes, we mask surprise / And guard our tongues and features* (Dickinson archive JA 1095).

Some were able to channel their feelings through their pen, in diaries and letters, and others wielded a paintbrush as their tool of choice. Those who made craft items found that through these artistic media they were able to express emotions that otherwise had to be kept in check, and that had no other acceptable outlet in a fraught and overcrowded internment camp. The variety of art and craftwork produced reified the emotions of internees, enabling them to find an outlet in a medium that could safely be made public. A watercolour by Wurzach artist Peter Hutton illustrates the value of a creative outlet for expressing pent-up emotions (Fig. 8.2).

Fig. 8.2 Watercolour from Wurzach by Peter Hutton. Courtesy of Gwen Bisson

Homesickness and Identity

Boxes were also useful artefacts on which to embroider or engrave aspects of personal identity. A finely plaited parcel string box was made in Liebenau camp, the lid of which was made of dyed string woven in the shape of a Union Jack. In Wurzach, a box was made out of Red Cross packing crate wood, using only a table knife and a piece of glass as tools, held in place with pins taken from the crate, and varnished with nail varnish. The box was painted with an image of a traditional English cottage, complete with a thatched roof and a cobbled path leading up to the front door. Such generic scenes of rural English idyll, centred on the traditional country cottage, were fairly common in the camps.

We should not be surprised that the images were of England rather than the Channel Islands; the majority of interned men were deported specifically because of their English birth. These images crop up on a variety of different items, often unexpectedly and incongruously. For example, a number of Christmas cards depict a traditional English village, complete with a church spire and houses with leaded windows, roses around the front door and not a hint of either snow or winter. An example of such a card was painted in Laufen, and depicts a country village in the middle of summer, with hollyhocks in full bloom (Fig. 8.3). This type of card was a generic scene of home, betraying the homesickness of the maker; thus, it made a meaningful present when given to other internees, especially given the grave shortages of paper in the camps at various times.

Fig. 8.3 Christmas card made in Laufen. Courtesy of the German Occupation Museum, Guernsey

Images of a traditional English home also crop up on badges and embroidered postcards (Fig. 8.4). Joan Coles, interned in Wurzach, was skilled in embroidery and needlework, and regularly produced items for the camp exhibitions of arts and crafts. At least three of her embroidered miniature pictures, a postcard and two little brooches, show English country cottages with flowers around the doorway.

Images of the Channel Islands are also relatively numerous, and can be interpreted in the same way as images of home. What is remarkable about these is that, in contrast to the generic English villages and cottages drawn from the

Fig. 8.4 Postcard made by Joan Coles in Wurzach. Courtesy of Jersey Heritage Collections

imagination, they depict specific island landmarks and were drawn from memory. Examples of this include two badges made from knots of wood, which depict the Corbière lighthouse and Janvrin's tomb in Jersey.

Greeting cards and watercolours were also popular media for depicting landmarks. A very detailed pen and ink sketch of Castle Cornet in Guernsey was drawn on a 1944 Biberach wedding anniversary card, but the most impressive artwork in this category was a painting by Sark artist Ethel Cheeswright. This was made as a thank-you gift for a German doctor in the town of Biberach, who had helped internees in the camp. It is among Cheeswright's most beautiful paintings and depicts a view of the cliffs of Sark, covered in spring flowers. Her views of the Channel Islands painted in the camp were reported in the "letters to the editor" section of the September 1943 issue of the CIMR which have "moistened the eyes of the ladies a little" (Fig. 8.5).

Another way in which the islanders were able to bring thoughts home into the camps was to set about transforming a part of the grey and drab campgrounds inside the barbed wire into a traditional English (or Channel Island) country garden, made possible by gifts of seeds from the Royal Horticultural Society. Two watercolours painted by internees show the results at Biberach: the first, by Sidney Skillett, shows a garden in full-bloom sunflowers growing side by side with lettuces and cauliflowers, with the barracks in the background. This garden brought considerable cheer to the camp (Garland 1945). One of Ethel Cheeswright's paintings shows a pleasant view of the camp with neat grass and flowerbeds in full bloom (Fig. 8.6). Such colour paintings give a gentler view of the camp especially when compared to the black-and-white photographs of Biberach.

Fig. 8.5 Painting of Sark by
Ethel Cheeswright.
Photograph by the author

Fig. 8.6 Painting of Biberach camp by Ethel Cheeswright. Courtesy of the German Occupation Museum, Guernsey

Confinement by Barbed Wire

The landscape beyond the barbed wire was also commonly depicted in artwork and artefacts made in camp. It represented a landscape of longing the first stage of what would, one day, be the journey home. This was particularly apparent at

Biberach, where the view of the *Wieland Linde*, a linden tree visible from the camp and planted by eighteenth-century Biberachian poet and writer Christophe Wieland to mark his engagement, occurs in several paintings, drawings and engravings done in camp.

Internee Byll Balcombe was known for his engraved German army-issue aluminium mugs which he made as gifts to other internees on special occasions, such as Easter, christenings, births, and wedding anniversaries, using a broken knitting needle and an old nail (Carr 2008). The Wieland Linde was, for him, a popular motif to symbolise love on wedding anniversary gifts. The tree was usually depicted alongside barbed wire in the foreground, perhaps showing his frustration at being interned and unable to wander at will beyond the camp.

Barbed wire featured on other artefacts and artwork in the camps, and was even used as jewellery. There was a brief enthusiasm in Biberach for wearing barbed wire brooches. It is not known whether these were made from actual barbed wire or hand-made barbs twisted and knotted using wire from another source; however, their use as personal adornments worn in full view of the guards makes an interesting statement. It is not clear whether they represented a statement of defiance: "interned but proud" against their captors, or whether the intention was to turn something that was hated and ugly into something that was desired and attractive. It could also have acted as a sign of what Winter (1999:46) calls "fictive kinship", or of belonging to the "association of internees"—a sign of communal identity still in use in the Channel Islands today.

Pride, Defiance, and the V-Sign

It is clear that pride in "being British" and keeping up morale was important in camp. Although this was done by displaying flags on lapels, hanging them on barrack room walls and incorporating them and patriotic colours into greetings cards, the activity which boosted morale most of all in camp was symbolic resistance.

In the Channel Island camps internees expressed their defiance against the occupiers through material culture. One of the most interesting ways in which this was carried out was through the "V-for-Victory" campaign, which was launched by the BBC's European Service in 1941 (Rolo 1943:136–139; Tangye Lean 1943:82), and was heard in the Channel Islands. The campaign encouraged the occupied peoples of Europe to chalk the letter V on walls to symbolise an Allied victory and to make the Germans feel that they were surrounded by a hostile resistance army. The campaign was later expanded to include the V-sound as well, using the Morse code for the letter V. People were encouraged to make this sound in public by clapping hands, ringing bells or knocking on doors. Beethoven's Fifth (or "V") Symphony was also used in the campaign because of the "*da-da-da-dum*" opening bars, which recalled the dot-dot-dot-dash of the letter "V" in Morse code (Blades 1977:179). The campaign was hugely successful until the Germans appropriated the letter V and started to use it to their own ends, proclaiming that it represented a German victory, and that those who used it were supporting them. Although this caused the campaign to peter out in some places, it went underground in the Channel Islands, and resurfaced in the internment camps of Germany, among other places.

The material culture brought home from the camps makes it clear that the V-sign campaign was renewed behind barbed wire by the internees. The question immediately arises as to what extent the guards were aware of this movement. There are two things to bear in mind: the first is that the Islanders had bribed the guards not to interfere too greatly in camp life using Red Cross chocolate, soap and cigarettes (Michael Ginns personal communication); the second is that people in Germany were forbidden from listening to the BBC or other foreign news services in case they were "infected" by the enemy propaganda (Rolo 1943:121; Sanders 2004:113), although it is not known to what extent this was obeyed. This order was mainly aimed at soldiers posted to occupied countries who could tune in more easily to the BBC.

Thus, the guards at the camps of Biberach, Wurzach, Laufen and Liebenau were unlikely to have been entirely aware of the V-signs in camp, nor would they necessarily have recognised the Vs for what they were if they saw them; all the Vs produced were encoded or hidden. If the guards were unaware of the signs or unlikely to react if they did see them, then why did the internees bother to produce such symbols of defiance? Not only was the act of resistance important for their self-respect and consumed some of the long hours which weighed heavily on their shoulders, it also created an invisible bond of solidarity with their friends and family

Fig. 8.7 Pencil sketch of Monty Manning by Eric Sirett. Courtesy of Peter Sirett

back in the Channel Islands. Together, they were defying the Germans, even if they were kept apart.

The most inventive examples of the V-signs made in the camps include a beard and moustache worn in a V-shape by Biberach internee Monty Manning; his likeness was captured in a pencil portrait by fellow internee and artist Eric Sirett (Fig. 8.7). In Wurzach, as at other camps, shoes were soled with plaited parcel string. One surviving shoe has a V-sign woven into the sole. A third example is an embroidered tablecloth, clearly dedicated with a monogram and crown in the centre to George V; coloured Vs are also embroidered all along the edges. Such a piece of needlework could easily go unnoticed as an item of symbolic defiance unless one was aware that George VI was the reigning monarch at that time.

Fighting Depression and Consuming Time

Finding ways to consume time and mentally evade the barbed wire, to avoid "lageritis" as it was called in Laufen, was key to enduring life in an internment camp. Although some struggled with this (e.g. Harris 1979:82), and battled debilitating depression in camp, as is clear from letters written while interned, others soon realised that keeping busy was all-important for their sanity. Although sports, theatre, music and educational activities were popular pastimes, people found that when they were back in the barrack rooms after a football match, a class, a play or a dance, they still had to contend with the worries and fear which ate away at their peace of mind. How long would the war last? Would they ever go home or see their loved ones again? What would happen to them if Germany won the war? Oral testimony, diary entries, and art and artefacts made in the camp show that finding a way to stop these thoughts became a priority for camp inmates.

The most effective items to make in these circumstances were those that consumed large amounts of time both to make and use, such as board games. Despite the help of the YMCA in sending equipment for indoor and outdoor games to internment camps, there were never enough packs of cards or dominoes to go round. So Islanders made their own, as can be illustrated by three examples. The first is a carved chess set, complete with a full set of painted pieces, made in Biberach from the wood of Red Cross packing crates (Fig. 8.8). The hinges of the chessboard were made from a food tin. The second is the example of a "shove ha'penny" board, which was made in Wurzach out of Red Cross packing crates. The hardboard was rubbed smooth with boot polish from next-of-kin parcels, and real ha'pennies were collected from various people and rubbed smooth on the steps of the schloss using saliva as a lubricant (Ginns personal communication). Cribbage boards were also made in the camps. One, now on display in the Channel Islands Military Museum in Jersey, was made of wood from a Red Cross packing crate; another, in private ownership in Sark, was made from a strip of leather with holes for the pegs. The name of the camp and the camp number of the owner were stamped into the leather. A third, also in private ownership, was made from a Red Cross biscuit tin pinned onto a wooden board, with broken knitting needles used as gaming pieces.

Fig. 8.8 Chess set made from Red Cross parcel crate wood. Courtesy of Mark Norman

Making board games seems to have been the preserve of the men of the camp, perhaps because it involved woodworking. My research has shown that the women tended to be more involved in needlework and many used their dressmaking skills in converting the old or second-hand clothes donated by the Red Cross. These clothes were vital to internees: while most deportees had packed trunks of clothes to be sent on after them, not all had arrived. After more than 2 years of rationing and extreme shortages during occupation, not everyone had plentiful supplies of clothes to pack in 1942 and 1943, and few of good quality. Many relied on next-of-kin parcels sent by relatives in the United Kingdom and the Channel Islands, but others spent their time adapting Red Cross clothes to fit themselves, their husbands, their growing children and even their children's dolls.

Making and clothing dolls was a pastime for a number of women. One internee of Wurzach, Florence Fish, made as many as 100 Heidi dolls. When she left one of these to the British Red Cross archives in London, she enclosed a note saying that she had made them from scraps of material provided by fellow internees. The hair, hat and basket of the doll were made from parcel string and the doll's socks were made from bandages. She also wrote to the curators that the reason she began making the dolls was that

> we had 200 children with us, mostly little girls. They, at that time, had nothing to play with so I started collecting scraps of material and that is how it all began . . . the only pleasant thing that stays in my memory are the faces of the little girls when they had their dollies, even though they were only rag ones. (BRCMA)

Women made a range of fashion accessories from the recycled Red Cross parcels. The most popular of these were belts made from folded cellophane cigarette wrappers (some with matching bracelets). Women also used strips of coloured cellophane to crochet colourful handbags. Summer hats made from parcel string were also known in the camps, as were summer sandals made from string soles and cellophane uppers. We know from sketches made by Mr Fish in Wurzach that Easter bonnets were also popular.

Sports and Theatre

Wurzach internee Joan Coles recorded in her diary on 27 April 1943 that the camp sports day was "one of the happiest days in the camp" since her arrival (Coles 1985:44). The material culture associated with these kinds of occasions include the hand-painted certificates for various races, and also the trophies that were made from recycled and engraved Red Cross food tins, as Edna Dorrian described in her diary.

Makeshift theatres were set up in all Channel Islander internment camps and plays and variety shows were well attended. Large numbers of theatre programmes and posters survive from all camps, made by the camp artists. In Biberach, the 'flats' or stage scenery were made from Red Cross packing cases. A sketch of a Biberach stage set by artist William Sandwith noted that the set was constructed from Red Cross cartons, packing cases, packing wrappers and various camp oddments. The theatre provided much entertainment for the internees and made them forget about being behind barbed wire for a short period. As Preston John Doughty said in his Wurzach internment diary after attending a performance on 26 September 1943, "although the Germans have got us behind barbed wire, they cannot stop us from smiling and enjoying ourselves" (JA ref. L/C/46/A/2).

Liberation and Repatriation

The happiness expressed on occasion during interned life was eclipsed during the spring of 1945 when the camps were liberated. This took place at different times in different places. For those in Biberach, Wurzach and Liebenau, it was the 23rd, 28th and 29th of April, respectively, and all were liberated by Free French troops. Those in Laufen were liberated on 4 May by the Americans. After their release, the former internees took the opportunity to explore the local landscape and towns and visit their friends in other camps by bicycle.

Two pieces of work dating from the period of liberation and repatriation stand out. The first is a greetings card made in Wurzach by Harold Hepburn for Jersey internee Pamela Tanguy. Hepburn's style is usually recognised by his images of schloss Wurzach filling the frame, with the inclusion of RAF spitfires in one corner, and German helmets and a swastika pennant in the other. This dual symbolism was so that, if ever he was challenged by a guard, he couldn't be accused of disseminating British propaganda (Michael Ginns, personal communication). However, on the card that celebrates repatriation, the hierarchy of the images are reversed and the German symbols have vanished. Dominating the frame is an airplane flying the internees back home and the schloss and town of Wurzach are reduced to tiny buildings in the background. The smoke trail of the plane reads "Goodbye Wurzach!" and one can almost sense the victorious air-punching of the artist as he paints the longed-for farewell to the days of internment.

A second item which celebrates liberation is a shell case left behind by fleeing German soldiers and engraved by Byll Balcombe in Biberach. The shell case is engraved with an image of Guernsey, draped with freesias and inscribed with a prayer in Guernesiaise, the Guernsey patois: *"L'Eternal nous protège! I'nous ordoune, amis, d'aimair la bénite ile ou sa grâce nous a mis!"* (The Eternal protect us! He orders us, friends, to love the blessed isle where his grace settled us!). On the other side, Balcombe engraved an image of the Weberberg, an area of the town often drawn by internees during their confinement. With an image of a rising sun, the caption commemorates the barbed wire entwined names of the internees Tom and Norah Dorrian, for whom the shell case was engraved, and their date of liberation. Balcombe's exaltation at his freedom is seen in the rays of the dawning sun which stretch out to the edges of the shell case, evaporating the strands of barbed wire around the Dorrians' names. The word *liberated* is stretched out beneath the breaking dawn (Fig. 8.9).

Fig. 8.9 Multiple perspectives of a single shell case engraved by Byll Balcombe in Biberach. Courtesy of Graham Jackson

Conclusion

I have shown how the material culture of internment, viewed as the reified articulations of spoken and unspoken emotions, evokes the individual and communal experiences of deportation and internment. It can also reveal the emotions experienced during internment as people expressed their homesickness, their frustrations, their boredom, their depression and, ultimately, their exaltation at liberation into the objects that they made.

Collections of drawings, letters, cards, embroideries, engravings, needlework, metalwork, woodwork and other surviving civilian PoW ephemera can often be of prime importance in giving us an insight into civilian experiences of war. Coupled with oral testimonies, diaries and memoirs we can begin to understand the emotions and experiences of those who are often perceived by their compatriots to have sat out the war in the apparent safety of internment camps, seemingly well-fed by the Red Cross, and saved from the experiences of occupation or bombing suffered by others.

I have also shown here that close inspection of the iconography on some individual artefacts or artwork, such as Balcombe's engraved shell case, Hepburn's greetings cards, or Coles' embroidered badges, are able to speak very clearly of the hopes and desires of the interned. Many of the items discussed here have also had a post-war role as memory objects, able to express the inexpressible on behalf of their owners when telling others of their experiences behind barbed wire.

Acknowledgements The author sincerely thanks the Guernsey Deportee Association, the Jersey ex-Internee Association, the Jersey Heritage Collections, the British Red Cross Museum and Archives, the Cambridge Heritage Research Group, the British Academy, the Société Jersiaise, Tom Remfrey, Michael Ginns, Gillian Lenfesty, Gisela Rothenhäusler, Reinhold Adler, Gwen Bisson, Richard Heaume, Graham Jackson, Mark Norman, Peter Sirett and the heirs of Edna Dorrian.

References

Archer, B. 2004 *The Internment of Western Civilians Under the Japanese 1941–1945: A Patchwork of Internment*. Routledge, London.

Becker, A. 2004 Art, Material Life and Disaster: Civilian and Military Prisoners of War. In *Matters of Conflict: Material Culture, Memory and the First World War*, edited by N. Saunders, pp. 26–34. Routledge, London.

Blades, J. 1977 *Drum Roll: A Professional Adventure from the Circus to the Concert Hall*. Faber and Faber, London.

Carr, G. 2008 The Trench Art of Byll Balcombe of Biberach. *Channel Islands Occupation Review* 36: 131–145.

Coles, J. 1985 *Three Years Behind Barbed Wire*. La Haule Books, Jersey.

Cresswell, Y. 1994 *Living with the Wire: Civilian Internment in the Isle of Man During the Two World Wars*. Manx National Heritage, Douglas.

Cresswell, Y. 2005 Behind the Wire: The Material Culture of Civilian Internment on the Isle of Man in the First World War. In *Totally Un-English? Britain's Internment of 'Enemy Aliens' in Two World Wars*, Yearbook of the Research Centre for German and Austrian Exile Studies 7, edited by R. Dove, pp. 45–61. Rodopi, Amsterdam.

Dorrian, E. n.d. Personal Diary. Guernsey Island Archives. AQ 299/22(1–16).

Doughty, P. n.d. I Was There: Our Trip on the Continent. Jersey Archives. L/C/46/A/2.

Dusselier, J. 2008 *Artifacts of Loss*. Rutgers University Press, New Brunswick.

Garland, G. 1945 A Brief History of the Guernsey Deportees to Dorsten and Biberach, Germany. September 1942–June 1945. Priaulx Library. LF940.53 LEN.

Harris, R. 1979 *Islanders Deported (Part I)*. CISS Publishing, Ilford.

Hinrichsen, K. 1993 Visual Art Behind the Wire. In *The Internment of Enemy Aliens in Twentieth Century Britain*, edited by D. Cesarani and T. Kushner, pp. 188–209. Frank Cass, London.

Müller-Härlin, A. 2005 Fred Uhlman's Internment Drawings. In *Arts in Exile in Britain 1933–1945: Politics and Cultural Identity. The Yearbook of the Research Centre for German and Austrian Exile Studies Volume 6*, edited by S. Behr and M. Malet, pp. 135–163. Rodopi, New York.

Remfrey, T. 2002 The Deportations from the Channel Islands in September 1942 and February 1943. *Channel Islands Occupation Review* 30: 5–14.

Rolo, C. 1943 *Radio Goes to War*. Faber and Faber, London.

Sanders, P. 2004 *The Ultimate Sacrifice*. Jersey Heritage Trust, St. Helier.

Saunders, N. 2003 *Trench Art: Materialities and Memories of War*. Berg, Oxford.

Sinclair, Y. 1944 Channel Island Monthly Review. *Journal of Channel Islands Refugees in Great Britain* 7(4): 71.

Tangye Lean, E. 1943 *Voices in the Darkness: The Story of the European Radio War*. Secker and Warburg, London.

Willmot, L. 2005 Nothing Was Ever the Same Again: Public Attitudes in the Occupied Channel Islands, 1942. *The Local Historian* 35(1): 9–20.

Winter, J. 1999 Forms of Kinship and Remembrance in the Aftermath of the Great War. In *War and Remembrance in the Twentieth Century*, edited by J. Winter and E. Sivan, pp. 40–60. Cambridge University Press, Cambridge.

Chapter 9
Archaeological Investigations of Second World War Prisoner of War Camps at Fort Hood, Texas

Judith Thomas

Abstract Camp Hood and North Camp Hood were two Second World War internment camps for German Prisoners of War (PoWs) located within the boundaries of Fort Hood, Texas. Since the end of the war, the structures assigned to temporary Second World War functions have been mostly destroyed. One camp was eradicated by the continual growth of the Fort Hood cantonment area. The location of the razed second camp is presently vacant and overgrown, but endangered by Fort Hood's future growth. Limited excavations of North Camp Hood Internment Camp and extensive scrutiny of archival documentation have recovered the requisite information to advise that the site is eligible for the National Register of Historic Places. The present military situation of reduced cultural resource funding and the expansion of training facilities, however, threaten to elide this important component of American military heritage. This chapter presents the results of the archaeological investigation of the PoW camp at Fort Hood, and examines the challenges to preserving this vestige of the American Home Front of the Second World War.

Introduction

The American Home Front heritage of the Second World War is fading. The Americans who participated in the Second World War are currently in their 80s and 90s, and this pool of men and women who hold living memories of this global war is rapidly diminishing. Similarly, the United States is losing physical evidence of its participation in the Second World War. With the exception of those in Hawaii, there are no battlefields in America to visit and visually remind us of this most important war. Instead, the tangible evidence of the Second World War in the United States is mostly limited to Home Front support facilities such as defense, production, and mobilization sites, and confinement camps. Scattered unevenly across America,

J. Thomas (✉)
Mercyhurst College, Mercyhurst Archaeological Institute, Erie, PA, USA
e-mail: jthomas@mercyhurst.edu

A. Myers, G. Moshenska (eds.), *Archaeologies of Internment*, One World Archaeology,
DOI 10.1007/978-1-4419-9666-4_9, © Springer Science+Business Media, LLC 2011

these finite heritage resources are certainly as relevant to America's history as are Civil War battlefields (Kelly 2004:34).

Unfortunately, with the passing years many of these historic resources have lost their integrity or disappeared entirely. In 2004, Roger Kelly, in light of the upcoming 60th anniversary of the Second World War, urged cultural resource managers to recognize the importance of America's Home Front heritage. He provides an outline of four major categories of Home Front properties: (1) controlled group camps (including internment camps) for Japanese Americans, military prisons, and "enemy alien" facilities for Axis diplomats and citizens believed to be a threat; (2) military-related facilities for defense, training, logistical operations, armament storage and transport, and battlefields; (3) industrial facilities that include shipyards, airplane assembly plants, and munitions deployment centers; and (4) civilian facilities such as defense-worker housing (Kelly 2004:36).

Kelly further suggests that American cultural resource managers should emulate recent work in Britain, where researchers and preservationists have inventoried extant Second World War era facilities and preserved a Prisoner of War (PoW) camp near Malton in North Yorkshire as a Second World War historical park (Kelly 2004:35). In the United States, the National Park Service has responded by submitting a National Register of Historic Places Multiple Property Documentation Form entitled "World War II and the American Home Front" as a National Historic Landmark Theme Study (Harper et al. 2004). This important study provides the broad historic context and guidelines necessary for assessing a wide variety of Second World War Home Front properties. Building upon the National Park Service work, the Department of Defense's Legacy Resource Management Program completed a historic context specifically for Second World War PoW camps on Department of Defense Installations (Listman et al. 2006).

The most extensive investigation of an American PoW camp was undertaken by Michael Waters of Texas A&M University. Since 1996, the investigations at Camp Hearne, Texas, which housed 3,000 German PoWs, have included archaeological excavations and extensive archival research, the results of which are presented in the book *Lone Star Stalag* (Waters 2004). The excavations at Camp Hearne provide a classic example of the productive interface between archaeology and historic documentation. In this case, the Camp Hearne research illustrates the consistencies and inconsistencies between the emic recall of prisoners and their keepers and the etic reality of the camp as a physical and social entity. Waters' project provides a model not only for the present study, but all examinations of rapidly disappearing Second World War Home Front heritage.

Located in Coryell and Bell Counties, Texas, the US Army's Camp Hood (later renamed Fort Hood) was established in 1943 as a tank training installation. The largest military base in the United States, Camp Hood became the home for two PoW camps during the Second World War: Camp Hood Internment Camp (CHIC) in the southern part of the reservation and North Camp Hood Internment Camp (NCHIC) in the northern sector (Fig. 9.1). In 2006, in response to the high probability of encroachment by the expanding military base, an archaeological investigation of the NCHIC remnants was conducted to assess the integrity of the site.

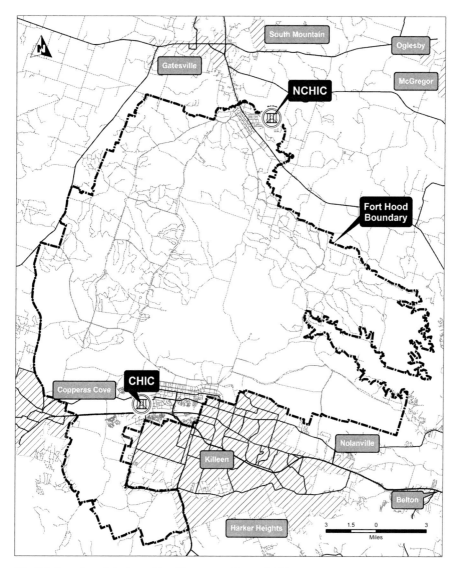

Fig. 9.1 Location of the Camp Hood Internment Camp (CHIC) and North Camp Hood Internment Camp (NCHIC) at Fort Hood, Texas. Prepared by David Pedler using spatial data from the Texas Natural Resources Information System (TNRIS)

Archival Research

Prior to the field investigation at the NCHIC, we conducted an examination of military records housed at the National Archives II in College Park, Maryland. A subsequent visit to the National Archives expanded the research to include information pertaining to CHIC, which was located in the cantonment area of south

Camp Hood. Perusal of primary sources, including letters, orders, memorandums, maps, real property records, and photographs, concerning Camp Hood during the war years revealed that the NCHIC was utilized for only 1 year, 1943–1944, and that CHIC existed throughout the war, closing in 1945. Primary sources at the National Archives Southwest Region in Fort Worth, Texas, and secondary sources, including local and general histories, national historic context studies, and reports of archaeological investigations at other Second World War PoW camps, were also examined. The author also attempted to locate photographs of the NCHIC through the International Committee of the Red Cross in Geneva, Switzerland, but that organization was unable to provide any photographs or other documentation.

A German institution established to assist the relatives of former German Armed Forces personnel housed at the *Deutsche Dienstselle*, Berlin, provided a list of 83 German soldiers imprisoned at Camp Hood (Rettig 2009). The data include the full name of the German soldier, birth date, place of birth, PoW number, rank, regiment, last known address, along with the date and place of death. Additionally, the information traces the prisoners' internment history with PoW camp names, dates, and final discharge location.

Physical Description of Camp Hood According to Archival Sources

Under the jurisdiction of the Provost Marshal General's Office (PMGO), which oversaw all matters pertaining to the operation of the PoW camps, the Corps of Engineers set the construction specifications for the PoW camps and carried out their physical construction. Research by Listman et al. (2006) revealed that the camp required 500 feet (152.4 meters) of unobstructed space outside the perimeter line, which itself consisted of two 8 feet (2.4 meters) tall cyclone wire fences topped with coiled barbed wire. The two fences were spaced 12 feet (3.66 meters) apart. Guard towers were located at the corners, and for larger camps, periodically spaced down the long sides. For the interior, camp plans required an open space of 40 feet (12.2 meters) between all buildings and at least 200 square feet (18.6 square meter) per prisoner for the recreation area. The standard barrack was a single-story, wood-frame building generally sided with tar paper. Measuring 20 feet × 100 feet (6.1 meters × 30.5 meters), the barrack accommodated 50 enlisted personnel at 40 square feet (3.7 square meter) per prisoner. Officers, however, were allowed 120 square feet (11.2 square meter) per prisoner, which reduced the number of prisoners to 16 per barrack. The wooden barrack floor was generally raised on block piers, which improved ventilation, helped reduce vermin infiltration, and discouraged tunneling. Each barrack had 12 windows on each long side and two windows with a door at each end. Some barracks had ventilation ducts along the roof ridge or in the apex of the gable ends. The other buildings in the PoW compounds were similar in construction and appearance.

There was a standard design for a PoW camp depending on the number of prisoners it was to hold. A company of 250 men would be housed together in a plan that included five barracks, one latrine, one mess hall, one chapel, one day room, and one workshop. Four companies, each with its own standard layout, would constitute one battalion compound of 1,000 prisoners. The number of battalion compounds which were separated from each other by fencing and a service road depended on the size of the PoW camp: A camp constructed for 3,000 prisoners would have three compounds which were referred to as Compound 1 or A, Compound 2 or B. Although there was a degree of variation, all PoW base camps had the same minimum facilities and were similar in appearance.

The archival research located a 1943 plan map (Fig. 9.2) and an aerial view of CHIC (Fig. 9.3), which reveal a single compound constructed to hold 1,000 prisoners or four companies. Although the requisite buildings are present, their placement differs from the prescribed, standard PoW camp layout. These dictate that all buildings should be aligned perpendicular to the central service road. At CHIC, however, the barracks, mess halls, and latrines are placed parallel to the central road while the administration, recreation, storage, guard, post exchange, visitor, and infirmary buildings are perpendicular to the road. Encircling the compound was a double-wire fence about 10–12 feet (3–3.7 meters) high. The two fences were about 10 feet (3 meters) apart, with a shallow ditch between these. This was known as the "dead line," marking the boundary that the prisoners could not cross (Eberhardt 1944:6). Guard towers were situated at the four corners. A recreational space within the double fence was located at the eastern end of the compound and a single-fence area was north of the compound. East of the PoW camp, the support garrison included four barracks and their latrine, officers quarters and officers latrine, a guard house, a mess hall, a post exchange, a work shop, and three administrative buildings. A description of the CHIC from an October 1944 inspection reveals that the theatre of operation type buildings were covered with a dark red sanded building paper and that numerous flower beds and walkways "presented a pleasing appearance" (Schwieger 1944:1). Presently, no photographs of the CHIC are known.

Although the archival research did not recover a plan map of the NCHIC, a 1943 aerial photograph clearly shows the layout of the NCHIC. The buildings are blurred but still perceptible. In contrast to the CHIC, the layout of NCHIC appears to conform to the standard layout for a 3,000-man prison camp. Presently, there are only a few known photographs of the camp. These were taken in June 1943 to document the escape of seven German prisoners (see below). One of the photographs (Fig. 9.4) shows the barracks with the appropriate fenestration, raised floors on piers, and ridge-line vents. The perimeter hog-wire fence was topped by inward-tilting, straight lengths of barbed wire, rather than the coiled wire specified by the Corps of Engineers.

North Camp Hood Internment Camp

Situated within the cantonment area of the very active Camp Hood in Bell County, Texas (Fig. 9.1), any remnants of CHIC succumbed to the continuing expansion of Fort Hood after the end of the Second World War. Presently, the Commissary and

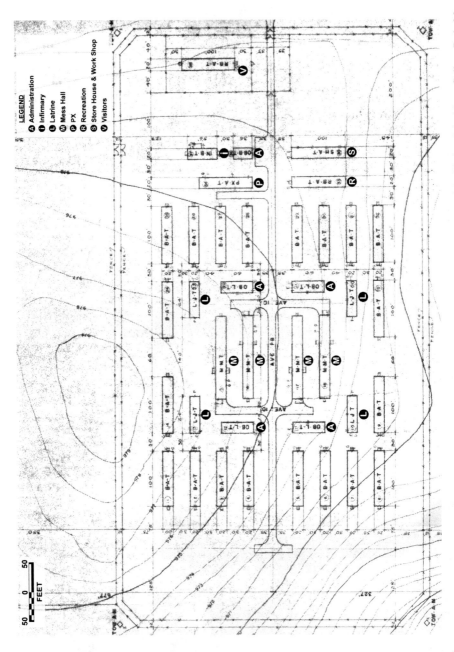

Fig. 9.2 Plan map of Camp Hood Internment Camp in 1943. By David Pedler based on an image courtesy of the National Archives, College Park, Maryland

Fig. 9.3 Aerial photograph of Camp Hood Internment Camp in 1943. Courtesy of the National Archives, College Park, Maryland

Main Post Exchange, with their accompanying parking lots, overlie any evidence of the CHIC. The NCHIC, however, is on the northern edge of Fort Hood where construction and tank training were minimal. Consequently, the remains of NCHIC are the only tangible evidence of the two Second World War PoW camps at Fort Hood.

Fig. 9.4 Photograph of the North Camp Hood Internment Camp, taken in 1943. From Edwards 1943

Site Description

Located in Coryell County, Texas, the NCHIC operated as a PoW camp during the Second World War from May 1943 to May 1944. Covering an area of about 60 acres (24.3 hectares) in the northern portion of the Fort Hood Reservation, the NCHIC is situated on a second terrace of the Leon River, abutting the western edge of the US Army's Longhorn Airfield (Figs. 9.5 and 9.6). Abandoned since about 1947, the site is densely overgrown with secondary vegetation that obscures the ground surface and masks most features. The inner PoW camp gravel roads, however, are discernable because the scrub growth in these areas is limited to grasses. Like other Second World War camps for 3,000 prisoners, the NCHIC was divided into three compounds. The PoW area was circumscribed by a series of wire fences that were under full guard. At the NCHIC, the Army support garrison is separated from the PoW compound by an access road. The original entrance to the NCHIC was from this access road into the center compound.

With the exception of the 1951 constructed Longhorn Airfield, which abuts the eastern edge of the site, the NCHIC has had little Army vehicular traffic or military training, and consequently, the landscape and features have not degraded since the initial razing. Although all superstructures were removed, many of the building footprints are discernable following the removal of rather dense overgrowth by changes in vegetation or the presence of the concrete foundation slabs that were used for the latrines, mess halls, store houses, and administrative buildings. In some areas of the site, bulldozed piles of broken concrete attest to the razing activities. In other areas, the concrete foundation slabs remain in place but are encroached by the vegetation. In 1986, an archaeological survey of Quadrat E 26, N 71, was conducted by the

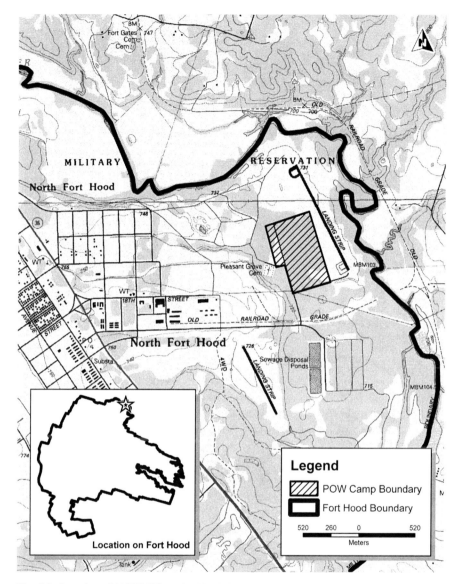

Fig. 9.5 Location of 41CV1638 on the North Fort Hood, Texas, 7.5' quadrangle map. Prepared by David Pedler using spatial data from TNRIS

Cultural Resource Program (CRP) at Fort Hood. This survey noted the abandoned military foundations but did not specify that it was the NCHIC, nor was the PoW camp registered as an archaeological site.

In 2006, the CRP arranged with Mercyhurst Archaeological Institute (MAI) to conduct its annual historic archaeological field school at the former PoW camp in

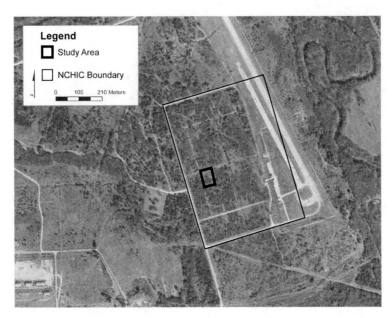

Fig. 9.6 Aerial photograph of the 41CV1638 area, taken in 2006. Photograph by Fort Hood Cultural Resource Program, Fort Hood, Texas

the summer of that year. The research objectives included (1) the identification, definition, and characterization of the site's extant architectural and archaeological remains; (2) a review of archival documents pertaining to the NCHIC; (3) registration of the site with the Texas Archaeological Research Laboratory; and (4) a determination of the site's eligibility for the National Register of Historic Places.

NCHIC Historical Background

In response to the menace of German Panzer armored units, the U.S. government established an anti-tank task force with temporary headquarters at Fort George Meade, Maryland, in 1941. After surveying a number of areas for a permanent location, the Tank Destroyer Tactical Firing Center headquarters settled on Coryell and Bell Counties, Texas, and in January 1942 began purchasing the land between Gatesville and Killeen. This area included hilly terrain and an environment thought to be similar to what the army would encounter in Europe and Africa. Named in honor of General John Bell Hood, the commanding officer of the Texas Brigade in the Confederate Army of Northern Virginia, Camp Hood was fully operational by December 1942. Camp Hood was renamed Fort Hood in 1950 when it became a permanent base. Acquisition of additional lands over the years has increased its total area to 216,915 acres (339 square miles). It is the largest military base in North America (Stabler 1999:22).

The orders to construct two internment camps at Camp Hood were issued by the Provost Marshal General to Captain Edward Sheridan, Corps of Engineers, on January 1, 1943. Sheridan's office diary entry of January 4, 1943, notes the construction of "the internment camps at Camp Hood, Texas (1,000) and Gatesville, Texas (3,000)" (Sheridan 1943). A memorandum dated May 3, 1943, relates that the CHIC was ready for occupancy and that the NCHIC would be ready "about May 12" (Byrd 1943). The NCHIC, however, received the first prisoners on June 4–5, 1943 (Marcy 1943:1). A series of four inspections took place over the next year, and their follow-up reports provide the only description of the physical facilities of NCHIC, and a glimpse of camp life.

According to the guidelines of the Geneva Convention of 1929, the International Red Cross (IRC) periodically visited all PoW camps. The first visit at NCHIC took place June 28–29, 1943. The Swiss Legation was represented by Mr. Verner Tobler, who was accompanied by Carl Marcy, Special Division of the State Department. Marcy's 1943 report of the visit provides the first description of the PoW camp. It also details the problems encountered by the prisoners and guards at the newly constructed facility. At the time of the visit, there were 800 prisoners at NCHIC: 300 had come directly from "ship's side" and 500 were transferred from Camp Chaffee, Arkansas (Marcy 1943:1).

The report notes that the standard sanitary facilities were draining poorly and that the camp did not have laundry facilities. Additionally, the medical facilities at that time consisted of one active dispensary located in Compound B which was not staffed by a full-time doctor (Marcy 1943:2). The major problem noted by the visitors revolved around the work program and the prisoners' unwillingness to participate in it. Labor assignments outside of the PoW camp consisted of piling lumber, working on drainage projects, and other tasks connected with the construction of North Camp Hood. The prisoners were paid 80 cents per day, with which they could buy supplies at the canteen. When the Swiss Legation visited NCHIC, only 100–150 men per day were being used for this "Class II" work, while the remaining prisoners maintained the compound. The greatest complaint from the PoWs was the Texas heat. The prisoners from Camp Chaffee had spent a year in Africa and they stated that working in the intense heat would further impair their health. Some requested that there be no work from 11:00 AM to 2:00 PM and others requested to be transferred to a more temperate climate (Marcy 1943:3). Their requests were denied.

Prisoners also complained to the Swiss Legation about the poor treatment of recaptured prisoners who took part in a prison break on June 8–9, 1943. The escape was believed to have been facilitated by grasses and weeds that were shoulder-high in some areas of the newly opened NCHIC, which allegedly permitted seven prisoners to crawl under the wire fence unseen by the 10 guards on duty (Eberhardt 1944:2). All were caught and returned. The complaints of mistreatment stemmed from the capture of three of the seven prisoners by a local sheriff who handcuffed them until they were picked up by the authorities. Two others were put in civilian prisoner clothing and held in a civilian jail. One escapee was held in a single room without a bed until the next day. These mistreatment allegations were dismissed as not serious by the Swiss representative (Marcy 1943:4). Repercussions of the escape, however, included an investigation into the NCHIC fencing, which was declared not up to code (Edwards 1943; Parse 1943). Attached to this memorandum are photographs of the fencing and the loci of the prisoners' escape (Fig. 9.4). In the background, the barracks of Compound B are visible.

The next inspection was made on November 13–14, 1943, by Captain Edward E. Shannahan of the Provost Marshal General's Office, Inspection Section, Operations Branch (Shannahan 1943). According to Shannahan, 920 NCHIC prisoners were being used for a variety of labor projects and the camp had a contract for work with a local farmer (Shannahan 1943:3). The food was found satisfactory and the prisoners were supplied with items that they preferred, such as flour, potatoes, and cabbage. Unlike many other PoW camps, there was no motion picture entertainment. Each compound, however, had an orchestra and theater guild. Additionally, the prisoners were allowed to circulate freely between the compounds in order to attend the shows that were held in the recreation rooms. A review of the military guard strength notes that there were four Military Police Escort Guard Companies stationed at the post (Shannahan 1943:6).

Although the inspection report noted only a few detrimental findings, it did conclude with negative remarks. Shannahan found that the grounds and general camp appearance gave a very unfavorable impression and that the security measures appeared to be loose. For example, Shannahan relates that when he accompanied Camp Commander Lt. Colonel Dudley Griggs to watch the prisoners being marched out on labor details, several prisoners were not wearing the required PoW uniforms stamped with "PW" on the back. Although Lt. Colonel Griggs sent the offenders back to get the proper clothes, the surprise of the prisoners and guards was noted by Shannahan. He surmised that normally the prisoners were not returned when improperly dressed (Shannahan 1943:4). Other examples of poor security included the lack of bed checks, simultaneous opening of both control gates at the main gate, superficial inspection of vehicles entering and leaving the camp, and a lack of officers available for emergency night duty. Shannahan ended his report with the observation that the prisoners apparently disciplined their own men without the Camp Commander's knowledge (Shannahan 1943:6–7).

A third visit to the NCHIC was made by the Swiss Legation on December 2, 1943. The emissary of the IRC at that time was Doctor Rudolph Fischer, who was accompanied by Charles Eberhardt, Special Division, Department of State. Eberhardt's report provides further details about the NCHIC as well as interesting comments that furnish insights of Eberhardt's impressions and personal prejudices. Focused primarily on the health and condition of the prisoners, the IRC report presents a much more detailed description of NCHIC prisoner life than the account provided by Shannahan. Eberhardt records that the PoWs arrived in five groups of 400–500 men throughout July and August. Eberhardt lists several prisoners who were shipped to other facilities as two "rabid Nazis," two "Poles," four PoW prisoners, thirteen prisoners set for repatriation, and five tubercular prisoners that were sent to Florence, Arizona (Eberhardt 1944:2). This visit found that although improvements had been made to the latrines, the laundry facilities remained poor.

By December 1943, NCHIC had three American doctors, one for each compound, and an American dentist who served all three compounds. With the exception of an advanced case of tuberculosis, no one became seriously ill or died that year (Eberhardt 1944:4). The food and cooking were noted as more than adequate and the prisoners' request for more potatoes and bread were met and added to the menu. Eberhardt found it surprising that the German prisoners had no knowledge of Thanksgiving and requested pork loin and bologna instead of a turkey (Eberhardt 1944:4). Although the canteen was commended for carrying a good line of all articles, it was cited for giving away too much on credit and pandering to the wants of the prisoners. Since the canteen was in debt for $3–4,000, an auditor was brought in to rectify the problem. Credit was canceled and the canteen profits were allocated to paying off these debts (Eberhardt 1944:4–5). Eberhardt's disapproval of this matter is evident in his writings.

> The former officer in charge of the canteen, appears to have been too generous; too eager to find everything and anything for which prisoners asked; to have spent both the Government's time and money as well as his own in endeavors to please and satisfy them and they took advantage of him and abused the privilege which this generousity [sic] had provided. (Eberhardt 1944:4)

Eberhardt further notes that although the prisoners seem to have impressed the Swiss Legation, with their many objections and claims of being "terribly abused," he, conversely, was not impressed (Eberhardt 1944:5).

Eberhardt reports that the recreation area was operational and that the three compounds had free daily passage into the area from 5:30 AM to 9:45 PM and most of Sunday. Soccer was the major sport, although the men also played volleyball, quoits, badminton, and croquet. Theatricals were presented in each camp at least once a week, and sometimes more frequently. The camp also operated schools with instruction in subjects including English and higher mathematics, taught by prisoner instructors. Religious services were conducted by a Catholic priest of German descent.

On the day of the December 1943 visit, 816 prisoners were working outside of the stockade and 137 were employed within the compounds. Work outside the PoW camp (but within the boundary of Camp Hood) consisted of working in the bakery, camp drainage, camp cleanup, fuel yard, maintenance yard, and wood detail. Inside work included carpentry, stove detail, and special orders. One job was for a local merchant who employed 50 men for 8 days to pluck turkeys. They worked 6 days a week for 8 hours a day, exclusive of traveling time. The prisoners were allowed 10 minutes of rest per hour. Pay was set at 80 cents per day or 10 cents per hour. Although about 900 prisoners worked every day, there were still some that refused to do so and they, reportedly, tried to enlist others to "soldier" and not work (Eberhardt 1944:6).

Noted in Eberhardt's report is the September 15, 1943, escape of four prisoners who were on post-cutting duty about 10 miles (16.1 kilometers) from the prison (Eberhardt 1944:3). Two were caught that same day while the other two remained at large for 2 days and were tracked down by blood hounds borrowed from a neighboring prison. Their punishment was 15 days' confinement. In response, four more guard towers were added, which brought the total to 10 (Eberhardt 1944:6). A second incident of prisoner unruliness is also documented. Noted as the possible first real attempt of sabotage by PoWs, Eberhardt relates that a group of prisoners were unloading railroad cars on a siding when some persons placed gravel in the axle boxes of several wheels of the railroad cars. The sabotage was discovered after the work force returned to NCHIC and, subsequently, the Federal Bureau of Intelligence was notified (Eberhardt 1944:3).

A list of complaints was handed to Doctor Fischer by the prisoner delegate on the last day of the December 1943 visit. The prisoners objected to the appropriation of canteen profits, the poor supply of clothing, the lack of soccer balls (they were routinely punctured by the barbed wire), and the poorly constructed barracks which permitted too much cold air to enter. The complaints were received and presented to the Camp Commander, who simply said that his quarters "were also drafty" and that the rest of their complaints were unwarranted. Eberhardt's concluding observations summarizes his feelings about the NCHIC:

> The writer feels that this is a "jinx" camp; that any officer who had been placed in command, would have had as much difficulty as or probably more than has the present Camp Commander. The prisoners as a group seem to be surly, unruly, non-cooperative and obstructive. (Eberhardt 1944:7)

The last IRC inspection at NCHIC occurred on April 8–9, 1944. Doctor Fischer, accompanied this time by Eldon F. Nelson, Special War Problems Division, Department of State, found the camp in the process of modification. Lt. Col. Griggs continued as the Camp Commander; however, the number of personnel at NCHIC was greatly reduced. Compound A was closed because many prisoners had been shipped to other facilities. At the time of this visit, there were 1,436 prisoners, of which 144 were noncommissioned officers and 1,292 were enlisted men (Nelson 1944:2). Reportedly, the largest group to leave was on March 25, 1944. At that time, 791 prisoners were sent to Fort Lewis, Washington (Nelson 1944:3). Nelson notes that many of the trouble-making PoWs, whom he had witnessed on his last inspection, were the ones that had been removed. The result was a marked improvement in camp morale. Other noted improvements included laundry tubs (although the latrines remained malodorous) and a 20 acre vegetable garden that was prepared for planting (Nelson 1944:2–3). Doctor Fischer and Nelson attended a large band concert and folk dancing event during their visit. Nelson notes that prisoners were no longer able to pass freely between compounds since an escape attempt. A separate memorandum reveals that a prisoner walked away from a work detail on January 22, 1944, but was apprehended later in the afternoon when he walked up to a farm house and asked for a drink of water.

Nelson reports that the educational program was no longer active because the majority of the instructors were among those transferred. The library, however, was well stocked with about 1,200 German books and 300 English books (Nelson

1944:4). The prisoners were getting more mail than they had earlier, which generally helped boost the morale. Nelson notes, however, that some prisoners were beginning to get returned mail with indications that the recipient no longer lived at that place or that the address no longer existed.

As before, the prisoners gave their requests to Doctor Fischer to be presented to the Camp Commander. Those who worked around water, as in the kitchens, wanted a second pair of shoes so that they would have a dry pair. They also did not like straw in their bed sacks. Lt. Col. Griggs replied that when they had been issued additional shoes, the prisoners cut them up. Other requests included film projectors, more holidays, more educational materials, and that those prisoners who could teach would not be transferred. Summarizing, Nelson claimed that the Swiss Legation ascertained that there had been considerable improvement at NCHIC. The physical appearance of the facilities had greatly improved and the morale was much better (Nelson 1944:7).

Nelson's report is the last inspection report of NCHIC. A May 9–10, 1944, inspection of CHIC (south camp) reveals that NCHIC was closed around April 1944 because there was not enough work in the surrounding area (PoW Special Projects Division 1944). On May 10, 1944, the NCHIC facilities became the Southern Branch of the US Disciplinary Barracks for holding Army personnel (Faulk and Faulk 1990:56). Listed as a Class 1 Installation of the Eight Service Command, the prison was reworked and soon held 800 officers and men who guarded about 2,500 prisoners. Prisoners were provided vocational training in motor maintenance, carpentry, printing, and shoe repair (Faulk and Faulk 1990:87).

At the close of the Second World War, Camp Hood reorganized into a peacetime facility. By November 1946, North Camp Hood was completely closed with the exception of the US Detention Barracks and the personnel responsible for its supervision (Scott 1965:204). In 1947, nearly 2,000 buildings, mainly at North Camp Hood, were declared surplus and sold (Faulk and Faulk 1990:91). With the passing of the Selective Service Act of 1948, however, Camp Hood became a permanent training center for the First and Second Armored Divisions. Consequently, more substantial housing and recreation facilities were erected and Camp Hood was renamed Fort Hood (Stabler 1999:22). In 1951, Operation Longhorn was conducted from March 25 through April 10 (Faulk and Faulk 1990:111). This expansive mock battle utilized all of Fort Hood and surrounding areas. In preparation for the exercise, Longhorn Air Field was constructed along the eastern edge of the former NCHIC. Although there is presently no documentary evidence of the precise closing of the Disciplinary Barracks, it is surmised that the prison closed prior to the building of the air field. With the closing of the prison, the land was abandoned, superstructures removed, and in some areas of the former NCHIC, clearing was performed with bulldozers. Although North Fort Hood has been utilized for National Guard and Army Reserve unit training since the end of the Second World War, there has been minimal impact on the site of the NCHIC. The extensive overgrowth of the site suggests that the area was not generally used for training exercises.

Archaeological Investigation

Field Methods

Abandoned since about 1947–1951, when Fort Hood removed the building super-structures, the NCHIC site is now heavily overgrown. Due to the size of the site (about 60 acres) and the dense thickets of mesquite, greenbrier, and mustang grape, it was necessary to select an achievable portion of the site for clearing in order to expose any structural features, establish a metric survey grid, and recover surface artifacts. The choice of the initial area for defoliation was determined by informa-tion supplied by Fort Hood CRM personnel and a brief reconnoitering of the site during a visit in March 2006. At that time, an intact concrete foundation slab with water drains and pipes was identified in what had been Compound 2. Based on these preliminary observations, it was deemed a suitable place to start the investigation. At the onset of the 2006 field season, MAI personnel cleared the designated site of vegetation. These activities focused on denuding the intact concrete slab and worked outward toward the central camp road. A total of 3,375 square meters was cleared. In the standard layout of a Second World War PoW camp, this cleared area housed the infirmary and administrative buildings which would have had concrete founda-tions. The extant cultural features were defoliated and exposed using trowels and root clippers.

Prior to excavations, a metal detector was used in the cleared area along tran-sects set 1 meters (3.3 feet) apart. During the 2006 investigation, thirteen 1 meter × 1 meter (3.3 feet × 3.3 feet) units were excavated. The units were located at the three entrances/exits of the concrete slab where human traffic would have been heaviest (Fig. 9.7). The archaeological investigation proceeded by the standard MAI proto-cols (Thomas 2007) and all recovered artifacts were transported to MAI's facilities in Erie, Pennsylvania.

Results

The 2006 investigation recorded three structural features (Fig. 9.7). These include a concrete slab foundation with chimney (Feature I), a stone-lined gravel walkway (Feature II), and the concrete slab foundation of a latrine (Feature III). Additionally, a total of 2,822 artifacts were recovered. The material recovered includes glass sherds (window glass from the former buildings as well as discarded soda and beer bottle sherds), concrete, brick, and ceramic tile from Feature I, and shotgun shells. Materials reflecting military use include tent stakes, plastic eating utensils, and a shoe sole. None of the recovered artifacts can, with certainty, be associated with the German prisoners of the NCHIC.

Feature 1: Concrete Foundation

Feature I is a rectangular concrete slab foundation with an off-center wing on the west side (Fig. 9.8). The long axis is oriented northwest-southeast and the poured

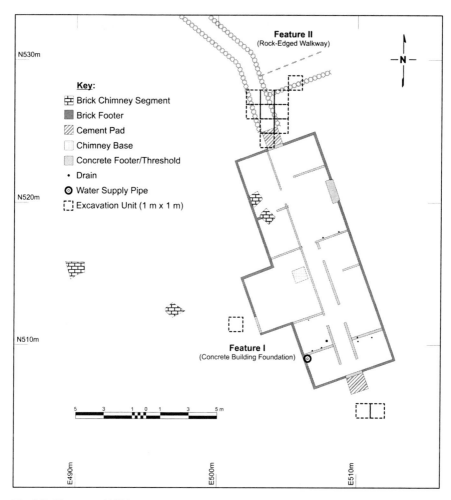

Fig. 9.7 Plan map of 2006 excavation of 41CV1638, North Camp Hood Internment Camp. Feature III (not shown) lies ca.55 meters (180.5 feet) northeast of Feature I. Drawn by David Pedler

concrete slab is edged with a three-course brick footer with one course extending above the ground surface. Indicated by thresholds made of a finer grade of cement than the main slab, there are three entrances into Feature I: one at each long end of the building and one into the wing. Wider than the usual 1.1 meters (3.5 feet) man doors in the main section, the entrance into the wing measures 1.4 meters (4.4 feet) and a small dimple in the center of cement threshold indicates that it was a double door. Outside the north and south entrances, a 1.22 meters (4 feet) square cement slab protects the entryway. A prepared gravel walkway (Feature II) abuts the north cement pad, indicating that the north entrance was the front of the building. A metal boot scraper (24 centimeters [9.4 inches] in length) is positioned outside of this entrance along the edge of the gravel pathway (Fig. 9.9).

Fig. 9.8 General view of Feature I, facing south. Photograph by J. Thomas

Fig. 9.9 Boot scraper located at the front (north) entrance to Feature I (the infirmary). Photograph by J. Thomas

Located within the wing are the structural remains of a brick chimney. The fallen chimney is scattered on and to the northwest of Feature I. The removal of the brick, concrete, and tile rubble from the surface of Feature I revealed the internal configuration of the building (Figs. 9.7 and 9.8). Interior walls were supported by concrete footers connected to the underlying concrete slab with lag bolts. Many of these footers are missing but their imprint on the concrete floor is easily discernable.

Feature I is divided into 10 rooms, including the wing room. A central hall that measures 1.06 meters (3.5 feet) wide ran the length of the building connecting the building entrances at each end. Entering from the front (north), the room to the left (east) apparently was open to the central hallway. Two small holes in the concrete floor suggest that there may have been a counter or possibly a low handrail fronting the hallway which enclosed the reception desks. Drains and water pipes signal the bathroom and three rooms which had sinks.

The Feature I footprint of about 56.4 feet × 20 feet agrees with the dimensions of other PoW buildings that were commissioned during the Second World War. The exterior double doors, lack of an interior doorway, and presence of a chimney suggest that the room in the building's wing possibly functioned as a heater/boiler room. Similar findings at the Camp Hearne PoW camp describe a heater room in the lavatories that was accessed only by external doors (Waters 2004:235). The presence of a chimney in Feature I, however, suggests the addition of an incinerator in this room. As identified on the 1943 map (Fig. 9.2) of the southern CHIC, the location and configuration of Feature I at NCHIC indicate that the structure was the infirmary for Compound 2. The 1943 aerial of NCHIC shows a building in this position in each of the three compounds which a cursory reconnaissance corroborated.

Feature II: Walkways

Feature II is a prepared pathway that serviced Feature I (Figs. 9.7 and 9.10). Constructed of limestone fossil gravel edged with limestone rock, the walkway

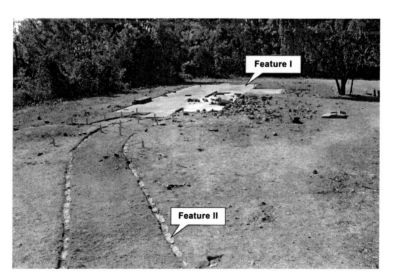

Fig. 9.10 General view of Features I (concrete slab) and II (walkway), facing south. Photograph by J. Thomas

is about 1.64 meters (5.3 feet) wide. Originating directly south of the Compound 2 east-west gravel road, Feature II trends southeastward curving to meet with the cement entrance pad outside of the north end of Feature I. Partially exposed during the 2006 excavations, a second prepared pathway intersects Feature II's southern section and extends eastward to where the barracks and latrine would have been. At the intersection of the two walkways, a bent metal pipe is firmly imbedded in the ground. Bent over from demolition activities, the pipe may have supported a sign or possibly a railing to the entrance of the building.

Feature III: Latrine

Feature III is a concrete slab that is the remains of a latrine in Compound 2. Located about 55 meters (180.5 feet) east of Feature I (Fig. 9.7), the latrine is presently covered with secondary growth, which limits its visibility. During the 2006 investigation, the latrine was located, identified, and mapped with a total station. Due to time constraints, Feature III was not cleared of vegetation; this limited our characterization of the feature. The location of Feature III is consistent with the standard layout of latrines in Second World War PoW camps in the USA. Situated between the mess hall and the barracks, this latrine would have served one company of 250 prisoners.

Discussion

The 2006 archaeological investigation of the North Camp Hood Internment Camp exposed a very small portion of a very large site and, as such, helped tell a small part of a much larger story. Limited to a 7-week field season and hindered by dense overgrowth, an area located in the center PoW compound (Compound 2) and around a concrete slab was targeted for archaeological examination. The clearing of 3,375 square meters exposed a stone-lined and graveled walkway that connected the inner compound road to the concrete foundation of what was initially described as an unknown structure (Thomas 2007). Although we posited that Feature I may have been an infirmary, it was a return to the National Archives that provided the necessary confirmation. Within the NCHIC, Feature I is the infirmary for Compound 2 and a cursory reconnaissance identified similar concrete foundations in the corresponding location in the other two compounds. Most importantly, the 1943 aerial photo demonstrates that Feature I was present during the PoW occupation of the NCHIC and was not added during the subsequent use of the property as a US Army Detention Barracks in 1944.

The investigations revealed evidence of the spatial division of the rooms. Thresholds, drains, pipes, and slight dimples in the concrete provide a glimpse of how the building was partitioned. Finally, the boot scraper set outside the entrance of Feature I adds a more personal element, reminding us that this building was frequented and used by Army personnel and their prisoners as they entered the infirmary.

The 2006 investigation did not recover any confirmed NCHIC-specific artifacts. This is not unexpected, however, considering the limited amount of archaeological testing that was conducted. The dense overgrowth inhibited the effectiveness of the metal detector. In the metal detector survey at Camp Hearne, however, the greatest artifact concentrations were identified in high traffic areas such as walkways and entrances to the barracks and behind the latrines where the prisoners did their laundry (Waters 2004:157). The lack of NCHIC artifacts from the limited excavation units placed at the entrances of Feature I does not preclude that period-specific cultural materials are in other areas of the site.

A pedestrian survey of the entire NCHIC site was conducted to address the 2006 research objective to identify and characterize the extant architectural features. Concrete foundations were noted and areas of bulldozing and grading were identified by piles of broken concrete. Although all three compounds have in situ concrete foundation slabs, Compound 1 contains the full complement of 17 building foundations in their original location and exhibits the least evidence of grading (Fig. 9.11). The concrete slabs of the mess halls, latrines, storage buildings, infirmaries, administrative buildings, and the post exchanges are present. More importantly, the space occupied by the buildings without foundations (the barracks) has sustained minimal damage. The high integrity of Compound 1 suggests that the possibility of intact archaeological deposits is potentially highest in this area.

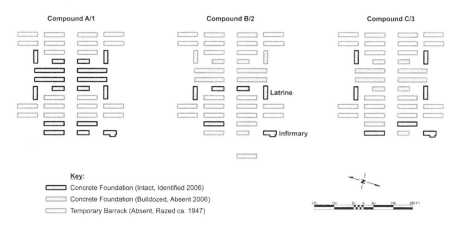

Fig. 9.11 Schematic plan of the North Camp Hood Internment Camp, showing the presence/absence of intact, bulldozed, and razed features. Drawn by David Pedler

In summary, the 2006 investigation of the NCHIC recovered the requisite information necessary to advise that the site is eligible for the National Register of Historic Places. It is clear that the archaeological remains of the NCHIC can be uniquely informative in a variety of areas such as the camp layout and attendant site-use behaviors. It is also evident that the investigation of NCHIC has helped to illuminate a critical moment in time. Though far from the battlefields of Europe and Africa, the events documented in central Texas are part of America and Germany's Second World War heritage.

Today, it is possible that Apache Attack helicopter training at Longhorn Air Field will require expansion into the areas of the NCHIC. Unfortunately, the continuing investigation of NCHIC was recently terminated by the contingencies of two wars; the funding for cultural resource management at Fort Hood is no longer available. Hopefully, the recognition that NCHIC is National Register eligible will at least act as a deterrent to further destruction of the site. It would be ironic if installations like the North Camp Hood Internment Camp and the Camp Hood Internment Camp, created by the exigencies of one war, should ultimately be destroyed by the demands of another.

Acknowledgments Funding for this research was provided by the US Department of Defense, the Department of the Army, and Mercyhurst College. The excavation was directed by J. Thomas under the guidance of J. Adovasio. This paper was edited, illustrated, and produced by D. Pedler. The author wishes to thank Karl Kleinbach, Sonny Wood, and Heidi Fuller of the Cultural Resource Program, Fort Hood, Texas, for their guidance and assistance.

References

Byrd, D. 1943 Memorandum to the Provost Marshal General, Washington, DC, dated 3 May 1943, Record Group (hereafter RG) 389, Provost Marshal General's Office (hereafter PMGO), Enemy PoW Information Bureau, Reporting Branch, Subject File, Modern Military Records Branch, National Archives, College Park, MD (hereafter MMRB, NA).

Eberhardt, C. 1944 Report on 2 December 1943, Inspection of Prisoner of War Camp, North Camp Hood, Camp Hood, Texas. RG 59, General Records of the Department of State Special War Problems Division, Inspection Reports on Prisoner of War Camps, 1942–1946, MMRB, NA.

Edwards, E. 1943 Memorandum to Chief of Engineers, Washington, DC, dated 25 August 1943. RG 389, PMGO, Records of WWII Prisoner of War 1942–1947, Construction & Condition of PoWs, MMRB, NA.

Faulk, O. and L. Faulk 1990 *Fort Hood: The First Fifty Years*. The Frank W. Mayborn Foundation, Temple.

Harper, M., J. Jeffries, W. Tuttle, N. Lichtenstein, and H. Sitkoff 2004 World War II and the American Home Front: National Historic Landmark Theme Study. National Historic Landmarks Survey, National Park Service, US Department of the Interior, Washington DC.

Kelly, R. 2004 America's World War II Home Front Heritage. *CRM Journal*, Summer .

Listman, J., C. Baker, and S. Goodfellow 2006 Historic Context: World War II Prisoner-of-War Camps on Department of Defense Installations. Department of Defense Legacy Resource Management Program, Project Number 05-256, Washington DC.

Marcy, C. 1943 Report on 28–29 June 1943, Inspection of Prisoner of War Camp, North Camp Hood, Camp Hood, Texas. RG 59, General Records of the Department of State Special War Problems Division, Inspection Reports on Prisoner of War Camps, 1942–1946, MMRB, NA.

Nelson, E. 1944 Report on 8–9 April 1944 Inspection of Prisoner of War Camp, North Camp Hood, Texas. RG 389, Entry 461, Box 2633, PMGO, General Records of the Department of State Special War Problems Division, Inspection Reports on Prisoner of War Camps, 1942–1946, MMRB, NA.

PoW Special Projects Division 1944 Memorandum dated 9 November 1944. Subject, Inspection 9–10 May 1944 of Camp Hood. RG 389, PMGO, Enemy PoW Information Bureau, Reporting

Branch, PoW Special Projects Division, Administrative Branch, Decimal File 1943–1946, MMRB, NA.

Parse, M. 1943 Memorandum to the Chief of Engineers, U S Army, Washington, DC dated 7 September 1943. RG 389, PMGO, Records of WWII Prisoner of War 1942–1947, Construction & Condition of PoW's, MMRB, NA.

Rettig 2009 Research produced by the Deutsche Dienststelle, für die Benachrichtigung der nächsten Angehörigen von Gefallenen der ehemaligen deutschen Wehrmacht, (WASt), Berlin.

Schwieger, D. 1944 Report on 19 December 1944, Inspection of Prisoner of War Base Camp, Camp Hood, Texas. RG 389, Entry 457, Box 1422, PMGO, General Records of the Department of State Special War Problems Division, Inspection Reports on Prisoner of War Camps, 1942–1946, NA.

Scott, Z. 1965 *A History of Coryell County, Texas*. The Texas State Historical Association, Lund Press, Minneapolis.

Sheridan, E. 1943 Entry for the Diary, dated 4 January 1943. RG 389, PMGO, Records of WWII Prisoner of War 1942–1947, Construction & Condition of PoWs, MMRB, NA.

Shannahan, E. 1943 Report on 13–14 November 1943, inspection of Prisoner of War Camp, North Camp Hood, Camp Hood, Texas. RG 389, PMGO, General Records of the Department of State Special War Problems Division, Inspection Reports on Prisoner of War Camps, 1942–1946, MMRB, NA.

Stabler, J. 1999 Historical Research Preliminary to National Register Assessments of 719 Historic Sites at Fort Hood, Bell and Coryell Counties, Texas. Research Report No. 36. Fort Hood Archeological Resource Management Series, United States Army, Fort Hood, Texas.

Thomas, J. 2007 Our Fading WWII Military Heritage: Archaeological Investigation of the Ft. Hood PoW Camp. Paper Presented at the 40th Annual Conference on Historical and Underwater Archaeology, Williamsburg, Virginia, 9–14 January 2007.

Waters, M. 2004 *Lone Star Stalag: German Prisoners of War at Camp Hearne*. Texas A&M University Press, College Station.

Chapter 10
Forgotten in the Wilderness: WWII German PoW Camps in Finnish Lapland

Oula Seitsonen and Vesa-Pekka Herva

Abstract In the later part of the Second World War, German troops were responsible for a front of nearly a thousand kilometers in Lapland, Northern Finland. The Germans built close to 100 prisoner of war and labor camps in the area, and imprisoned some 30,000 Russian soldiers there. Since Lapland's infrastructure was very poor, the prisoners were used as a workforce for tasks such as building and improving roads and bridges. The prison camps and military bases, as well as their archives, were almost completely destroyed during the German retreat from Finland, in 1944–1945, in the Lapland War between the Finns and the Germans. In this chapter we report on preliminary fieldwork at the German base of Peltojoki, and we discuss how archaeology can contribute to the study and understanding of military sites from the recent past.

Introduction

Finland had close ties with Nazi Germany during the Second World War, even though there was no formal alliance between the two countries. As a result of this cooperation, from 1941 to 1944 German troops were responsible for a nearly 1,000 kilometer long front in Finnish Lapland, extending from Lake Oulu to the Arctic Ocean (Fig. 10.1). The Germans also established many prisoner of war (PoW) camps, mostly for Soviet prisoners, in Lapland, the Northern wilderness of Finland. Prisoner labor was used for constructing and modernizing infrastructure (Westerlund 2008:48).

The material remains of the PoW camps and other military structures in Finland have attracted relatively little attention from either historians or archaeologists

O. Seitsonen (✉)
Department of Geosciences and Geography, University of Helsinki, Helsinki, Finland
e-mail: oula.seitsonen@helsinki.fi

V.-P. Herva
Department of Archaeology, University of Oulu, Oulu, Finland
e-mail: vesa-pekka.herva@oulu.fi

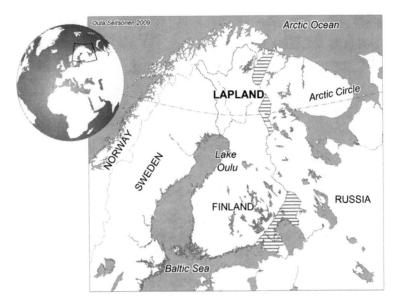

Fig. 10.1 Location of Finnish Lapland within Europe and some of the localities mentioned in the text. Areas ceded to Soviet Union after the Second World War are depicted with horizontal lineation. Drawn by Oula Seitsonen

(but see Huttunen 1989, 1990; Koskela and Pietiläinen 2004; Postila 2002; Westerlund 2008). One reason for this neglect, no doubt, is a perceived lack of extant evidence. The Germans destroyed their military sites and associated documents during their retreat from Finland in 1944–1945. There are, furthermore, very few firsthand written accounts of German PoW camps in the Lapland wilderness. Some archival material about the camps may survive in closed Russian archives (Westerlund 2008:18–23). Since there is little remaining documentary evidence, archaeology and material culture studies can make an important contribution to the knowledge and understanding of the camps. Archaeology and material culture studies, however, are of course not simply poor substitutes for document-based historical research. When conducted within an appropriate theoretical framework, an archaeological approach can provide new perspectives on PoW camps and other military sites.

After a description of the military and historical background to the German camps in Lapland, we focus on the site of Peltojoki in Muotkan Ruoktu, Inari, where preliminary archaeological fieldwork was conducted in September 2009. This research is part of the larger project "Landscapes of Finnish Conflicts: Archaeological Studies in Finland and Karelian Isthmus" (LoFC), based out of the Department of Archaeology at the University of Helsinki. This chapter discusses the archaeological potential of the Peltojoki site and other internment camps. We are particularly interested in how material culture studies can elucidate the dynamics of the interaction between people and things in the northern wilderness,

Fig. 10.2 Typical fjell landscape of the Finnish Lapland in the Pallastunturit area in mid-June. Photograph by Oula Seitsonen

an environment that was unfamiliar and threatening both to the Germans and to their prisoners (Fig. 10.2).

Historical Background: The Germans and Their PoW Camps in Lapland

Finland had enjoyed close ties with Germany since the early twentieth century and the two countries, while not formal allies, cooperated during the Second World War. German troops arrived to Finland in 1941 as part of Hitler's Operation Barbarossa, the attack on the Soviet Union, and Finland depended on German material and other help in the situation where its own war with the Soviet Union seemed to be just a matter of time. Finland had its own reasons to join forces with Germany against the Soviet Union in 1941. The presence of the German troops in Northern Finland made it possible for the Finns to concentrate forces on the Karelian front in the southeastern part of the country (Mann and Jörgensen 2002:75–76). While effectively allying itself with Germany, Finland was eager to maintain the impression of two separate wars against the Soviet Union, and it tried to avoid conflict with the Allies, particularly the United States (Mann and Jörgensen 2002:93; Ziemke 1963:283–284). Great Britain, however, declared war on Finland in 1941, although that resulted only in a solitary bombing attack in the Petsamo region (Mann and Jörgensen 2002:84–85; Tovey 1948; Ziemke 1963:286).

The northern front of Operation Barbarossa became essentially stationary by the end of 1941 (Fig. 10.3), largely because the German troops were poorly prepared for the conditions of Lapland (e.g. Kallioniemi 1990:15; Westerlund 2008:311; Westwood 2005:27). Lapland was "completely unsuitable for the military actions", as the commander of German troops in Finland, Eduard Dietl, had observed when Germany started to plan the war in the arctic (Mann and Jörgensen 2002:70). It is instructive that Finland and the Soviet Union, when engaged in the Winter War in

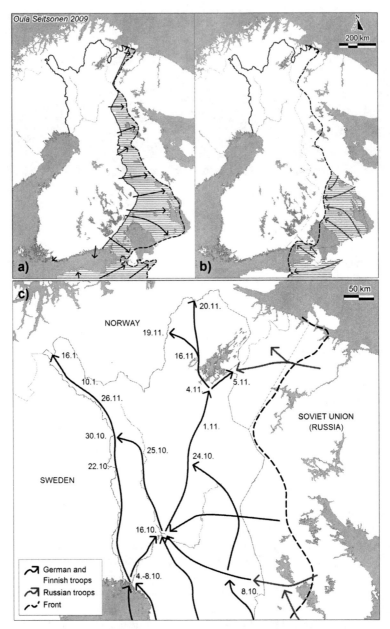

Fig. 10.3 Front-lines during the Continuation and Lapland Wars: (**a**) The advance of the Finnish-German offensive in 1941 to the stationary front-lines, (**b**) The major Russian offensive in the summer 1944, (**c**) Troop movements during the Lapland War in the fall 1944; dates show the advance of the Finnish troops. Drawn by Oula Seitsonen after Korhonen (1963) and Mann and Jörgensen (2002)

1939–1940, had left the 800 km long Northern front guarded only by the occasional ski patrol, with military outposts sometimes tens of kilometers apart (Mann and Jörgensen 2002:70, 72). The northern wilderness was an alien environment for modern warfare, especially the *Blitzkrieg* tactics first employed in Central Europe.

The northern front was principally occupied by the German 20th Mountain Army (*Gebirgs-Armee-Oberkommando 20*), along with supporting Finnish troops, some SS groups, Luftwaffe personnel, and the building forces of *Organisation Todt*. At the peak of the German military buildup there were over 200,000 German soldiers in Northern Finland (Jokisipilä 2005:19; Kaltenegger 2006:169–171). The Germans officially took some 9,000 Soviet PoWs on the northern front, and some 20,000 prisoners were brought to Finland as a workforce (Westerlund 2008:62–64). The presence of the Germans and their prisoners brought an unprecedented internationalism to the sparsely inhabited, peripheral Northern Finland, where some of the local inhabitants had never seen a foreign person before (Jokisipilä 2005:21, 25; Junila 2000; Lähteenmäki 1999).

Stalag 309 in Salla, Eastern Lapland (today in Russia), was the only official German PoW camp in the Finnish territory (Fig. 10.4), but there were actually over a hundred temporary German PoW camps, punishment camps, and work camps in the northern half of Finland, and the Finns also established some twenty camps (Westerlund 2008) (Appendix). The distribution of the known German camps follows passable roads (Fig. 10.4). Since prisoner labor was used to improve the infrastructure of Lapland (Westerlund 2008:50–56, 312), the prisoners were moved to new locations as the need for workers arose, and this continuous relocation may also partly explain the absence of accessible records. Figure 10.4 includes sites with at least a few weeks of PoW activity, as inferred from the fragmentary evidence compiled from different sources by Westerlund (2008:300), and preliminary archaeological surveys. Camps accommodated about 300 prisoners on average, but there is little information about the precise number of prisoners in individual camps (Westerlund 2008:29).

The prisoners were usually accommodated in improvised turf huts, cardboard and plywood tents, and wooden barracks (Westerlund 2008:140–142 (Fig. 10.5)). Even in more static camps, such as *Stalag 309*, the prisoners first had to build their own turf huts, which were later replaced with wooden barracks (Westerlund 2008:33). The prisoners were kept behind barbed wire in at least some camps (Lähteenmäki 1999:158), but recollections from informants suggest that not all camps had barbed-wire fences or structures such as guard towers. Informants also recall that Finnish children were allowed to approach the prisoners and exchange bread for wooden bird figurines that the prisoners had carved.

The eyewitness reports and second-hand information gathered by Finnish liaison officers suggests that conditions varied between camps. Descriptors ranged from "adequate" to "inhuman" (Alftan 2005:117, 122; Lähteenmäki 1999:150–151). Finnish liaison officers sometimes complained that the treatment of prisoners was "too soft-handed", but prisoners could also be treated extremely brutally (Alftan 2005:117, 122; Lähteenmäki 1999:148, 150; Westerlund 2008:40, 64–69, 85). The official death rate in German-run camps was around 20%, and was slightly higher in

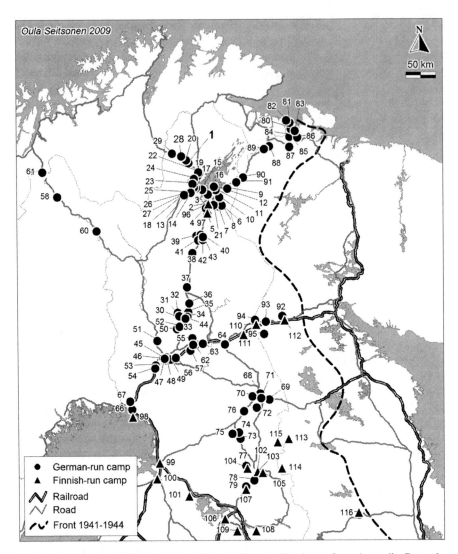

Fig. 10.4 Distribution of POW camps in Northern Finland. Numbers refer to Appendix. Drawn by Oula Seitsonen after Westerlund (2008), and field surveys by the war Historical Society of Lapland and the LoFC project

Finnish-run camps (Westerlund 2008:316). The locals often describe the road from Kaamanen to Karigasniemi as "being founded on the Russian prisoners"—there are stories about prisoners having been executed and buried into the foundations of the road, and one of our informants claims to have witnessed such an execution as a child.

The Soviet Union launched a major assault in the summer 1944 (Fig. 10.3), and by September had forced Finland into a cease-fire treaty, which demanded that the

Fig. 10.5 Soviet PoWs in front of their barracks somewhere in the Finnish Lapland during the Second World War. Photograph by Max Peronius

Finns drive out the German troops, on an unrealistic schedule (Ahto 1980:76; Mann and Jörgensen 2002:171). At first, both the Finns and Germans merely pretended to be at war, but the increasing Soviet pressure soon turned the mock war into a real war (Ahto 1980; Alftan 2005:175). The German military, disappointed with the betrayal of their Finnish brothers-in-arms and concerned about the progress of the Allied forces into Germany, resorted to scorched earth tactics during their retreat to Norway (Fig. 10.3). They took some 9–11,000 PoWs with them and at least 1,000 unfit prisoners were left behind. There is some evidence to suggest that the Germans had moved over 10,000 PoWs to Norway and Germany already before the outbreak of hostilities between Finland and Germany in the fall 1944 (Westerlund 2008:112).

This Lapland War (as it would come to be known) resulted in a compara-tively small number of casualties—both sides lost about 1,000 men killed and 3,000 wounded (Kallioniemi 1990:269; Kaltenegger 2006:171; Mann and Jörgensen 2002:185). Material losses were enormous. The Germans destroyed not only their former bases and camps, but also burned down every Finnish village within their reach, in total some 16,000 buildings. Over 1,000 road bridges, some 100 railroad bridges and 40 ferries were blown up; 170 km of railroad, 9,500 km of road and almost 3,000 culverts were destroyed; and most electricity poles cut down. Tens of thousands of head of cattle and reindeers were killed, and over 130,000 land-mines and other explosives planted in the landscape. In the years after the end of the war, these mines would kill about 2,000 people (Kallioniemi 1990:55–61, 266). Unexploded ordnance is still found in Lapland, and it remains a potential threat for archaeological studies of military sites.

Material Heritage of the Second World War in Finland

The archaeology of the recent and contemporary past has become an established field of study (e.g. Buchli and Lucas 2001a; Graves-Brown 2000; Holtorf and Piccini 2009). In tandem with this development, war and conflict in the modern era have attracted the interest of archaeologists, along with related broader issues such as imprisonment and other institutional confinements (e.g. Casella 2007; Dewar and Fredericksen 2003; Dobinson et al. 1997; Gilead et al. 2009; González-Ruibal 2008; Myers 2008; Saunders 2001; Schofield et al. 2006).

In Finland, specifically, war and conflict have been the subject of archaeological research only on a modest scale, but a change has begun to occur in the 2000s (e.g. Lahelma and Sipilä 2004; Raninen 2005; Seitsonen and Kunnas 2009; Sipilä and Lahelma 2006). Archaeological fieldwork has been conducted at a handful of sites, including at the location of the 1809 Battle of Koljonvirta (Marin 2005; Poutiainen 2005). First World War fortifications around the capital of Helsinki, and the industrial city of Tampere, have also recently been studied by archaeologists (Adel 2009; Lagerstedt 2008; Lagerstedt and Saari 2000).

Second World War sites are generally not legally protected in Finland, but the need to conserve certain sites has recently been recognized. For example, parts of the Salpa Line, built after the Winter War, are now protected, and the importance of certain other sites, such as the Winter War battlefield of Raatteentie in North-Eastern Finland, for tourism is also recognized (Niukkanen 2009:91). Raatteentie is considered important Second World War heritage because it saw a legendary Finnish battle against the Soviet troops and is therefore part of the "heroic story" of the small Finnish nation against the gigantic war machine of the Soviet Union (cf. Buchli and Lucas 2001b; Price 2005). Second World War sites in Lapland, by contrast, have a less glorious (and ostensibly more dubious) pedigree due to their association with the German troops and their prisoners. Second World War remains in Lapland have tended to be viewed simply as war junk: obstacles that spoil the natural beauty of the Lapland wilderness. Eagerness to keep Lapland "clean", and the lack of formal protection, threaten these sites and leave them open to exploitation by collectors of war memorabilia. The former German soldiers, Soviet prisoners, and their descendants, on the other hand, might understandably regard the northern Second World War sites as memorials.

Historians have written several overviews of the war in Lapland (Ahto 1980; Kallioniemi 1990; Korhonen 1963; Mann and Jörgensen 2002; Ziemke 1963), but these generally focus on military actions and seldom discuss particular sites, people or material culture. There are a few studies of the relationships between the civilians, soldiers, and prisoners (Junila 2000; Lähteenmäki 1999; Wendisch 2006), but the experiences of ordinary privates, and especially prisoners, have hardly been covered at all (but see Westerlund 2008). The dearth of archival material and first-person accounts adds to the difficulty of studying life in PoW camps.

Some potential informants chose to forget traumatic wartime experiences; others give selected information to researchers, or their memory can simply fail (Lähteenmäki 1999:220; Banks 2007; Fraser and Brown 2007; Zarankin and Funari

2008). Some personal memoirs of Hitler's arctic war were written by the leaders of the German troops (Erfurth 1951, 1954; Rendulic 1952, 1964), but prison camps and the treatment of the prisoners are not mentioned in these sources. Archaeological research on the German PoW camps in Lapland can provide a view into the ignored, forgotten, and concealed subaltern histories of the conflict (cf. Buchli and Lucas 2001b:171; Harrison and Schofield 2009:191).

Today, the German military sites in Finnish Lapland are in varying states of deterioration. Because the buildings were mainly made of wood and turf, and many were burnt down when camps were abandoned, little survives on the surface. A piece of a concrete wall is the only standing structure at Peltojoki, for instance, and most hikers probably pass German sites in the wilderness without ever knowing what was once there. The Germans also destroyed the supplies that they could not take with them during the retreat, which means that dumps of burned and broken *matériel* can be found at camp sites and along the retreat routes.

To tap into the full potential of the material remains, it is essential to recognize that archaeological material is primarily useful for other purposes than reconstructing the course of events in a narrow sense. The archaeology of the recent past can all too easily slip into mere illustration and recapitulation of pre-existing historical narratives. For example, burnt binders found at Peltojoki (Fig. 10.8) might be showcased as evidence of the destruction of the German camp archives, but such an approach only serves to trivialize archaeological research—nothing new is said nor are new views into the past generated. A more useful approach is to focus on and explore relationships between people, material culture, and the world in a particular historical and environmental context. This approach can potentially open up new perspectives on the seemingly familiar past.

The publicity resulting from the fieldwork at the Peltojoki camp suggests that there is a wider popular interest in the archaeology of the Second World War in Finland. This interest is probably connected to national myths and traumas, ranging from the glorified "Spirit of the Winter War", which apparently unified the country in a common struggle (Mälkki 2008), to the complicated Finnish-German relationships (Silvennoinen 2008), which eventually led to the devastation of Lapland (Ahto 1980). The archaeology of Second World War sites has the potential for future tourism, which is crucial to the economy of Lapland. Somewhat ironically, Lapland has been a popular destination for German tourists for decades.

The Peltojoki Military Base and PoW Camp

In August 2009, the Peltojoki base (Fig. 10.4) was chosen as the location for the first small-scale archaeological study of a German PoW camp. The site is located in Muotkan Ruoktu in Inari, at the intersection of the River Peltojoki and the Kaamanen-Karigasniemi road, which was built by the Germans in 1941–1943 using PoWs as the labor force. A preliminary mapping of the site was conducted in 2007 when the surface was still littered with metal finds, but unfortunately in between the two field seasons, the metal was collected and sold as scrap. Various features are visible on the surface and these were mapped during the 2009 campaign. The test excavation of seven discrete features shows that the site merits more extensive fieldwork.

The Peltojoki base was in use at least from 1942 (certain finds from the site were even stamped "1942") when it served as a camp for Soviet PoWs who were building the road and the bridge on the river, supervised by Wehrmacht troops and possibly Organization Todt staff (Huttunen 1990). Several tin cans found at the site are stamped *Wehrmacht*, one barrel top *Heer*, and one piece of porcelain *Fl.U.V.* (*Flieger Unterkunft Verwaltung* or Flight Barracks Administration); perhaps this find indicates the presence of air-force personnel (the nearest known airfield built by the Germans is in Kaamanen, about 20 km to the southeast). A local informant who visited the camp as a child around 1943 did not have recollection of specific installations associated with prisoners, such as barbed wire fences. It is not known how long the site served as a PoW camp.

Certain defensive structures documented at the site may imply that a bridge guard at least was maintained there throughout the war (Fig. 10.6). The base was also refurbished at some point as a supply depot which operated during the retreat of the German troops in the fall 1944 (Huttunen 1990). The Germans destroyed the camp before retreating from Lapland, and the latest date for that is mid-November 1944; the Finnish Defense Forces reached the southern end of the Kaamanen-Karigasniemi road on 16 November and made contact with the German rear guard on 19 November in Karigasniemi close to the Norwegian border (Kallioniemi 1990:254; Korhonen 1963:82).

A total of 44 structures likely dating to the Second World War have so far been identified and mapped at the Peltojoki site. According to one of our informants, one structure is a Second World War era ground cellar which was reused after the war as living quarters. This was further supported by the stratigraphy and finds within the remains of an outside toilet identified at the site; this structure had also been used both during and after the war. Rubbish pits (Fig. 10.7), foxholes, and other depressions were common features at the site. The remains of a kitchen and two other larger buildings, about the size of Finnish-manufactured prefabricated modular barrack (see Westerlund 2008:135), were also identified, along with an animal shed with a turf foundation, possible tent placements, and the aforementioned outside toilet on the fringe of the site.

The barrack-like buildings were probably used for accommodation, and the tents could have been used either for accommodation, or they may relate to the use of the site as a supply depot. The animal shed illustrates the important role of some 60,000 horses (and an unknown number of mules and reindeers) that the Germans had in Lapland, since the rudimentary infrastructure in fact favored draught animals over motor transportation (Westerlund 2008:292). A local informant who had visited the kitchen and mess hall of the base in 1943 with his mother recalled that one building in the camp also served for delousing the German soldiers.

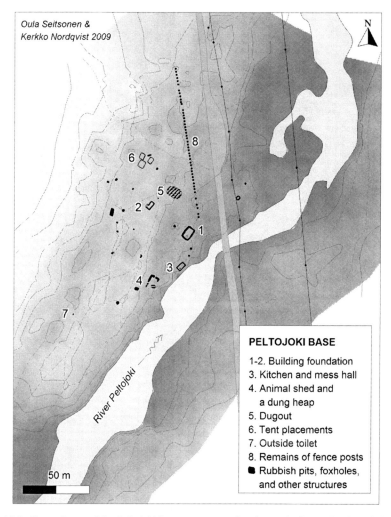

Fig. 10.6 General map of the Peltojoki base, contours at 2 m intervals. Drawn by Oula Seitsonen and Kerkko Nordqvist

Spatial Organization and the Built Environment

Spatial organization and the built environment are arguably reflective and con-stitutive of people's thought and behaviour; that is, their understanding of, and relationship with, the world (Rapoport 1969; Akkerman 2001; Myers 2009). This also applies in such cases as recent military camps which may initially seem to be designed and built on the basis of purely pragmatic considerations (Schofield

Fig. 10.7 On the foreground a trash pit full of tins and other rubbish, and in the background the remains of a concrete kitchen wall in the Peltojoki base, before the excavation. Photograph by Oula Seitsonen

2005:52–53). Looking at spatial organization and the built environment provides a potential approach for understanding ways of life in PoW camps in Lapland.

Only five of the 44 mapped structures at the site represent the remains of more or less substantial buildings: a robust dugout, kitchen building, animal shed, and two barrack-like buildings. The location of the larger barrack by the road to the camp and close to the gate might suggest that it was manned by soldiers, perhaps a commandant or duty officer and guards (Schofield 2005:54; Westerlund 2008:370). The kitchen is located by the river, likely for obtaining cooking water from the clear Peltojoki River, and the animal shed is in the back. The three tentatively identified tent placements are in the northern side of the camp, behind the dugout. The purpose of the tents is unclear, but they may have accommodated German soldiers or prisoners, or served as storage space. A test pit produced two tin cans, but whether or not they had anything to do with the actual function of the tents is not known. There is a rubbish pit with unidentifiable machine parts near the tents which might indicate that machinery was stored in the tents and destroyed on the spot when leaving the camp.

The built environment of the Peltojoki camp appears to have been ephemeral, and the rare photographs of other German wartime camps in Northern Finland convey the same impression. While the impermanence of buildings is understandable, the organization of the space in camps is more perplexing. The buildings and other features documented during the fieldwork are scattered around, and while the five main structures mentioned above are not entirely incoherently located or aligned, the camp does not exactly look like a neatly and tightly organized unit. The photographs of German bases that we have been able to study so far appear to indicate that at least some sites were denser and laid out in a more rectilinear manner. On the other hand, it is possible that there were many more buildings which can no longer be identified on the surface; some piles of stones at the site, for example, might relate to the fireplaces of otherwise completely destroyed buildings. Nevertheless, a key aspect of our planned future research is to address the spatio-functional organization of the camp. That, coupled with a comparative perspective, provides a basis for understanding how the spatial arrangement and built environment of the camps mediated and manipulated particular sets of thought and behaviour.

The present survey data suggest that the built environment at Peltojoki was adapted to the local topography. Bushes must have been cleared from the sectors of fire at least, which would have made the place more open than it is now. There are otherwise few traces of significant reclaiming of the site from nature. The cultural space of the camp may not have been manifestly separated from the surrounding wilderness. Whether or not, and to what degree, PoW camps in Lapland were enclosed by fences is not known, but at Peltojoki there is no archaeological or other evidence for the use of barbed wire. Of course, barbed wire may have been removed after the war and reused in, for instance, reindeer fences (Huttunen 1990). A row of sturdy pole remains was located on the side of the camp facing the road, but it is unclear whether this feature represents the fence of the camp or is a later feature. It is also possible that fences and barbed wire may not have even been seen as necessary, as the surrounding wilderness basically did the work of barbed wire, particularly in the winter.

Soldiers' Things

Upon their coming to Lapland, the Germans were quite out of place in this new environment, and even the most well-trained German Mountain Jaegers (many of whom were, in fact, Austrian) were unprepared for the harsh conditions encountered on the Lapland front (e.g. Kallioniemi 1990:15). Some Soviet soldiers taken prisoner were more accustomed to the local conditions than the Germans and were aware of the hazards of the tundra and taiga environment, and were thus able to build adequate shelters (e.g. Westerlund 2008:33). Yet the Soviets also had troops drafted from distant lands, and the prisoners registered in the Lapland camps include soldiers from, for instance, Ukraine and the Caucasus (PoW Database n.d.; Westerlund 2008:99); their war and imprisonment experiences were undoubtedly no less strenuous than those of the Germans. The Finns were in an enviable position in this respect, as most of them had been used to the wilderness since their childhood. A German Colonel provides a sardonic yet apparently apt portrayal of the difference between the brothers-in-arms and later enemies: "Finns put a slice of bread into the pocket and go [to the forest], whilst for Germans you have to drag along a field kitchen" (Junila 2000:104–105).

In general the Germans were both ill-trained and ill-equipped for the kind of war waged on the Arctic front, and the Finnish troops had to train their German allies in such basic skills of wilderness warfare as cross-country skiing and making fires (e.g. Alftan 2005:190–192). A Finnish liaison officer was amused to see how German soldiers filled full backpacks for mere 3 days' ski patrol trips and took even firewood and alcohol with them into the wilderness (Alftan 2005:196–197, 199). The clothing of German soldiers was initially unfit to the Lapland conditions, especially in winter, but the situation improved over time; Swedish fur hats and Finnish *Lapikas* skiing boots can be seen in wartime photographs taken in Lapland (Franz Repper Collection n.d.).

By 1944 the German high command also prepared an official forest fighting manual for the Finnish conditions, with the help of Finnish officers (Merkblatt 1944). The limited infrastructure of Lapland, combined with the intimidating wilderness, was a constant source of trouble for the German war machinery. However, Finnish veterans recall that by the time the Lapland War broke out most of the German troops had adapted quite well to local conditions and had become strong adversaries for the Finns (Kallioniemi 1990:15).

The test trenches excavated during the 2009 season at Peltojoki were primarily intended to provide guidance for further fieldwork rather than produce substantial data, but some preliminary observations are possible. One of the most intriguing topics for future study is waste management in the camp. Of the five partly excavated rubbish pits three mainly produced destroyed *matériel*, which contained everything from gas masks to reels of cable, nails and skis. These pits are clearly connected to the destruction of the camp in 1944 during the German retreat to Norway (Fig. 10.8). Only one relatively small pit near the kitchen building produced ordinary household waste, mainly German tin cans and porcelain, whereas another pit close to the possible tent placements yielded only glass, almost solely shards of alcohol bottles: One bottle cork shows that Delbeck wine or champagne was consumed at the site. This concentration of glass, if indeed formed while the camp was still running, might indicate well-organized and to some degree specialized rubbish disposal practices, which contrasts with the seemingly makeshift spatial organization of the camp. By the same token, the scarcity of ordinary household waste may indicate that the main garbage dump or dumps of the camp are yet to be found. Locating them in the future would provide an important means for studying life in the camp.

It is possible that rubbish was simply thrown into the river. A concentration of porcelain was detected on the bottom of the river by the kitchen, some of which was collected during the fieldwork. It seems likely, however, that the pottery in the river is related to the destruction phase of the camp. The porcelain in this particular concentration and the shards found in the rubbish pit near the kitchen include a Finnish ware produced by the Arabia factory, as well as wares produced in German factories. A few pieces have readable stamps: two pieces are stamped with *Johann Haviland, Bavaria* and one with the Reich eagle and *Fl.U.V., 1942, Bohemia*. Some sherds of earthenware bottles and military cups have been identified as German products.

Fig. 10.8 One of the trash pits used to destroy military *matériel*, which could not be taken along during the retreat in the fall 1944; *inset*: burned binders from the trash pit. Photographs by Oula Seitsonen

The presence of Finnish porcelain at the site is unsurprising, but the seeming rarity of German wares is intriguing, given that an entire warehouse of German military kitchen utensils (blown up in the fall of 1944) is known to have been located in Kaamanen, not far from Peltojoki. One aim of the future research is to study how and why the Germans engaged with their material culture in the context of PoW camps, which in turn provides a new perspective on how the soldiers and their prisoners accommodated themselves, materially and cognitively, to the particular circumstances in the Lapland wilderness.

Conclusion

One of the main themes of this project is to study Soviet prisoners confined in PoW camps in the wilderness of Finnish Lapland, but the initial work ended up revealing more information about German soldiers than their prisoners. The material remains that the Germans left behind illustrate the clash between technology and nature, which more or less characterized the entire German military campaign in the North. Similarly, the initial fieldwork conducted at the Peltojoki military base and PoW camp in 2009 did not reveal finds or structures which could straightforwardly be connected to the prisoners but it did provide an overview of the camp—especially its spatial organization—which will facilitate future work at the site. The fieldwork also produced the first archaeologically recorded assemblage of Second World War German military *matériel* in Finland.

There is seemingly a discrepancy between the built environment of the Peltojoki camp and the rubbish disposal practices thus far discovered. The camp appears to have been relatively loosely organized and its buildings are quite insubstantial. That a temporary military base should show such features is unsurprising, of course, and a similarly makeshift built environment can be observed in photographs of other German camps in Northern Finland. It is clear that such differences were related to various factors, from the specific function of sites to the length of time that particular camps were used. The portable material culture shows a rather higher degree of standardization, as might be expected in a military setting and especially at a site that also functioned as a supply depot. However, the initial observations of ordered rubbish disposal practices seem at odds with the apparently loosely organized space in the Peltojoki camp. The dominance of Finnish wares over German porcelain at the site also adds to this intriguing scenario.

What these observations mean exactly, and how well they will hold up in the light of future research, are open questions at the moment, but the point is that various issues call for further study. These issues, once further explored, have the potential to broaden our perspectives on PoW camps beyond conventional historical research. In summary, the study of German military sites and installations in Finland by archaeologists opens up new ways of understanding how soldiers and prisoners lived their lives in a context of confinement and in the wilderness environment which was alien and hostile to many of them. Yet the study of PoW camps need not be only about war and conflict, but can also address other issues, such as the wide-ranging ways of thinking and acting in relation with material culture in particular historical and environmental circumstances. Thus, the archaeology of PoW camps can potentially contribute to broader studies of human thinking and behaviour.

Acknowledgements We would like to thank the volume editors, Antti Lahelma, and Wesa Perttola, for reading and commenting on earlier drafts. Despite this assistance, the authors are responsible for any remaining mistakes. Additional thanks are also due to Yrjö Norokorpi of the Finnish Forest Administration, Jari Leskinen, Aki Romakkaniemi, and Kai Romakkaniemi of the Lapland War Historical Society, and Hans Niittyvuopio of Muotkan Ruoktu. Finally, for assistance in the field, we thank Kerkko Nordqvist, Anu Herva, Ulrika Köngäs, Heidi Nordqvist, Sanna Seitsonen, and last but not least two charming little girls, Elsa and Sohvi Seitsonen.

Appendix: German and Finnish Prisoner of War, Punishment and Work Camps in the Northern Half of Finland (Based on Westerlund 2008:32, Appendix 1–2)

German camps

Nr.	Municipality	Location	Nr.	Municipality	Location
1	Inari	Peltojoki	37	Sodankylä	Sattanen
2	Inari	Ivalo	38	Sodankylä	Siltaharju
3	Inari	Ivalo Rajankangas	39	Sodankylä	Tankavaara Purnumukka
4	Inari	Törmänen Alajoki	40	Sodankylä	Tankavaara Ylisenvaara
5	Inari	Palkisoja	41	Sodankylä	Tankavaara Pikku Tankavaara
6	Inari	Nangujärvi Saiholompola	42	Sodankylä	Tankavaara Peuravaara
7	Inari	Southern end of Lake Nangujärvi	43	Sodankylä	Tankavaara Vosavaara
8	Inari	Nangujärvi Kettujärvi	44	Sodankylä	Jokelaisenaapa
9	Inari	Nellimö Paksuniemi	45	Rovaniemi	Korkalovaara
10	Inari	Mustola Paloselkä	46	Rovaniemi	Ounasvaara
11	Inari	Sarminiemi	47	Rovaniemi	Ounasjoki
12	Inari	Pikku Kaamassaari	48	Rovaniemi	Saarenkylä
13	Inari	Juutuanjoki	49	Rovaniemi	Pallari, Oikarainen Road 5 km
14	Inari	Ranta-Antti beach	50	Rovaniemi	Road to Arctic Ocean 61.5 km
15	Inari	Kankivuono	51	Rovaniemi	Haukivaara
16	Inari	Mahlatti Mahlatsaari	52	Rovaniemi	Mukkala
17	Inari	Nukkumajoki	53	Rovaniemi	Hirvas
18	Inari	Konesjärvi Pikkupaanteenvaara	54	Rovaniemi	Muurola Kuusivaara
19	Inari	Vuontisjärvi	55	Rovaniemi	Rovaniemi-Kemijärvi Road 59 km
20	Inari	Kielajoki	56	Rovaniemi	Kulus Olkkajärvi
21	Inari	Hanhijärvi	57	Rovaniemi	Misi, Railroad 42 + 7 km
22	Inari	Kaamanen Haaraldinjärvi	58	Enontekiö	Iitto
23	Inari	Sikovuono	59	Enontekiö	Siilasjärvi Siilastupa
24	Inari	Hyljelahti	60	Enontekiö	Palojoensuu
25	Inari	Solojärvi Haukkapesäoja	61	Enontekiö	Kilpisjärvi Malla
26	Inari	Karipääjärvi Jurmurova	62	Kemijärvi	Rovajärvi
27	Inari	Illestinkaira	63	Kemijärvi	Ketola, Rovaniemi-Kemijärvi Road 71 km
28	Utsjoki	Kaamasmukka	64	Kemijärvi	Joutsijärvi
29	Utsjoki	Luomusjoki	65	Kemijärvi	Korpijärvi
30	Sodankylä	Seipäjärvi Saarijärvi	66	Kemi	Vallitunsaari
31	Sodankylä	Seipäjärvi	67	Alatornio	Kalkkimaa
32	Sodankylä	Seipäjärvi Myllyvaara	68	Kuusamo	Kuusamo
33	Sodankylä	Vuojärvi	69	Kuusamo	Kuusamo-Kiestinki Road 20 km
34	Sodankylä	Road to Arctic Ocean 86.5 km	70	Kuusamo	Kaikkonen
35	Sodankylä	Road to Arctic Ocean 93 km	71	Kuusamo	Sänkikangas
36	Sodankylä	Road to Arctic Ocean 96 km	72	Kuusamo	Penttilänvaara

Appendix (continued)

German camps			Finnish camps		
Nr.	Municipality	Location	Nr.	Municipality	Location
73	Taivalkoski	Korvua	96	Inari	Ivalo
74	Taivalkoski	Tervajoki	97	Inari	Palkisoja
75	Taivalkoski	Isokumpu	98	Kemi	Ajossaari
76	Taivalkoski	Inkee	99	Oulu	Oulu
77	Suomussalmi	Rapuanvaara	100	Liminka	Liminka
78	Suomussalmi	Kerälänkylä, eastern end of Lake Sakarajärvi	101	Pelso	Pelso
79	Hyrynsalmi	Hyrynsalmi	102	Suomussalmi	Suomussalmi
80	Petsamo	Liinahamari	103	Suomussalmi	Taivalalanen
81	Petsamo	Peuravuono	104	Suomussalmi	Pesiö
82	Petsamo	Nurmensätti	105	Suomussalmi	Haukiperä
83	Petsamo	Kap Romanow	106	Kajaani	Kajaani
84	Petsamo	Parkkina	107	Hyrynsalmi	Hyrynsalmi
85	Petsamo	Näsykkä	108	Hyrynsalmi	Tipasoja
86	Petsamo	Titowka	109	Hyrynsalmi	Tuhkala
87	Petsamo	Ylä-Luostari	110	Salla	Kuolajärvi Kairala Saukkojänkä
88	Petsamo	Kolosjoki	111	Salla	Kotala Church
89	Petsamo	Salmijärvi Jäkälävaara	112	Salla	Alakurtti Kaitaankangas
90	Petsamo	Nautsi	113	Uhtua	Vuonninen
91	Petsamo	Jäniskoski	114	Uhtua	Vasovaara
92	Salla	Alakurtti	115	Uhtua	Lonkka
93	Salla	Kairala	116	Rukajärvi	Tiiksjärvi
94	Salla	Nurmi			
95	Salla	Lampela			

Note: Since the Finnish place names were difficult for Germans, they often named locations by the distance travelled along road from some central location (Alftan 2005:64).

References

Adel, V. 2009 I maailmansodan aikaisten linnoitusten inventointi Tampereen Pispalassa. *Pirkan maan alta. Arkeologisia tutkimuksia* 10: 71–81.

Ahto, S. 1980 *Aseveljet Vastakkain*. Kirjayhtymä, Helsinki.

Akkerman, A. 2001 Urban Planning in the Founding of Cartesian Thought. *Philosophy and Geography* 4(2): 141–167.

Alftan, R. 2005 *Aseveljet:Saksalais-Suomalainen Aseveljeys 1942–1944*. WSOY, Helsinki.

Banks, I. 2007 Ghosts in the Desert: The Archaeological Investigation of a Sub-Saharan Battlefield. *Journal of Conflict Archaeology* 3: 1–28.

Buchli, V. and G. Lucas (eds.) 2001a *Archaeologies of the Contemporary Past*. Routledge, London and New York.

Buchli, V. and G. Lucas 2001b Models of Production and Consumption: Archaeologies of the Contemporary Past. In *Archaeologies of the Contemporary Past*, edited by V. Buchli and G. Lucas, pp. 21–25. Routledge, London.

Casella, E. 2007 *The Archaeology of Institutional Confinement*. University Press of Florida, Gainesville.

Dewar, M. and C. Fredericksen 2003 Prison Heritage, Public History and Archaeology at Fannie Bay Gaol, Northern Australia. *International Journal of Heritage Studies* 9(1): 45–63.

Dobinson, C., J. Lake, and J. Schofield 1997 Monuments of War: Defining England's 20th-Century Defence Heritage. *Antiquity* 71: 288–299.

Erfurth, W. 1951 *Suomi sodan myrskyssä 1941–1944*. WSOY, Porvoo.

Erfurth, W. 1954 *Sotapäiväkirja vuodelta 1944*. WSOY, Porvoo.

Franz Repper Collection n.d. *Original photos.* http://www.gaissmair.net/Repper_collection.htm (Accessed 07 September 2009)

Fraser, H.A. and M. Brown 2007 Mud, Blood and Missing Men:Excavations at Serre, Somme, France. *Journal of Conflict Archaeology* 3(1): 147–171.

Gilead, I., Y. Haimi, and W. Mazurek 2009 Excavating Nazi Extermination Centres. *Present Pasts* 1: 10–39.

González-Ruibal, A. 2008 Time to Destroy: An Archaeology of Supermodernity. *Current Anthropology* 49(2): 247–279.

Graves-Brown, P. 2000 *Matter, Materiality and Modern Culture*. Routledge, London.

Harrison, R. and J. Schofield 2009 Archaeo-Ethnography, Auto-Archaeology: Introducing Archaeologies of the Contemporary Past. *Archaeologies* 5(2): 185–209.

Holtorf, C. and A. Piccini (eds.) 2009 *Contemporary Archaeologies, Excavating Now*. Peter Lang, Frankfurt am Main.

Huttunen, P. 1989 Saksalaisten Linnoittamistyöt Lapin Sodassa 1944. *Faravid. Pohjois–Suomen Historiallisen Yhdistyksen Vuosikirja* Xiii:157–176. Pohjois–Suomen Historiallinen Yhdistys, Rovaniemi.

Huttunen, P. 1990 *Muotkanruoktu (Peltojoki-Peäldujuuha)/Vankityöleiri, Huoltolaitos?* Unpublished Survey Report. National Board of Antiquities, Finland.

Jokisipilä, M. 2005 Napapiirin Aseveljet. In *Aseveljet:Saksalais-Suomalainen Aseveljeys 1942–1944*, pp. 9–51. Wsoy, Helsinki.

Junila, M. 2000 *Kotirintaman Aseveljeyttä*. Bibliotheca Historica 61. Suomalaisen Kirjallisuuden Seura, Helsinki.

Kallioniemi, J. 1990 *Suursodan Loppunäytös Pohjoisessa:Lapin Sota 1944–1945*. Teospiste, Raisio.

Kaltenegger, R. 2006 *Saksan Armeijan Vuoristojoukot 1939–1945*. Koala, Helsinki.

Korhonen, A. 1963 *Viisi Sodan Vuotta*. Wsoy, Helsinki.

Koskela, J. and S. Pietiläinen 2004 *Saksalaiset Oulussa 1942–44:Raportti Historiallisen Ajan Sotilaskohteiden Arkeologisesta Inventoinnista Oulun Kaupungin Alueella Keväällä 2004*. Unpublished Research Report. Archaeological Laboratory, University of Oulu, Finland.

Lagerstedt, J. 2008 *Ensimmäisen Maailmansodan Maalinnoitteet Suomessa: Sotilaskäytöstä Suojelukohteiksi*. Unpublished MA Thesis. Department of Archaeology, University of Helsinki.

Lagerstedt, J. and M. Saari 2000 *Krepost Sveaborg – Helsingin Maa – Ja Merilinnoitus Ensimmäisen Maailmansodan Aikana*. http://Www.Novision.Fi/Viapori/ (Accessed 28 March 2009)

Lahelma, A. and J. Sipilä 2004 Pasifistiset Pyyntikulttuurit? Sodan Paradigmateoria Ja Kivikauden Suomi. *Muinaistutkija* 4:2–22.

Lähteenmäki, M. 1999 *Jänkäjääkäreitä Ja Parakkipirkkoja. Lappilaisten Sotakokemuksia 1939–1945*. Historiallisia Tutkimuksia 203. Suomen Historiallinen Seura, Helsinki.

Mälkki, J. 2008 *Herrat, Jätkät Ja Sotataito:Kansalaissotilas- Ja Ammattisotilasarmeijan Rakentuminen 1920- Ja 1930-Luvulla "Talvisodan Ihmeeksi."* Bibliotheca Historica 117. Suomalaisen Kirjallisuuden Seura, Helsinki.

Mann, C. and C. Jörgensen 2002 *Hitler's Arctic War: The German Campaigns in Norway, Finland, and The USSR 1940–1945*. Ian Allan Publishing, Hersham.

Marin, S. 2005 *Koljonvirran Sotahistoriallinen Alue Ja Sen Merkitys Paikallisidentiteetille*. Unpublished MA Thesis. University of Oulu, Finland.

Merkblatt 1944 *Waldkampf Und Spähtruppausbildung In Finnland. Vom 14.2.1944 (18a/26)*. http://Www.Gaissmair.Net/Waldkampf.Pdf (Accessed 07 September 2009)

Myers, A. 2008 Between Memory and Materiality: An Archaeological Approach to Studying the Nazi Concentration Camps. *Journal of Conflict Archaeology* 4(1): 231–245.

Myers, A. 2009 Bodies and Things Confined: Archaeological Approaches to Studying Control and Detention. *Anthropology News* 50(1): 8–9.

Niukkanen, M. 2009 *Historiallisen Ajan Kiinteät Muinaisjäännökset. Tunnistaminen Ja Suojelu.* Museoviraston Rakennushistorian Osaston Oppaita Ja Ohjeita 3. Museoviraston Rakennushistorian Osasto, Helsinki.

Postila, T. 2002 *Schutzwall–Sodanaikainen Puolustusasema Urho Kekkosen Kansallispuistossa.* Metsähallitus Sarja A 71. Metsähallitus, Vantaa.

Poutiainen, H. 2005 *Iisalmi Koljonvirta:Taistelualueen Arkeologinen Tutkimus.* Unpublished Research Report, Mikroliitti Oy.

PoW Database n.d. PoW Database, Prisoner of War Deaths and People Handed Over In Finland 1939–1955. Online Database. http://Kronos.Narc.Fi/Frontpage.Html (Accessed 09 September 2009)

Price, J. 2005 Orphan Heritage: Issues in Managing the Heritage of the Great War in Northern France and Belgium. *Journal of Conflict Archaeology* 1(1): 181–196.

Raninen, S. 2005 Tuskan Teatteri Turun Kärsämäessä:Ajatuksia Ja Sitaatteja Roomalaisesta Rautakaudesta, I Osa:Maarian Kärsämäki Ja Itämeren Maailma. *Muinaistutkija* 4: 40–71.

Rapoport, A. 1969 *House Form and Culture.* Prentice-Hall, Englewood Cliffs.

Rendulic, L. 1952 *Gekämpft, Gesiegt, Geschlagen.* Welsermühl Verlag, Wels und Heidelberg.

Rendulic, L. 1964 *Soldat In Stürzenden Reichen.* Damm Verlag, Munich.

Saunders, N. 2001 Matter and Memory in the Landscapes of Conflict: The Western Front 1914–1999. In *Contested Landscapes: Movement, Exile and Place,* edited by B. Bender and M. Winer, pp. 37–53. Berg, Oxford.

Schofield, J. 2005 *Combat Archaeology: Material Culture and Modern Conflict.* Duckworth, London.

Schofield, J., A. Klausmeler, and L. Purbrick (eds.) 2006 *Re-mapping the Field: New Approaches in Conflict Archaeology.* Westkreuz Verlag, Berlin.

Seitsonen, O. and L. Kunnas 2009 Ahvola 1918: An Archaeological Reconnaissance of a Finnish Civil War Battlefield. *Journal of Conflict Archaeology* 5: 57–80.

Silvennoinen, O. 2008 *Salaiset Aseveljet:Suomen Ja Saksan Turvallisuuspoliisiyhteistyö 1933–1944.* Otava, Helsinki.

Sipilä, J. and A. Lahelma 2006 War as a Paradigmatic Phenomenon: Endemic Violence and the Finnish Subneolithic. *Journal of Conflict Archaeology* 2: 189–209.

Tovey, J. 1948 The Carrier Borne Aircraft Attack on Kirkenes and Petsamo. *The London Gazette* 38300. http://Ibiblio.Org/Hyperwar/Un/Uk/Londongazette/38300.Pdf

Wendisch, I. 2006 *Salatut Lapset–Saksalaissotilaiden Lapset Suomessa.* Ajatus, Helsinki.

Westerlund, L. 2008 *Saksan Vankileirit Suomessa Ja Raja-Alueilla 1941–1944.* Tammi, Helsinki.

Westwood, D. 2005 *German Infantryman: Eastern Front 1943–45.* Warrior 93. Osprey, London.

Zarankin, A. and P. Funari 2008 Eternal Sunshine of the Spotless Mind: Archaeology and Construction of Memory of Military Repression in South America (1960–1980). *Archaeologies* 4(2): 310–327.

Ziemke, E. 1963 *Saksalaisten Sotatoimet Pohjolassa 1940–1945.* Wsoy, Helsinki.

Chapter 11
Materialities and Traumatic Memories of a Twentieth-Century Greek Exile Island

Nota Pantzou

Abstract In the twentieth century, over one hundred locations in Greece served as places of political exile and imprisonment for men, women and children. A distinctive example of these painful places is the island of Ai Stratis in the North Aegean Sea. The island was used for political banishment from the 1920s through to the 1960s. This paper will provide a historical and material biography of Ai Stratis before discussing the materiality of this traumatic heritage, and will finish by exploring the potential for an archaeology of exile in Greece.

Introduction

In recent years, interest has grown considerably both in the public and academic realms with regard to sites that are imbued with distressing connotations, or associated with ethnic conflicts, political or social oppression, violence and death. Within the domain of archaeology, the emergence of sub-disciplines such as battlefield archaeology (e.g. Carman and Carman 2001), conflict archaeology (e.g. Schofield et al. 2006), Cold War archaeology (e.g. Uzzell 1998) and the archaeology of slavery clearly demonstrates that concrete efforts are made to record and study this diverse and discomforting tangible heritage. As far as issues of protection and management are concerned, one example of the need to maintain these cultural spaces is the inclusion in UNESCO's World Heritage List of cultural properties such as Robben Island Prison in South Africa and the death camp of Auschwitz in Poland. At the same time, the rise of dark tourism, the "visitation to places where tragedies or historically noteworthy death has occurred" (Tarlow 2005:48), indicates the fascination that these sites and landscapes can exert on the wider public (see Lennon and Foley 2000; Stone 2006; Tarlow 2005). Yet attitudes towards uncomfortable monuments are not always related to stories of acceptance and maintenance.

N. Pantzou (✉)
Museum of Political Exiles of Ai Stratis, Athens, Greece
e-mail: nota.pantzou@gmail.com

A. Myers, G. Moshenska (eds.), *Archaeologies of Internment*, One World Archaeology,   191
DOI 10.1007/978-1-4419-9666-4_11, © Springer Science+Business Media, LLC 2011

Prisons, plantations, convict sites and concentration or indoctrination camps are bearers of traumatic memories and landmarks of what Meskell (2002:558) defines as "negative heritage". Conflictual sites, as Meskell affirms, deserve our attention for a particular reason: their negative associations greatly dictate their wavering between celebration and erasure (Meskell 2002:571). Her definition of this type of heritage and her idea on its shifting and twofold dimension are valuable for understanding the biographies and ambiguous positions of confined or open spaces and monuments of negative memory within state agendas and collective imagery. However, in acknowledging the ambiguity of heritage, I believe that the concept of traumatic heritage can describe more efficiently its nature and dynamics, especially as approached under the scope of this study. That is because negative heritage seemingly also implies the existence of "positive" cultural resources, whereas *traumatic* is a more inclusive term, since social or political traumas can gradually be healed and turned into a positive transformation or change.

It is in this context of redemption and negation that the absence of systematic research and attempts to archaeologically document and to thoroughly preserve the material aspects of traumatic heritage in Greece should be considered. However, two essays which address the materiality of the Greek Civil War from an archaeological perspective merit our attention. Yannis Hamilakis (2002) explores the signification and symbolic appropriation of classical antiquity in both the political "rebirth" of those detained for their beliefs on the prison island of Makronisos and in the counter memories of the detainees against the regime. Dimitris Papadopoulos in a phenomenological approach to space, deals with the impact of the Greek Civil War upon the human, natural and built landscape of Prespa lakes, emphasising on the "war's material destruction and its social, traumatic long-term effects" (2005:11, 2008). Why do we encounter such a lack of interest? Why have there been no excavations to date? Why have painful sites not been turned into heritage sites? What is the status of traumatic heritage in twentieth- and twenty-first-century Greece? To narrow down the potential research area, the focus of this study is centered on Ai Stratis, an island that was used to hold political detainees, whose biography mirrors the complexities and material legacy of the Greek Civil War. This decision is based on the role of exile islands as landmarks of this civil struggle and on Ai Stratis' longevity as place of internment throughout the twentieth century: parameters that allow for a more holistic examination of the character and position of this heritage in narratives and national imagination.

The term Civil War instantly brings to mind images of bloodshed, genocide and extreme violence, though the irremediable rupture that such strife causes both on the public and private domain rarely appears in any dictionary definitions. Civil conflicts stigmatise places, people and memories in unique ways. It is not surprising then that Civil War heritage holds a marginal place within official narratives and collective imagination. In reality, this traumatic tangible or intangible heritage's conservation, management, representation and interpretation are greatly conditioned by the politics of remembering and forgetting, shifting between the status of a source of disgrace and a means of reconciliation. One such example of the ambiguous position of this type of heritage is the Long Kesh/Maze Prison in Belfast (see Chapter 15 by Purbrick, this volume). As McAtackney (2006:7) explains when issues of site maintenance occur, sentiments vary and opinions often split between those who prefer "to see the prison, and all it represented, obliterated and forgotten whereas the other extreme wished the site to be fully retained as a 'Museum of the Troubles'". Under these circumstances, a particular archaeological approach needs to be developed accounting for the fragile and ambivalent character of this unpleasant past, considering that it can be more susceptible to dissonance or obliteration.

In employing the example of Ai Stratis, the intention is that it will operate as a model for mapping the future of the archaeology of exile in Greece. In this regard, I shall provide a brief chronology of state orientation towards places of confined living and present and analyse material traces of exile on the landscape and social fabric through an examination of Ai Stratis' historical and material biography. This is only a preliminary endeavour to address issues of interpretation, negotiation and protection of traumatic heritage in Greece. The hope is that this study will evolve into a more integrated investigation of both state and public attitudes towards the past Ai Stratis represents, aspiring to incorporate this cultural resource as a legitimate part of the Greek cultural heritage.

Civil Polarisations and Political Exile in Twentieth-Century Greece

Archaeologists and historians are prone to emphasise dates and fixed chronologies. For the Greek Civil War, the years between 1946 and 1949 often define the chronological limits of the civil atrocities that took place, on a first level between the Democratic Army (the Leftists) and the National Army (the Rightists/government army), and on a second level between the state and the "dangerous–often leftist" citizens (see Carabott and Sfikas 2004; Clogg 2006; Mazower 2000; Panourgia 2009:81–116). Although this traumatic epoch of modern Greek history is confined to these fixed chronologies, one needs to look back in order to understand the onset and components of this sociopolitical rupture. More importantly, one has to explore the years that followed the Civil War in order to trace its aftermath on the political sphere and on public life, and the imprint it left on both collective memory and personal history.

As with all civil wars, the Greek Civil War (*Emfilios Polemos*) is a complex phenomenon that transcends space and time, and moves beyond battlefields. It is in these years (1946–1949) that mass executions occurred, that the number of political prisoners increased,[1] that the first indoctrination camps were set up (Voglis 2002:100) and that the Greek islands were swamped with political exiles. During this time around 60,000 Greeks sought refuge in socialist countries,[2] 600,000 people out of a population of 7.3 million were displaced,[3] and more than 45,000 were killed.[4] In September 1949, there were 18,000 leftists imprisoned in Greece,[5] and by the end of the Civil War more than 50,000 political prisoners had passed through the internment site of Makronisos alone.[6] Unquestionably, this social and political fracture deeply affected the lives of a large segment of Greek society and bequeathed to Greeks a heritage emblematic of the national disunion.

According to the dictionary, exile is "the condition of someone being sent or kept away from their own country, village, especially for political reasons". What is of interest is that this measure to control political opponents by expelling and politically deactivating them has been enforced since classical antiquity. Cleisthenis, often referred to as the father of the Athenian democracy, is considered to have established exile as a political procedure, forging a long tradition that has extended beyond the ancient Greek world. The Roman philosopher Seneca the Younger, Dante Alighieri, Napoleon I, as well as Leon Trotsky are some of the most famous political exiles. But why is exile in twentieth-century Greece worthy of our attention? How could it help us understand the Greek Civil War and specifically this distressing heritage's locus in Greek psyche? The answer is found in the intensity of the phenomenon in the twentieth century as demonstrated by the immense number of people in exile, the amount of locations that served as exile places, and the long duration of this enforced condition.[7] From the 1920s to the mid-1970s, thousands of civilians spent up to 30 years of their lives being detained for their political beliefs and almost 100 locations have functioned as sites of exile or imprisonment around Greece over the same period. Of those locations, around 30 are barren and far-flung islands. These places are physical reminders of a period when the interest of the Greek nation-state shifted from the enemies beyond its national borders to the "enemies within". Exile and imprisonment as practices of punishment and apparatuses of political control were used systematically by several consecutive Greek governments throughout the twentieth century, against political opponents and especially those suspected of leftist beliefs and accused of "anti-national feelings" (see Lampropoulou 1999; Panourgia 2009:226–230; Voglis 2002:92–96). Therefore, despite the fact that the years between 1946 and 1949 often define the official chronological boundaries of the Civil War, it is apparent that the beginning and the end of such conflicts and polarisations cannot be confined to fixed dates and landmarks.

Landscapes of Greek Exile: The Case of Ai Stratis

Ai Stratis is just one of many islands where men, women and children were sent into exile. Notably it is the island with the longest history of use for political detainees. In other words, its persistence as a place of repression will contribute to detecting the shifts in its biography and could possibly represent a source of valuable historical and material evidence. Ai Stratis is an island in the North Aegean Sea, around 18 nm south-west of Lemnos, and today has about 210 inhabitants. Shortly after its annexation to Greece (1912), between circa 1926 and 1967—with the exception of few brief periods—it served as a place of exile for approximately 10,000 people. In total, four phases can be discerned in the biography of Ai Stratis as an exile island: first phase from 1920s to the mid-1940s, second phase between 1946 and 1949, third phase from 1950 to 1963 and the fourth phase covers the period of Military Junta (1967–1974). Successive governments' and regimes' preference for Ai Stratis is not accidental. Its remoteness from mainland Greece, arid landscape and scarce population explain why it became synonymous with exile.[8] Suffice to say that the Aegean islands have been used as places of political exclusion since the Roman times. For example, historical sources suggest that "politically dangerous" Romans and Byzantines were exiled on the desert-like island of Giaros (Church and Brodribb 2009; see also Panourgia 2008:402–403).

The first people to be detained in Ai Stratis in the mid-1920s were mostly workers involved in strikes, lumped together with brigands and petty thieves. At that period the local community numbered around 1,000 people. Already in the nineteenth century many of its inhabitants had migrated to Egypt, Libya, Sudan and Asia Minor as a result of the grinding poverty and the island's limited resources (Giannos 1983:97–98; Ministry of the Aegean 2000:190–191). It is from 1929 onwards, with Venizelos' Idionymo, law which aimed to criminalise both subversive political actions and ideas, that exile as a legal measure and practice of coercion was institutionalised, and that Ai Stratis was established as a site of oppression and confinement. From 1929 up until 1943 (the first phase of operation of Ai Stratis as place of exile), political exiles stayed in houses which were rented to them by the locals. It is only during the Greek Civil War that the practice of establishing mass internment camps gathered momentum in Greece (Voglis 2002:100). During this period (the second phase of banishment on Ai Stratis), Ai Stratis not only was revived as a place of banishment, but also, due to the new legislative framework, turned into a concentration camp (Panourgia 2009:26; Voglis 2002:94).[9] According to Laskaridis (2006:108–109), a survivor of Ai Stratis, 5,500 people, among them women and minors, were transferred to the island due to the measures of enforced evacuation and administrative banishment between 1946 and 1947. In those days, the majority of female exiles rented islanders' houses, whereas male detainees chiefly lived in tents in the hinterlands of the village. Their compound was set amidst fields and gardens (Farsakidis 2006:119).

After the period of extensive warfare ended, a new chapter opened for Ai Stratis. From 1950 until 1963 (the third phase of exile to Ai Stratis), the island functioned as the main place of exile for those dissidents labelled as "unrepentant". This meant that even when the hostilities terminated in the summer of 1949, people remained in exile. Following this, the camp was divided into three sections (Flountzis 1986:15; Laskaridis 2005:28). It occupied the space that extends around the hill of Agios Minas and is cut across by two small creeks, Tenediotis and Paradisis. With the passing of years, the number of political exiles gradually dropped and in 1963 the camp officially closed. Yet, the colonels of the Military Junta (1967–1974) included Ai Stratis in their network of sites of detention and used it for individual banishment cases (Giannos 1983:126).

What are the material impressions of exile upon the landscape of Ai Stratis? Given that the island received about 10,000 exiles over the course of approximately 40 years, it reasonably follows that this reality has left a strong imprint on space and memory. For some internees, their recollections of Ai Stratis are notably powerful and extended such as for Laskaridis who spent there almost 13 years of his life. Thus, a way to reconstruct Ai Stratis' past is to refer in brief to landmarks of life in exile as reflected in oral accounts and personal memoirs. These markers signify the organisation of the inmates' everyday life and provide a vivid image of the physicality of exile.

Little information is available with respect to the first phase of Ai Stratis (1920s to early 1940s). No camp operated then and political exiles, despite their marginal status, shared space with the local residents (Ministry of the Aegean 2000:197–200). However, signs of concrete symbolical and social confinement of the political exiles make their appearance earlier than the Civil War period. During the Second World War, between 1941 and 1942, 130 political exiles, among them women and people in need, were restrained within the old school of Ai Stratis (now the building housing the Museum of Democracy, see below), awaiting their surrender to the German forces (Bosis 1947). Even though they had requested to be released in order to join the resistance movement, the Greek police refused to let them go, regarding them as "enemies of the nation". By winter 1942, 33 of them had died of hunger (Bosis 1947:149).

While no more than 200 detainees were simultaneously banished to the island before the outbreak of the Civil War, during the 1946–1949 period, there were instances where 1,000 people were shipped over in a single day following "sporadic arrests" (Laskaridis 2006:107). This is the time when the camp of disciplined existence is taking shape (Panourgia 2008:397). The political exiles played an instrumental role in the formation of the camp because of their initiatives towards ameliorating their living conditions (see Flountzis 1986). In this sense, a second more dense community was born in Ai Stratis.

Irrespective of its members' diverse origins, religious and ethnic affiliation, and even political orientation, this living organism developed into a vibrant community with its own structure and internal rules. One such manifestation was the creation of the "symbiosis groups of political exiles", the OSPE (Kenna 2004:78–93; Voglis 2002:94). Their basic aim was to set a routine and to struggle against "time that stood still" and the restrictions imposed upon them by the regime. As one survivor of Ai Stratis told me, immediately after their arrival they assembled tents, constructed kitchens, ovens and toilets trying to improve their living standards (see also Papageorgiou 2006:75–76). Next, political exiles concerned themselves with setting up working parties of carpenters, blacksmiths, barbers and even shoemakers, classes for the illiterate and for those who were keen to learn foreign languages, a profession, or about art (Flountzis 1986:92–95; Papageorgiou 2006:76; Voglis 2002:94). All their actions and activities were supervised by the gendarmerie which was based at Maraslios, the local school in the environs of the village (Fig. 11.1). Guard posts and an isolation unit further enforced this sense of confinement and as they stood scattered across the landscape they served as constant reminders of the identity of this community.

Similar conditions also existed throughout the third phase of Ai Stratis as a prison island (1950–1963), which is recorded as the most organised and affluent period in

Fig. 11.1 The camp of Ai Stratis. In the background Maraslios. Courtesy of the Museum of Political Exiles of Ai Stratis

terms of living conditions and material culture. This is, to a great extent, due to two factors. First, the synthesis of the camp in the post Civil War era was altered considerably. The majority of the incorrigibles were social-minded and politically active civilians, as well as members of the Greek intelligentsia. Interestingly, political prisons and camps acted as a matrix, an environment for the propagation of ideas and knowledge, and the moulding of personalities (see Voglis 2002:164–166, 206). Ai Stratis similarly provided fertile ground for the exchange of ideas and political transformations (see Flountzis 1986:155–174). Second, male exiles' and, after 1953, female exiles' stay in the island lasted from as a little as a couple of months to several years. This parameter of permanence determined also the manner in which living space was arranged and how aspects of everyday life were built.

Over the course of the third stage of exile at Ai Stratis, apart from the communal kitchens, wells and workshops, a new infirmary was built, some tents were gradually transformed into shacks, and an indoor as well as an outdoor theatre operated hosting dance events, concerts and theatrical plays staged meticulously by the detainees (see Farsakidis 2006:144; Flountzis 1986:79–93; Van Steen 2005:366–372) (Fig. 11.2). As has been seen in other internment contexts (see e.g. Burström 2009), their interest in enhancing living conditions extended even into activities of archaeological character. Efthifron Iliadis, a professional antiquarian, conducted a systematic investigation of Ai Stratis' Byzantine heritage, and he even carried out excavations of an ancient cemetery while interned in Makronisos (Domenikou 2008: 88–89; see also Ellinoudi 2008).

Another aspect of the exiles' enforced living in this landscape is that in seeking to appropriate this space they created new routes, new habits, new place names and new

Fig. 11.2 Political exiles attending a concert. Courtesy of the Museum of Political Exiles of Ai Stratis

landmarks (see Farsakidis 2006:117). In view of the fact that they were not allowed to blend in with the islanders, they employed their segregation and internment to construct a reality that catered for their needs. One such landmark, for example, is the memorial erected by the internees for the dead of exile on the hill of Agios Minas in 1946, after having exhumed the remains of their fellow inmates from different locations (Ministry of the Aegean 2000:152). This symbolic act sent a clear message to the regime, as represented on Ai Stratis by guards and policemen. By treating those dead as heroes, they first valorised their sacrifice and simultaneously ascribed a heroic meaning to their own decision to endure exile and their refusal to reform.[10]

The gendarmerie appropriated space in a similar fashion. To stress its correctional role, the police force coexisted with schoolchildren under Maraslios' roof. In the same spirit, the old school of Ai Stratis was utilised both as an isolation ward in the Second World War and as an infirmary for the exiles in a later phase (Giannos 1983:123). Such practices were not exclusively characteristic of the Ai Stratis' case. At the island of Chios, female exiles of the Civil War period were detained in a school building (Gavriilidi 1976; Konstantopoulou 1976:64) and while exiled at the island of Trikeri in a monastic compound (Theodorou 1976). Evidently the regime exhibited unique qualities in rehabilitating built spaces for its concrete purposes.

What is left to see? What are the material remnants of exile? It is noteworthy that the official closure of the camp was not followed by destruction of buildings and erasure of structures reminiscent of strategies of state control, such as in the case of Makronisos. In Makronisos, the state tried to eliminate every physical reminder of the existence of the camp by demolishing the architecture of oppression and selling the debris as building material to the mainland. In Ai Stratis, however, nature most efficiently achieved what state strategies failed to deliver. In 1968 a catastrophic

Fig. 11.3   The village of Ai Stratis in 2005. Photograph by Nota Pantzou

earthquake destroyed most of the houses and forever altered the landscape of exile (Fig. 11.3) (Ministry of the Aegean 2000:213–217; Giannos 1983:131). This was also accomplished by the subsequent relocation of the settlement by state decision. The earthquake, together with the Junta's policies, ensured the rebirth of Ai Stratis and this traumatic site's redefinition in local memory. As for the remaining standing structures related to the camp, they were simply left to decay: only Maraslios and the school/infirmary building still stand unscathed having being restored.

Added to this, when in the 1980s a number of painful cultural places, such as Makronisos and Trikeri (a female exile camp), were designated as historic sites, as part of the national reconciliation project (see Close 2002; Ministry of Culture et al. 1994:192; Panagiotopoulos 2000), the island of Ai Stratis was not deemed worthy of legal protection. Nevertheless, the then Minister of Culture, Melina Merkouri, issued a ministerial decree according to which the state undertook the responsibility of procuring a building to house a Museum of Ai Stratis. The Museum of Political Exiles of Ai Stratis, a non-governmental organisation founded by survivors of Ai Stratis in 1988, eventually opened its doors to the public in 2006 in Athens. A year later a public museum was inaugurated on the island by Kostas Karamanlis, the former Greek Prime Minister and former president of the right-wing party New Democracy, and was named the Museum of Democracy.

At first sight, these initiatives seem to indicate the active role of the state in safeguarding these landmarks of traumatic heritage. The reality is far more complex and disappointing. For instance, the historic sites of Makronisos and Giaros (designated in 2001) are totally neglected. Their state of conservation is extremely poor because the first site has been consistently exploited for pastoral ends and utilized as a refuse dump, whereas the second site has been used as an area where military training exercises take place. Undoubtedly, each endeavour to rehabilitate or obliterate this traumatic heritage illustrates complex current valuations and evaluations of the past. The value of the past fluctuates, exhibiting its ever-evolving position in the social and political landscape. Yet the heritage of exile does not exclusively consist of immovable cultural resources. Artefacts can also represent valuable sources of data, although it is often necessary that they be examined separately in order to fully reveal their stories.

The Material Culture of Exile

Defining the material culture of exile is not an easy task since diverse circumstances have determined its fate. Given the ambiguous locus of this distressing heritage and shifting status in state rhetoric and social memory, it is not surprising that much movable material of possible archaeological interest has been discarded, or remains concealed and hidden. There are several examples, where former political exiles destroyed or hid letters and photos or other reminders of their painful experience in order to save themselves and their families from the social stigma and the danger of detention (e.g. Fourtouni 1986:71–72). These physical reminders of suffering seem to open a window into the material world of exile and embody the detainees' everyday struggles and anguish. In modern contexts, these fragments of life in exile operate as a material link between the survivors and the outside world.

I would like to distinguish between personal objects referring to the personal belongings of the survivors, and local objects, meaning the tools, furniture, and machinery that facilitated their adaptation to the daily routine of exile. Certainly this categorisation is not final. By suggesting this distinction, the intention has been basically to provide a framework that will pave the way for a preliminary analysis of the material remains of internment. More precisely, into the first category fall artefacts such as photos taken in exile, correspondence with family and friends, handmade cards or art and crafts produced by workshops run by the detainees, books (some of them also handmade), handmade suitcases from carton or wood, souvenirs and gifts from fellow inmates, documents, newspaper clippings, blankets and all sort of household utensils (like teapots and plates) that an exile could take with him/her when released (Fig. 11.4).

In the second category one encounters utalitarian objects such as makeshift tables, beds, chairs, lamps, kitchen utensils and tools. But, among all these material manifestations of life in exile, there are some objects of political and highly emotional value, such as torture tools, uniforms worn by the guards or any material evidence of state propaganda. On the basis of the information provided about the manner in which political exiles organised their every day life, we can roughly group movable material evidence also according to four themes: self-organisation, political organisation (the political aspect of life in exile), recreation/education and communication. The fourth category includes material records that on the one hand

Fig. 11.4 A fish gun made by an exile. Courtesy of the Museum of Political Exiles of Ai Stratis

reflect the efforts of the exiles to maintain contact with family and outside world, and that on the other hand represent how the outside world, i.e. state and the public in general perceived or treated the internees.

The distinction between personal and local objects is helpful to the extent that it reveals what is saved from oblivion and what is not. It is remarkable, that irrespective of or on certain occasions because of their distressing value, personal objects are carefully kept and preserved by either the political exiles themselves or their families. The purpose of safeguarding the material traces and memories of this traumatic past for posterity is because former exiles want their stories to be heard and the wounds to heal (Farsakidis 2006:117; Manousos 2005:71–72). As stated in the preface of a collection of testimonies written by female exiles, concerning their urge to chronicle their stories from detainment: "They decided that what they had experienced, what they were still to experience, must not be forgotten; it was their responsibility to be the keepers of history as they themselves had lived it" (Fourtouni 1986:95). Therefore artefacts directly linked to stories narrated by former internees and the material evidence surviving on the landscape can help decipher this heritage and fulfil survivors' wishes.

Greek Traumatic Heritage

Not long ago, whilst discussing the topography of Ai Stratis with a former exile, I was struck by the fact that he could not comprehend why I was interested in knowing about the arrangement of space and the exact location of the campsite and communal buildings. He told me that no one had ever asked him anything similar before.[11] Although there are several personal accounts on how life was organized in exile, there is little information on the organization of space. As years pass by and time eradicates the traces of this period from the landscape and former detainees' memory, it becomes even more difficult for them, when they revisit the prison island, to map the limits of the camp or identify remaining structures. As no methodical archaeological surveys have been conducted, nor a specific heritage protection framework introduced so far, there is a pressing need to focus attention on this disintegrating heritage.

For the development of an archaeology of exile or internment in Greece it is vital to shed light on the underlying factors behind existing attitudes towards this traumatic past. First, the heritage of political internment in Greece should certainly not be equated to the treatment of the Greek National Resistance legacy, a source of national pride. According to a brief survey, approximately 12 museums exist all over Greece that commemorate the Greek Resistance to Nazi and Italian Occupation (which lasted 4 years), whereas the museums that represent the national disunion are no more than 4 (covering a period of 60 years). This of course comes as no surprise considering the complex intersections of personal memory, politics and traumatic heritage, and the much expected compound and slow processes that involve this heritage's integration into the national or local imagination, heavily conditioned by the politics of remembering and forgetting.

Second, pertaining to the lack of archaeological research on the subject, archaeology in Greece is principally directed towards the study of Minoan civilisation, Mycenaean kingdoms, Classical city-states, Hellenistic kings, and the Byzantine Empire. There is nothing glorious about indoctrination camps and prison islands. Most importantly, the contemporary past in Greece lies within the expertise of art historians, architects and civil engineers as determined by the structure of the Greek Ministry of Culture.[12] Despite this, one cannot overlook the vast amount of literature relating to Greek civil polarisations and the practices of political persecution that has been produced in the field of history and political science in the last decade (e.g. Margaritis 2002; Mazower 2000; Nikolakopoulos et al. 2002; Panourgia 2009; Voglis 2002). At the same time, personal memoirs have proliferated and the associations and societies founded by former exiles and political prisoners organise pilgrimages to places such as Ai Stratis, Trikeri, Giaros and Makronisos on an annual basis. The foundation of the Museum of Democracy is also indicative of an emerging trend within both the social and political domain, towards dealing with this distressing past.

The first steps towards reconciliation were taken in the 1980s with the designation of historic sites and the scheduling of historic buildings. Unfortunately it appears that a "gap period" followed in relation to the negotiation of exile memories and the material aspects of political banishment. This shift can be understood if examined in view of the effects that temporal distance has on people's perception and approaches (see Lowenthal 1985). The more remote the elements of this past are, the more people tend to detach them from their associations with loss, pain and violence. As Uzzell (1998:18) aptly states: "Our feelings and emotional responses to the past are partly a function of time". In this case, 62 years have passed since the end of the Greek Civil War and roughly 37 years from the abolishment of exile as an apparatus of political segregation. It seems that the framework is being laid for moving Ai Stratis and related cultural spaces officially into heritage discourse. However, this does not necessarily mean that these places are becoming "less of a memorial and more of a tourist attraction" (Uzzell 1998:20). I believe that there is still a long way to go before sites of oppression become tourist destinations and heritage attractions in Greece. More profoundly, there is an impelling motive to concentrate on securing the material existence of this heritage exiled from public space and memory through raising awareness and activating mechanisms that will celebrate its complexity and lay emphasis on its educational role and lasting importance without neglecting the valuable input of its remaining keepers, aiming at what Uzzell (1989) calls a hot interpretation of the past.

Notes

1. During the period 1935–1943, 950 people were detained in Ai Stratis (Ministry of the Aegean 2000:195), whereas the number of detainees during the Greek Civil War period exceeded 5,000 (Laskaridis 2005).
2. Voglis 2002: 228.
3. Kokkori 2009: 66.
4. Margaritis 2009: 24.
5. Voglis 2002: 97.
6. Bournazos 2000: 117. It is important to have in mind that all numbers are approximate. I have also to specify here that no reliable records exist.
7. It is important to clarify that exile and administrative banishment are the same thing.
8. Within the context of this study, exile should not be confused with the practice of self-exile. As for the terms of release, one could only escape exile by signing the declaration of repentance, a direct negation and denunciation of one's political beliefs.
9. During the Civil War period, the types of internment were three: prisons, indoctrination camps (Makronisos, Trikeri, Chios, Giaros) and exile islands which in 1947 were turned into camps of disciplined existence (such as Ai Stratis, Ikaria, Limnos etc). The former inmates use the term exile to refer to their detainment in both indoctrination camps and camps of disciplined existence.
10. On the semiotics and politics of human remains see Verdery 1999.
11. This is an informant that has been interviewed on numerous occasions by journalists and scholars.
12. Comprehensive studies regarding the management and representation of Makronisos and Giaros have been produced by teams consisted mainly of architects, on Giaros see Stavridis 2006: 295; and for the Makronisos' case see Ministry of Culture et al. 1994; see also Law 3028/2002 "For the Protection of Antiquities and in general of the Cultural Heritage" Ministry of Culture 2002: 3003–3004.

Acknowledgements I thank Harilaos Sismanis, Aris Tsouknidas and Giorgos Farsakidis for their support. Thanks are also due to Ioannis Vovos, Katerina Stefatou, Neni Panourgia, Myrsini Pichou, Niels Andreasen, Laura McAtackney and Dimitris Papadopoulos for reading drafts of this chapter.

References

Bosis, K. 1947 *Ai Stratis. I Machi Tis Pinas Ton Politikon Exoriston Sta 1941.* Ekdosis Tis Kentrikis Epitropis Tou KKE, Athens.
Bournazos, S. 2000 To Mega Ethnikon Scholion Makronisou.1947–1950. In *Istoriko Topio Ke Istoriki Mnimi. To Paradigma Tis Makronisou*, edited by P. Panagiotopoulos, pp. 117–145. Filistor, Athens.

Burström, M. 2009 Selective Remembrance: Memories of a Second World War Refugee Camp in Sweden. *Norwegian Archaeological Review* 42(2): 159–172.

Carabott, P. and T. Sfikas (eds.) 2004 *The Greek Civil War: Essays on a Conflict of Exceptionalism and Silences*. Ashgate, Aldershot.

Carman, J. and P. Carman 2001 Beyond Military Archaeology: Battlefields as a Research Resource. In *Fields of Conflict: Progress and Prospects in Battlefield Archaeology, Proceedings of a Conference Held in the Department of Archaeology, University of Glasgow*, edited by P. Freeman and T. Pollard, pp. 275–281. BAR International Series 958, Oxford.

Church, A.J. and W.J. Brodribb 2009 *Tacitus: The Annals*, Trans. [online] Available at: http://classics.mit.edu/Tacitus/annals.html [Accessed 25 December 2009].

Clogg, R. 2006 *A Concise History of Greece*. Cambridge University Press, Cambridge.

Close, D. 2002 The Road To Reconciliation? The Greek Civil War and the Politics of Memory in the 1980s. In *The Greek Civil War: Essays on a Conflict of Exceptionalism and Silences*, edited by P. Carabott and T. Sfikas, pp. 257–278. Ashgate, Aldershot.

Domenikou, A. 2008 *Efthifron Iliadis. O Mikrasiatis Kallitechnis Ke Archeopolis*. Vivliopolio Ton Vivliophilon, Athens.

Ellinoudi, A. 2008 O Desmotis-Protos Anaskafeas Tis Makronisou. *Kiriakatikos Rizospastis*, 25 May.

Farsakidis, G. 2006 *San Vgis Ston Pigemo Gia Tin Ithaki*. Tipoekdotiki, Athens.

Flountzis, A. 1986 *Sto Stratopedo Tou Ai Strati, 1950–1962*. K. Kalopoulos, Athens.

Fourtouni, E. 1986 *Greek Women in Resistance*. Thelpini Press, New Haven.

Freeman, P. and T. Pollard 2001 *Fields of Conflict: Progress and Prospect in Battlefield Archaeology*, p. 272. Archaeopress, Oxford.

Gavriilidi, N. 1976 Gia To Parartima Me Tis Epikindines. In *Stratopeda Ginekon*, edited by V. Theodorou, pp. 223–266. Athanassiou, Peristeri.

Giannos, I. 1983 *Istoria Tis Nisou Agiou Efstratiou (Ai Strati)*. Athens.

Hamilakis, Y. 2002 The "Other Parthenon": Antiquity and National Memory at Makronisos. *Journal of Modern Greek Studies* 20: 307–338.

Kenna, M. 2004 *I Koinoniki Organosi Tis Exorias: Politikoi Kratoumenoi Ston Mesopolemo*. Alexandria, Athens.

Kokkori, G. 2009 Nekres Zones, Xerizomenoi Anthropoi, Erima Choria. In Emfilios Polemos 60 Chronia Apo Tin Lixi Tou. *Eleftherotipia, Istorika* 61–72.

Konstantopoulou, A. 1976 Gia To Stratopedo Ginekon Tis Chiou. In *Stratopeda Ginekon*, edited by V. Theodorou, pp. 39–80. Athanassiou, Peristeri.

Lampropoulou, D. 1999 *Grafontas Apo Tin Filaki: Opsis Tis Ipokimenikotitas Ton Politikon Kratoumenon, 1947–1960*. Nefeli, Athens.

Laskaridis, V. 2005 *Imerologia Tis Exorias*. Epochi, Athens.

Laskaridis, V. 2006 *Apo Ton Dekemvri Ston Emfilio Ke 134 Mines Exoria*. Vivliorama, Athens.

Lennon, J. and M. Foley (eds.) 2000 *Dark Tourism: The Attraction of Death and Disaster*. Continuum, London.

Lowenthal, D. 1985 *The Past Is a Foreign Country*. Cambridge University Press, Cambridge.

Manousos, D. 2005 *Gioura: To Aparto Kastro*. Entos, Athens.

Margaritis, G. 2002 *I Istoria Tou Ellinikou Emfiliou Polemou (1946–1949)*. Part II. Vivliorama, Athens.

Margaritis, G. 2009 Geniki Episkopisi Tou Ellinikou Emfiliou. In Emfilios Polemos 60 Chronia Apo Tin Lixi Tou. *Eleftherotipia, Istorika*, 9–36.

Mazower, M. (ed.) 2000 *After the War Was Over: Reconstructing the Family, Nation and State in Greece, 1943–1960*. Princeton University Press, Princeton.

McAtackney, L. 2006 The Negotiation of Identity at Shared Sites: Long Kesh/Maze Prison Site, Northern Ireland. Paper Presented at the UNESCO University and Heritage 10th International Seminar "Cultural Landscapes in the 21st Century", Newcastle. April, 2005.

Meskell, M. 2002 Negative Heritage and Past Mastering in Archaeology. *Anthropological Quarterly* 75(3): 557–574.

Ministry of Culture, Ministry of Public Works, SADAS-PEA, Technical Chamber of Greece, ICOMOS, National Technical University of Athens, and PEKAM (eds.) 1994 *Makronisos: Istorikos Politistikos Topos*. Ministry of Culture, Athens.

Ministry of Culture 2002 *For the Protection of Antiquities and in General of the Cultural Heritage*. Ministry of Culture, Athens.

Ministry of the Aegean, 2000. *Ai Stratis: Fotografika Ichni [1940–1970], Archio Vasili Manikaki*.

Nikolakopoulos, I., A. Rigos, and G. Psallidas (eds.) 2002 *O Emfilios Polemos: Apo Ti Varkiza Sto Grammo*. Themelio, Athens.

Panagiotopoulos, P. (ed.) 2000 *Istoriko Topio Ke Istoriki Mnini. To Paradigma Tis Makronisou*. Filistor, Athens.

Panourgia, N. 2008 Desert Islands: Ransom of Humanity. *Public Culture* 20(2): 395–421.

Panourgia, N. 2009 *Dangerous Citizens: The Greek Left and the Terror of the State*. Fordham University Press, New York.

Papadopoulos, D. 2005 'Liminal' Lakes: Shifting Topographies and the Limits of Archaeology in a Border Wetland. Paper Presented at the 11th European Archaeological Association Conference, Cork, Ireland. 5–11 September.

Papadopoulos, D. 2008 I Alli Klironomia: Mnimi, Ilikotita Ke I Topografia Tou Emfiliou Sti Prespa. In *Mnimes Ke Lithi Tou Ellinikou Emfiliou Polemou*, edited by R. van Boeschoten, T. Vervenioti, E. Voutira, V. Dalkavoukis, and K. Batha, pp. 171–195. Epikentron, Thessaloniki.

Papageorgiou, P. 2006 *Sti Dini Tis Katochis Ke Tou Emfiliou: Mnimes Exorias Ai Stratis-Makronisos*. Yperorios, Samos.

Schofield, J., A. Klausmeier, and L. Purbrick (eds.) 2006 *Re-mapping the Field: New Approaches in Conflict Archaeology*. Westkreuz Verlag, Berlin.

Stavridis, S. (ed.) 2006 *Mnimi Ke Empiria Tou Chorou*. Alexandria, Athens.

Stone, P. 2006 A Dark Tourism Spectrum: Towards a Typology of Death and Macabre Related Tourist Sites, Attractions and Exhibitions. *Tourism: an Interdisciplinary International Journal* 54(2): 145–160.

Tarlow, P. 2005 Dark Tourism–The Appealing "Dark" Side of Tourism and More. In *Niche Tourism, Contemporary Issues, Trends and Cases*, edited by M. Novelli, pp. 47–58. Elsevier Butterworth-Heinemann, Oxford.

Theodorou. V. 1976 Pali Sto Trikeri. In *Stratopeda Ginekon*, edited by V. Theodorou, pp. 403–406. Athanassiou, Peristeri.

Uzzell, D. 1989 The Hot Interpretation of War and Conflict. In *Heritage Interpretation: The Natural and Built Environment*, edited by D. Uzzell, pp. 33–47. Belhaven Press, London.

Uzzell, D. 1998 The Hot Interpretation of The Cold War. In *Monuments of War: The Evaluation, Recording and Management of Twentieth-Century Military Sites*, edited by J. Schofield, pp. 18–20. English Heritage, London.

Van Steen, G. 2005 Forgotten Theater, Theater of the Forgotten: Classical Tragedy on Modern Greek Prison Islands. *Journal of Modern Greek Studies* 23(2): 335–395.

Verdery, K. 1999 *The Political Lives of Dead Bodies: Reburial and Postsocialist Change*. Columbia University Press, New York.

Voglis, P. 2002 *Becoming a Subject: Political Prisoners During the Greek Civil War*. Berghahn Books, New York.

Chapter 12
The Engineering of Genocide: An Archaeology of Dictatorship in Argentina

Andrés Zarankin and Melisa Salerno

Abstract Dictatorships and state terrorism were sociopolitical realities shared by most Latin American countries from 1960 to 1980. These regimes pursued the persecution and extermination of ideas and people considered to be dangerous. The history of political repression in Latin America was frequently silenced by official discourses. Archaeology represents an alternative way to learn more about the 1960–1980 period of violence. In this chapter, we discuss the role played by certain material devices in the identification and punishment of political opponents. We will take the most recent dictatorship in Argentina (1976–1983) as our case study, and we will focus on two different but interrelated expressions of material culture: architecture and dress. Both of these were fundamental in the engineering of genocide, as they were used in the definition and denial of victims' identities.

Introduction

The capacity for invention is one of the distinguishing features of human beings compared to other forms of life on Earth. As archaeologists, we are familiar with the many and varied practices developed by humans through time. Artifacts and structures are continually created within cultural contexts, through which they gain specific meanings and purposes. Buildings, tools, medicines, means of communication and transportation, ostensibly, make our lives easier. Our capacity for invention has a dark side too, which, instead of fascinating, frightens. Here, we refer to the people and things that work together toward the stigmatization, torture, and murder of those considered to be enemies.

A. Zarankin (✉)
Federal University of Minas Gerais, Belo Horizonte, Brazil
e-mail: zarankin@yahoo.com

M. Salerno
National Council for Scientific and Technical Research, Buenos Aires, Argentina
e-mail: melisa_salerno@yahoo.com.ar

A. Myers, G. Moshenska (eds.), *Archaeologies of Internment*, One World Archaeology, 207
DOI 10.1007/978-1-4419-9666-4_12, © Springer Science+Business Media, LLC 2011

For many centuries, dominant groups have been interested in developing new methods for identifying and dealing with their enemies, who are often understood as a threat to social order. This need increases in times of conflict, perhaps due to the anxiety caused by an unknown number of opponents. In some cases, the identification of persecuted people depends on the recognition of certain aspects of their appearance: the Nazis believed the Jews had an easily recognizable appearance, which was used to justify their inferiority and extermination (Mills 2002). A similar trend was observed after the 11 September 2001 attacks in New York City, when government agents began to identify men of "Middle Eastern appearance" as potential terrorists (Mogul and Ritchie 2007). Once identified, the enemies are isolated, controlled, and sometimes killed in locations created specifically for that aim. The Nazi concentration camps are an infamous historical example (Sofsky 1999); the "black sites" established under the administration of President George W. Bush are a contemporary one (Amnesty International 2005, 2006; ICRC 2007).

In recent years, researchers have shown great interest in discussing different aspects of the postmodern world through the analysis of material culture (Beaudry et al. 1991; Johnson 1996; Orser 1996). From an interpretive point of view (Hodder 1991; Hodder et al. 1995), archaeologists have focused on the role played by objects and structures in the constitution of social life. The analysis of material culture has proved useful in understanding the production, reproduction, and change of specific practices and identities, regardless of time and space variables. In this context, and particularly from the 1990s onward, researchers have studied the exercise and consequences of violence in their own societies. Among other things, this possibility was connected to the recognition that archaeology was not a neutral scientific endeavor, but was in fact closely associated with politics and subjectivity.

Following recent developments in archaeologies of conflict (e.g., Schofield et al. 2002; Huyssen 2003; Saunders 2004; Funari and Zarankin 2006, 2008; González-Ruibal 2008; Schofield 2009; Funari et al. 2009), this chapter discusses the role played by certain material devices in the repression of political dissidence in the recent past. We will focus on a specific Latin American case study: the most recent military dictatorship in Argentina. Latin America is frequently discussed by human rights researchers for its history of oppressive regimes, and Argentina in particular has become tragically recognized for the violence of its latest dictatorial rule. Here we will consider two material expressions used by Argentinean repressive forces in the identification and punishment of their enemies: dress and architecture. Both these factors were fundamental to the engineering of genocide[1] in the country between 1976 and 1983.

---

[1] The term "genocide" is widely used by the legal system, civil rights movements and social sciences in Argentina to refer to the systematic murder of politically persecuted people during the most recent dictatorship (Feierstein 2007). In this context, the term is not exclusively used to define the attempt to destroy an ethnic or a national group, but any given group (be it racial, religious or political, among others) in part or in its entirety (Melson 1992; Charny 1994). Among other things, the use of the term genocide was relevant for prosecutors to transform the actions of the military regime into crimes against humanity which could not possibly prescribe (the average period in which homicides prescribe in Argentina is of ten years).

During this most recent dictatorship, military forces in Argentina used physical appearance (mainly dress) as a way to identify people that would be stigmatized. Through this and other means they tried to define subversion as a social category, which gathered together all forms of disagreement with government policies. Once identified, these newly created enemies were transferred to Clandestine Detention Centers (CDCs) where they were held captive indefinitely (most of the time, until they were killed and their bodies hidden in unmarked graves). The materiality of these spaces and the actions taken by military agents (some of which were associated with dress) aimed to destroy the apparently dangerous character of the victims.

Taking these ideas into account, we will here discuss some of the mechanisms employed by the Argentinean military government to define and subsequently deny the identity of its opponents. We will use varied lines of evidence, including official discourses, survivors' testimonies and the results of archaeological excavations. Included in the latter are the excavations undertaken at a CDC located in the city of Buenos Aires known as *Club Atlético*, and the fragments of clothing associated to some of the bodies exhumed at Lomas de Zamora Cemetery.

Military Dictatorships in Latin America

The history of military dictatorships in Argentina should be understood within a larger sociopolitical context, as the regimes were part of a conflict on regional and global scales (Zarankin and Salerno 2008). Since the victory of the independence movements, Latin America swayed between democratic and authoritarian governments (Meyer and Mena 1989). During the 1960s and 1970s, several countries in Central and South America came under rule of dictatorships. For instance, Argentina (1966–1973, 1976–1983), Bolivia (1964–1982), Brazil (1964–1985), Chile (1973–1990), Ecuador (1963–1966), Honduras (1963–1971, 1972–1982), Panama (1968–1989), Peru (1968–1980), and Uruguay (1973–1985). Other countries suffered under dictatorial governments which dated back to previous decades. For instance, the Dominican Republic (1930–1978), El Salvador (1931–1982), Guatemala (1921–1986), Haiti (1957–1990), Nicaragua (1936–1979), and Paraguay (1949–1989).

In the 1960s and 1970s, most Latin American dictatorships were military regimes. They were ruled by particular forms of government, commonly known as *juntas* (Feitlowitz 1999). Juntas referred to political committees or boards composed of military officers. Once in power, they instituted a series of martial laws, which implied an exception to ordinary legislation (the political order defended by national constitutions). In general, military juntas held extraordinary powers due to supposed "states of emergency"—situations where judicial institutions were ostensibly unable to ensure the safety and well-being of the nation. These powers were an ordinary means to limit or suspend civil liberties, such as the freedom of speech and the right to due process.

After the 1959 Cuban Revolution, left-wing movements spread across Latin America (Avelar 1999). As Wright (2007) suggests, the fast growth led to the creation of revolutionary groups, increasing number of strikes and protests, and farmers and workers' discontent and organization. In some cases, left-wing political parties managed to gain significant positions in democratic elections. On other occasions, left-wing movements encouraged militarized actions, mainly guerrilla operations, against the governments of the moment (Wright 2007). Despite their significant diversity, left-wing movements usually shared a common basis in Marxist ideology. Therefore, they stressed the connections between capitalism and inequality, and the possibility of constructing a fairer society.

Latin American dictatorships used repressive forces on the pretext of protecting the best interests of their nations. They conducted dirty wars against any and all forms of political opposition. Repressive methods included exile, murder, and enforced disappearance (the deprivation of liberty by agents of the state, followed by the concealment of the whereabouts of the disappeared person, who is left outside of the protection of the law-United Nations 2006). State terrorism frequently resorted to psychological campaigns to spread fear, diminish political resistance, and encourage witch hunts and denunciations among the population. Latin American dictatorships, as with all dictatorships, took great pains to control information (Herman and Chomsky 2002). They censored the media, and concealed or destroyed the official documents that cataloged their actions. Dominant narratives were intended to silence the voices of the victims, manipulating public opinion with the aim to legitimate state-sponsored violence.

Repression in Latin America developed within an international context dominated by the Cold War (Acuña 2003). This war was expressed as a rivalry between capitalism (represented by the United States of America) and socialism (represented by the Soviet Union) beginning after World War II. This period was characterized by a permanent state of tension, a tension perhaps magnified due to the lack of any explicit declaration of war. The United States of America felt that the growth of left-wing movements in Latin America threatened their national security (Lernoux 1980), and thus supported the aspirations of military elites in the region. Dictatorships were expected to control any dissidence directed against capitalism. The United States often provided political, economic, and military support to these regimes, including intelligence services and military instruction, for example at the infamous *School of the Americas* (Gill 2004).

Many similarities exist in the repressive methods employed by Latin American dictatorships between the 1960s and the 1980s. Some of these patterns account for the existence of a coordinated strategy among several countries of the region. It is well established that Latin American governments elaborated a joint plan of political repression in 1975. *Plan Cóndor* (Operation Condor) was a military program developed in the Southern Cone. It included Argentina, Brazil, Chile, Bolivia, Uruguay, Paraguay, and peripherally, Peru and Ecuador. *Plan Cóndor* was designed to conduct intelligence activities, and persecute and exterminate political opposition (Nilson 1998; McSherry 2002; Calloni 2006).

We will now turn to the specific case of military dictatorship in Argentina. On 24 March 1976, a military coup overthrew the democratically elected president,

Isabel Martínez de Perón (General Juan Domingo Perón's widow), on the pretext that her government was unable to control the action of subversive groups which threatened the order supposedly dictated by tradition. A junta consisting of Lieutenant-General Jorge Rafael Videla, Admiral Emilio Massera, and Brigadier-General Orlando Agosti took power. The *Proceso de Reorganización Nacional* (National Reorganization Process, 1976–1983) which followed is the most sinister period in Argentinean history. It was aimed at destroying popular resistance through the physical annihilation of its enemies: any institutions or people who resisted their power (IACHR 1980; CONADEP 1984).

The Engineering of Genocide in Argentina

As in most South American countries, political repression in Argentina was organized by a paramilitary structure: a clandestine service of the state military forces. During the most recent dictatorship, enforced disappearance was a key aspect of political violence. It depended on the identification of persecuted people, and their subsequent kidnapping and imprisonment in unknown locations (CDCs). Political prisoners had no legal rights and were at the mercy of their captors. They were brutally tortured and frequently killed. Both testimonies and archaeological evidence point out that the *Desaparecidos* (The Disappeared) were thrown from military airplanes or helicopters into the *Río de la Plata*, or were shot and buried in unmarked mass graves (Bellelli and Tobin 1985; EAAF 1992; Doretti and Fondebrider 2001).

Thousands of people of all ages and occupations including workers, students, professionals, and teachers were kidnapped by military agents in Argentina, and most were never seen or heard from again. In 1983 and 1984, the *Comisión Nacional sobre la Desaparición de Personas* (National Commission on the Disappearance of People) registered more than 9,000 cases of enforced disappearance between 1976 and 1983 (CONADEP 1984). Human rights organizations such as *Asociación Madres de Plaza de Mayo* (Association of Mothers of the Plaza de Mayo) (2005) and the *Servicio de Paz y Justicia* (Peace and Justice Service) registered more than 30,000 cases.

In spite of survivors' testimonies and legal investigations, several aspects of political repression still remain unknown and unexplained. In general, military forces attempted to hide the evidence of their crimes—as mentioned before, government authorities ordered the destruction of official documents on paramilitary operations. Furthermore, they commanded the dismantling of CDCs, and they denied the existence of mass graves. It is within this context of secrecy and denial that archaeology—a discipline centrally concerned with the study of material remains—became involved in shedding light on dictatorship and disappearance in Argentina. The first work on the subject was interested in finding and identifying the bodies of the victims (EAAF 1991, 1992, 1993; Doretti and Fondebrider 2001). In recent years, some researchers have started to study the structures and objects associated with repression (Funari and Zarankin 2006, 2008; Zarankin and Salerno 2008).

Enforced disappearance is intimately connected to the imposition, manipulation, and destruction of victims' identities at the hands of victimizers. The identification of enemies depended on the creation of a new social category. The concept of subversion was used to stereotype, demonize, and stigmatize those chosen for political persecution. Once the victims were kidnapped and imprisoned, the military agents employed repressive strategies to deny their identities. These methods distanced people from their own self-understanding as individuals. Paradoxically, they also distanced them from the stereotype of subversives that the dictatorship had previously created to define them. The military forces intended to transform victims into passive, helpless, and dominated beings. For those not in prison, the detainees were nowhere to be found and became *desaparecidos*. Murder, in a sense, was an extension of the victims' disappearance.

Identities reside in bodies which have a deep connection with the material world (Tarlow 2002; Joyce 2005). On the one hand, bodies have a material existence. On the other, they allow us to relate ourselves with the material things that surround us, such as other people and objects. Some expressions of material culture play an active role in the definition of identities (Beaudry et al. 1991); that is to say, in the definition of social differences and similarities. As a consequence, they have the potential of classifying and distributing bodies in different social contexts. These expressions of material culture produce and are, in turn, produced by meaningful practices and practical meanings that are mostly performed through the body. If identities account for who we are and what we do—and simultaneously who others are and what they do—then material culture has a significant influence on self-understanding and the understanding of others (Jones 1995; 1999). In this chapter we discuss the role that certain expressions of material culture could have played in the definition and denial of persecuted people's identities during the most recent dictatorship in Argentina. We will particularly focus on dress and architecture, as these two elements were fundamental to the identification and forced disappearance (kidnapping, imprisonment and even death) of the victims.

The Appearance of the Enemy

The identification of the enemy by the military dictatorship depended on the development of a new process of social categorization (Salerno 2009). Categories do not always match what people think of themselves; that is to say, they do not necessarily involve self-determination, but rather, the imposition of social identities (Jenkins 1996). Categorization might be understood as a strategy of domination: part of the mechanisms dominant groups use to impose their will upon others (De Certeau 1980; Frazer 1999). Nation-states frequently employ categorization as a means to catalog, organize, and control their populations (Foucault 1976). It is worthwhile to remember that nation-states are supported by repression and propaganda, and the way they classify people can thus have a major impact on citizens' lives. Official discourses (including government decrees, military authorities' statements, and publicity spots, among others) will provide information that will help us decipher some of the ideas that the government wanted to impose on society.

Social categories frequently use stereotypes with the aim of diminishing the efforts of evaluating and classifying individuals and groups. The construction of stereotypes is associated with the selection of a series of attributes, which apparently define the members of a given category—leaving aside some other characteristics. This process of generalization reduces the possibility of distinguishing diversity within a class (Archenti 2005). Between 1976 and 1983, the military government in Argentina decided to classify people according to their proximity to the military world. The official discourse of the time placed each citizen along a social continuum, with good/healthy/positive/ordered/capitalist representing the ideal pole, and evil/sick/negative/chaotic/socialist representing the least ideal.

In general, people were placed on three different positions. The military forces occupied one extreme of the continuum. They were in charge of the *Proceso de Reorganización Nacional*, and they were the ultimate authority in the country. During the 1970s, the government stressed that Argentina was increasingly dominated by terrorism, violence, and chaos (Junta Militar 1980[1976]:11). Official discourses pointed out the need to face a profound moral and ethical crisis. The military forces believed that their duty was to return peace, faith, and health to the nation (APA 1978:3; AUA 1998:13). From their own perspective, citizens could occupy two different positions in the social continuum: "good citizens" wanted to collaborate with the government and they were willing to live their lives in peace and order. Alternatively, "bad citizens" represented a threat to the republic, as they expressed an ideological and practical opposition to life conditions in the country. These were labeled "subversive" (Consejo de Defensa 1975:1; Junta Militar 1980[1976]:7).

Of interest to us here is the fate of those who were thought to fit the category subversive—those who were eventually subject to enforced disappearance. It is important to remember that the identification of these individuals demanded their previous stigmatization. For Goffman (2003:11), stigmas are a series of undesirable attributes which discredit people in social interaction. Stigmas may transform people into weak, dangerous, and evil beings, usually detached from mainstream society (Goffman 2003:12). Subversion was particularly useful to create a distorted imaginary about the other. In general terms, it mixed up ideas about the strange with ideas about the enemy. Without a doubt, subversion as a social category facilitated political persecution. By means of a "psychological" campaign on the part of the government (Ejército 1975:1), the existence and proliferation of subversion in Argentina was thought to be recognizable by the "good" citizens.

According to Goffman (2003:14), the stigmas include defects of personality, such as domineering passions, and false or rigid beliefs. During the last dictatorship in Argentina, subversion was considered to be part of these defects, as it represented an extreme political behavior. Official discourses frequently associated subversion with international terrorism (Junta Militar 2008 [circa 1976]) promoted by the "faithless and antichristian Marxism" (APA 1978:5). Furthermore, these discourses defined subversion as a "disease" (AUA 1998:14; Gente 1977 in SDH 2004): a state of disorder which demanded a major intervention of the state to be cured or to be isolated and annihilated (Schindel 2000). As any other disease, subversion was supposed to affect peoples' bodies and have specific symptoms. Most of them were seemingly reflected in bodily image. From this perspective, it is possible to point out that the appearance and consolidation of subversion as a social category was closely connected to the construction of stereotypes and stigmas concerning external appearance.

On several occasions, military discourses claimed that certain expressions of material culture (mainly dress and adornment) were fundamental to social classi-fication. This idea was based on the assumption that appearance had the potential to reveal the essence of people—independently of their attempts to hide it. Goffman (2003:56) stressed that stigmatized individuals could be analytically divided into the "discredited" and "discreditable." The condition of the former was thought to be known or easily detected, while that of the latter was thought to be unknown or difficult to perceive during social interaction. In the most recent dictatorship in Argentina, discredited and discreditable people were associated with different styles of physical appearance.

In the early days of the regime, military forces spread the idea that subversion referred to guerrilla men and women who participated in left-wing political orga-nizations. Official discourses stressed that these people could be identified by a military appearance. Museums of subversion made explicit use of this idea. In these macabre museums, Argentinean citizens were taught several strategies to recognize their supposed enemies, exaggerating and caricaturing their appearance (Pigna and Seoane 2006). In general, these subversive mannequins wore uniforms and badges (along with weapons, political flags, and pamphlets). These articles were thought to provide significant information on political affiliation and specific ranks within different organizations. It is rather unbelievable that the enemies of the state would in fact dress as they were depicted in the museums—doing so would quickly render them identifiable and punishable targets.

A short time later, the government widened their scope. They stated that sub-version not only involved guerrilla men and women, but it also included seemingly harmless people: students, teachers, and priests, among others. Subversion quickly stopped being represented by an easily identifiable paramilitary enemy. Official discourses gave some clues to recognize subversion in informal dress, clearly dis-tinct from military style clothing. According to the security forces, subversive individuals were untidy and dirty (Garaño and Pertot 2002). Dressing practices rejected by official discourses were associated with the subversive intention of changing the accepted social order. Informal appearance—as that of intellectual and young people—was frequently connected to the hippie movement (Saulquin 2006). During the 1960s and most of the 1970s, jeans, long hair, beards, and bright colors were symbols of nonconformity. This kind of appearance was considered to be an expression of resistance to dominant traditions, such as capitalism and state policies.

The Disappearance of the Persecuted

Once subversion became defined as a social stigma, the military government began to punish all individuals who fit the category. These stigmatized individu-als were kidnapped, tortured, and killed whenever possible. The procedure involving clandestine detention and imprisonment was termed *chupar* (to swallow), and it was conducted by paramilitary groups called *patotas* or *grupo de tareas* (task groups). Most of the time, political prisoners were taken to CDCs.

CDCs were used by different Latin American dictatorships in the 1970s, mainly those participating in *Plan Cóndor*. However, they only became massively and systematically organized in Argentina between 1976 and 1983. CDCs combined the worst traits of previous punitive traditions including medieval practices of torture and the panopticon regimes of the Enlightenment, particularly the distribution of prisoners in isolated spaces and the organization of time through daily routines (Foucault 1976). Some other characteristics, presented in detail below, were exclusive to CDCs.

Until recently, little archaeological research had been conducted on CDCs in Argentina (but see Bozzuto et al. 2004; EIMePoC 2008; Zarankin and Niro 2009). This situation is probably associated with the horror they inspire and the need some people have to deny recent history. It is necessary to overcome these obstacles in order to understand how victims were punished and their identities transformed during the dictatorship. As previously mentioned, in this case we will take into account two different but related expressions of material culture: architecture and dress. As most CDCs were destroyed at the end of the military government, the archaeological study of their material remains is a unique tool to learn more about dictatorship and its aftermath. The analysis of these remains can be completed by studying survivors' testimonies which shed light on people's experience during their imprisonment.

The *Club Atlético* CDC

We use the *Club Atlético* CDC as our main case study, but we also draw on data from other CDCs in Argentina. The *Club Atlético* received its code name from the initials of the real name of the institution: *Centro Antisubversivo* (antisubversive center). This CDC was in operation in the basement of the Federal Police Warehouse in Buenos Aires between February and December 1977. During that period, approximately 1,500 people were kidnapped and taken there. Most of them were never seen again. *Club Atlético* was demolished at the end of 1977 in an attempt to hide and deny its existence. On top of the remains, the military government built part of the *25 de Mayo* Highway. This highway acts as a seal which makes it difficult to access the surviving remains of the CDC.

In 2002, the government of the city of Buenos Aires supported the development of an archaeological project conducted by Marcelo Weissel (2002). The project originated as a response to the request of *Club Atlético* survivors. These people believed that archaeologists would be able to find the remains of the CDC in the intersection of *Paseo Colón* Avenue and *25 de Mayo* Highway. A Commission for Work and Consensus was then created. It was made up of *Club Atlético* survivors and victims' relatives, human rights organizations (such as *Madres de Plaza de Mayo, Hijos por la Identidad y la Justicia contra el Olvido y el Silencio, Centro de Estudios Legales y Sociales,* and *Abuelas de Plaza de Mayo*), the Human Rights Department

Fig. 12.1 Archaeological excavations at *Club Atlético* clandestine detention center. Photograph by Andrés Zarankin

of the city of Buenos Aires, and a group of experts, including engineers, architects, conservation professionals, and archaeologists. It is interesting to note that in this commission, archaeologists were only consultants, and the decisions on the excavation process were made by all commission members.

In 2003, this archaeological intervention was cut off as a result of political and academic differences between archaeologists and the commission. Thus, the City of Buenos Aires opened a bidding process for a new excavation project. The proposal *Archaeology as Memory: Archaeological Interventions at Club Atlético Clandestine Center of Detention and Torture* (Bianchi Villelli and Zarankin 2003a) was eventually chosen. In this case, archaeologists tried to excavate the structure of the building and recover the objects associated with the operation of the CDC (Fig. 12.1). At the same time, they intended to reinforce memory and call everybody's attention on a history which was frequently denied by official discourses. They wanted to make a true contribution to justice, as they were committed to meet the requests of survivors and victims of repression in Argentina.

Architecture

Club Atlético followed some of the principles of nineteenth-century punitive institutions, including the norm of prisoners' isolation from the outside world and from the other people inside the building. As social identities are relational, these circumstances transformed the way people defined themselves (and were, in turn, defined by the others). According to Foucault (1976:240), "loneliness is the first condition for total submission . . . isolation ensures the dialogue between the prisoner and the power which is exercised over him". In CDCs, architecture and dress had special importance in this process.

Prisons, concentration camps, and CDCs intend to reduce contact between supposedly dangerous people and society. This is why these institutions strictly control the comings and goings of people and things. In the case of CDCs, isolation is complete and all encompassing. Prisons and concentration camps are easily recognizable from the outside: everybody knows where they are, their existence is officially accepted, and they are ruled by laws which—in principle if not in practice—guarantee some level of respectful treatment of prisoners. CDCs operate within preexisting buildings (CONADEP 1984; Calvo 2002; Daleo 2002; Di Ciano et al. 2001), modifying their interior to create repressive institutions. *Club Atlético* operated in the basement of an official institution: except for those inside the building (and not always all of them, as prisoners had trouble with identifying where they were), nobody knew where it was; it did not officially exist, and thus this absolute secrecy offered absolute impunity. Perhaps, then, prisons and concentration camps can be described as places, while CDCs such as *Club Atlético* can be defined as non-places. These non-places eventually transformed people into *desaparecidos* (Zarankin and Niro 2009).

The military authorities wanted CDC prisoners to know that they had been completely separated from the outside world. Survivors' testimonies point out that in these institutions people were given a code, a number and/or a letter, which replaced their real name (AEDD 2006). One of the first things that military agents did when victims arrived at CDCs was to take every personal belonging away from them. Thus, they were forced to undress. They were later tortured and asked to dress again (CONADEP 1984). Enforced nakedness achieved several interrelated goals: first, it was intended to blur the cultural condition of prisoners, denying their rights as human beings; second, it was intended to break the boundaries of modesty, fostering feelings of humiliation among the victims. Third, it was intended to facilitate torture and increase the experience of pain. This procedure shows some resemblances with those used in other repressive institutions such as Nazi concentration camps (Chapter 5 by Myers, this volume) or American black sites (ICRC 2007). When the torture was over, CDC prisoners were forced to dress in uniforms or clothes previously worn by other captives (Actis et al. 2006). The use of clothes different from their own made prisoners feel distant from the objects which reminded them of their life before imprisonment.

As previously mentioned, the goals of CDCs were not only to separate prisoners from the outside world, but from the rest of the people inside the building as well. The spatial organization of *Club Atlético* provides an interesting example of these circumstances. *Club Atlético* can be divided into two distinct areas: the top floor served as an administrative center, while the basement contained the torture rooms and the prison cells. This organization divided and classified people into two opposing groups: military agents/dominants/above and enemies/dominated/below. Official documents such as architectural drawings offered little information on the basement, as its transformation into a prison was expected to be secret. In order to broaden our understanding of the building, we used a series of drawings elaborated by survivors. Archaeological drawings could not be completed by the interpretation of material remains, as more than 80% of *Club Atlético's* surface remains unexcavated (it lies under the highway). However, archaeological drawings were compared with survivors' sketches, showing remarkable coincidences between them. These graphics were finally analyzed through a series of models, such as Hillier and Hanson's *Gamma Model* (1984).

The *Gamma Model* discloses the underlying structure of a given building by dividing it into a series of spaces and determining the degree of connectivity among them. Hillier and Hanson (1984) claim that most structures can be divided into two different groups: distributive and non-distributive. Distributive structures have multiple spaces accessible from more than one entrance point, while non-distributive structures have multiple spaces accessible from only one opening. Distributive structures have a more democratic character, as the exercise of power and control is homogenously distributed among different spaces (Hillier and Hanson 1984; Markus 1993). In contrast, non-distributive structures concentrate power and control in specific areas, as all of the spaces within these buildings are organized hierarchically. Gamma Model also allows researchers to determine accessibility. Accessibility accounts for the distance between specific spaces within a building and the outside, thus measuring isolation and access difficulty.

The structure of *Club Atlético's* basement was highly segmented and non-distributive. It was intended to separate prisoners in different cells and restrict their circulation within the building. During the excavation, it was possible to identify the

Fig. 12.2 *Club Atlético* prison cell wall with inscription that reads: "God, please help me". Photograph by Andrés Zarankin

remains of prison cells. Some of the walls had writings upon them, giving testimony of the horrifying life conditions in the CDC (Fig. 12.2). In most cases, prisoners only left their cells when they were taken to the torture room. Thus they knew little about other people at the CDC. The military forces considered it was necessary, as they did not want survivors to report the presence of other prisoners or agents if they were ever released. Torture rooms were located at the center of the basement. This was a simple way to ease the task of taking prisoners to the questioning room and allowing other detainees to hear the screams of their partners. Without a doubt, *Club Atlético* reveals that a key element of the CDCs was their cellular and panoptical properties. *Club Atlético* also reveals the CDCs as spaces dominated by violence and repression.

Dress

Inside *Club Atlético* and other CDCs, dress was also a means to reinforce prisoners' isolation and the transformation of their identities. Handcuffs, leg-irons, blindfolds and hoods were usually part of a prisoner's outfit. The main goal of blindfolds and hoods is to suppress the sense of sight. In our society, vision has a strong relationship with knowledge. If knowledge is power, then the gaze is part of its dynamic. Those who play the role of watching have the opportunity to exercise control over things (Thomas 2001). In CDCs, blindfolds and hoods transformed prisoners into passive, observed, and dominated objects—certainly different from the active, dangerous, and stigmatized subversive individuals that dominant discourses had previously defined. These instruments denied prisoners the possibility of recognizing their capturers and the ways in which they could be attacked (Actis et al. 2006). Furthermore, they made people develop other senses (such as sound and smell) to identify moments of tension and calm (CONADEP 1984). Handcuffs and leg-irons complemented the blindfolds and hoods. Together, these devices reduced prisoners' sensory perceptions and physical movements. A similar strategy is currently used at the black sites of the American-led War on Terror (ICRC 2007).

Finally, we would like to add that the archaeological project at *Club Atlético* made it possible to find extensive remains (Bianchi Villelli and Zarakin 2003b). Some objects were associated with the functioning of the CDC. The other materials were debris used to cover the building once it was demolished. Survivors and victims' relatives participated in the excavation and the analysis of the remains (Fig. 12.3). It was a powerful way of simultaneously producing knowledge and social action (Funari 2001). For example, in the first fieldwork season, archaeologists found a ping-pong ball under the remains of the elevator. They were surprised to learn that torturers used to play ping-pong as a way of entertaining themselves. The detainees were kept blindfolded, but they could listen to the ping-pong ball coming and going somewhere nearby. The ping-pong ball proved to be a powerful symbol of the whole detention camp system.

The place where survivors and victims' relatives suspected that *Club Atlético* was located was finally dug out by archaeologists. The material remains of the clandestine center of detention and torture were transformed into a place of memory.

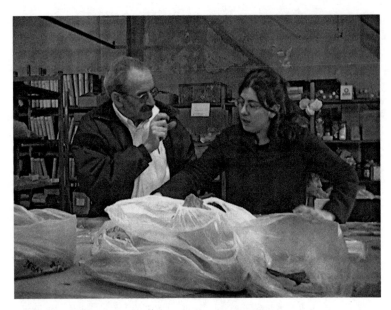

Fig. 12.3 Archaeologist Marcia Bianchi Villelli working at the field laboratory with a *Club Atlético* survivor, Mario Villani. Photograph by Andrés Zarankin

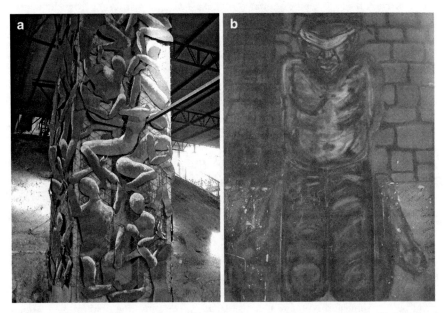

Fig. 12.4 Artistic representation commemorating those who were imprisoned at *Club Atlético*. Photograph by Melisa Salerno

Club Atlético informs Argentineans about the tragic consequences of dictatorship in the country. It offers the opportunity of reflecting on the importance of fundamental rights such as those of life and freedom. Furthermore, *Club Atlético* represents a significant place for survivors and relatives who want to commemorate their dead. The remains not only serve as a meeting point but also as a place for expression and the reappropriation of people's history. The archaeological excavation was surrounded by several artistic representations (Figs. 12.4a, b).

The Final Stage: Death

Most prisoners in *Club Atlético* were killed. The multiple connections between dress, identity, and death were studied through the analysis of an archaeological assemblage. The collection was composed of approximately 300 fragments of clothing from almost 80 garments and shoes. These remains were associated with 38 bodies of people killed during the most recent dictatorship in Argentina (Salerno 2006, 2009). The bodies were exhumed by the *Equipo Argentino de Antropología Forense* (Argentinean Forensic Anthropology Team, or EAAF) at Lomas de Zamora Cemetery between 2004 and 2005. All these bodies showed signs of extreme violence, such as multiple bullet wounds. Since 1984, EAAF has been working in Argentina and in other countries to locate unmarked mass graves and identify the victims of state repression. They use documentary and archaeological information to achieve this goal.

When we began to study the clothing remains from Lomas de Zamora Cemetery we thought it would be possible to transform dress into a complementary line of analysis for the identification of the bodies. Forensic researchers usually compare the garments that witnesses believe the victims were wearing the last time they were seen alive, with the garments eventually found on the bodies. In our case study, bodies exhibited clothes different from those victims wore at the moment they were kidnapped. Furthermore, bodies frequently had few or no pieces of apparel associated with them. In these cases, we were able to find some pieces of underwear and/or a few pieces of clothing covering the upper or lower part of the body. The information obtained through the analysis of clothing remains provided additional evidence on the circumstances surrounding the death of the victims. Most shirts, t-shirts, sweaters, pants, and skirts presented signs of damage such as bullet holes (Fig. 12.5). Blindfolds and ties were also found on the hands and feet of some bodies.

The presence of bodies naked, half-dressed, or wearing clothes different to the ones expected by witnesses' testimonies contributed to the interpretation that these people had been imprisoned in CDCs (Table 12.1). It is relevant to remember that military units forced prisoners to change clothes when they arrived at these CDCs. Moreover, people condemned to death were often forced to wear clean clothes under the promise that they would be released. They were frequently shot in fake confrontations with security agents, and entered the morgue as "*NN*" (*ningún nombre,*

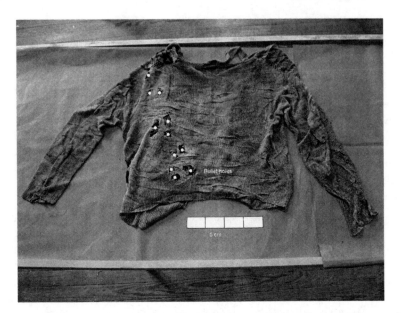

Fig. 12.5 A sweater with bullet holes, excavated at Lomas de Zamora Cemetery. Photograph by Melisa Salerno

Table 12.1 The presence of naked and dressed bodies

	Number
Fully-dressed bodies	12
Half-dressed bodies	18
Naked bodies	8
Total	38

or "no name" corpses) (EAAF 1991, 1992, 1993; Doretti and Fondebrider 2001). Nakedness, torture, and dress changes made the identification of bodies a difficult task. As a whole, they represented a repressive strategy which perpetuated the disappearance of people's identities.

Conclusions

In this chapter, we discuss some of the strategies used by Latin American dictatorships to identify and punish their enemies. We particularly focused on the most recent dictatorship in Argentina as our case study. Material culture played an important role in this analysis. On the one hand, written sources on political repression are scarce and biased. In general, military authorities hid or destroyed the evidence on the worst aspects of their crimes (that is to say, the kidnapping and murder of people). On the other hand, material culture was fundamental to the engineering of genocide. As we have shown in this chapter, some expressions of material culture such as dress and architecture were found to be useful in political violence because of their close connection with the body and identities.

The definition of enemies' identities was one of the first steps that the recent military dictatorship in Argentina took to justify state repression. Subversion as a social category must be thought as a construction which was frequently defined in essentialist terms. Physical appearance was thought to be a simple way to identify subversives. Once they were recognized by the military agents, they were sent to CDCs until their fate was decided. CDCs were designed to annihilate political dissidence by means of an illegal network of repression. The spatial organization of these buildings and the way prisoners were forced to undress, among many other things, were necessary to isolate prisoners from the outside world and the rest of the people inside the CDC. Isolation was a key element in the transformation of prisoners' identities. In this way, detainees were transformed into dominated beings.

Beyond social, political, and legal consequences, the repressive strategies disclosed in this chapter suggest the existence of a significant turn in political violence. The most recent dictatorship in Argentina did not create new methods for identifying and punishing the enemy. The military government stepped over a different threshold: secrecy. The disappearance of thousands of people between 1976 and 1983 gives us some clues about it. The materiality of repressive institutions provides information on the historical changes in the annihilation of the enemies. In the last century, we did not only see the continual development of the nineteenth century prison with the intention of producing docile and useful bodies, we also saw the appearance of black sites: secret prisons where no clear rules seem to exist. Secrecy offers the possibility of going beyond cultural limits.

Argentinean as well as other Latin American CDCs might have set a precedent for contemporary black sites. Their operational principles might have been one of the cornerstones of a new generation of non-places. CDCs fulfilled the expectations of all repressive institutions: getting rid of political opponents without taking full responsibility for the actions. Clandestine repression in Argentina was intimately associated with the disappearance of people both alive and dead. Those who managed to get out of CDCs could never escape the horror of being there. The archaeological study of political violence in Argentina provides a vital tool to reconstruct the history of the victims. It is our commitment as archaeologists to defend the right of survivors, victims' relatives, and all of society to know.

Acknowledgments We thank the National Council for Scientific and Technical Development (Brazil), the Federal University of Minas Gerais (Brazil), and the National Council for Scientific and Technical Research (Argentina) for their support. The Argentinean Forensic Anthropology Team gave us the opportunity to study the garments from Lomas de Zamora. We also thank Adrian Myers and Gabriel Moshenska for their invitation to participate in this volume, and for their valuable comments and suggestions on this work. Finally, we thank Bruno Sanches Ranzani da Silva for helping us with the translation. We are solely responsible for the ideas presented here.

References

Actis, M., C. Aldini, L. Gardella, M. Lewin, and E. Tokar 2006 *Ese Infierno: Conversaciones de Cinco Mujeres Sobrevivientes de la ESMA*. Altamira, Buenos Aires.

Acuña, C. 2003 *Por Amor al Odio. La Tragedia de la Subversión en la Argentina, Tomo I*. Del Pórtico, Buenos Aires.

Amnesty International 2005 United States of America/Yemen: Secret Detention in CIA "Black Sites", 11 June 2009. http://www.amnesty.org/en/library/asset/AMR51/177/2005/en/413e36cb-d493-11dd-8a23-d58a49c0d652/amr511772005en.pdf

Amnesty International 2006 United States of America Below the Radar: Secret Flights to Torture and Disappearance, 11 June 2009. http://www.amnesty.org/en/library/asset/AMR51/051/2006/en/3edf2253-d447-11dd-8743-d305bea2b2c7/amr510512006en.html

Archenti, A. 2005 Imaginario y Representación: Sobre Algunas Formas de Clasificación Social. *Abordajes* 2: 27–29, 10 October 2008. http://www.sada.gba.gov.ar/abordaje.pdf

Asociación Ex-Detenidos Desaparecidos (AEDD) 2006 Testimonios, 10 October 2008. http://www.exdesaparecidos.org.ar/aedd/testimonios.php#

Asociación Madres de Plaza de Mayo 2005 *La Dictadura, la Impunidad y la Compleja Trama de Complicidades, 1976–2005*. Asociación Madres de Plaza de Mayo, Buenos Aires.

Asociación Patriótica Argentina (APA) 1978 *Argentina y sus Derechos Humanos*. Libertad, Buenos Aires.

Asociación Unidad Argentina (AUA) 1998 *Subversión. La Historia Olvidada. Documento Histórico*. AUNAR, Olivos.

Avelar, I. 1999 *The Untimely Present: Postdictatorial Latin American Fiction and the Task of Mourning*. Duke University Press, Durham.

Beaudry, M., L. Cook, and S. Mrozowski 1991 Artifacts and Active Voices: Material Culture as Social Discourse. In *The Archaeology of Inequality*, edited by R. McGuire and R. Paynter, pp. 150–191. Blackwell, London.

Bellelli, C. and J. Tobin 1985 Archaeology of the Desaparecidos. *Society for American Archaeology Bulletin* 14(2): 6–7.

Bianchi Villelli, M. and A. Zarankin 2003a. Arqueología como Memoria. Intervenciones Arqueológicas en el Centro Clandestino de Detención y Tortura "Club Atlético". Manuscript on file, Comisión de Trabajo y Consenso del Proyecto "Recuperación de la Memoria del Centro Clandestino de Detención y Tortura Club Atlético", Dirección General de Derechos Humanos, Gobierno de la Ciudad Autónoma de Buenos Aires, Buenos Aires.

Bianchi Villelli, M. and A. Zarankin 2003b. Arqueología como Memoria. Intervenciones Arqueológicas en el Centro Clandestino de Detención y Tortura "Club Atlético". Informe de Avance -Bimestre Julio/Agosto. Manuscript on file, Comisión de Trabajo y Consenso del Proyecto "Recuperación de la Memoria del Centro Clandestino de Detención y Tortura Club Atlético", Dirección General de Derechos Humanos, Gobierno de la Ciudad Autónoma de Buenos Aires, Buenos Aires.

Bozzuto, D., A. Diana, A. Di Vruno, V. Dolce, and V. Vázquez 2004 "Mansión Seré": Debates y Reflexiones. In *Resúmenes del XV Congreso Nacional de Arqueología Argentina*, p. 207. Universidad Nacional de Río Cuarto, Río Cuarto.

Calloni, S. 2006 *Operación Cóndor: Pacto Criminal*. Editorial Ciencias Sociales, La Habana.

Calvo, A. 2002 La Academia de la Bonaerense. *Revista de la Asociación de Ex–Detenidos Desaparecidos* 2(6): 9–12.

Charny, I. 1994 Towards a Generic Definition of Genocide. In *Genocide: Conceptual and Historical Dimensions*, edited by G. Andreopoulus, pp. 64–94. University of Pennsylvania Press, Philadelphia.

CONADEP 1984 *Nunca Más: Informe de la Comisión Nacional Sobre la Desaparición de Personas*. Eudeba, Buenos Aires.

Consejo de Defensa 1975 Directiva del Consejo de Defensa N° 1/75 (Lucha contra la Subversión). Nunca Más. Documentos Militares, 11 June 2009. http://www.nuncamas.org/document/document.htm

Daleo, G. 2002 Escuela de Mecánica de la Armada; "Esto No Tiene Límites", Jorge Acosta Dixit. *Revista de la Asociación de Ex–Detenidos Desaparecidos* 1(5): 9–14.

De Certeau, M. 1980 *La Invención de lo Cotidiano. Vol. 1. Artes de Hacer*. Universidad Iberoamericana, México City.

Di Ciano, L., M. Benítez, and Z. Enríquez 2001 Cerca de Casa, los Dueños de la Vida. *Revista de la Asociación de Ex–Detenidos Desaparecidos* 1(3): 9–13.

Doretti, M. and L. Fondebrider 2001. Science and Human Rights: Truth, Justice, Reparation and Reconciliation, a Long Way in Third World Countries. In *Archaeologies of the Contemporary Past*, edited by V. Buchli and G. Lucas, pp. 138–144. Routledge, New York.

Ejército Argentino 1975 Plan del Ejército (Contribuyente al Plan de Seguridad Nacional). Anexo 15 (Acción Psicológica). Nunca Más. Documentos Militares, 11 June 2009. http://www.nuncamas.org/document/document.htm

Equipo Argentino de Antropología Forense (EAAF) 1991 Antropología Forense: Nuevas Respuestas para Problemas de Siempre. *Gaceta Arqueológica Andina* 20: 109–118.

Equipo Argentino de Antropología Forense (EAAF) 1992 Excavando la Violencia: Arqueología y Derechos Humanos en el Cono Sur. In *Arqueología en América Latina*, edited by G. Politis. Biblioteca del Banco Popular, Buenos Aires.

Equipo Argentino de Antropología Forense (EAAF) 1993 La Antropología Forense: Informe de Situación. *Publicar en Antropología y Ciencias Sociales* 3(3): 109–118.

Equipo de Investigación por la Memoria Política Cultural (EIMePoC) 2008 *"El Pozo" (Ex Servicio de Informaciones). Un Centro Clandestino de Detención, Desaparición, Tortura y Muerte de Personas de la Ciudad de Rosario, Argentina*. Prohistoria, Rosario.

Feierstein, D. 2007 *El Genocidio como Práctica Social. Entre el Nazismo y la Experiencia Argentina. Hacia un Análisis del Aniquilamiento como Reorganizador de las Relaciones Sociales*. Fondo de Cultura Económica, San Diego.

Feitlowitz, M. 1999 *A Lexicon of Terror: Argentina and the Legacies of Torture*. Oxford University Press, New York.

Foucault, M. 1976 *Vigilar y Castigar; El Nacimiento de la Prisión*. Siglo XXI, México.

Frazer, B. 1999 Reconceptualizing Resistance in the Historical Archaeology of the British Isles: An Editorial. *International Journal of Historical Archaeology* 3(1): 1–10.

Funari, P. 2001 Public archaeology from a Latin American perspective. *Public Archaeology* 1(4): 239–243.

Funari, P. and A. Zarankin (eds.) 2006 *Arqueología de la Represión y la Resistencia en América Latina (1970–1980)*. Brujas, Córdoba.

Funari, P. and A. Zarankin 2008 "Eternal Sunshine of the Spotless Mind": Archaeology and Construction of Memory of Military Repression in South America (1960–1980). *Archaeologies* 4(2): 310–327.

Funari, P., A. Zarankin, and M. Salerno (eds.) 2009 *Memories from Darkness: Archaeology of Repression and Resistance in Latin America*. Springer, New York.

Garaño, S. and W. Pertot 2002 *La Otra Juvenilia. Militancia y Represión en el Colegio Nacional de Buenos Aires (1971–1983)*. Biblos, Buenos Aires.

Gill, L. 2004 *The School of the Americas: Military Training and Political Violence in the Americas*. Duke University Press, Durham.

Goffman, E. 2003 *Estigma: La Identidad Deteriorada*. Amorrortu, Buenos Aires.

González Ruibal, A. 2008 Time to Destroy: An Archaeology of Supermodernity. *Current Anthropology* 49(2): 247–279.

Herman E. and N. Chomsky 2002 *Manufacturing Consent: The Political Economy of the Mass Media*. Panteón Books, New York.

Hillier, B. and J. Hanson 1984 *The Social Logic of Space*. Cambridge University Press, Cambridge.

Hodder, I. 1991 *Reading the Past: Current Approaches to Interpretation in Archaeology.* Cambridge University Press, Cambridge.

Hodder, I., S. Shanks, A. Alexandri, V. Buchli, J. Carman, J. Last, and G. Lucas 1995 *Interpreting Archaeology: Finding Meaning in the Past.* Routledge, London.

Huyssen, A. 2003 *Present Past: Urban Palimpsests and the Politics of Memory.* Stanford University Press, Stanford.

Inter-American Commission on Human Rights (IACHR). 1980 Report on the Situation of Human Rights in Argentina, 11 June 2009. http://www.cidh.oas.org/countryrep/Argentina80eng/toc.htm

International Committee of the Red Cross (ICRC) 2007 ICRC Report on the Treatment of Fourteen "High Value Detainees" in CIA Custody, 11 June 2009. http://www.humansecuritygateway.info/documents/ICRC_Report_TreatmentOfFourteenHighValueDetainees_CIACustody.pdf

Jenkins, R. 1996 *Social Identity.* Routledge, London.

Johnson, M. 1996 *An Archaeology of Capitalism.* Blackwell, Oxford.

Jones, S. 1995 Discourses of Identity in the Interpretation of the Past. In *The Construction of European Communities*, edited by P. Graves, S. Jones and C. Gamble, pp. 119–153. Routledge, London.

Jones, S. 1999 Historical Categories and the Praxis of Identity: The Interpretation of Ethnicity in Historical Archaeology. In *Historical Archaeology: Back from the Edge*, edited by P. Funari, M. Hall, and S. Jones, pp. 219–232. Rouledge, London.

Joyce, R. 2005 Archaeology of the Body. *Annual Review of Anthropology* 34: 139–158.

Junta Militar 1980 [1976] Documentos Básicos y Bases Políticas de las Fuerzas Armadas para el Proceso de Reorganización Nacional. Congreso de la Nación, Buenos Aires.

Junta Militar 2008 [Circa 1976] Comercial contra la subversión. http://www.youtube.com/watch?v=IQRgUHO-d5M (Accessed 1 October 2009)

Lernoux, P. 1980 *Cry of the People: The Struggle for Human Rights in Latin America and the Catholic Church in Conflict with US Policy.* Penguin Books, New York.

Markus, T. 1993 *Buildings and Power; Freedom and Control in the Origins of Modern Building Types.* Blackwell, Oxford.

McSherry, P. 2002 Tracking the Origins of a State Terror Network: Operation Condor. *Latin American Perspectives* 29(1): 36–60.

Melson, R. 1992 *Revolution and Genocide: On the Origins of the American Genocide and the Holocaust.* University of Chicago Press, Chicago.

Meyer, L. and J. Mena 1989 Introducción. In *Los Sistemas Políticos en América Latina*, edited by L. Meyer and J. Mena, pp. 17–21. Siglo XXI /Universidad de las Naciones Unidas, México City.

Mills, M. 2002 Poisoning Young Minds in Nazi Germany: Children and Propaganda in the Third Reich. *Social Education* 66(4): 228–230.

Mogul, J. and A. Ritchie 2007 In the Shadows of the War on Terror: Persistent Police Brutality and Abuse of People of Color in the United States. A Report Prepared for the United Nations Committee on the Elimination of Racial Discrimination on the Occasion of its Review of the United States of America's Second and Third Report to the Committee on the Elimination of Racial Discrimination.

Nilson, C. 1998 *Operación Cóndor: Terrorismo de Estado en el Cono Sur.* Lholé-Lumen, Buenos Aires.

Orser, C. 1996 *A Historical Archaeology of the Modern World.* Plenum Press, New York.

Pigna, F. and M. Seoane 2006 *La Noche de la Dictadura. Memoria Fotográfica Inédita a 30 Años del Terror, Caras y Caretas.* Buenos Aires, Argentina.

Salerno, M. 2006 Informe del Análisis de Indumentaria del Cementerio de Lomas de Zamora. Manuscript on file, Equipo Argentino de Antropología Forense, Buenos Aires.

Salerno, M. 2009 "They Must Have Done Something Wrong…": The Construction of "Subversion" as a Social Category, and the Reshaping of Identities through Body and Dress. In *Memories from Darkness: Archaeology of Dictatorship and Repression in Latin America (1960–1980)*, edited by P. Funari, A. Zarankin, and M. Salerno. Springer, New York.

Saulquin, S. 2006 *Historia de la Moda Argentina. Del Miriñaque al Diseño de Autor*. Emecé, Buenos Aires.

Saunders, N. (ed.) 2004 *Matters of Conflict: Material Culture, Memory and the First World War*. Routledge, London.

Schindel, E. 2000 Palabra, Cuerpo y Ausencia. Los Desaparecidos en el Discurso Oficial de la Prensa Escrita, 1978–1998. Scholarship Report UBA/ADUBA 1998. Manuscript on file, Facultad de Ciencias Sociales, Universidad de Buenos Aires, Buenos Aires.

Schofield, J. 2009 *Aftermath: Readings in the Archaeology of Recent Conflict*. Springer, New York.

Schofield, J., W. Johnson, and C. Beck (eds.) 2002 *Matériel Culture: The Archaeology of Twentieth Century Conflict*. Routledge, London.

Secretaría de Derechos Humanos (SDH) 2004 Educación y Terrorismo de Estado. SUTEBA ¿Usted Sabe qué Lee su Hijo en Este Momento…, 1 October 2009. http://www.suteba.org.ar/archivonotas/pag12-1220N0.pdf

Sofsky, W. 1999 *The Order of Terror: The Concentration Camp*. Princeton University Press, Princeton.

Tarlow, S. 2002 The Aesthetic Corpse in 19th Century Britain. In *Thinking Through the Body: Archaeologies of Corporeality*, edited by Y. Hamilakis, M. Pluciennik, and S. Tarlow, pp. 85–97. Kluwer Academic/Plenum Publishers, New York.

Thomas, J. 2001 Archaeologies of Place and Landscape. In *Archaeological Theory Today*, edited by I. Hodder, pp. 165–186. Polity Press, Cambridge.

United Nations 2006 International Convention for the Protection of All Persons from Enforced Disappearance, 28 September 2009. http://www.unhcr.org/refworld/docid/47fdfaeb0.html

Weissel, M. 2002 Informe Final Investigación Arqueológica. Manuscript on file, Secretaría de Obras y Servicios Públicos, Gobierno de la Ciudad Autónoma de Buenos Aires, Buenos Aires.

Wright, T. 2007 *State Terrorism in Latin America: Chile, Argentina, and International Human Rights*. Rowman and Littlefield, Lanham.

Zarankin, A. and C. Niro 2009 The Materialization of Sadism: Archaeology of Architecture in CDCs. In *Memories from Darkness: Archaeology of Dictatorship and Repression in Latin America (1960–1980)*, edited by P. Funari, A. Zarankin, and M. Salerno. Springer, New York.

Zarankin, A. and M. Salerno 2008 Después de la Tormenta. Arqueología de la Represión en América Latina. *Complutum* 19(2): 21–32.

Chapter 13
A Political Archaeology of Latin America's Recent Past: A Bridge Towards our History

Gonzalo Compañy, Gabriela González, Leonardo Ovando,
and David Rossetto

Abstract In Latin America, archaeologists have begun to apply their theories and methodologies to the 1960s and 1980s, a period that witnessed the rise and fall of numerous oppressive dictatorships. The era of dictatorship was characterized by the implementation of economic, political, and social projects and by the disappearance and killing of thousands of people. These extreme methods were part of a range of strategies aimed at effecting widespread social transformation. How can the archaeologist study these fearsome acts of repressive governments – is the discipline of archaeology able to continue working within its usual paradigms, or does the study of morbid topics such as mass graves and torture call for new theories and methods? In this chapter, we consider the role of the archaeologist in negotiating, understanding, and interpreting these complex, painful pasts in Latin America.

Introduction

Latin American archaeologists have begun to apply their theories and methodologies to the period spanning the 1960s to 1980s, which saw the rise and fall of several oppressive dictatorships. In Argentina, archaeologists are now studying the traces of the 1976–1983 dictatorship. Though the first archaeological interventions were limited to the recovery and identification of bodies from mass graves by the Argentine Forensic Anthropology Team (EAAF), archaeologists have recently extended their

G. Compañy (✉), L. Ovando, D. Rossetto
Political-Cultural Memory Research Group (E.I.Me.Po.C.), Universidad Nacional de Rosario,
Rosario, Argentina
e-mail: zalocvive@yahoo.com.ar; leoovando@yahoo.com.mx; david.a.rossetto@gmail.com

G. González
Political-Cultural Memory Research Group (E.I.Me.Po.C.), Universidad Nacional de
Rosario/CONICET, Rosario, Argentina
e-mail: glgonza2@yahoo.com.ar

A. Myers, G. Moshenska (eds.), *Archaeologies of Internment*, One World Archaeology,
DOI 10.1007/978-1-4419-9666-4_13, © Springer Science+Business Media, LLC 2011

work to include the study of other significant sites relating to state oppression, including Clandestine Detention Centres (CDCs).

These disciplinary developments take place within a specific historical and political context in which initiatives to address the past, such as the Truth Commission and the creation of an "official memory" through memorials and museums, are on the rise. These projects have largely been directed by the state itself. It could be argued that this "memory work" cannot be separated from the social-political crisis unleashed in the latter part of 2001. It is in this particular context that human rights organizations made certain advances: in 2003, they were successful in repealing the "impunity laws" that had limited legal proceedings against those responsible for the kidnapping, torture, and deaths of "the disappeared". This marked the beginning of new charges against the repressive forces of the dictatorship. In 2003, human rights organizations were also successful in gaining access to a number of buildings that served as CDCs during the dictatorship, including the Navy Mechanics School or *Escuela de Mecánica de la Armada* (ESMA). These changes in state treatment of the memory of the recent past represented a significant victory for human rights organizations in Argentina. Both the reopening of the legal processes and the re-examination of those symbolic places opened up an area as yet unexplored by archaeologists.

All members of our research team were born during the Dictatorship era. We were toddlers and school children when Argentina returned to democracy, and the work of the Truth Commission was part of the background of our young lives. The Dictatorship, spoken and unspoken, has been omnipresent in our lives, and we must acknowledge this in our work. It is in this spirit that we begin with the narration of experiences related to the recovery of a former CDC in Rosario, Argentina. Our work explores the physical space of this CDC and includes testimonies from individuals who were detained there during the dictatorship. *El Pozo* (The Pit), also known as *Servicio de Informaciones* (Information Services), functioned as one of the main CDCs in Rosario and its region. Between 1976 and 1979, *El Pozo* held kidnapped or "disappeared" persons. It was a place of torture and death. In this chapter, we use the name *Pozo*, because it was regularly used as a synonym of *CDC*, and also because

> There were many cases of this kind of naming for detention centres, such as: "Pozo de Bandfield" or "Pozo de Quilmes", etc. Also designated as "Pozo" (Pit) were those places with a cellar or a basement that were used for the confinement and hiding of the detained-disappeared." (Equipo de Investigación por la Memoria Político Cultural 2008:52)

In the last few years, it has become increasingly common for researchers working on the recovery of historical memory to argue for a specific epistemological approach that would allow them to work beyond traditional disciplinary boundaries. Like our colleagues, our work in El Pozo in 2002–2004 led us to call for a new archaeology, one that accounts for our own position in history. We maintain that the definition of one's position constitutes one of the fundamental steps necessary to start any recovery project in these spaces of memory. In our own case, this positioning required an explicit recognition of the human, historical, and political dimensions that rest at the foundations of the very processes we were trying to study.

El Pozo

CDCs were designed and used by the state's security forces as nodes of intelligence gathering and repression that operated between 1976 and 1983. Although the Dictatorship began in 1976, the first experimental detention centres opened in 1975 in Tucumán Province, under the name of *Lugar de Reunión de Detenidos* (Prisoner Gathering Place) (Mántaras 2005). These were part of a repressive system which sought to reduce and counteract social movements that opposed the ruling political elite. The work in these places of horror was directly related to intelligence mechanisms amongst it can be included the captivity, interrogation, torture, and ultimately death. The captive person entered the clandestine centre under a condition called *detenido-desaparecido* (disappeared-detained). There was no legal form which described this person's fate or whereabouts. A former disappeared member of the Montoneros, Hugo Papalarado, testified about his experience in El Pozo: "In here you are already dead; because you are [considered] dead by everyone outside, it didn't really matter if you were still alive inside" (Testimony of Hugo Papalardo, Montoneros 2002). At the same time, the State denied every act that could relate it to the disappearances, and the repressive structure was ultimately justified by a discourse of the war on subversion. In this context, CDCs worked as a sort of operating room or theatre, a place to perform a surgery that would generate a newly organized and terrorized society. While before the 1976 coup d'état, CDCs were one form of repression, during the dictatorship they became the principal mode of that repression (Calveiro 2004).

El Pozo operated under the supervision of Santa Fe's Provincial Police Information Services and was located in the Central Police Station, a building that stands in Rosario's downtown. Today, it serves as the Provincial Government House. Approximately, 3,000–4,000 people passed through El Pozo as *detenidos-desaparecidos*. The fate of the arrested person was determined in this facility through interrogation and torture. This decision could result in a conditional release, a pass towards the legalization of the arrest, or disappearance.

We entered El Pozo by the same door the *detenidos-desaparecidos* had used decades earlier. We encountered graffiti that offered a sort of paralyzing welcome: The message referred to the former Police Chief of Rosario, Feced, the man primarily responsible for the operation of El Pozo during its years as a CDC. The message read, *Feced Pase* (welcome Feced, walk in) (Fig. 13.1). This, along with other graffiti, acted as a constant reminder of how alive and fresh the voices that struggled under the Dictatorship remained. A feeling that time had stopped hovered around the empty rooms of the building. This feeling of frozen time is referenced in the testimony of former prisoner, Ana María Ferrari as she recollects revisiting El Pozo:

When I entered in the Information Services I perceived the same odour. It was like time never passed, like if this place had been locked all this time, perhaps there was a little more humidity but the odour was the same. (Testimony of Ana María Ferrari, *Juventud Peronista Zona Norte* 2005)

Fig. 13.1 Graffiti at the
entrance to "El Pozo".
Courtesy of the Equipo de
Investigación por la Memoria
Político Cultural
(E.I.Me.Po.C.) photographic
archive

The site consists of a first floor, a basement, and a second floor; interconnected rooms, some of them modified after the Information Services stopped operating as a detention centre. A desk with an empty photo album, the same that was used back then to show pictures of *detenidos-desaparecidos*, images of *operativos*. Walls with the paint peeling off, engravings beneath the paint, names, dates, lines, drawings, doodles, broken glasses, and lights that didn't work. It required courage even for us to enter that same door, to face the same odour, *Feced Pase*.

As we entered, we were received by the same dark corridor, a narrow space with a high ceiling that continued up a short flight of stairs, no more than four or five steps. After that, we found ourselves in a rectangular room (Fig. 13.2). Later, through testimonies, the reading of legal procedures, and the active work with survivors, we came to know that this place worked as a sort of "waiting room" where the *detenidos-desaparecidos* waited, tied and blindfolded, crowded, and piled up, to begin their path through El Pozo.

On the opposite side of the entrance stairs there is a door that leads to a second short corridor *Boulevard Perdiste* (Boulevard "you lost") that ends in a round room *La Rotonda* (The Roundabout), which leads to the torture room, the Guzman Alfaro office, the *Lofiego el ciego* (the blind man), and the archive office. With the exception

Fig. 13.2 "The waiting room" on the first floor. Courtesy of the Equipo de Investigación por la Memoria Político Cultural (E.I.Me.Po.C.) photographic archive

of this last room, all the others had broad windows and balconies that faced out on to the street (Figs. 13.3 and 13.4).

> They knew that political prisoners won't escape because there are reprisals... Sometimes we even negotiated being alone for a moment on the balconies, it was a classic bully mechanism. (Testimony of Luis Cuello, Partido Socialista de los Trabajadores 2003)

The absence of bars forming a boundary between the outside and the inside allowed us to question how we, as archaeologists, related to objects described in the testimonies of *detenidos-desaparecidos*. The rectangular room mentioned above is connected to a little room called *debajo de la escalera* (under the stairs) (Fig. 13.5). From this room it was possible to access the basement and the second floor called *La Favela*. This room is significant because the fate of the *detenidos-desaparecidos* depended very much on whether they were taken to the second floor or to the basement.

> One night, they took us out of that round part (*La rotonda*)... they took us to the little room under the stairs, the one underneath '*La Favela*'. We started to talk, I was very scared, then he told me to calm down... he started to quietly whistle our song, I began to calm down, I thought: 'Well at least there's a partner here'. (Testimony of Carmen Lucero, Unión de Estudiantes Secundarios 2005)

Once again, in facing the empty space of El Pozo, its dimensions and its characteristics, locations, and meanings, we were confronted with the question of how to recover the spatiality of the CDC. Given our knowledge that when the CDC operated the assignment of *detenidos-desaparecidos* to one room or another directly affected their chances for survival or disappearing, our work started to uncover signs of resistance and struggle for survival.

La Favela (Fig. 13.6) originally consisted of a little room where *detenidos-desaparecidos* were held while they awaited their fate. Today, this has been extended to cover all the rooms of the second floor. This modification took place in the latter part of 1978; there have been numerous other structural changes made since 1978. These modifications have primarily affected the torture room. In the basement, we were overwhelmed by the advanced state of deterioration. While this operated as a space of torture, it was also a space where *detenidos-desaparecidos* could keep in contact with each other. Here, prisoners were not bound or blindfolded. The basement was divided into three rooms: the little room (Fig. 13.7), the women's room (Fig. 13.8), and the men's room, each bigger than the last. The first two were used as women's quarters. There was also a small bathroom and a small round room in the middle of the basement that matched the footprint of the round room on the first

Fig. 13.4 The "torture room" and its door towards a balcony on the first floor. Courtesy of the Equipo de Investigación por la Memoria Político Cultural (E.I.Me.Po.C.) photographic archive

floor. There was a space by the men's room that was used as a kitchen, and a small set of stairs to the street level ending in a metal door (Figs. 13.9 and 13.10).

> During the day, we climbed the little stair that lead to Dorrego street, we spent *whole hours watching the street*. Once one of the military infantry approached from outside and commented: those [the repressors] are tough guys aren't they? (Testimony of Luis Cuello)

The space revealed just how close prisoners were to freedom. This proximity with the outside, mediated only by a door, appears as shocking as the engravings that cover the walls of the basement: engravings of names, initials, dates, and drawings created prior to 1979, the year when the Information Services ceased operating the site as a CDC. The specificity of the archaeological survey on these inscriptions, our attempts to conserve them, and the search for an appropriate methodological tool for their recording and survey, did not necessarily question the place of our practise as archaeologists. The wall stood as an object beyond the ethical commitment with the theme; but in order to be able to survey the wall and its writing it was necessary to understand those *"whole hours watching the street"*.

> Imagine yourselves in a situation where you don't know if you are going to survive, if you are getting transferred, aren't you going to want to leave a trace of your passing through that place… You can't imagine the way we lived down here and in what level of desperation

Fig. 13.5 The "waiting room" and the "under the stairs" room during a flood, on the first floor. Courtesy of the Equipo de Investigación por la Memoria Político Cultural (E.I.Me.Po.C.) photographic archive

we counted the days, another day we lived through, another day we survived. It is very hard imagining someone in this situation not trying to leave a trace, a sign, something that could say that he was there. (Testimony of Ana María Ferrari)

It never came to my mind to write, but I believe that a person who doesn't know if he's going to live or not might start writing, as an act of transcendence... 'Here, I leave my name'. (Testimony of Hugo Papalardo)

It is very probable, yes, if the guy over there that was sleeping in the lower bed, in a moment of solitude, the first thing he would do, would be writing something in the wall. Most of all, if you weren't sure if you were going to be able to get out of here... so the first thing you would do would be writing your name or something in the wall, like 'well, I leave something'. (Testimony of Hugo Papalardo)

The inscriptions on the wall, the layout of the rooms, and their spatial distribution, began to acquire a new perspective when viewed against the testimonies of those who were there as *detenidos-desaparecidos*. What we later called *Bajadas* (Descend) with the survivors were reunions or visits where they assisted the archaeologists and other members of the research team, often in the company of family or friends. Once there, the survivor reconstructed the passage and experiences lived through the spaces in El Pozo. At the end of this walk, the activity was closed with a workshop where we all discussed and thought over the survivor

Fig. 13.6 "La Favela" on the second floor. Courtesy of the Equipo de Investigación por la Memoria Político Cultural (E.I.Me.Po.C.) photographic archive

Fig. 13.7 The "women's room" in the basement. Courtesy of the Equipo de Investigación por la Memoria Político Cultural (E.I.Me.Po.C.) photographic archive

Fig. 13.8 "The kitchen" or "the small room" in the basement. Courtesy of the Equipo de Investigación por la Memoria Político Cultural (E.I.Me.Po.C.) photographic archive

Fig. 13.9 The "men's room" in the basement. Courtesy of the Equipo de Investigación por la Memoria Político Cultural (E.I.Me.Po.C.) photographic archive

experiences, but not just those related to her confinement but mainly about those related with her history, her political activities, and then about her life as a survivor after the release. The survivor returning to her place of confinement initially caused an encounter with a painful past, a ferocious meeting with sensation and images

Fig. 13.10 Stairs and metal bridge that lead to the street in the "men's room" at the basement. Courtesy of the Equipo de Investigación por la Memoria Político Cultural (E.I.Me.Po.C.) photographic archive

imprinted on their corporal memory – "I never talked about this", "at first I didn't want to get close to this building" – but at some point, she managed to transcend this fixation on horror. The act of re-encounter with this history could no longer be limited to what it was lived during her confinement, nor to the traumatic aspect of it. The *survivor* lived through a traumatic experience, not only survived the confinement but also survived a life that contains them, that goes beyond them. The survivor carries the history of a life that cannot be reduced to a history of trauma. A trauma inscribed in the past that emerges, and should not be taken nor told as a distant story, apolitical, ahistorical, an exclusive tale of confinement and death, a descriptive comparison of the many CDC, life experiences as detailed methodologies of torture. It is not about recovering that past, a part of that which we can barely name, and thus splits the time, but about how to transmit the "rest of the things of the world and life" (Casullo 2001:259).

Another way of taking action, or intervening on the empty spaces of El Pozo was through another set of workshops that we called *bajadas con la comunidad* (a descent with the community). These consisted of working with those who attended to discover what they knew, thought, and felt about that place and its history. The *descent* took place in two stages: the first consisted of a walk through the

different rooms and spaces of the CDC. In every space, we read fragments of testimonies that gave some meaning to the rooms. These histories were selected and
compiled from the different activities with the survivors as well as from extracts of
judicial rulings. The second stage was a reflexive workshop. The intention of this
workshop was to try to express in words the sensations, feelings, and thoughts that
came up during the first part. The triggers were questions such as: "What do I know
about this history?", "What do I feel about this place, about this history?", "What
does my own history have to do with that history?", and finally "What does this
present have to do with that history?"

> People should be able to say 'this is also my history'. Anyone who was born in Rosario
> has something to do with this. I started to hear about this from a few schoolmates back
> then. It belongs to us. I am not responsible for the people that died in here, but those people
> have a lot to do with me. A person that was born in a place without detention centres also
> has something to do with all who disappeared. History is not a written paper, we all make
> history. (Testimony of Fernanda)

> This thing of provoking the question, 'This is also me', 'This could be me', 'could it be
> me?' (Testimony of Piero)

The moment this individual asks himself these questions, he is able to recognize
himself as part of a generation pierced through the same axis: a lack of information
and knowledge of what happened in that particular period of history, a lack of a generational collective project, disappointment, and a general devaluation of the self.
From there he (and we) begins to comprehend that maybe it was nothing but *horror* that constantly generated and reproduced paralysis, rupture, and isolation. There
were common arguments like "I know nothing about politics", "I've never been told
of what happened here", "I've got nothing to add to this history", that account for
this apparent paradox. A paradox that shows that what ties us as a generation is precisely isolation, fragmentation. Once recognized in her/his generational bond this,
not just an individual but a subject standing from a generational us, is interpolated,
at the same time that interpolates a generational other impersonated in a protagonist
of that history: the survivor. In this tension, the possibility of a dialogue that starts
to enable a generational transmission is established.

> The worst that one could do is to transmit the fear, because new generations have to make
> their own new experiences and shake off the fear, if not we end up working as their [the
> military] transmission channel. (Testimony of Hugo Papalardo)

> After this experience you can keep on living and never taking charge of it... there's the
> paradox, between your life and what you are seeing. It's like in the arts: nothing but showing
> a paradox, it is in itself a parenthesis. (Testimony of Elisa)

The intention behind these activities was to enable the words, the questions; to generate an active space of thinking about the horror, about the silence created by
phrases such as: *don't ask about it, don't get involved, we don't talk about that
here, if it happened it happened for a reason, leave the past behind*; for later moving towards a recognition of a broader situation, a general (generational) situation
through the acknowledgement in the 'other' of the 'self', the belonging to a present
tightly related to that past.

Only when you find yourself facing death you can struggle for life. . . when you get out (of 'El Pozo') you are going to live life very differently. . . there's something else behind reason in the writings in the wall. . . it's a feeling. . . if we don't have it, if we don't learn it (the feeling) we can't fight back. . . because reason it's going to highlight only the data. . . if you don't find the death, you won't find life. (Testimony of Roy)

CDCs would then represent confinement, though not only of the subjects that were there as *detenidos-desaparecidos,* but also represent confinement as a reduction: the history of a life to the experience of a trauma, a historical process to the present/past dichotomy, politics to a party affiliation, a generation crossed by socio-historical bindings to the summation of individuals on a certain age range, the dimension of the *humane* to a division of good and evil. El Pozo cannot be simply described, cannot be simply told just by its materiality, cannot be filled with objects, cannot be delimited by the archaeological discipline and just by that allow us to believe ourselves to be positioned towards it. Its survivors cannot simply be interviewed as a means to recover *traces* of those who had died, because in that action, we continue to negate the survivor's life. El Pozo is experienced in the everyday, in a truncated generational transmission; in the negation and silencing of the political identities of those who were confined as *detenidos-desaparecidos*; in the economical models installed in that dictatorship; in a fragmented society; in archaeologists barely capable of thinking ourselves *within* history (Equipo de Investigación por la Memoria Político Cultural 2008).

This work has led us to define a political dimension of archaeology: a position that enables an active questioning of the processes and events that lead us to comprehend the reason of existence of these types of places; beyond the details of their inner functioning or the conditions under which the *detenidos-desaparecidos* were being interrogated. From this problematic framework, we feel it is appropriate to ask: what are the implications of the materiality of a CDC in the recovery of *historical memory*? What happens, and what does not? What do we see, and what do we not allow ourselves to see when we cannot conceive traces beyond its materiality?

Clandestine Detention Centres and the Archaeologist

When entering a CDC like *El Pozo*, we find ourselves within a physical space; we find material remains, empty spaces, and emptied spaces overloaded with meaning and disputed by many different voices. Voices that demand active participation, and the acknowledgement of their rights in history, in this present. These claims necessitate the recovery of a previous history, and call for an examination and acknowledgement of the processes that lead to the installation of the CDCs and the later silence that concealed their operations, effectively allowing their work to continue. How is it possible to develop an archaeology that doesn't deny these voices? Voices that, in their own accounts, start from the horror of forced silence, from their own divisions, their own isolation, their own horror.

We ask ourselves then, if it is possible to transcend this horror that paralyses, that inhibits any possibility for collective action, for any action, for the acknowledgement of the subject, for a transmission and the construction of a historical identity, in the end; to transcend the restriction that might enable a transforming action over the established order. It is also pertinent to ask ourselves if the reduction of a study to the material remains is a sort of curtailment to the possibility of a reconnection between those voices, between those subjects. The processes that brought us to this point required the redefinition of specific archaeological assumptions, such as those that claim that the field should start with material at least 100 years old; or even our rusted custom of over describing the steps we followed to generate a detailed architectural description. This is how, when facing this stream of conflicted claims, a fight for the creation of historical and political meaning, we can ask ourselves why some archaeological investigation lines limit themselves to the study of material traces, why the archaeological work ends where the trace's materiality ends? What are then the remains of a CDC, a clandestine centre for forced disappearances, torture, and death? the remains of a survivor and her/his account? the remains of a historical memory, remains of history, and a society?

These questions take us back to thinking about a political dimension that includes an element of archaeological practice, as well as other disciplines: moreover to re-imagine a political archaeology that starts from the acknowledgement that we are *historical subjects* before we are scholars; entwined in "a history, a culture, a generation, a 'must do', a 'who am I' in this particular context, as a founding condition to begin to think of an *Other*" (Equipo de Investigación por la Memoria Político Cultural 2008:561). A survivor *other*, a generational *other* as part of a community that constantly interpellates our role as archaeologists, and as part of a common historical process. We began to work from the paralysing horror represented by a name written on the wall of this CDC. The graffiti causes us to try to imagine the sound of the bodies during the interrogations, to perceive the darkness through their blindfolds.

There is also horror in the numerous threats that we received because of our attempt to work on this problematic theme. Horror remained as the background setting until the day the person we were trying to reach in our discourse stopped being just another archaeologist able to comprehend our same specific language (how a certain theoretical-methodological model could or could not be applied in this place); until we noticed how the others, by the action of this horror, stopped being political subjects to be reduced as victims. The victims of a history that for many years could not even be named. "We don't speak about that, because the words represent the death of the narrator" (Guelerman 2001:44).

How can we transmit that which, at the same time, cannot be named nor forgotten? This uncertainty describes our dilemma concerning that past that appears as a spectre anchored in the memory of those who experienced it with their bodies. It becomes a part of a hole into the real (Martorell 2001), whose boundaries are not the techniques of torture, nor the architecture of a CDC, not even those material objects related to those events; but the memories that are necessary for the present to be lived. This is where archaeology finds a place in the search of the humane, the acknowledgement of the subjects, beyond objects and informants. Archaeology becomes an enquiry through which our knowledge, as researcher subjects, is questioned when facing that which cannot be talked about. Knowledge needs to be constructed with those who have survived that terror to be able to narrate their own history around the socio-political processes that formed the last civilian-military dictatorship in Argentina. Our task, then, was to attempt an archaeology capable of rethinking and reconnecting that traumatic past with this fragmented present; by recovering not as much the traces of horror, but rather the sense of the humane.

> As symbolizing beings, we carry the possibility of transmitting a past built by 'others' in the past. And in this fighting arena, in this search for new meanings to enunciate the horror – beyond the ideas of betrayal, erratic ideologisms, the hard attempt to mention the defeat, the infinite pain – it inscribes the raw certainty of facing the vital sense of death: *being able to* say what we die for... implies *knowing how to* say what we live for. (Equipo de Investigación por la Memoria Político Cultural 2008:591)

Our work is a search for the boundaries of the transmittable, that is to say: until which point is it valid to propose an archaeological practise oriented towards the almost exclusive study of the traces of horror represented by the activities and the general functioning of the CDC? Where does a trace start or end? Would they start with an engraving in the wall? And if that is the case, could the engraving be separated from the history that includes the engraver? In this sense, our political-ethical place doesn't begin with an archaeological *being* but rather with our condition of historical subjects, that is with a political archaeology, one that starts by asking ourselves what we investigate for, where we begin, who we dig for, and who we dig against.

Conclusion

Recovering a historical memory from places such as El Pozo that symbolize state repression and terror requires an acknowledgement not so much that these places materialize horror but that these places are *made of* horror. They materialize the logic of state terrorism and become the emblems of the continuity of the established order.

The recovery of historical memory during work on these emblematic places relates to a search for that aspect of the humane that horror confined, but also with the recovery of a subject that has been exiled from history and bound to its remains, to its horror. The recovery of historical memory starts from the recovering of the question. The questioning begins with the acknowledgement of our characteristics as historical subjects; it takes us to the acknowledgement of the possibilities that come with this recognition. We are historical subjects not only because we are entwined with history, but also because we have the capability to change it, whether by action or omission. The recovery of historical memory may have less to do with the establishment of answers, than with enabling the questioning. Where are we when we are out of history? What are we participants in when we don't participate?

These facts, that shake the consciousness of the civilized world, are not however the biggest suffering that you have brought to the Argentine people, nor the worst violations to human rights that you incur. In the political economics of this government we should seek, not only the explanation for their crimes, but a bigger atrocity that punishes millions of human beings with the planned misery. (Walsh 1977:182)

Horror emerges then as a false clue. Maybe, from the archaeological discipline in Argentina we have been limiting ourselves to the dictatorship/democracy dichotomy, regarding the second as a whole without fissures. From this tranquillity, we approach with some certainty the horrors left by the first one. The focus then is not for the repressive methods used in CDCs nor the techniques we used to register them, but rather those processes that conditioned, favoured, and enabled the creation of those places and their latter silencing and negation. There is a need for a historicization.

The fact that we as archaeologists position ourselves from a non-neutral place when facing a problem of this kind seems to be related to the particular context that propitiates this kind of investigation, given that the non-neutrality corresponds to a position that goes far beyond the specific problem. In other words, taking on board the events of horror forces us to take a non-neutral position. In this sense, and as social scientists, maybe we should not disable the questioning about the implications of our practice; questions that allow (or at least don't inhibit) the possibility for a dialogue between the different subjects in the construction and re-construction of this history. The affirmation that we, as archaeologists, should limit ourselves to the materiality and that our subjects are merely "informants" is thus a form of disciplinary negation.

Acknowledgements We extend our gratitude to the survivors of El Pozo who worked with us on this project, and without whom the project would not have been possible. We would also like to thank Silvia Bianchi, coordinator of The Political-Cultural Memory Research Team, and the other members of the team. Finally, we would like to thank Erin Kaipainen for her revising of our English.

References

Calveiro, P. 2004 *Poder y Desaparición: Los Campos de Concentración en Argentina*. Colihue, Buenos Aires.

Casullo, N. 2001 *Fragmentos de Memoria, la transmisión cancelada*. Norma, Buenos Aires.

Equipo de Investigación por la Memoria Político Cultural 2008 'El Pozo' (ex Servicio de Informaciones) Un centro clandestino de detención, desaparición, tortura y muerte de personas de la ciudad de Rosario, Argentina. Antropología Política del pasado reciente. Prohistoria, Rosario.

Guelerman, S. (ed.) 2001 *Escuela, Juventud y Genocidio: Memorias en Presente*. Norma, Buenos Aires.

Mántaras, M. 2005 *Genocidio en Argentina*. Cooperativa Chilavert Artes Gráficas, Buenos Aires.

Martorell, E. 2001 Recuerdos del Presente: Memoria e Identidad. In *Memorias en Presente*, edited by S. Guelerman, pp. 133–170. Norma, Buenos Aires.

Walsh, R [1977]. 2001 *Carta Abierta de un Escritor a la Junta Militar: Operación Masacre*. Ediciones del Sol-Clarín, Buenos Aires.

Chapter 14
Hohenschönhausen: Visual and Material Representations of a Cold War Prison Landscape

John Schofield and Wayne Cocroft

Abstract The Cold War prison complex at Hohenschönhausen is notorious as a former forbidden zone of the East Germany's *Ministerium für Statssicherheit* (Stasi). Set in a far-flung suburb in eastern Berlin, Hohenschönhausen has, since 1994, been a memorial site, increasingly visited as part of organised coach tours to landmarks of Berlin's troubled past. As with other recently occupied prisons around the world, former prisoners guide visitors around the stark interior, with first-hand accounts of torture and atrocity. It is a visit one remembers. But the prison itself is only part of the story, albeit a central focus for the wider landscape of Hohenschönhausen – a place of industry and espionage, a secret city of the Stasi and of the Cold War. In 2005, the authors spent 2 days surveying and generating a characterisation of this wider landscape to improve interpretation and presentation for prison visitors, on site and online. An unexpected dimension to this study was a realisation that, for some, the habits of the Cold War remain.

Introduction

In a review of the film *The Lives of Others* (2007), Peter Bradshaw wrote:

> Nothing could provide a more effective antidote to Ostalgie – that is, the tongue-in-cheek nostalgia for the days of the Berlin wall in which educated Germans are said sometimes to indulge. This fierce and gloomy drama, written and directed by first-timer Florian Henckel von Donnersmarck, was a notable winner of the 2007 best foreign film Oscar. It is an indictment of the sinister brutalities of the Stasi, the German Democratic Republic's (GDR) secret police, whose tentacular network of informers was so vast that fully 2% of the entire civilian

J. Schofield (✉)
Department of Archaeology, University of York, York, UK
e-mail: john.schofield@york.ac.uk

W. Cocroft
English Heritage, Cambridge, UK
e-mail: wayne.cocroft@english-heritage.org.uk

A. Myers, G. Moshenska (eds.), *Archaeologies of Internment*, One World Archaeology,   245
DOI 10.1007/978-1-4419-9666-4_14, © Springer Science+Business Media, LLC 2011

population was on the payroll – a network of fear and shame worthy of George Orwell's
Nineteen Eighty-Four.

One might add to this the nostalgic leanings of the unreformed, and those with
genuinely positive attitudes towards what they consider to have been the benefits of
the German Democratic Republic (GDR), such as full employment and childcare
provision.

Over 2 days in 2005, presumably while this film was being made, two
archaeologists surveyed the material traces of a place that was central to the telling
of this story – the infamous Stasi prison of Hohenschönhausen in eastern Berlin.
The aim of this survey was to document the wider landscape in which the prison
was situated, using methods of extensive or rapid survey and landscape characterisation, alongside a visualisation and photographic recording of subtler traces that
persist from the recent past. This was archaeological survey of two very different
kinds (the very extensive and the very detailed), in an extreme landscape where the
threat of Hohenschönhausen seemed tangible. It was, for us, a survey unlike any
other.

Historical Context, Physicality and the Film

In 1994, the former *Ministerium für Statssicherheit* (Stasi) prison at
Hohenschönhausen was designated as a memorial site, commemorating the
victims of post-war political repression. It lies at the centre of a former forbidden
zone of Stasi administration buildings, workshops and stores, surrounded by a
neighbourhood dominated by secret police housing (the flats evoked so eloquently
in *The Lives of Others* – whereby one rose up the block as one progressed through
the Stasi, which was achieved through one's success in spying and reporting on
others) (Fig. 14.1). Some of these buildings have found new uses, while others
remain empty. The flats – we were told – still house some former Stasi officials.

But the story begins earlier than this. To the north-east of Berlin's city centre,
Hohenschönhausen grew during the late nineteenth century as an industrial suburb of factories and railway marshalling yards. Alongside this development, other
areas maintained a semi-rural character comprising single-storey cottages with large
gardens and communal open areas. This piecemeal development continued into
the twentieth century, including a machine works, built about 1910, and during
the late 1930s the Nazis built a large communal kitchen and laundry to serve this
working-class neighbourhood.

Since the fall of the Berlin Wall in 1989 the full extent of Soviet, and later East
German, brutal subjugation of their political opponents has been exposed. We now
know that in many instances the surviving infrastructure of repression constructed
by the Nazis was seized and reused. To the north of Berlin, the concentration camp
at Sachsenhausen was taken over and new accommodation blocks were constructed.
In 1945, after the fall of Berlin, any large building complex that remained reasonably intact was eagerly seized by the occupying powers. The communal kitchen

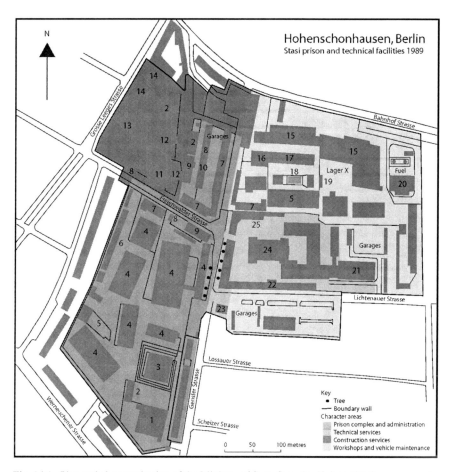

Fig. 14.1 Plan and characterisation of the Ministry of State Security Hohenschönhausen complex in 1989. Drawn by Wayne Cocroft. KEY: *1* Canteen; *2* Mechanical & Electrical plant; *3* Main unit of the Ministry for State Security HA XX—Hauptabteilung XX des MfS—Main unit of the Ministry for State Security responsible for investigating internal opposition; *4* Technical operatives; *5* Vehicles; *6* Offices and camp rooms; *7* Service building; *8* Guard room; *9* Communications; *10* Electrical transformers; *11* Main unit IX of the Ministry for State Security, Unit 11 reconnaissance for National Socialists and war criminals—HA IX/11—Hauptabteilung IX des MfS, Abteilung 11 Aufklärung von NS und Kreigsverbrechen; *12* Armed and Chemical Service; *13* Supply Service unit—VD/6—Versongungsdienst Abteilung 6; *14* Work group for Minister for fortifications construction—AGM 1B—Arbeitsgruppe des Ministers für das Schutzbausen; *15* Workshops; *16* Canteen; *17* Service building Abteilung IV; *18* Swimming pool; *19* Fuel bay; *20* Boiler house; *21* Main unit of the Ministry for State Security, investigating affairs HA IX—Hauptabteilung IX des MfS (Surafrechtliche Ermittlungen); *22* Central Medical Service of the Ministry for State Security—ZMD Zentralmedizinischer Dienst des MfS and Prison hospital; *23* Camp commandant; *24* Main prison building—Unit XIV of the Ministry for State Security imprisonment affairs—Abt.XIV—Abteilung.XIV des MfS (Stafvollung); *25* Prison workshops

building at Hohenschönhausen was both sufficiently distant from the city centre to have avoided the worst of the fighting and bombing of the Second World War, and remote enough to not attract unwanted attention. It was ideal for the purpose of confinement.

For anyone arrested by the Soviet occupation authorities, Hohenschönhausen, known then as Special Camp No. 3, was often their initial interrogation and holding camp. Soviet sources indicate that between July 1945 and June 1946, 886 people died here, although some argue the true figure was closer to 3,000 (Gendenkstätte Berlin 2006). Many were simply buried in adjacent bomb craters that peppered the areas around the railway yards. By October 1946, when the Soviets dissolved this camp, around 20,000 prisoners had passed through its gates, many en route to reactivated former Nazi concentration camps. The Soviets continued to operate the complex as the Central Soviet Detainment Prison until March 1951 when they handed it over to the incipient East German secret police service, K5.

From the Soviets, the East Germans inherited a collection of former industrial buildings and the 1930s kitchen complex. The whole complex was crudely closed off with wooden and barbed wire fences (Erler and Knabe 2005:30). Internally, the cellars of the former kitchen were converted into rows of dark cells, known to the prisoners as the *U-boat*. Detainees, some of whom were architects and other skilled workers, were used on Stasi and other state building projects. In a later twist, the detainees were released and became Stasi employees still engaged on state construction projects (Erler and Knabe 2005:32). Over the following decades, the complex was extended as the prison was enlarged, and as the Stasi took on new functions, new buildings were added.

Throughout its history, East Germany increasingly made use of standardised building components in its civil and state construction projects, and this is evident at Hohenschönhausen. In its early years, the complex was surrounded by a simple wooden stockade boundary with wooden watchtowers, giving it an almost medieval appearance. By the late 1950s, the boundary was replaced by an outer brick wall. On Freienwalder Strasse, barbed wire supports remain that are similar to those used on the early 1960s phases of the Berlin Wall. Probably, in the early 1970s, the main prison compound was replaced and BT11-type guard towers, identical to those used on the Berlin Wall, were placed at its corners. Elsewhere, standard prefabricated slabs were used for road surfaces; other standardised components included lifting barriers and lamp-posts.

In common with other totalitarian countries, the Stasi acted as a state within a state. Under East German control Hohenschönhausen became the main holding prison for those awaiting trial. Typical prisoners in the camp included former Nazis, those who opposed the East German regime, reform-minded members of the party, and some people kidnapped from the west. Prisoner numbers reached a peak after the June 1953 uprising against communism that was marked by spontaneous demonstrations in Berlin and elsewhere in East Germany.

As is evident in *The Lives of Others*, by the 1970s, the Stasi employed tens of thousands of people, including informants, with the potential to reach down into nearly all sections of East German society (Ash 1997; Funder 2003). Through the

Hauptabteilung Aufklärung des MfS (HVA) (Main Administration Reconnaissance), led by Markus Wolf, the Stasi gathered foreign intelligence and spread the influence of the GDR through training and supplying friendly countries. To support this organisation, a vast headquarters was built elsewhere in Berlin, in Normannenstrasse. In parallel, the Hohenschönhausen complex grew to meet many of the more mundane and specialised functions of the organisation. This included garages for storing and servicing vehicles, general building sections and a special construction section dedicated to state fortifications. Surveillance devices were also built here. In addition to these practical tasks, there was a Nazi records section, containing information that might be used to embarrass leading figures in West Germany or to blackmail people into working for the Stasi. The main administration section for the remainder of the Stasi's 17 prisons was also located here. By the late 1980s, the Stasi directly employed around 100,000 people, with about a further 260,000 informants (Childs and Popplewell 1999:82, 86).

Hohenschönhausen, then, was the main remand prison in the former GDR for people detained by the former Ministry of State Security, the *Stasi*. The prison therefore rightly plays a significant role in the film *The Lives of Others*. Even though it only features two or three times, in scenes of interrogation; it is ever-present. The threat of something, an awareness of its existence, is more unsettling for the audience than its prominent display or frequent referencing would ever be. It is likely this was true also for the citizens of the GDR, whose lives were typically overseen by the Stasi and its network of informants. For them, it was probably ever-present too, perhaps even more threatening in its remote existence and mythical status.

Hohenschönhausen could easily have been the central character of the film: the place gaining strength through repeated reference as the story progressed. But the Stasi officer, the Brechtian playwright and his actress girlfriend all gave compelling and persuasive performances ultimately offering some distraction from the power of place that is such a feature of *The Lives of Others*. The real-life stories surrounding this film provide another layer to the dramas that it portrayed. The film's director, Henkel von Donnersmarck, and the lead actor Ulriche Mühe – who died of cancer shortly after the completion of filming – were successfully sued for libel over an interview in which Mühe asserted that his former wife had informed on him through their 6 years of marriage. She denied the claims, though hundreds of pages of government documents record the activities (Guardian 2007; Zacharek 2007).

Landscape and Archaeology

Around the time this film was being made, we found ourselves in Berlin with time on our hands. We had visited the prison at Hohenschönhausen once before, on an organised visit with a guided tour. Two things drew us back there in 2005: one was a desire to revisit the prison building, now a memorial and museum, accessible for visitors and where, like on Robben Island, South Africa, one is taken around by former detainees who have particular insight and perspectives on this place. Second, we wished to explore the wider landscape which we had begun to investigate on our previous visit: the empty industrial buildings and rumours of their functionality had intrigued us. We like secret places; places where archaeological methods have the potential to reveal more than other sources have yielded thus far. We were certainly aware of the wider prison landscape, but were unclear as to how well this secret area, this *verboten stadtteil*, was understood, and what archaeological traces of it might survive. We proposed to explore these questions by taking both an extensive view of the area (recognising and documenting landscape character) and a more microscopic view of the subtler traces of Hohenschönhausen's troubled past. We felt that by taking this dual approach, an interesting and informative documentation of this place might present itself. Here, we focus on the more detailed enquiry; the broader landscape study is described elsewhere (Cocroft and Schofield 2010).

Our method was simple. With notebooks, maps and a camera, we traversed the entire area of the prison landscape, first tracing the outer perimeter, largely following the roads immediately beyond the blocks of flats. These had been clearly modernised but were undoubtedly of Eastern European character. One former block, now a hotel, appeared to provide a view over the entire area. Having spent some time negotiating permission to gain access to a top-storey bedroom, we were taken into a room with uninterrupted views north over the site. Other than that, all our views were from street level. This elevated view had obvious resonance: as we have seen, one's seniority determined one's position in the block, confirming the impression and reality of control: of being watchful, of observing others, or being able to observe others. In a scene cut from the film, the Stasi official in *The Lives of Others* is seen coming home from work, taking up his binoculars and watching neighbours in adjacent blocks. One family was then reported by him for handling illegal goods, and the husband arrested. This really, and regularly, happened.

Having completed a path around the perimeter, we set about crossing the site by whichever routes were accessible. We followed roads, deserted car parks, alleyways and crossed waste ground where buildings had been demolished. These vacant plots were also informally field-walked, to search for artefacts. Access to buildings had been impossible to arrange, but some limited views could be gained into empty buildings through windows and doorways. Our notes and photographs incorporated traces of the site's former use still evident in the contemporary landscape. We photographed buildings, their décor and aspects of plan form and landscape context; we recorded smaller structures, as well as graffiti and signage, ground surfaces, wall textures and fabrics, the above-ground district heating system so characteristic of Soviet-era towns and cities, and other traces such as drain covers. We created a map of the site, both on paper in conventional form and in the collection of images we had made. We tried to roughly date the buildings as well as characterise their form and function. For lunch, we ate in the workers' canteen, a facility from the GDR that retained much of its former character – in the décor, and in the menu. Interestingly, this was also the only place where we were prevented from taking photographs.

Our methods borrow heavily from the principles of landscape characterisation, by which areas of landscape are considered distinctive for reasons that include present occupation and use, alongside the historic processes that have helped shape what exists today (Fairclough 2008). Our characterisation takes account of the area's former industrial and residential functionality, the new and adapted industrial buildings, the prison, the traces of closure, secrecy and surveillance, and the textures and contours of walkways, roads and hard-standings. Our photography, and the urge for photographic recording as archaeology, is influenced by our involvement with survey work at the former Royal Air Force (RAF) Station Coltishall (Cocroft and Cole 2007; Dunlop 2008), and knowledge of studies elsewhere, where artists perform a vital role in the recording of former militarised landscapes (Boulton 2009).

This felt like a progressive and interesting step in considering archaeologies of the contemporary past: a combination of conventional archaeological methods, tailored to a very unconventional setting; a photographic documentation of the quotidian and the everyday; and a social setting which gave the project an edge, in the sense of genuine unease at being observed – literally, on one occasion. This was not the sort of interested bystander one usually experiences on an archaeological excavation. This actually felt quite intimidating. The man who watched us was of stocky build, and was probably in his early to mid-50s. He wore a checked, short-sleeve shirt, and simply walked up and down the pavement opposite us for the best part of 2 hours. We never saw him actually look at us. We mentioned this at lunch-time to staff at the Museum, who confirmed he probably was former Stasi. We moved to a new location after lunch and he didn't follow us. Some former Stasi officials, we were told, have not worked since The Change, and many find it hard to break habits. If all you have ever done is watch people, perhaps it is hard to stop. We never saw him again.

How one makes sense of such a complex and highly charged location was also partly the subject of our enquiry. The prison itself was already well researched and documented. Our concern was to encourage the memorial to understand and promote its own position within a wider landscape context, much as English Heritage and the National Trust in England encourage visitors to Stonehenge to extend their gaze to the wider landscape, and to explore that landscape by providing guidance and information: What can visitors expect to see, and how do those less obvious traces interconnect with the more prominent monumental form? Here, our concern was the plan-form of this area and how it developed through the twentieth century, particularly from the 1950s to 1970s; the buildings, viewed externally; and the subtler traces of landscape, such as the textures of road surfaces, graffiti, piping, walls and boundaries. The photographs that accompany the words of this chapter represent our results: a predominantly visual encounter with a rather unfamiliar and challenging landscape.

Stories in Stones

The Lives of Others raised the profile of Hohenschönhausen. On Oscar night, for example, the extract shown to a global audience referred specifically to Hohenschönhausen – a place suddenly transformed, in potential at least, from one notorious amongst East Germans, to a name familiar around the world. Creating a record of this landscape and also beginning to understand its archaeology and character took on renewed significance and purpose in the light of this film and its global success. Yet, as we undertook the survey, we were unaware of the film's preparation.

One of the things that perhaps set *The Lives of Others* apart, and which caught the imagination of former East Germans and those who remember that era, was the authenticity of the film: both in the production and the philosophy behind it. Hohenschönhausen was not featured in the film: the director of the memorial apparently refused permission, objecting to making the Stasi man into a hero (Funder 2007). But all of the equipment used for surveillance, for example, was original. One can also take an archaeological view of this. We were pleased, for example, to hear Florian Henckel von Donnersmarck, the screenwriter and director, say in an interview that: "I think places store memories; that feelings felt in a particular place don't just disappear – they are somehow still in the stones" (Lions Gate Home Entertainment 2007). That is largely why we think an archaeological investigation of this place is worthwhile: that in the results of the work, and by simply undertaking a survey, we contribute to unlocking some of those memories. That is what we hope we have achieved at Hohenschönhausen – to tell a story and create a framework within which the inevitable process of change can be managed in an effective and appropriate way, helping Hohenschönhausen to retain or store its memories for the future.

Photo Essay

Fig. 14.2 Rear view of the refurbished 1970s plattenbau apartments on Werneuchener Strasse which overlook the complex. To the right is the derelict main canteen on Gensler Strasse

Fig. 14.3 View of the north side of Gensler Strasse from one of the apartments on Werneuchener Strasse. In the foreground is the canteen, in the middle the triple-fenced computer centre of HA/XX, Hauptabteilung Directorate XX, responsible for communications technology and computer espionage, and to its rear the buildings of the technical services

Fig. 14.4 Barred windows of the main canteen on Gensler Strasse

Fig. 14.5 Traces of the sliding gate barring entry to the computer centre of Hauptabteilung XX. In the 1990s, there was an attempt to run a commercial business from this building; it failed and the building is now derelict

Fig. 14.6 Freienwalder Strasse. Once inside the complex further barriers and guardrooms controlled access into inner compounds. The windowless building to the rear housed a communications facility

Fig. 14.7 To the rear is the surviving frontage of the early twentieth-century light engineering factory on Freienwalder Strasse, later used by the HA IX –11, Hauptabteilung des MfS, Abteilung 11 Aufklärung von NS und Kreigsverbrechen, Main unit IX of the Ministry for State Security, Unit 11 reconnaissance for National Socialists and war criminals. In the foreground are the remains of the complex's district heating system, formerly a common feature in Eastern Europe

Fig. 14.8 Within the complex, entry into many buildings was controlled by individual entry points, in this case the building of the HA IX/11

Fig. 14.9 Looking for artefacts on the site of the demolished engineering works on Freienwalder
Strasse

Fig. 14.10 Freienwalder Strasse looking away from the prison towards the main entrance to the
complex. To the *left* is the communications facility and to the *right* the offices of the chemistry
service and criminal technical institute

Fig. 14.11   Manhole cover, made in the GDR

Fig. 14.12   Entrance to an electrical transformer and plant building

Fig. 14.13 Control office for access into Lager X, Camp X, which was mainly responsible for vehicle maintenance. Above, bars have been cut from the windows

Fig. 14.14 Many tourists pass through the landscape of the secret enclave unaware of its existence and focussed on their anticipation of the prison experience. The standard BT11-type guard towers, as used on the Berlin Wall during the 1970s, probably indicate that the outer wall was replaced at this date

Fig. 14.15 The main prison building. The lower brick portion represents the 1930s National Socialist communal kitchen; post-war it was raised in height

Fig. 14.16 The inner prison court, probably added during the 1950s or 1960s

Fig. 14.17 1980s prison surveillance

Fig. 14.18 Prison corridor with cells to either side and locked gates to either end

Acknowledgements We are grateful to the staff of the Gendenkstätte Berlin-Hohenschönhausen for welcoming us and sharing their knowledge of the area. In particular, we are indebted to Silke Bauer, Reinhard Bernauer and the historian Peter Erler. All photographs by the authors.

References

Ash, T.G. 1997 *The File: A Personal History*. Vintage, London.

Boulton, A. 2009 Cood bay Forst Zinna: Film, art and Archaeology. In *Europe's Deadly Century: Perspectives on 20th Century Conflict Heritage*, edited by N. Forbes, R. Page, and G. Perez, pp. 12–17. English Heritage, Swindon.

Bradshaw, P. 2007 Review of the Lives of Others. Guardian Newspaper, 13 April 2007. http://www.guardian.co.uk/film/2007/apr/13/worldcinema.drama

Childs, D. and R. Popplewell 1999 *The Stasi-the East German Intelligence and Security Service*. Macmillan, London.

Cocroft, W. and S. Cole 2007 *RAF Coltishall, Suffolk, a Photographic Characterisation*. English Heritage Research Department Report 68. English Heritage, Swindon.

Cocroft, W. and J. Schofield 2010 Hohenschönhausen, Berlin–Explorations in Stasiland. *Landscapes*. 11(1): 67–83.

Dunlop, G. 2008 The War Office: Everyday Environments and War Logistics. *Cultural Politics* 4(2): 155–160.

Erler, P. and H. Knabe 2005 *Der Verbotene Stadtteil Stasi-Sperrbezirk Berlin-Hohenschönhausen*. Jaron Verlag, Berlin.

Fairclough, G. 2008 'The Long Chain': Archaeology, Historical Landscape Characterization and Time Depth in the Landscape. In *The Heritage Reader*, edited by G. Fairclough, R. Harrison, J. Jameson, and J. Schofield, pp. 408–424. Routledge, London.

Funder, A. 2003 *Stasiland: Stories from Behind the Berlin Wall*. Granta, London.

Funder, A. 2007 Tyranny of Terror. *The Guardian*, 5 May 2007. www.Guardian.Co.Uk/Books/2007/May/05/Featuresreviews.Guardianreview12

Gendenkstätte Berlin–Hohenschönhausen 2006 *The Stasi-Prison*. Berlin, Museum Leaflet.

Guardian 2007 Ulrich Mühe 1953–2007. *The Guardian*, 25 July 2007. http://www.Guardian.Co.Uk/Film/Filmblog/2007/Jul/25/Ulrichmuehe19532007 (Accessed 17 April 2010)

Lions Gate Home Entertainment 2007 *The Lives of Others*. DVD.

Zacharek, S. 2007 The Lives of Others. *Salon.com*, 9 February 2007. http://www.Salon.Com/Entertainment/Movies/Review/2007/02/09/Lives_Of_Others/ (Accessed 16 April 2010)

Chapter 15
The Last Murals of Long Kesh: Fragments of Political Imprisonment at the Maze Prison, Northern Ireland

Louise Purbrick

Abstract The prison called both Long Kesh and the Maze is regarded as a symbol of the Northern Ireland conflict. Since its closure in 2000, the meaning of its history, the significance of its legacy and its possible futures have been disputed. The majority of the site has been demolished, access to its buildings restricted and plans for re-development have faltered. Using records of the prison made prior to the demolitions, this chapter interprets a fragment of the material culture of the prison; it examines a series of murals in one of its H Blocks, and argues that close attention to the materiality of this site can contribute to some understanding of the violence of the conflict itself.

Introduction: Representing the Troubles

The low lying boggy land of a former Royal Air Force base at Long Kesh, close to Lisburn, south of Belfast, was a place of incarceration from 1971 until 2000. This chapter examines a series of murals found intact in 2002 inside one of the structures built on this land, and it considers their meaning and the relationship of meaning to site. The use of the site as a prison corresponds to a period of conflict in Ireland, usually referred to as the Troubles, which spanned over 30 years from August 1969, when the British Army was sent to Northern Ireland and began a long-term, large-scale deployment, to a peace process that has continued into the early twenty-first century. Jonathan Tonge opens his recent book, *Northern Ireland*, by stating that this conflict was "by far the worst seen in Western Europe since the Second World War" and by announcing its death toll: 3,665 people. Republican forces were responsible for 2,148 deaths, loyalists for 1,071 and 365 people were killed by British troops (Tonge 2006:1).

L. Purbrick (✉)
School of Humanities, University of Brighton, Brighton, UK
e-mail: l.purbrick@bton.ac.uk

A. Myers, G. Moshenska (eds.), *Archaeologies of Internment*, One World Archaeology,
DOI 10.1007/978-1-4419-9666-4_15, © Springer Science+Business Media, LLC 2011

The conflict in and about Northern Ireland is one of the most studied of recent wars, but the scholarship that has ensured that is Northern Ireland is an "extensively interpreted region" has also produced "dissensus", "multiple disagreements" and a "meta-conflict", that is, "a conflict about what the conflict is about" (McGarry and O'Leary 1995:1–2). Four basic interpretations have been delineated by John Whyte according to the identification of different pairs of antagonists: Britain versus Ireland, the south versus the north of Ireland, capitalist versus worker, Protestant versus Catholic (Whyte 1990:114). Interpretations are also grouped into those that attribute internal or external causes of the conflict and cast it as either ethno-national or colonial in nature, respectively (McGarry and O'Leary 1995:5; Tonge 2006:12–15). The division between two communities within Northern Ireland is at the centre of ethno-national explanations of conflict. On the one hand, Unionists and loyalists identify themselves as British and defend the continued existence of Northern Ireland through which the union with Britain has been maintained since its creation by the partition of Ireland in 1920. On the other hand, nationalists and republicans seek recognition as Irish, and feel trapped within the arbitrary border of an artificially constituted British state.

Within a colonial explanation, the battle is between those seeking Irish independence, and British forces paired with Unionists, the beneficiaries and surrogates of British rule. As Britain's oldest colony, Ireland has been the subject of protracted colonial intervention of which the Troubles was a recent phase. Currently, ethno-national interpretations are dominant in public arenas, not least because the 1998 Good Friday Agreement which instituted the present power-sharing or "consociational" arrangements for Northern Ireland's internal government, is based upon balancing the opposing demands and desires of the two traditions and has transformed a war over territory into one of identity (Tonge 2006:13).

Ethno-national interpretations of the conflict are premised upon the analysis of contemporary political discourse and not other forms of evidence, such as its material record. Assumptions about an inevitable and perpetual opposition of identities has led to hesitancy around much of the most substantial material culture of the Troubles, lest its meanings are impossible to balance and an unmanaged version of events spills out in public. For example, the large structures of British military occupation, such as watchtowers, have been removed and access to the prison site discussed here (regularly referred to as a symbol of the Troubles) has either been limited or prohibited since its closure. Following the archaeological imperative to examine rather than avoid material culture, I suggest that such investigative effort could extend our understanding of the conflict.

Murals are the most familiar forms of Northern Ireland's material culture and are one of the few that have been the subject of sustained analysis. The origins of loyalist murals have been traced to the early twentieth century commemorations of William III's 1690 victory at the Battle of the Boyne, and republican ones to the street activism that accompanied prison struggles of the late 1970s (Jarman 1997; Rolston 1991, 1992, 1995, 2003). Neil Jarman, writing in 1998, stated:

In little more than a decade mural painting has developed into one of the most dynamic media for symbolic expression in the north of Ireland. On any journey, real or virtual, through the working-class estates of Belfast one is bombarded by a panoply of visual statements. In recent years these images have become increasingly elaborate and extensive in their design and professional in their execution. Nowadays scaffolding is often erected in front of walls which are to be transformed and painters may spend days working to cover a wall with symbols, icons and images. We have come a long way from 1970 when two men were sentenced to six months' imprisonment for painting a tricolour at Annadale Street, or from 1980 when a 16-year-old youth was shot dead while painting republican slogans on a wall by a policeman who said he thought the paintbrush was a gun. Nowadays such activity is largely acknowledged as an established, if not entirely legitimate, political practice. (Jarman 1998:81)

Since the high point of mural painting in the 1990s, its practice has altered considerably and it is often bound up with peace process attempts to produce neutral urban spaces. The redevelopment of mural sites, removal and relocation of murals or their replacement with public art are now more likely to be the matter of debate.

Conflict and Imprisonment

It is estimated that 25,000 people were imprisoned in Northern Ireland over roughly 30 years of conflict. Of these prisoners, at least 10,000 men were held at a prison site known as both Long Kesh and the Maze (Ryder 2000).[1] The first were internees. Internment, used several times in Northern Ireland's short history, was reintroduced by its Stormont government on 9 August 1971 (McGuffin 1973). Nissen huts had been erected on the runways of Long Kesh airbase earlier in the year in preparation for mass arrests. At the beginning of 1972, the internment centre comprised five compounds, each of four Nissen huts enclosed in high wire (Fig. 15.1). Re-named Her Majesty's Prison (HMP) Maze with the introduction of British Direct Rule in the same year, it continued to grow until there were 22 compounds by the end of 1974. Over this time, sentenced prisoners had been allocated to compounds alongside internees. Crucially, sentenced prisoners held special category status. Following a 30-day republican hunger strike in Belfast's Crumlin Road jail in 1972, the then Secretary of State for Northern Ireland Willie Whitelaw had conceded that all politically motivated prisoners did not have to wear a uniform or undertake work, and could receive more letters, parcels and visits than ordinarily sentenced prisoners (McKeown 2001:28–29). Thus special category prisoners had more or less the same rights as those remanded or interned, which is to say that once within the prison system they were treated as if not in fact convicted.

Imprisonment was a strategy of war in Northern Ireland as in conflicts all over the world. Conflicts that take place within contemporary democracies have adapted and subverted existing judicial and penal systems to criminalize types of organization, forms of expression or acts of violence that might in a conventional battlefield earn the captured the status of Prisoner of War. For example, the 1973 *Northern*

Fig. 15.1 A compound at Long Kesh in 2006. Photograph by Louise Purbrick

Ireland (Emergency Provisions) Act contained a schedule that codified a conflict-related offence (producing explosives, using firearms, holding weapons, making petrol bombs, throwing them) and proscribed organizations (Northern Ireland 1974). There were trials for scheduled offences, but these were conducted in a court without a jury. "Diplock courts", as they were known, also allowed convictions on uncorroborated confessions. Successive British administrations have found it politically expedient to define conflict over Northern Ireland as a problem of law and order and to consider violence as criminal or pathological rather than political.[2] Both internment (always readily understood as war measure) and special category (recognition of the political nature of particular affiliations or violent acts) compromised the British position and caused sufficient embarrassment to phase out the use of internment and withdraw special category status (Gardiner Report 1975).

Those sentenced after 1 March 1976 were sent to a new hastily constructed prison adjacent to the Long Kesh internment centre. It was built to install a conventional penal regime of rehabilitation for its individual male occupants, based on a cellular structure. Cells were arranged in eight low-rise blocks (Fig. 15.2), 96 single units divided equally into four wings, each forming an upright of an H shape (Fig. 15.3). The H Blocks, however, did not contribute to the "normalisation" (Gormally et al. 1993) of imprisonment as its architects had intended; it became a site of resistance to the de-politicization of the conflict and thus a front-line in its own right. The first republican prisoners sent to the H Blocks sought to win back special category status and refused to wear prison uniforms. Their action, known as being "on the blanket" because when denied their own clothes they wrapped themselves in the

Fig. 15.2   View of the H Blocks in 2006. Photograph by Louise Purbrick

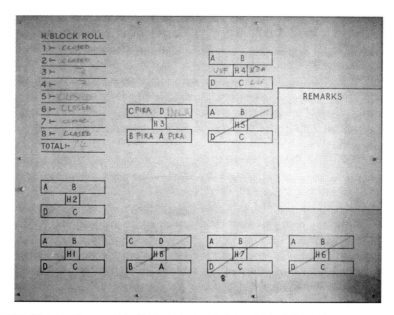

Fig. 15.3   Working diagram of the H Blocks in the administration buildings. Photograph by Louise Purbrick

cell bedding, developed into a long, large-scale collective prison protest that escalated into a no-wash campaign in which prisoners refused to use bathrooms and to slop-out, and, ultimately, the hunger strikes of 1980 and 1981 (Campbell et al. 1994). Ten republican prisoners died from starvation, the first and best known being Bobby Sands. Their deaths secured substantial freedoms within the H Blocks: prisoners' right to wear their own clothes was granted just days after the hunger strikes ended and an initial first step in the wider recognition of their political status, which included acknowledgement of their membership of collective organizations, republican or loyalist, that eventually control their own wings and set the conditions for mural painting to flourish within the prison.

At the Long Kesh/Maze Site

Two prison systems, structurally adjacent and politically overlapping, existed at Long Kesh/Maze. The internment compounds had not been used as a prison since the late 1980s, when the remaining sentenced prisoners were transferred to the H Blocks. The very last prisoners of Long Kesh/Maze were moved out of the H Blocks in September 2000; most had been released 2 months earlier under the terms of the Good Friday Agreement that provided for "an accelerated programme for the release of prisoners ... convicted of scheduled offences in Northern Ireland" (Belfast Agreement 1998:25). From this moment on there has been continual debate about the historical significance and possible future use of the site (Purbrick 2006).

What remains as material record of the record of imprisonment at Long Kesh/Maze? One H Block (H6), one compound (Cage 19), a section of the perimeter wall, administration buildings, a prison chapel and the prison hospital are at least externally intact. The rest was demolished between 2006 and 2008. Despite the scale and complexity of the site that encompassed 22 compounds, eight H Blocks, and a vast paraphernalia of containment within a two-and-a-half mile perimeter wall, its record of political imprisonment is fragmentary and partial. Similarly, my account is also incomplete.

Since 2000, I have been involved in the creation of a record of the material culture of Long Kesh/Maze and have contributed to the debate about its future use. Apart from two external views (Figs. 15.1 and 15.2), This chapter draws upon my observations, field notes and photographs made at the prison site between 2002 and 2004 while working with photographer Donovan Wylie. At that time, Wylie's concern was to demonstrate the scale of the prison through representing its repetitious spaces of incarceration. He showed the walls as a system of control, describing their purpose through his photography but without much reference to those who occupied the spaces within them (Fig. 15.4). My contribution to this work at Long Kesh/Maze was as an art historian, offering an analysis of its prison architecture and history of its occupation; it was not to make an additional or alternative account, although when I found traces of prison life I made a record with pen and paper, an old 35 millimeter camera and a disposable camera. Most traces were found on walls and

Fig. 15.4 "Inertias". Copyright Donovan Wylie. Reproduced with permission

while what remained in 2002 could only be a tiny fraction of the layers of decoration made over 30 years of imprisonment, they are nevertheless indicative of the political occupation of the jail.

Marking and covering prison walls are rejections of the prison regime announced in its architecture; they attempt to reconstruct a prison life from within its confines. The fractions of evidence of political imprisonment in Northern Ireland that I observed have since been destroyed with the demolition of the majority of the prison. Destruction raises as many questions about what is considered historically significant and what is shunned or disregarded as any act of preservation. Material culture is never pristine, and a fragmentary material record is always an effect of historical processes, but is particularly problematic at a site that was, and is, highly contested: Long Kesh/Maze was occupied by opposing political forces whose different historical relationships to the site have held its development in stalemate. Fragments, however, are the stock in trade of archaeologists and historians.

When I arrived in Long Kesh/Maze in November 2002, I entered a deserted but not empty prison. It was in limbo. Even in the compounds, which had been disused for 15 years, things had been abandoned, but not gathered up or thrown away. There were pieces of prison paperwork trodden into the compound floor, markings and coverings on interior of the Nissen huts that remained as well as some furniture lying around (Fig. 15.5). A whiteboard displaying a list of names and rack numbers indicating the shelf space where prisoners left any possessions they

Fig. 15.5 Chair at Long Kesh in 2002. Photograph by Louise Purbrick

could not take into the camp had not been wiped clean (Fig. 15.6). The people were absent; there were neither prisoners nor prison officers. A skeleton maintenance staff remained.

The decommissioning of Long Kesh/Maze, a process of removing remaining prison property and determining the fate the buildings in the disused internment camp and the more recently inhabited H Blocks of the cellular jail was not yet underway. Thus, in the H-Block administration buildings, records lay around that were only later collected by the Public Record Office Northern Ireland (PRONI) (Fig. 15.7). Someone had left their coat hanging on the back of one office door and football kits, half heartedly pulled out of a washing machine, were twisted up on the floor of the sports hall. Certain H Blocks, H3, H4 and H5, were placed in warm storage, ready for re-use. Press reports circulated claims that Long Kesh/Maze would be pressed into service as an immigration holding centre. Thus, parts of the prison were being maintained while others prepared for closure. The clearing out of cells, which would have been a regular practice during the life of Long Kesh/Maze when prisoners had finished the term of their sentences and their cell spaces were made ready for others still detained, was extended with the implementation of the Good Friday Agreement. As entire wings and blocks became unoccupied, the interiors of the cells were dismantled: standard cell furniture, furnishings and fittings (beds, shelves, curtains, lighting) were removed and stored. They were then cleaned but with varying degrees of thoroughness, and some re-fitted, while others left to deteriorate. Thus, the H Blocks were in different states of decoration and decay. All walls of the warm storage blocks had been painted in the pale institutional colors familiar from hospitals and re-furnished in contrasting domestic fabrics. The blocks H1, H2

Fig. 15.6 Rack numbers at Long Kesh in 2002. Photograph by Louise Purbrick

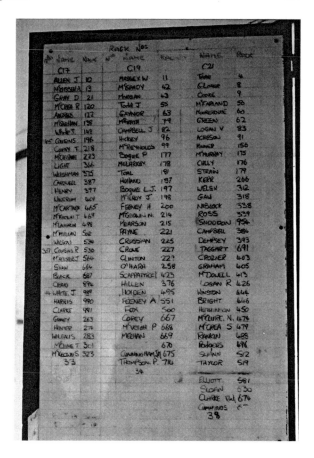

and H8 had all fittings and furniture removed, the walls had been cleaned and there had been some repainting.

The cell doors seemed to have been missed by the cleaners and fragments of writing were still visible. In the offices extending from the administrative area in the centre of the H Blocks, known as the circle, were piles of discarded prison issue artifacts: bibles, paper towels, curtains and pillow cases. Damp pervaded everywhere, swelling the walls, floors and ceilings, bubbling and flaking the paint. The condition of blocks H6 and H7 was much the same but their cleaning seemed fairly superficial and had left more traces of wall markings and wall coverings: evidence of posters, stickers and graffiti. The cleaning of the H Blocks was incomplete and it was partial. A flip chart in an upstairs office of the administration buildings had been turned to reveal a page used in a briefing session for maintenance staff. It carried an instruction to paint over the murals. All had been covered over, except in one block, H7.

Fig. 15.7 Paperwork in administration buildings at Long Kesh in 2002. Photograph by Louise Purbrick

The Last Murals

On the walls of C wing, H7, was a large mural of a battlefield transformed into a graveyard (Fig. 15.8).[3] A skeletal figure, with a death mask for a face and clothed in a uniform of pale blue trousers and red jacket evocative of a nineteenth-century British soldier, charges out of a dark landscape. Carrying a tattered flag like a spear, the skeleton soldier appeared in the desperate and courageous stance associated with "going over the top" and the uneven ground behind him suggests the muddy mounds of trench warfare. The mounds are also newly dug graves whose wooden crosses read: *Greysteel, Sinn Fein, IRSP, INLA, IRA*. A grim reaper stalks in the background. *Shankill Road* was painted on the radiator below the mural. A text painted on the wing wall explained the mural's purpose and to whom it belonged:

> This mural is dedicated to all the brave men who have fought with "2nd Batt" West Belfast UFF. Since 1973 they have taken the war almost single-handedly to the Republican Movement. From having so little to achieving so much that their memory must forever live on. *Quis Separabit* [who will separate us].

The skeleton soldier is an adaptation of "Eddie", heavy metal band Iron Maiden's mascot. His stance and, indeed, the composition of the entire mural draws upon the cover image of the band's 1983 single *The Trooper*, a rock music interpretation of Alfred Tennyson's, *Charge of the Light Brigade*. This misdirected, disastrous but most famous advance of the Crimean War is a less important historical reference for loyalists than the Battle of the Somme, expressed through the First World War landscape that has replaced the dry rocky background of the original image.

Fig. 15.8 Mural in H7, C
Wing, in 2002. Photograph by
Louise Purbrick

However, the incarnation of Iron Maiden's Eddie as a trooper does articulate the
reckless courage of the last defenders of Empire, whose appeal to loyalists is demonstrated by its duplication in mural form: several different versions painted on gable
ends in Derry and Belfast.[4]

The trooper Eddie is unmistakably a loyalist; the tattered flag he carried displays
the red hand of Ulster. Loyalist Eddie, with the layers of meaning typical of appropriated art forms, was located at the top of the H7's C wing, near the entrance to
its dining room. On the walls on the dining room were painted four male forms that
represented UFF 2nd Batt. All were shown in black military style uniforms distinguished by balaclava headwear as opposed to a more conventional helmets or caps.
All displayed guns and were accompanied by the song title and slogan *Simply the
Best*.

In the floor plan of the H Block, dining rooms are found at each corner of the
cross bar that forms the H and is its administrative circle, but they are entered only
from the wing. Dining rooms are located on either side of the intersection of wings.
C wing continues through double airlock gates into D wing to complete the upright
the H. In the D wing dining room of H7, a poem was painted in large script under

the headline, *2nd Battalion on Tour*. The headline appeared on a banner, paint trying to capture the appearance of the folds of a ribbon created when pinned to a wall. The poem read:

I First Produced my RPG. Then I Produced My Rocket
I Shouted No Surrender and Connelly House Got It
We'll kill Them at Their Work
We'll Shoot them in the Head
We'll kill Them in Their Bookies
Then It's Home To Bed

A Freedom Fighter

Bordering the poem and completing the ensemble were two images. To the left was an adaptation of a red-edged triangular *men at work* road sign, featuring a silhouetted figure in a balaclava and rocket in the centre. "ON HOLD" was boldly displayed in black capitals along the bottom. Below the road sign image, were three place names also painted in black capital letters:

ROCK BAR
CONNELLY HOUSE
LOWER FALLS SF

To the right was a shield-shaped emblem displaying a clenched fist, a version of the Red Hand of Ulster, surrounded by a repetition of military affiliation: 2nd Batt. West Belfast (Fig. 15.9). The H7 mural series is addressed to a local audience; all murals contain acronyms and place names that assume intimate knowledge of the conflict in Northern Ireland. UFF is the regularly used shortened form for the Ulster Freedom Fighters, the loyalist group described as the "nom de guerre" (McKay 2000:24) of the Ulster Defence Association (UDA), its "flag of convenience" (Tayor 1999:116), and its "cover name" used "to claim responsibility for the killing of Catholics."[5] The UDA, formed in 1971, was the largest loyalist organization: estimates place the number of members in the mid 1970s at 30,000–40,000 (many of whom were also members of the part-time British Army force, the Ulster Defence Regiment). The UDA is identified in Sutton Index of Deaths as responsible for 112 fatalities (Sutton nd);[6] it was not proscribed, however, until 1992. The UFF was established 2 years into the life of the UDA, in 1973, to be, in the words of one of its founders, "more effective" that its parent organization and "willing take the war to the IRA" (Harding Smith in Taylor 1999:115), a phrase repeated on walls of H7. The Sutton Index lists 147 people killed by the UFF.

There are a number of references to UFF actions in the mural series. *Their Bookies* is an allusion to the killing of five Catholics in Sean Grahams Bookmakers on 5 February 1992. The place names, *Greysteel, Rock Bar, Connolly House* and *Lower Falls* work in a similar way. On 30 October 1993, two UFF opened fire on people drinking in the Rising Sun bar in Greysteel, County Derry, in 30 October 1993, killing seven. They shouted "trick or treat" before the used their weapons, an AK47 and a Browning pistol (Taylor 1999:225). A week before, on 23 October, an

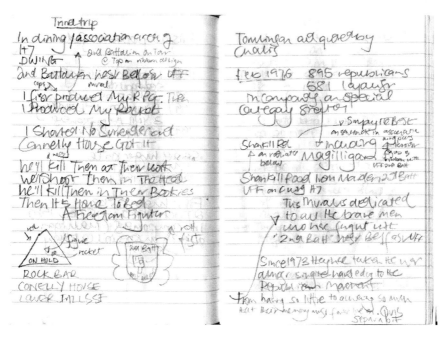

Fig. 15.9 The author's 2003 notebook. Photograph by Louise Purbrick

IRA bomb prematurely detonated in a fish shop on the Shankill Road; the intended target was the Loyalist Prisoner Association offices above run by the UFF but ten people downstairs in the shop were killed in the explosion: the IRA member, the fish shop owner, his daughter and seven of their customers (McKittrick et al. 1999).[7]

The other UFF actions indicated on the walls of H7 took place the following year. On 10 January 1994, UFF launched a missile at a public house called the Rock Bar on the Falls Road, West Belfast, a Catholic-nationalist area. They used an RPG, a shoulder-held rocket propelled grenade. The grenade ricocheted off the pub's protective metal grille exploding in the street. The UFF drove away firing shots (Wood 2006:181). The attack on Connolly House, Sinn Fein's offices in Andersonstown, another Catholic-nationalist area of West Belfast, 3 months later was very similar: the same type of weapon was used damaging the front of the building (Wood 2006:182). There were no fatalities from either UFF action; Sinn Fein's Andersonstown offices were empty at the time of the attack, but both were significant shows of force, threatening displays of loyalist armory and their ability to invade nationalist areas. These actions are claimed as the achievement of a particular UFF unit, West Belfast 2nd Battalion C Company, led by the notorious Johnny Adair, who was arrested in relation to at least one of these rocket attacks. All are indicative of his leadership but also of a longer period of loyalist assaults on a so-called "pan nationalist front" (McKay 2000:95) that included representatives of constitutional nationalist parties as well as supporters of the republican movement.

The UFF actions that took place in the early part of 1994, that is, in months follow-ing the signing of the Downing Street Declaration may also be considered a violent sign of the political uncertainty felt by loyalist and unionists as they anticipated some form of British withdrawal from Ireland.

Of the acronyms written on the crosses scattered over the graveyard battlefield in the Eddie as loyalist trooper mural, perhaps only one requires no explanation: Irish Republican Army (IRA). The shortened form of Irish National Liberation Army (INLA), the Irish Republican Socialist Party (IRSP) and SF for Sinn Fein are less commonly used. This collection of letters blurs the political with the military and elides fiercely contested divergent republican traditions. All are also encompassed by the pronoun repeated three times with poem attributed to A Freedom Fighter: *them*. *Them* is "the other side", the entire Catholic community and any of its repre-sentatives. The mix of acronyms and pronouns on the walls of H7 are indications of the dual sectarian strategies of UFF. On the one hand, they targeted representatives of the republican movement aided, as the Stevens Inquiry revealed, by the receipt of intelligence information from British security forces including the Special Branch of the Royal Ulster Constabulary and MI5 (Taylor 1999:206–210). On the other hand, they engaged in the indiscriminate killing of Catholic people. Deliberate attacks on those who could be described as uninvolved, non-participants, civilians, bystanders or innocent, if these were not such very difficult terms to use, have been defended by UFF members as a "clear strategy and methodology" of pressurizing the IRA by attacking the community assumed to give it "support" (Harding Smith in Taylor 1999:116). This is what is meant by "taking the war to the IRA".

The Work of Murals

Murals are a visual shorthand for the Troubles. Those covering the gable ends of houses in working-class areas of Northern Ireland's towns and cities are recog-nizable to those who have never set foot in them. "The media", as McCormick and Jarman point out, "use murals to convey a sense of authenticity to films and dramas ostensibly set in Belfast, even when this requires the painting of a paramil-itary mural in Dublin, Cardiff or Manchester" (McCormick and Jarman 2005:50). Tours of murals are now an essential component of tourist visit to Belfast. However, Jarman maintains that a mural's intended audience is, or at least it was during the conflict, local: "It targets the image at people who will more readily understand the nuances and allusions" (Jarman 1997:210). That murals provide instant geograph-ical and historical associations required by television and film script writers while their content is not fully comprehended suggests that have layers of meaning and multiple effects.

Murals mark out the segregated and sectarian geography of Northern Ireland; they announce the boundaries of Catholic (nationalist-republican) and Protestant (unionist-loyalist) areas and ensure the separation persists. They define the space; they declare its allegiance. For those from both near and far, an inhabitant who lives alongside them or tourist who views from a distance, they can invite or deter entrance. "They are expressions of power and they are attempts to demonstrate control over space and place", (McCormick and Jarman 2005:50). But murals are no straightforward reflection of unfettered loyalist power in a protestant estate or uncontested republican control over of Catholic streets. Mural painting exists in a relationship between communities and those who claim to represent them. While the tourist would be acutely aware of being in a space that belongs to someone else, their precise location, their specific imagery and pattern of upkeep is bound up with the political struggles within their localities. A newly painted or re-painted mural may be roundly welcomed or quietly tolerated; it may simultaneously demonstrate support for a particular political or military group or the suppression of opposition to that group. It can articulate the collective identity of a particular place and impose it upon a population whose lives are less fixed than the paint on the bricks around them.

The H7 mural series works in the same way as the gable-end murals, although the relationships within which they exist are rather rarefied in the highly structured space of Long Kesh/Maze. Nevertheless, they too demarcate the segregation between loyalists and republicans that has characterized the Northern Ireland conflict and was an organizing principle of the prison. The poem, slogans, battalion badges and mottos, black figures with their balaclavas as well as the loyalist trooper in his graveyard battlefield are all declarations of the territorial limits of the UFF within Long Kesh/Maze and the extent of their power over the wings of the H Block and the individual cells attached to them. To those who visited C and D wing of H7, including any prisoner officers, the mural series demonstrates that the UFF controls the space, having the ability to manipulate and dominate it. To those prisoners who are affiliated to the UFF, the array of emblems would be a familiar sight, a daily welcome back into the group, reassuring them of their place within it and its reminding them of its authority. The mural painting not only asserts loyalist supremacy over Catholic people but also the UFF dominance over other loyalists groups, such as the Ulster Volunteer Force (UVF) and even other battalions within the UFF itself. Thus, whatever reassurance the murals might offer, they are also an encouragement, command and warning to UFF members to remain loyal to its organization.

The position of mural painting in power struggles within and between communities mean that they are unstable art forms, the objects of conflict rather than simply records of it (McCormick and Jarman 2005:50). The instability of mural painting has extended through the peace process in Northern Ireland; alterations and removals have accelerated to the point that mural painting is "being disappeared" (McCormick and Jarman 2005:54).[8] Their concern is not that murals remain in place and preserved; it is their disappearance from public debate that they seek to address, arguing that the removal of mural painting is relatively unnoticed despite its significance. The wide reproduction of murals as the rapidly readable signs of place in both print and film form may make it appear as they are always there. However, mural conservation, such as at Free Derry Corner, where walls are continually repainted to form a commemorative corridor is the exception. "They are but rarely regarded as objects worthy of preservation" (McCormick and Jarman 2005:69).

Murals are, therefore, never permanent: they are temporary interventions into public space, which were and, in some cases, are maintained only while they remain relevant politically, culturally or socially to the community close by. Much like conventionally commissioned public art, responsibility for the work and its physical condition does not reside with its creator but with the commissioner. The are a few mural painters, Bobby Jackson and his family, The Bogside Artists or Gerard Kelly (also known as Mo Chara), with reputations as muralists sufficient for them to claim ownership and exert some control over their work – but most mural painters most are not unnamed and unknown beyond the groups who commission the mural and communities in which it exists. They may adapt trade skills, use self-taught methods or practices acquired from other local mural painters in the creation of pieces for a particular community or military campaign or group and would simply share the interest of those who required the mural in its destiny, its upkeep or abandonment.

The removal of the H Block murals as the prison was cleaned up in preparation for re-use or closure followed the normal lifecycle of such painting. With no nearby community interested in maintaining them, they disappeared. Painting over murals within the prison is not so very different from doing so in housing estate; it is an act of repossession of space. At Long Kesh/Maze, it re-asserted the authority of the prison in deserted H Blocks where formerly it had little or no control. The Northern Ireland Prison Service accepted that prisoners ran their own wings. The most immediately pressing question raised by the H7 UFF mural series is not why were they destroyed but why were they preserved while others were erased. One of the maintenance workers responsible for clearing the cells explained to me that they just "didn't get around to it". Notes left in the administration buildings show that H7 was not the last block to be emptied of prisoners but Loyalist Eddie charging over the graves of republicans and Catholics, the poems celebrating loyalist violence and weaponry, mottos announcing the supremacy of the UFF remained on the H Block walls until they were broken up in the demolition of the jail.

Other Walls

Recent writings in the archaeology of conflict have suggested that difficult, hot, contested or dissonant material culture is valuable for its critical properties, an ability to instigate a dialogue about the past (Fairclough et al. 2008). Furthermore, rather than reaffirming a narrative of national unity achieved through war, those material remains that fracture such reassurances of ultimate victory can insist that historical differences, which may underpin conflict or persist in its aftermath are recognized or, at least, not painted over.

The H7 mural series certainly pose difficulties not least of which are the questions of how to make such artifacts accessible and then how to display them without causing hurt and offence. They easily could have fulfilled the criteria of dissonance by instigating a debate about a series of issues that lie at the heart of conflict-resolution: What is the nature of sectarianism? What are the historical and political conditions in which sectarianism persists and conflict erupts? Unfortunately, lack of access to H7 means that I can only hint at the purposes they might have served. Few people saw them: the loyalists imprisoned in the block, the prison officers who worked in it while it was open or as it closed, the photographers, artists, surveyors and historians who were granted access by the Northern Ireland Prison Service or the Northern Ireland Office to the prison in its moment of limbo. Once it was decommissioned and transferred to the Northern Ireland Executive, the devolved government, it was possible to apply for a place on a tour guided by a civil servant which encompassed the perimeter wall and one of its towers, the internment camp, the H Block administration buildings, the hospital and H3, a warm storage block that had been thoroughly cleaned and blandly repainted. Requests to visit H7 were denied.

Restricted access could be bemoaned as a lost opportunity to view last murals of Long Kesh in situ. However, in situ is not, of course, quite the same as in context and the H7 murals had already undergone a process of decontextualization simply by being left. They became unrepresentative. The clearing and cleaning of the H Blocks had removed all substantial signs of republican presence within the prison despite the fact that its single largest group always had been the IRA. I found only one fragment that might have been associated with a republican prisoner: a tiny green and red image cut from a newspaper was taped above a cell door. It was an advertisement for a car accessory, a sign that would dangle on the inside of a rear windscreen showing two traditionally Catholic football kits, Celtic and Manchester United, embracing each other. The overwhelming absence of republican imagery allows the remaining inscriptions, such as the UFF murals, to dominate a deserted space that was once contested through different forms of political representations. The H7 mural series obscures the composition and complexity of the whole prison and they do not necessarily articulate a loyalist prisoner's experience.

Other fragments suggest that life within Long Kesh/Maze was not entirely dominated by political and military groups. Where cleaning was most superficial, in H6 and H7, more traces could be found within the cells. Some were political, for example, the remains of stickers showing the allegiance between loyalist and British fascist organizations (Fig. 15.10). Others were more personal. Several cells were wallpapered (Fig. 15.11). Prisoners had papered their walls from the early days of the prison. Wallpaper was pasted on the partitions within the Nissen huts that constituted the sleeping compartments of the internment centre compounds (Fig. 15.12). It is a domestic form, pretty and homely (Entwisle 1970:18, 139; Hoskins 2005:198). Indeed, wallpapers used in Long Kesh/Maze are most likely to be from the homes of prisoners, spare rolls left over from a redecoration scheme brought in by their families. Surrounded by patterns that recall a place beyond the jail or, at least, mimic a domestic setting, the cell becomes a space of escape not only from the prison authorities but also from the prisoners' organizations that maintained a landscape of political affiliation in shared arenas immediately outside it (along the wing and in the dining rooms). Wallpaper looks out of place in the prison and, perhaps, that is the point; it evokes another world, both personal and private, that is quite at odds with the collective political identities enforced in mural painting. Furthermore, the wallpaper is nostalgic rather than triumphal; it is wistful

Fig. 15.10 Remains of "Combat 18 IRA Scum" sticker, H7 in 2003. Photograph by Louise Purbrick

Fig. 15.11 Wallpapered cell in H7 in 2003. Photograph by Louise Purbrick

and full of longing. It appears as an attempt to make yourself at home in jail. The majority of prisoners in Long Kesh/Maze were lifers.

Wallpaper provides a more reassuring account of war and imprisonment than that offered by UFF murals; it tells a humanitarian and universal narrative of the separation of families and the loss of a home. Its universalizing properties belie the specific political conditions in which it was used, however. Substantial redecoration

Fig. 15.12 Wallpapered partition in a Nissen hut in 2002. Photograph by Louise Purbrick

of a cell within a supposedly maximum security prison is a measure of the freedom won through the struggles for political and collective recognition. Republican actions between 1976 and 1981, the blanket protest, no-wash campaign and hunger strikes, were by far the most significant, but their mass escape of 1983 and the loyalist vandalism of 200 cells the previous year also played a part in securing prisoners command over their own time while imprisoned and over their own, albeit restricted, space. Nevertheless, the humane domestic wallpaper brings the problem of the UFF murals into sharp relief. Their celebration of the death of Catholics and republicans cannot be easily accommodated in the framework within which the material culture of conflict is usually interpreted and understood.

Some Questions in Conclusion

Artifacts of conflict from bullets, torn uniforms, shoes, bones and bloodied walls and handkerchiefs are used to reveal the extent to which a vague notion of war is ranged against an equally generalized notion of human integrity; it causes suffering. The persistence of entrenched difference and the gleeful routine of killing expressed in words and tempo of the UFF's wall poem present war as the actions of some people against others. Staring straight out of the walls of H7 is an account of the relationship between hierarchy, hatred, violence and conflict. For this reason they are an important, although disappeared, record of sectarian warfare: they reveal motivations for violence that are rarely, if ever, addressed.

However, it may be that future interpreters or curators of the material culture of the conflict show relief that the mural of Iron Maiden's Eddie as loyalist trooper, the Freedom Fighter poem and surrounding slogans were demolished along with the rest of H7. The UFF mural series is not an easy subject to write about – even within a book such as this – and poses even greater difficulties for a heritage practice in which the result is usually putting material culture out on public display. One way of addressing the specificity of the series, its associations with a single loyalist group and thus its inability to represent the other prisoner communities in a segregated jail would be to re-create the wall markings and murals painted by each group and reconvene all for exhibition.

Notwithstanding the problem that such a comparative approach is likely to be doomed by the juxtaposition of artistic reproduction and archaeological remains, there is the matter of comparative collecting and the limitations of representativeness. Should the size of the largest military group involved in the conflict be reflected through a greater number of assembled images? Or, could display space be allocated according to which one was the "most important" protagonist and killed the greatest number of people? Would it be appropriate to look for murals or wall markings of comparable content, equally ferociously sectarian, regardless of different political beliefs? Spelt out so crudely, attempts at achieving representativeness, especially if this is understood as a search for some kind of balance, produce a relatively inaccurate history. In a peace process based on power-sharing political institutions, such as in Northern Ireland, balance is a priority and the past tends to take its most politically expedient form.

Notes

1 For higher figures, see: Coiste na n-larchimí, A museum at Long Kesh or the Maze? *Report of Conference Proceedings* 14 June 2003, p. 27.

2 The clearest articulation of this was by Margaret Thatcher at press conference on 21 April 1981, during the hunger strike. She stated: "Crime is crime is crime, it is not political", *Conflict Archive on the Internet* (hereafter CAIN) Web service, "The Hunger Strike of 1981 – A Chronology of Main Events" http://cain.ulst.ac.uk/events/hstrike/chronology.htm (visited 7.11.09).

3 For a color version taken while the H Blocks were still occupied, see *The Guardian's* Maze Prison picture gallery http://www.guardian.co.uk/world/gallery/2008/apr/29/northernireland?picture=333820433 (visited 10.4.10).

4 See Jonathan McCormick, "A Directory of Murals", CAIN webservice
   http://cain.ulst.ac.uk/mccormick/album10.htm;
   http://cain.ulst.ac.uk/mccormick/album14.htm;
   http://cain.ulst.ac.uk/mccormick/album15.htm (visited 7.11.09) and Bill Rolston, Contemporary Murals in Northern Ireland – Loyalist Tradition, CAIN webservice, http://cain.ulst.ac.uk/bibdbs/murals/slide4.htm (visited 7.11.09). Iron Maiden's Eddie as trooper has also inspired tattoos (McKay, 2000:96).

5 CAIN Web Service "Abstracts on Organisations", http://cain.ulst.ac.uk/othelem/organ/uorgan.htm (visited 7.11.09)

6 Malcolm Sutton, *An Index of Deaths from the Conflict in Ireland* (The Sutton Index of Deaths), http://cain.ulst.ac.uk/sutton/index.html (visited 7.11.09).

7 The names and biographical details of those killed in these three incidents can be found in David
   McKittrick et al. (1999 pp. 1277–1280, 1328–1333 and 1335–1337).
8 One important and often cited example of such a disappearance are the murals that covered the
   Lower Shankill area of West Belfast in the latter years (2000–2002) of Johnny Adair's dominance within UFF. The names, mottos and slogans of the UFF and the UDA were repeatedly
   painted accompanied by portraits of local loyalists (e.g. Adair himself and Billy Wright) as
   well as royal figures (William III and Princess Diana). Defacement of these murals accompanied feuding between within the UFF with the end of Adair's regime declared when many were
   painted over in magnolia (McCormick and Jarman, 2005:63–4).

References

Belfast Agreement 1998 *The Belfast Agreement: An Agreement Reached at the Multi-Party Talks
    on Northern Ireland.* The Stationary Office, London.
Campbell, B., L. McKeown, and F. O'Hagan (eds.) 1994 *Nor Meekly Serve My Time: The H-Block
    Struggle 1976–1981.* Beyond the Pale, Belfast.
Entwisle, E. 1970 *The Book of Wallpaper: A History and an Appreciation.* Kingsmead Reprints,
    Bath.
Fairclough, G., R. Harrison, J. Jameson, and J. Schofield (eds.) 2008 *The Heritage Reader.*
    Routledge, London.
Gardiner Report 1975 *Report of a Committee to Consider, in the Context of Civil Liberties and
    Human Rights, Measures to Deal with Terrorism in Northern Ireland.* Her Majesty's Stationery
    Office, London.
Gormally, B., K. McEvoy, and D. Wall 1993 Criminal Justice in a Divided Society: Northern
    Ireland Prisons. In *Crime and Justice: A Review of Research Volume 17*, edited by M. Tonry,
    pp. 51–135. Chicago University Press, Chicago.
Hoskins, L. 2005 *The Papered Wall: The History, Patterns and Techniques of Wallpaper.* Thames
    and Hudson, London.
Jarman, N. 1997 *Material Conflicts: Parades and Visual Displays in Northern Ireland.* Berg,
    Oxford.
Jarman, N. 1998 Painting Landscapes: The Place of Murals in the Symbolic Construction of Public
    Space. In *Symbols in Northern Ireland*, edited by A. Buckley, pp. 111–125. Institute of Irish
    Studies, Belfast.
McCormick, J. and N. Jarman 2005 Death of a Mural. *Journal of Material Culture* 10(1): 49–71.
McGarry, J. and B. O'Leary 1995 *Explaining Northern Ireland: Broken Images.* Blackwell, Oxford.
McGuffin, J. 1973 *Internment.* Anvil Books, Tralee.
McKay, S. 2000 *Northern Protestants: An Unsettled People.* Blackstaff Press, Belfast.
McKeown, L. 2001 *Out of Time: Irish Republican Prisoners Long Kesh, 1972–2000.* Beyond the
    Pale, Belfast.
McKittrick, D., S. Kelters, B. Feeney, and C. Thornton 1999 *Lost Lives: The Stories of the Men,
    Women and Children who Died as a Result of the Northern Ireland Troubles.* Mainstream
    Publishing, Edinburgh and London.
Northern Ireland 1974 *Northern Ireland Emergency Provisions Act 1973.* Her Majesty's Stationery
    Office, London.
Purbrick, L. 2006 Long Kesh/Maze, Northern Ireland: Public Debate as Historical Interpretation.
    In *Re-mapping the Field: New Approaches in Conflict Archaeology*, edited by J. Schofield,
    A. Klausmeier, and L. Purbrick, pp. 72–80. Westkreuz-Verlag, Berlin-Bonn.
Rolston, B. 1991 *Politics and Painting: Murals and Conflict in Northern Ireland.* Associated
    University Press, Cranbury.
Rolston, B. 1992 *Drawing Support: Murals in the North of Ireland.* Beyond the Pale, Belfast.

Rolston, B. 1995 *Drawing Support 2: Murals of War and Peace*. Beyond the Pale, Belfast.

Rolston, B. 2003 *Drawing Support 3: Murals and Transition in the North of Ireland*. Beyond the Pale, Belfast.

Ryder, C. 2000 *Inside the Maze: The Untold Story of the Northern Ireland Prison Service*. Metheun, London.

Sutton, M. n.d. An Index of Deaths from the Conflict in Ireland. http://cain.ulst.ac.uk/sutton/index.html (Accessed 21 April 2010)

Taylor, P. 1999 *Loyalists*. Bloomsbury, London.

Tonge, J. 2006 *Northern Ireland*. Polity, Cambridge.

Whyte, J. 1990 *Interpreting Northern Ireland*. Clarendon, Oxford.

Wood, I. 2006 *Crimes of Loyalty: A History of the UDA*. Edinburgh University Press, Edinburgh.

Chapter 16
Lockdown: On the Materiality of Confinement

Eleanor Conlin Casella

Any meaningful exploration of internment immediately raises an unsettling cluster of underlying questions. Why does confinement exist? Why would a modern state expend tremendous resources (both financial and political) to maintain groups of people within an institutional compound? Who becomes subjected to confinement, and under what sort of circumstances? When we turn towards our unique archaeological exploration of these stark environments, further paths of exploration emerge. How do people experience confinement? How do the built and natural landscapes of these places reinforce the process of internment? What mechanism do the various types of occupants use to sustain a sense of social being? And ultimately, what material conditions characterise daily life within these institutions?

With scholars, reformists, philanthropists, social engineers, clinicians, and politicians writing about confinement since the late eighteenth century, a vast interdisciplinary literature exists on the institutional landscape that characterises places of internment. While historians and architects have examined how early communal forms of social welfare and punishment transformed into the stark penitentiaries, asylums, fortified compounds, and extermination camps of the twentieth century (Evans 1982; Ignatieff 1978; Irwin and Austin 1994; Katz 1986; Markus 1993; Pratt 2002), criminologists, legal theorists, and philosophers have debated the relative civic effects of imprisonment (a particular type of confinement) as a mode of punishment, deterrence, and retribution (Garland 1990; Hirsch 1992; Howe 1994; Humphreys 1995).

Others from sociology, anthropology, and culture studies have considered the lived experience of institutionalisation by exploring the psychological impact of the institutional environment on inmates (Clemmer 1940; Sykes and Messinger 1960; Foucault 1977; Goffman 1961; Rhodes 2001), staff (Liebling and Price 2001), dependant children and families (Owen 1998), and even the researchers themselves (Fleisher 1989). Evocative literary works and survivors memoirs have offered insight on the internal worlds and personal experiences of these terrible places

E.C. Casella
School of Arts, Histories & Cultures, University of Manchester, Manchester, UK
e-mail: e.casella@manchester.ac.uk

A. Myers, G. Moshenska (eds.), *Archaeologies of Internment*, One World Archaeology, 285
DOI 10.1007/978-1-4419-9666-4_16, © Springer Science+Business Media, LLC 2011

(Atwood 1996; Colijn 1997; Genet 1949; Jeffrey 1997; Levi 1986; Waters 1999; Wilde 2000). Finally, archaeological perspectives, including those contained within this volume, have begun to illuminate the material and spatial conditions of the modern institution. This work has revealed a profound dissonance between ideal designed landscapes of disciplinary intention, and embodied landscapes of insubordination and compromise. As a compendium of studies based around modern places of internment, this edited volume offers a new perspective on the underlying *materiality* of confinement. It suggests, in other words, some important ethical and political directions for appreciating the broader significance and impact of its ubiquitous presence within contemporary society.

Places for Others: A Diachronic Approach

With its dependence on confinement as *the* primary mode of management for non-citizen populations – in addition, of course, to its own non-productive, dangerous, and dependent citizens – the modern state has been characterised as a *carceral society* (Casella 2007; Garland 1990; Parenti 1999). Indeed, the very presence of confinement opens murky ethical questions of whom can be seen to qualify as a citizen of the nation-state (see Farrell and Burton, Chapter 6). And yet, the evolution of this ubiquitous phenomenon was neither inevitable nor accidental. Its enthusiastic adoption and rapid diffusion linked directly to wider transitions in Western (and later colonial) societies, including the complex social and economic dislocations wrought by industrialisation, a shift in responsibility for strategic labour management and social welfare to the public sector, and the emergence of a particular articulation of power between the modern nation-state and its (sanctioned) citizenry.

In the introduction to this volume, the editors attempt to distinguish between *internment* and *imprisonment* as somehow related to "unjust" versus "just" forms of spatial restriction (Moshenska and Myers, Chapter 1). Beyond the difficult ambiguities posed by the deployment of a moral judgement as the underlying basis for definition (a problem acknowledged by the editors in their discussion), such a juxtaposition also fails to consider how either term may be distinguished from *confinement* – a concept of wider relevance, one that could be used to situate these case studies within the broader historical evolution of this particularly wrenching form of population management. In other words, is internment materially different than other contemporary or previous forms of confinement? And if so, why?

Further, as a unique technology of population management, confinement holds significance to varying degrees across different cultures, and indeed different historic moments. Although the editors of this volume locate *internment* to the twentieth century, such an exclusive temporal link remains a matter of great historical and archaeological debate, with the proliferation of asylums, workhouses, encampments, and "industrial schools" equally representing the mass confinement of specific non-criminal and civilian populations throughout the seventeenth, eighteenth, and nineteenth centuries (Baugher 2001; Beisaw and Gibb 2009; Casella 2007; Huey 2001; Markus 1993; Rothman 1990). Ultimately, the particular historic trajectory of this stark phenomenon – broadly traced from the early proto-institutional monasteries and almshouses of late-medieval Europe, to the various detention facilities for economic migrants and asylum seekers established throughout the developed nations of our own contemporary world – remains a crucial subject for both scholarly analysis and ethical critique.

Thus, by shifting our research focus, as these various chapters do so effectively, onto the *materiality* of confinement, we can consider the strategic development, global proliferation, and human legacy of this painful phenomenon. We can apply the powerful diachronic perspective of our discipline to explore how confinement itself emerged as a sinister, if not capricious, expression of the nation-state's power over those populations deemed to be unproductive, dangerous, or merely different. González-Ruibal (Chapter 4), for example, details the wider historical and European context of concentration camps established during the Spanish fascist regime of General Franco in order to consider their evolution from detention centres to labour camps, and ultimately prisons used for political repression. In his study of civilian internment on the Isle of Man during the two World Wars, Mytum (Chapter 3) adopts a similar historically comparative approach to demonstrate how changing accommodation strategies employed by the British government resulted in not only dramatically different physical experiences of confinement but also divergent perceptions of the various ethnic and gender groups within the internee populations.

Weiss (Chapter 2) also adopts just this explicitly historical perspective in her comparative analysis of confinement in late nineteenth century South Africa in order to trace similarities between the closed labour camps of the South African diamond fields and later civilian camps established by the British during the Anglo-Boer War of 1899–1902. By not only exploring the ambiguous relationship these British wartime compounds shared with contemporary late nineteenth century German camps in colonial South-West Africa and later Nazi concentration camps across 1940s Europe, but also tracking their political and architectural mechanisms backwards into the earlier privately run barrack compounds established for African mineworkers, Weiss' comparative study exposes how disciplinary technologies and political projects of racial rule continuously combined to reinscribe the labouring body under various instances of colonial internment. Further, it is only through this close diachronic analysis that the seamless evolution of state- and market-sanctioned violence – modes of power inherent to all forms of confinement – emerges from her research.

Other contributors to this volume have adopted this essential diachronic approach to demonstrate the ongoing legacy of confinement to survivors, relatives, descendants, and contemporary communities. Thus, while archaeological survey of the Catalina Prison Camp, a mid-twentieth century labour camp in Arizona, produced few substantial material remains, Farrell and Burton (Chapter 6) found that the site's association with Gordon Hirabayashi, a Japanese-American student who gained notoriety following his high-profile refusal to comply with federal relocation orders during the Second World War, offered an invaluable opportunity for the recognition, remembrance, and redefinition of this shameful episode in American history. Drawing upon oral histories gathered as part of their public outreach programme, these scholars demonstrated how commemoration activities at the site provided a reconciliation of painful historic fractures within the wider Japanese-American community over questions of patriotism and military draft resistance, civil rights, and citizenship.

This process of reintegrating both shattered pasts and fractured communities gains urgency when the specific historical trajectory has been compressed into the very recent past. A number of case studies within this volume consider the powerful role of archaeology as both a unique technique for providing material evidence of recent trauma and violence, and as a forum for articulating personal and collective testimony for these experiences. Pantzou (Chapter 11), for example, argues for the application of archaeological recording methods to *Ai Stratis*, an Aegean island used for the isolation of Greek political exiles until 1974, as a means for "securing the material existence of this heritage" in order to "shed light on the underlying factors behind existing attitudes towards this traumatic past". Similarly, faced with the methodological challenge of "empty spaces and emptied space overloaded with meaning and disputed by many different voices", Compañy et al. (Chapter 13) consider the responsibility that accompanies an acknowledgement of these voices in the present. Involved with the archaeological examination of buildings used as Clandestine Detention Centres (CDCs) during the Argentine dictatorship of the late 1970s, these scholars echo Farrell and Burton by observing that a recognition of these voices requires a recovery of the previous history, an examination of the processes that resulted in the establishment of these sites, and produced the silences that concealed their operation and thereby continued their uselife.

And yet, perhaps in some cases, an explicit engagement with the unique historical trajectory of a place of confinement leads more appropriately to the destruction or loss of direct material signatures of the violence within (see Feldman 1991). Perhaps, as Purbrick (Chapter 15) observed in her study of the sectarian murals within the Long Kesh/Maze Prison of Northern Ireland, the process of these inflammatory paintings "being disappeared" reflects the transience of their meaning, as they are often "maintained only while they remain relevant politically, culturally or socially to the community close by". Or would the act of painting them over suggest a new material layer in the specific historical trajectory of this place of internment? As I've explored elsewhere (Casella 1997), the very act of removing or "ruining" a place of tragedy may provide a material means for the associated community to transform their grief into a collective statement of commemoration. Perhaps, in certain contexts, the reintegration of shattered pasts requires us to recognise heritage "destruction" as a conscious *transformation*, rather than a politically questionable *obliteration*, of that painful past?

Together, the studies contained within this volume serve to expose the origins, development, and operation of confinement as a unique, historically contingent, and peculiarly modern social practice. Or, as acknowledged by Compañy et al. (Chapter 13):

> We are historical subjects because we are entwined with history, but also because we have the capability to change it, whether by action or omission. The recovery of historical memory may have less to do with the establishment of answers, than with enabling the questioning. Where are we when we are out of history? What are we participants in when we don't participate?

By adopting this crucial diachronic approach to our research on places of confinement, we may understand not only how these tragic places came to be, but also how they are remembered by communities today. We destabilise the perceived inevitability of their existence, and by illuminating their specific historical trajectory, give voice to the possibility of alternatives.

Towards a Materiality of Internment: Uniformity and Diversity

Turning to specifically consider the *materiality* of internment, an underlying tension immediately emerges from the case studies compiled within this volume. On the one hand, the disciplinary mechanism of confinement produces a compelling material signature of *uniformity*, as expressed through both the anonymous landscapes of barracks, corridors, and fence lines, and the identical sets of institutional provisions issued to all inhabitants – a category applied to both the internees, and the authority figures (guards, soldiers, interrogators) who maintain confinement. Nevertheless, those same built spaces and portable objects frequently contain material evidence for the diverse social identities of those within these compounds and camps. In other words, while the built landscapes and institutional objects associated with internment create a powerful force of uniformity, those who experience internment simultaneously create signatures of *diversity* by using the material world to maintain a sense of personal self and communal belonging. Archaeological research on confinement allows us to not only recover physical evidence of each of these dimensions, but to illuminate the nature of this dynamic material tension as well.

Many studies contained within this volume offer intriguing perspectives on the repetition inherent to places of confinement. By contrasting the uniform textures of road surfaces, boundary walls, and architectural features within their photographic essay on the *Hohenschönhausen* complex of Cold War era East Berlin, Schofield and Cocroft (Chapter 14), for example, document the material relationship between standardised building components and the maintenance of state power under totalitarian regimes. Other contributors asked whether the uniformity of the built environment itself created a standardised approach to confined subjects, even when the actual internees could be perceived as offering varying levels of social "risk". In his comparison of two Scottish-based encampments related to the Second World War, Banks (Chapter 7) echoed Weiss (Chapter 2) by demonstrating the material similarities between contemporary places for the confinement of labourers (Canadian forestry workers) and captured prisoners of war (German PoWs). While this study interprets a characteristic landscape feature of confinement, specifically wire boundary fences, as holding multiple purposes dependant upon the type of internee, underlying similarities in both the compound layouts and built features – the bunkhouses, cook house, dining hall, work sheds, foremen/guard zones, and inevitable perimeter fences – expose a deeper embrace of uniformity in both the practical management of communal male labour and state accommodation for non-citizen inhabitants.

Other scholars approached this question of uniformity by exploring strategies adopted by inhabitants to relieve the dreadful monotony of institutional life. Mytum (Chapter 3) draws upon autobiographies, diaries, and archival sources to detail the many creative projects developed by male PoW internees on the Isle of Man – artistic crafts, musical events, and theatrical productions designed for "the eating away of time through years in camp". In documenting these endeavours, this study acknowledges the psychological trauma created by the uniformity of everyday life under confinement.

When taken to violent extremes, the material signature of uniformity adopts a sinister corporeal form. In their archaeological study of a Clandestine Detention Center (CDC) and associated municipal cemetery related to the Argentine dictatorship of the late 1970s, Zarankin and Salerno (Chapter 12) observe how the disciplinary tactics of internment – particularly, the homogenous distribution of power across all inmates – stripped political prisoners of their human identities, ultimately producing "No Name" bodies that required forensic intervention to establish and reclaim their personhood. As their chapter reminds us, archaeology offers an essential tool for counteracting the intentional and politically motivated obliteration of material evidence for the violence required to sustain internment. By systematically recording the material evidence of uniformly horrible living conditions, uniformly tortured bodies, uniformly enclosed, and fortified spaces, archaeology provides a necessary testimony of the very physical and historical existence of this unique form of social management.

And yet, as observed earlier, the physical remains of internment simultaneously contain meanings that destabilise this force of uniformity. In a direct echo of Mytum's archive-based study of wartime internee crafts and theatrical productions on the Isle of Man, Carr (Chapter 8) has examined the materiality of objects and artworks created by Channel Islander internees during the Second World War. Faced with the monotony of institutional life, members of this British civilian community scavenged the material world of their camps for the necessary resources "to consume time and mentally evade the barbed wire". Through their resulting handicrafts and artworks – a body of objects that ranged from barbed wire handmade jewellery, engraved German army-issue aluminium commemorative mugs, and boxes decorated with Union Jacks or English country scenes, to an ornate tablecloth embroidered with a monogram and crown dedicated to King George V (a surreptitious reference to the "V-for-Victory" campaign) – internees asserted their own personal aesthetics, communicated their collective resistance and shared political sentiments, and materially recorded their diverse experiences of life under confinement.

An alternative example of material diversification can be found in Seitsonen and Herva's (Chapter 10) analysis of *Peltojoki*, a German camp for captured

Soviet PoWs. Located within Lapland, a region of Northern Finland, this Second World War base contained various structures and service buildings that indicated a standardised, if ephemeral, built environment characterising this military camp. In contrast, the portable material remains collected from rubbish tips offered evidence of divergence from the uniformity of military-issue provisions. Struggling to adapt to the harsh winter conditions of the Lapland wilderness, German soldiers appeared to have augmented their military clothing with Swedish fur hats and Finnish ski boots, as represented in surviving photographs. Further, the recovered ceramic assemblage suggests an increasing adoption of Finnish wares, with local factory porcelains appearing in addition to German military-issued Bavarian and Bohemian wares.

Material signatures of diversification can therefore be interpreted as indicators of both an active resistance to, and strategic adaptation of, the uniformity that characterises the institutional landscape of confinement. Ultimately, it is by appreciating the dual and simultaneous role of the material world – as both a compelling force of disciplinary standardisation, and as an active medium of diverse self-expression, collective resistance, and technological adaptation – that we can begin to offer new archaeological perspectives on the experience of confinement.

Confined Lives: From Oppositional to Pluralistic Modes of Power

Ultimately, places of confinement are fabricated through the interplay of social relations of power. While a number of contributions to this volume document the creative means by which internees destabilise, challenge, and modify their experience of internment, it is essential to avoid placing too much emphasis on a perceived open landscape of action that is brutally denied to people enduring confinement. As observed in lengthy historical detail by González-Ruibal (Chapter 4), the totalitarian environment of confinement is one of domination. Further, the painful embodied experiences of deprivation, hunger, thirst, and limited hygiene, combine in all too many cases with arbitrary punishment (if not torture) to maintain a state of fear, suffering, and humiliation for those confined. Incarcerated bodies become emblazoned with markers of difference, with this exclusionary materiality communicated through their dress (Zarankin and Salerno, Chapter 12), their access to food (Myers, Chapter 5), or their racially inscribed skin (Weiss, Chapter 2). Both cultural and natural landscapes are strategically drafted into this brutal imposition of control, as demonstrated by Pantzou (Chapter 11) in her study of Ai Stratis, an island in the North Aegean Sea that served as a Greek political prison from 1929 through 1974. While an earthquake in 1968 destroyed most of the built heritage associated with the concentration camp, the very isolation of this "barren and far-flung" island from the Greek mainland itself provided an effective tool for sustaining exile as both a means of punishment and an apparatus of political control.

Nonetheless, the material legacy of confinement involves far more than a straight-forward expression of domination. How, for example, does this experience of isolation, deprivation, and humiliation forge a sense of shared belonging among internees? How does it create a "Society of Captives" to quote the title of a par-ticularly influential early criminological study (Sykes 1958)? Archival research on Second World War era German PoW camps established in Fort Hood, Texas, (Thomas, Chapter 9) not only illuminated the mundanity of everyday life under internment, but also documented how internees shared an all-too-familiar social world of petty bureaucratic procedures, perpetual food complaints, underpaid camp maintenance works, and inadequate provision of clothing, recreational resources, and accommodation facilities. Life within a wartime PoW camp – whether based in Texas, Scotland, Southern Africa, or the Isle of Man – generated a comparable materiality, a shared social and material struggle against the boredom, deprivations, and unfree labours that characterises everyday life for those confined.

But more significantly, Thomas' study also exposed social fractures within this confined community, noting that while the majority of German internees worked at camp labour projects, others refused and instead "tried to enlist others to 'soldier' and not work". Further, an improvement in general morale appeared to accom-pany the transfer of "trouble-making PoWs" in March 1944. Far from a cohesive "counter-hegemony" or collectively maintained "hidden transcript" (Scott 1990), the constitution of inmate society (or perhaps, societies?) emerges as a messy clus-ter of sympathetic desires, aspirations, interests, antipathies, enmity, obligations, and competition. Associated material signatures impose simultaneous messages of centripetal and centrifugal tension, as Purbrick (Chapter 15) acknowledged in her sophisticated reading of the sectarian murals within the Long Kesh/Maze Prison of contemporary Northern Ireland. Adopting the term "dissensus" to address the complex array of antagonists involved in this multi-dimensional conflict, Purbrick recognises the polyvalent semiotics of the penal murals for the fractured inmate communities of this infamous British penitentiary, finding their position "in power struggles within and between communities mean that they are unstable art forms, the objects of conflict rather than simply records of it".

Ultimately, an archaeological exploration of confinement reveals a far more com-plex network of power relations than a simple binary opposition between forces of domination and expressions of resistance. It is because of these ambiguities that ethnographers have developed the concept of *heterarchy* to describe social power as a set of nested relationships and moments of opportunity, rather than totalitarian linear structures of domination and resistance (Ehrenreich et al. 1995; Crumley 1987). By emphasising the lateral, transient, and circumstantial nature of power relations, this model has exposed the "several cross-cutting personal criteria [which] contribute to status, influence, and power" (Levy 1999:73). As I have previ-ously argued (Casella 2007:76–81), this anthropological approach provides a useful framework for generating a politically engaged understanding of the ambiguous material dynamics of confinement.

How do these heterarchies operate within these austere societies? When we turn to explore the shifting and fractured communities within places of confinement, material relationships of trade, exchange, and black market activity immediately emerge. Decades of previous interdisciplinary research exists on the unofficial (or, more typically, semi-sanctioned) internal trade economy that remains perpetually nurtured under confinement (see Sykes 1958; Feldman 1991; Goffman 1961; Heffernan 1972; Garofalo and Clark 1985). This shadow political-economy, while quietly recognised (if not relied upon) by officials, offers a rich material demonstration of the fractured internal world experienced by internees, inmates, patients, and prisoners of confinement. Or as recognised by Myers (Chapter 5) in his evocative material study of the human "detritus" created by Nazi genocide and extermination camps during the Second World War, "[a] scrap of paper, cloth, metal, wire, or string was, if not of immediate use to the owner, useful to another and hence held trade value". Desires for anything not institutionally provided (food, luxuries, sexual activity, personal safety) fosters the black market trade, making this economic phenomenon a ubiquitous aspect of confinement (Williams and Fish 1974). Further, the broader process of gift exchange, as a non-monetary based economy, generates nested links of obligation, competition, altruism, favour, threat, collaboration, and enmity that vigorously fractures the oppositional structures of those who confine and those who are confined. Indeed, when we apply classic exchange models from economic anthropology (Renfrew 1975; Sahlins 1972; Polanyi 1957) to analyse the interior operation of these black markets, a baroque interplay of altruistic, balanced, and negative exchanges reveals the fractured materiality of surviving life inside the perimeter wall (Casella 2010).

Conclusion: Why Does Confinement Exist?

As a collection of papers on the archaeology of internment, this volume makes three important contributions to the wider scholarly analysis of confinement. It emphasises the historical contingency of this particularly wrenching form of population management, and thereby not only rejects its inevitability, but opens the possibility of alternatives for the future as well. Through the explicit and refreshing material focus of the contributing papers, the volume illuminates the simultaneous processes of uniformity and diversity that characterise not only places of confinement, but also our archaeological research on places of confinement. Finally, by not only offering an essential testimony to the brutal material experiences of confinement, but also interrogating the internal fractures, operations, and exchanges within confined communities, this volume offers new pluralistic understandings that encompass both the imposition of state power over (non)citizenry, and those moments of opportunity seized by those confined to create their own moments of action, belonging, and identity.

Ultimately, we return to the initial question posed in this discussion. Why does confinement exist? Popular justifications for internment will always raise far more complex questions of social power. Why does a state imprison segments of its population? As in the case of criminal incarceration, many perceive civilian and military confinement as a form of punishment – an infliction of hard treatment by an authority on a group of people who are characterised by some perceived failure. Others champion a rehabilitative purpose, justifying confinement as a disciplinary mechanism for transforming dangerous, dependent, or simply different individuals into self-sufficient and reintegrated citizens.

With the increasing application of internment to unsanctioned economic migrants, a more cynical perspective has begun to prevail. Confinement has become identified as a powerful means of socio-economic neutralisation – of human warehousing. But regardless of which explanation triumphs, the underlying concept of social power infuses these justifications. Whether accepted as a force of retribution, reformation, or segregation, the authoritative exertion of state power is inevitably summoned to explain the endurance (if not expansion) of this stark, authoritative, and ultimately painful form of population management.

References

Atwood, M. 1996 *Alias Grace*. Bloomsbury Publishing, London.

Baugher, S. 2001 Visible Charity: The Archaeology, Material Culture, and Landscape Design of New York City's Municipal Almshouse Complex, 1736–1797. *International Journal of Historical Archaeology* 5(2): 175–202.

Beisaw, A. and J. Gibb 2009 *The Archaeology of Institutional Life*. The University of Alabama Press, Tuscaloosa.

Casella, E.C. 1997 To Enshrine Their Spirits in the World: Heritage and Grief at Port Arthur, Tasmania. *Conservation and Management of Archaeological Sites* 2(2): 65–80.

Casella, E.C. 2007 *The Archaeology of Institutional Confinement*. University Press of Florida, Gainesville.

Casella, E.C. 2010 Broads, Studs and Broken Down Daddies: The Materiality of 'Playing' in the Modern Penitentiary. In *Social Archaeologies of Trade and Exchange*, edited by A. Bauer and A. Agbe-Davies. Left Coast Press, Walnut Creek.

Clemmer, D. 1940 *The Prison Community*. Christopher Publishing House, Boston.

Colijn, H. 1997 *Song of Survival: Women Interned*. White Cloud Press, Ashland.

Crumley, C. 1987 A Dialectical Critique of Hierarchy. In *Power Relations and State Formation*, edited by T. Patterson and C. Gailey, pp. 155–169. American Anthropological Association, Washington.

Ehrenreich, R., C. Crumley, and J. Levy 1995 *Heterarchy and the Analysis of Complex Societies*. American Anthropological Association Archaeological Paper No. 6. American Anthropological Association, Arlington.

Evans, R. 1982 *The Fabrication of Virtue*. Cambridge University Press, Cambridge.

Feldman, A. 1991 *Formations of Violence: The Narrative of the Body and Political Terror in Northern Ireland*. University of Chicago Press, Chicago.

Fleisher, M. 1989 *Warehousing Violence*. Sage Publications, Newbury Park.

Foucault, M. 1977 *Discipline and Punish*. Translated by A. Sheridan. Vintage Books, New York.

Garland, D. 1990 *Punishment and Modern Society*. Clarendon Press, Oxford.

Garofalo, J. and R. Clark 1985 The Inmate Subculture in Jails. *Criminal Justice and Behavior* 12(4): 415–434.

Genet, J. 1949 *The Thief's Journal*. Grove Press, New York.

Goffman, E. 1961 *Asylums*. Anchor Books, New York.

Heffernan, E. 1972 *Making It in Prison*. Wiley, New York.

Hirsch, A. 1992 *The Rise of the Penitentiary*. Yale University Press, New Haven.

Howe, A. 1994 *Punish and Critique: Towards a Feminist Analysis of Penality*. Routledge, London.

Huey, P. 2001 The Almshouse in Dutch and English Colonial North America and Its Precedent in the Old World: Historical and Archaeological Evidence. *International Journal of Historical Archaeology* 5(2): 123–154.

Humphreys, R. 1995 *Sin, Organized Charity, and the Poor Law in Victorian Britain*. St. Martin's, New York.

Ignatieff, M. 1978 *A Just Measure of Pain*. Pantheon Books, New York.

Irwin, J. and J. Austin 1994 *It's About Time: America's Imprisonment Binge*. Wadsworth Publishing, Belmont.

Jeffrey, B. 1997 *White Coolies*. Angus and Robertson, Pymble.

Katz, M.B. 1986 *In the Shadow of the Poorhouse*. Basic Books, New York.

Leibling, A. and D. Price 2001 *The Prison Officer*. Prison Service Journal, London.

Levi, P. 1986 *If This Is a Man: Remembering Auschwitz*. Summit, New York.

Levy, J. 1999 Gender, Power, and Heterarchy in Middle-Level Societies. In *Manifesting Power*, edited by T. Sweely, pp. 62–78. Routledge, London.

Markus, T. 1993 *Buildings and Power*. Routledge, London.

Owen, B. 1998 *In the Mix: Struggle and Survival in a Women's Prison*. State University of New York Press, New York.

Parenti, C. 1999 *Lockdown America: Police and Prisons in the Age of Crisis*. Verso, London.

Polanyi, K. 1957 The Economy as an Instituted Process. In *Trade and Market in the Early Empires*, edited by K. Polanyi, C. Arensburgh, and H. Pearson, pp. 243–270. Free Press and Falcon's Wing Press, Glencoe.

Pratt, J. 2002 *Punishment and Civilization*. Sage Publications, London.

Renfrew, A.C. 1975 Trade as Action at a Distance: Questions of Integration and Communication. In *Ancient Civilisation and Trade*, edited by J.A. Sabloff and C.C. Lamberg-Karlovsky, pp. 3–59. University of New Mexico Press, Albuquerque.

Rhodes, L.A. 2001 Towards an Anthropology of Prisons. *Annual Review of Anthropology* 30: 65–83.

Rothman, D. 1990 *The Discovery of the Asylum*, 2nd Edition. Little, Brown and Company, Boston.

Sahlins, M. 1972 *Stone Age Economics*. Aldine-Atherton, Chicago.

Scott, J. 1990 *Domination and the Arts of Resistance: Hidden Transcripts*. Yale University Press, New Haven.

Sykes, G. 1958 *The Society of Captives*. Rinehart, New York.

Sykes, G. and S. Messinger 1960 The Inmate Social System. In *Theoretical Studies in Social Organization of the Prison*, edited by R. Cloward, pp. 6–10. Social Science Research Council, New York.

Waters, S. 1999 *Affinity*. Virago Press, London.

Wilde, O. 2000 De Profundis. In *The Complete Works of Oscar Wilde*, edited by M. Holland and R. Hart-Davis. Henry Holt and Company, LLC, New York.

Williams, V.L. and M. Fish 1974 *Convicts, Codes, and Contraband: The Prison Life of Men and Women*. Ballinger, Cambridge.

Subject Index

A

Accelerated modernity, period of, 3
Adair, Johnny, 275
Aegean islands, 195, 288
Aerial bombings, 54, 69
Aerial views/photographs
    Camp Hood, 154
    Deaconsbank Camp, 118
    Knockaloe Camp, 46
    Longhorn Airfield, 155–156
Africanistas, 54
Agios Minas, 195, 198
Agosti, Orlando, 211
Ai Stratis, Greek exile island, 191–193
    civil polarizations and political exile,
        193–194
    heritage of, 201–203
    landscapes of, 194–200
        banishment phases, 195
        camp divisions, 195
        earthquake devastation, 199
        exchange of ideas/knowledge,
            197–198
        memorials, erection of, 198
        school buildings, living in, 198–199
        time passing skills, 196
    personal/local objects, 200–201
AK47/Browning pistols, 274
Albatera (Valencia), 55, 65, 70
Alighieri, Dante, 194
Amache Relocation Center, Colorado,
    102–103
Ama-overalls, 29
American Civil War, 8, 81, 113–114,
    147–148
American Constitution, 89, 99, 102, 106,
    108–109
American Home Front heritage, 147–148
American PoW camps, 7, 148

America the Beautiful, 105
Anarchists, 3, 55, 59
Ancien Regime, 60–61, 66
Anglo-Boer War, 10, 21, 23, 26, 287
Animal sheds, 120–121, 180, 182
Annihilation, 23, 71, 211–212, 213, 223
Another Time Another Place, 114
Anthropogeographie, 23
Anti-British Nazi propaganda, 23
Anticommunism/antiliberalism, 63
Anti-Francoist guerrilla, 70
Anti-German sentiments, 34, 41
Anti-national feelings, 194
Anti-social elements, 113
Anti-Spain, 55
Anti-tank task force, 156
Apache Attack helicopter training, 168
Apartheid policies, 22–23, 25, 27–29, 31
Aranda de Duero, 65
Arbeit Macht Frei, 11, 75–76
*Archaeology as Memory: Archaeological
    Interventions at Club Atlético
    Clandestine Center of Detention
    and Torture*, 216
Archaeology of extermination, 5
The Archaeology of Institutional Confinement,
    7
Archaism, 53, 61–63, 71
Ardverikie Estate, 121
Argentina, archaeology of dictatorship in,
    207–209
    appearance of the enemy, 212–214
        discredited and discreditable, 214
        faithless and antichristian Marxism, 213
        good/bad citizens, 213–214
        guerrilla men and women, 214
        informal appearance, 214
        official discourses, 212
        process of generalization, 213

9 781441 996657